The Princeton Review®

I0803429

PSAT/ NMSQT®

PREP

with 3 Practice Tests,
2026 Edition

The Staff of The Princeton Review

PrincetonReview.com

Penguin Random House

The Princeton Review

The Princeton Review
110 East 42nd Street, 7th Floor
New York, NY 10017
editorialsupport@review.com
princetonreview.com
penguinrandomhouse.com

Published in the United States by Penguin Random House LLC, New York.

ISBN: 979-8-217-11884-7
eBook ISBN: 979-8-217-11885-4
ISSN: 2687-8755

The material in this book is up-to-date at the time of publication. However, changes may have been instituted by the testing body in the test after this book was published. If there are any important late-breaking developments, changes, or corrections to the materials in this book, we will post that information online in the Student Tools. Register your book and check your Student Tools to see if there are any updates posted there.

Editor: Selena Coppock
Production Editors: Kathy Carter & Nina Mozes
Production Artist: Jennifer Chapman

Manufactured in the United States of America.

10 9 8 7 6 5 4 3 2

2026 Edition

EU Contact:
Penguin Random House Ireland
32 Nassau Street
Dublin D02 YH68
https://eu-contact.penguin.ie

For customer service, please contact **editorialsupport@review.com**, and be sure to include:

- full title of the book
- ISBN
- page number

Acknowledgments

Special thanks to Kenneth Brenner, Sara Kuperstein, Amy Minster, and Scott O'Neal for their contributions to this edition.

Thanks also to Aleksei Alferiev, Anne Bader, Kevin Baldwin, Grace Cannon, Tania Capone, Paul Christiansen, Nicole Cosme, Wazhma Daftanai, April Davis, Gina Donegan, Harrison Foster, Anne Goldberg-Baldwin, Beth Hollingsworth, Brian Hong, Brad Kelly, Kevin Keogh, Aaron Lindh, Jomil London, Dave MacKenzie, Sweena Mangal, Jason Morgan, Amanda Nowotny, Robert Otey, Elizabeth Owens, Danielle Perrini, Gabby Peterson, Denise Pollard, Xander Posner, Jess Thomas, Christina Torturo, Kathy Ruppert, Jimmy Williams, and Suzanne Wint.

The Princeton Review would also like to thank Jennifer Chapman, Kathy Carter, and Nina Mozes for their time and attention to each page.

Special thanks to Adam Robinson, who conceived of and perfected the Joe Bloggs approach to standardized tests, and many other techniques in this book.

Contents

Get More (Free) Content at PrincetonReview.com/prep

As easy as 1·2·3

1 Go to PrincetonReview.com/prep or scan the **QR code** and enter the following ISBN for your book: **9798217118847**

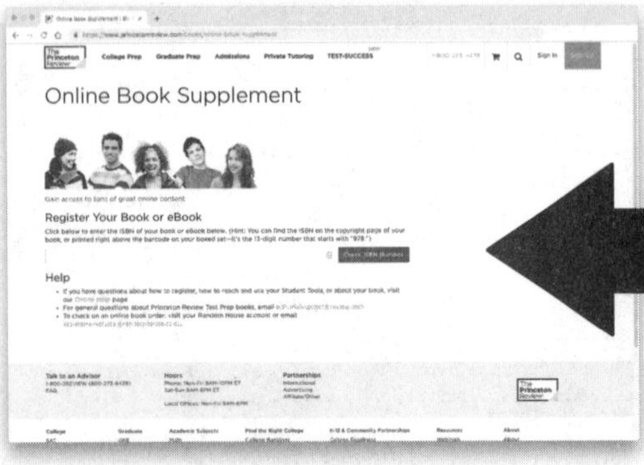

2 Answer a few simple questions to set up an exclusive Princeton Review account. *(If you already have one, you can just log in.)*

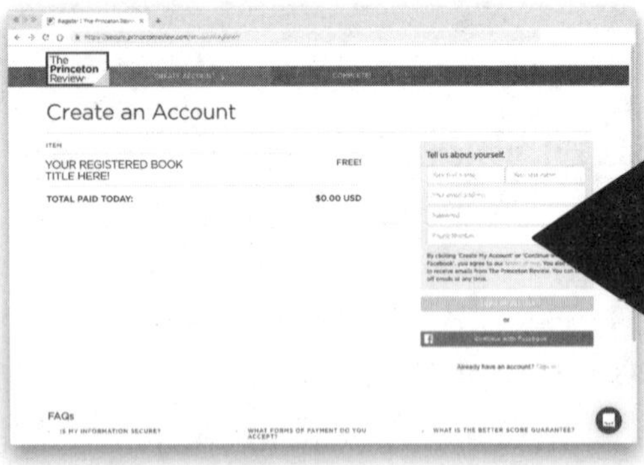

3 Enjoy access to your **FREE** content!

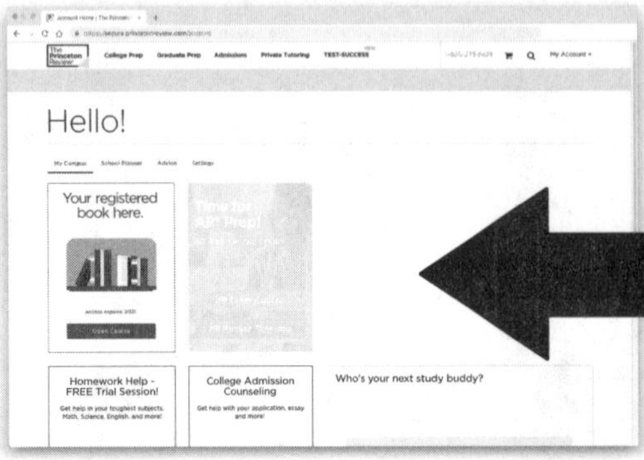

Once you've registered, you can...

- Access and print out two more full-length practice tests as well as their corresponding answers and explanations
- Use our online tools to take your practice tests digitally or use our online proctor to time you while you take the test in the book, then enter your answers online
- Enter your answers in our online bubble sheet to get an approximate scaled score with explanations
- Get valuable advice about the college application process
- If you're still choosing between colleges, use our searchable rankings of *The Best 391 Colleges* to find out more information about your dream school
- Access printable resources, including a study guide, a score conversion table, and more
- Check to see if there have been any corrections or updates to this edition

Need to report a potential **content** issue?

Contact **EditorialSupport@review.com** and include:

- full title of the book
- ISBN
- page number

Need to report a **technical** issue?

Contact **TPRStudentTech@review.com** and provide:

- your full name
- email address used to register the book
- full book title and ISBN
- Operating system (Mac/PC) and browser (Chrome, Firefox, Safari, etc.)

Look For These Icons Throughout The Book

 **ONLINE PRACTICE TESTS**

 **ONLINE ARTICLES**

 **PROVEN TECHNIQUES**

 **APPLIED STRATEGIES**

 **STUDY BREAK**

 **MORE GREAT BOOKS**

Part I
Orientation

Chapter 1
What Is the Digital PSAT/NMSQT?

The Digital PSAT/NMSQT—from now on, we'll just call it the PSAT—is a standardized test given primarily to high school juniors to give them a "preliminary" idea of how well they could do on SAT question types. The test is also used to determine which students are eligible for National Merit Scholar recognition. This chapter will give you a general overview of the test and how it is used, along with the basics to start your preparation. We'll also give you a glimpse at the other tests in College Board's Suite of Assessments: the PSAT 8/9 and the PSAT 10.

THE DIGITAL PSAT/NMSQT

College Board's "Suite of Assessments" ranges from the PSAT 8/9 to the SAT. If you are reading this book, you are likely most interested in the PSAT at this time, so we'll start there. Just like the other tests in the Suite, the PSAT contains a Reading and Writing section and a Math section, each divided into two modules. The content of all the tests in the Suite is similar, and the number of questions and time per module are identical.

> **Psst...**
> College Board makes the PSAT 8/9, the PSAT 10, and the PSAT/NMSQT. But when we refer to just the plain old "PSAT" in this book, we're referring to the PSAT/NMSQT.

This is what College Board says about the Reading and Writing section:

"The section focuses on key elements of comprehension, rhetoric, and language use that the best available evidence identifies as necessary for college readiness and success. In this section, students answer multiple-choice questions requiring them to read, comprehend, and use information and ideas in texts; analyze the craft and structure of texts; revise texts to improve the rhetorical expression of ideas; and edit texts to conform to core conventions of Standard English."

Here is The Princeton Review's take: Be prepared to justify your selected answer with evidence from the text and/or graph provided. This test is not about making up anything; it's about finding the correct answer based on the text.

College Board has this to say about the Math section:

"The digital SAT Suite Math section focuses on key elements of algebra, advanced math, problem solving and data analysis, and geometry and trigonometry (except for the PSAT 8/9 which does not test trigonometry) that evidence identifies as necessary for college and career readiness and success. Over the course of the Math section, students answer multiple-choice and student-produced response (SPR) questions that measure their fluency with, understanding of, and ability to apply the math concepts, skills, and practices that are most essential for readiness for entry-level postsecondary work."

Here is The Princeton Review's take: Expect to see Algebra I and II, some Geometry, and questions that have charts, graphs, data tables, scatterplots, and other forms of data.

The Digital Suite of Assessments has a built-in Desmos calculator that can be used on all Math questions. In addition, students may bring their own approved calculators if they prefer. Even though this tool is always at hand, it is up to the test-taker to determine whether the calculator will help solve a question. According to College Board, "students who make use of structure or their ability to reason will probably finish before students who use a calculator."

The bottom line: Write down your work and use the calculator for tedious calculations. Note, however, that a calculator most likely will not be necessary to solve most of the questions.

All questions in the Reading and Writing section are multiple-choice. Most of the Math questions are multiple-choice, but about 25% of the questions are "student-produced responses," for which students enter their own answers. Each correct answer earns points, and there is no penalty for an incorrect response or a question left blank.

The bottom line: Don't leave anything blank!

When Is the PSAT Given?

The Digital PSAT is administered in a testing window of several days. Your school will announce the exact dates at the beginning of the school year, and you can find out more about the testing windows at PrincetonReview.com or through College Board at CollegeBoard.org.

Keep on Schedule
You'll officially take the PSAT in the fall of your junior year. Plan to take the SAT anytime between the winter of your junior year and the fall of your senior year.

How Do I Sign Up for the PSAT?

You don't have to do anything to sign up for the PSAT; your school will do all the work for you. Test registration fees can vary from school to school, so be sure to check with your school counselor if you have questions about how much the PSAT will cost you.

What About Students with Special Needs?

If you have a diagnosed physical or learning disability, you will probably qualify for accommodations on the PSAT. However, it's important that you get the process started early. The first step is to speak to your school counselor who handles learning disabilities. Only your counselor can file the appropriate paperwork. You'll also need to gather some information (documentation of your condition) from a licensed practitioner and some other information from your school. Then your school counselor will file the application for you. You will need to apply for accommodations only once; with that single application you'll qualify for accommodations on the PSAT, SAT, and AP Exams. There is one exception to this rule: if you change school districts, you'll need to have a counselor at the new school refile your paperwork.

Does the PSAT Play a Role in College Admissions?

No! The PSAT plays no role in college admissions. It's really just a practice test for the SAT. The one exception is for that very small group of students, about 4 percent of all students nationwide, whose PSAT scores qualify them for National Merit recognition. (We'll tell you more than you ever wanted to know about that in the next chapter.) Recognition as a commended scholar, semifinalist, or finalist for National Merit is a fairly impressive addition to your college admissions portfolio and is something that you should certainly pursue if you are seriously in contention for it.

What Happens to the Score Report from the PSAT?

Only you, your high school, and the National Merit Scholarship Corporation (which co-sponsors the PSAT) will receive a copy of your score report. It won't be sent to colleges.

Do I Need to Prepare for the PSAT?

You might be thinking, *If colleges don't see my PSAT score, why do I need to bother doing well on this test? Do I even need to prep for it?* That's a very good question because the truth is that you don't necessarily need to prepare for or do well on the PSAT. If you don't think that you could score in the top 4% of PSAT test-takers in your state—even with a little bit of preparation—then there's virtually no benefit to scoring better-than-okay on the PSAT. That being said, if you plan to take the SAT, your PSAT preparation will transfer, so there's no harm in preparing for a slightly easier version of a test you will be taking soon enough. However, if you plan to take the ACT instead of the SAT, aren't aiming to qualify for National Merit, and don't have any other reason to do well on the PSAT, you have our permission to put this book down in favor of a more worthwhile activity.

WHAT DOES THE PSAT TEST?

As you begin your prep, it's useful to remember that the PSAT is not a test of how capable you are academically, how good of a person you are, or how successful you will be in life. The PSAT simply tests how well you take the PSAT. That's it. And performing well on the PSAT is a skill that can be learned like any other. The Princeton Review was founded more than 40 years ago on this very simple idea, and—as our students' test scores show—our approach is the one that works. It can feel extremely daunting to hear that changes to tests could heavily influence your college admission outlook. However, remember that any standardized test is a coachable test. A beatable test.

The PSAT doesn't measure the stuff that matters. It measures neither intelligence nor the depth and breadth of what you're learning in high school. It doesn't predict college grades as well as your high school grades do. Colleges know there is more to you as a student—and as a person—than how you do on a single test.

Who Writes the PSAT?

The PSAT is written and administered by College Board and used for scholarships by National Merit Scholarship Corporation. You might think that the people at College Board are educators, professors of education, or teachers. They're not. They are people who just happen to make a living writing tests. In fact, they write hundreds of tests, for all kinds of organizations.

The folks at College Board aren't really paid to educate; they're paid to write and administer tests. And even though you'll be paying them to take the PSAT, you're not their customer. The actual customers College Board caters to are the colleges, which receive the information they want at no cost. This means that you should take everything that College Board says with a grain of salt and realize that its testing "advice" isn't always the best advice. (Taking testing advice from College Board is a bit like taking baseball advice from the opposing team.)

Every test reflects the interests of the people who write it. If you know who writes the test, you will know a lot more about what kinds of answers will be considered "correct" answers on that test.

HOW IS THE PSAT STRUCTURED AND SCORED?

Category	PSAT/NMSQT
Time Overall	134 minutes plus break
Components	• Reading and Writing section • Math section
Number of Questions	• Reading and Writing: 54, including 4 experimental questions • Math: 44, including 4 experimental questions
Answer Choices	• Reading and Writing: all multiple-choice with 4 answers per question • Math: 75% multiple-choice with 4 answers per question, 25% student-produced responses
Time by Section	• Reading and Writing: 64 minutes in two 32-minute modules • Math: 70 minutes in two 35-minute modules
Relationship Between Modules	• Module 1 has a broad mix of levels of difficulty. • Performance on Module 1 determines the difficulty of Module 2. • Students who do well on Module 1 will get a Module 2 that is harder, on average. • Students who do less well on Module 1 will get a Module 2 that is easier, on average.
Scoring	• The score is based on the number of questions correct and the difficulty of the questions seen. • Students who do well on Module 1 are put into a higher bracket of possible scores. • Students who do less well on Module 1 are put into a lower bracket of possible scores. • Section scores range from 160 to 760. • The total score is the sum of the section scores and ranges from 320 to 1520.

All Reading and Writing questions are attached to short passages, with one question per passage. There will be a wide range of text complexities presented, and the passages will cover a variety of topics from history, science, and literature (even some poetry).

The Math content has a strong focus on algebra, problem-solving, and analytical topics, and it includes some high-level content such as trigonometry. Some questions require student-produced responses, and these will be scattered throughout the Math modules. As previously stated, calculator use will be allowed on all math questions.

As you can see from the table above, both sections (Reading-Writing and Math) are divided into two modules. On the Digital PSAT, your performance on the first module in each section will determine the makeup of your second module. Do well on the first module, and you will see a harder (on average) mix of questions on the second module. Miss more questions in the first module, and you will get an easier (on average) difficulty for the second module. You always want to do as well as possible, of course, but remember this: to earn a top score, you must achieve the hard second module on both sections.

To help you do your best, we recommend that you review the explanations for the questions in the drills and the practice tests, even if you answer a question correctly. You may discover techniques that help to shave seconds from your solutions. A large part of what's being tested is your ability to use the appropriate tools in a strategic fashion, and while there may be multiple ways to solve a given problem, you should focus on the most efficient path to a solution.

Scoring on the PSAT

The PSAT is scored on a scale of 320–1520, which is the sum of the two section scores that range from 160–760. The two sections are the Reading and Writing section and the Math section. Wrong answers are not penalized, so you're advised never to leave a question blank—even if that means blindly picking a letter and clicking it for any uncompleted questions before time runs out.

So, how do the two modules work together to determine your score in a section? Well, if your raw score is high enough on the first module, you will automatically be bumped into a possible score range that is overall higher than you would be in if you had a lower raw score on the first module, though the two ranges may overlap some. Some questions within a module are also weighted, so doing better on those will increase your score more than doing well on easier, non-weighted questions. As such, your score is determined not only by how many questions you answer correctly but also by how hard the questions were that you did. Although the scoring curve on each Digital PSAT may calculate your score slightly differently, you will always have two jobs: understanding which questions you should focus on and building your stamina to stay sharp through both modules in each section. Throughout this book, we will show you how to do just that.

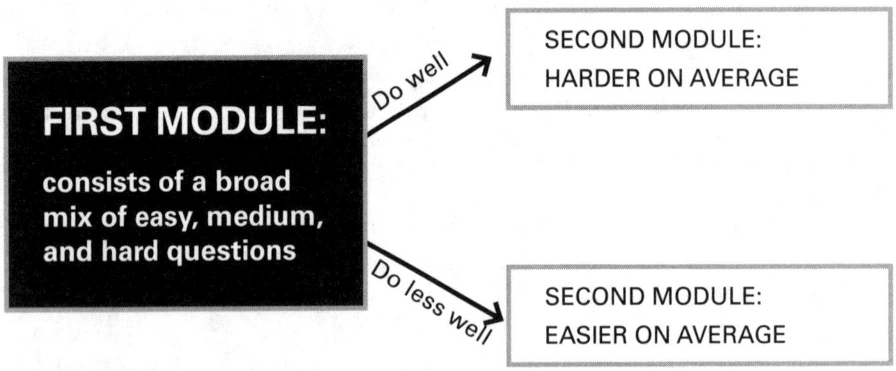

On the Digital Suite, only your section scores and total score will be reported. You won't see a score for each individual module or be shown whether you received the easier or harder second module.

What Does the PSAT Score Mean for My SAT Score?

The SAT is scored on a 1600 scale, whereas the PSAT is scored on a 1520 scale. However, because the PSAT and SAT are aligned by College Board to be scored on the same scale, your PSAT score indicates the approximate SAT score you would earn were you to have taken the SAT on that same day. Since the PSAT is slightly easier, you can't score quite as high on it as you can on the SAT.

PSAT 10

Now that we've covered some basics about the PSAT, let's discuss how it works with the other tests in the SAT Suite of Assessments. Though there is a test called the PSAT 10, it is identical to the structure of the PSAT/NMSQT in terms of both number of questions and time limits per section. Just as with the SAT and the PSAT, the PSAT 10 includes a Reading and Writing section and a Math section. The major differences between the PSAT and the PSAT 10 are who takes the PSAT 10 and when: 10th-graders, sometime in the spring. Additionally, the PSAT 10 test does not qualify you for National Merit Scholarship consideration.

PSAT 8/9

The PSAT 8/9 is designed for eighth and ninth graders, as the name would imply. The Digital version of the test will also match the other tests in the Suite in terms of structure, timing, and number of questions. The content of each section is comparable to the content of the SAT and PSAT, but it is a little easier and is therefore scored on a somewhat lower scale.

WHAT'S WITH ALL THESE TESTS?!

So, if the PSAT 8/9, the PSAT 10, and the PSAT/NMSQT all have the same sections, number of modules, number of questions, and time to take them, what exactly ARE the differences among the tests? There are two main ones: the content covered on each test and the possible score ranges. See the chart below for a comparison of all the tests in the Digital SAT Suite of Assessments.

Test	PSAT 8/9	PSAT 10 and PSAT/NMSQT	SAT
Reading and Writing Content	Information and Ideas (≈26%) Craft and Structure (≈28%) Expression of Ideas (≈20%) Standard English Conventions (≈26%)	Information and Ideas (≈26%) Craft and Structure (≈28%) Expression of Ideas (≈20%) Standard English Conventions (≈26%)	Information and Ideas (≈26%) Craft and Structure (≈28%) Expression of Ideas (≈20%) Standard English Conventions (≈26%)
Text Complexity	Grades 6 through 11	Grades 6 through college-level	Grades 6 through college-level
Math Content	Algebra (≈42.5%) Advanced Math (≈20%) Problem-Solving and Data Analysis (≈25%) Geometry (≈12.5%)	Algebra (≈35%) Advanced Math (≈32.5%) Problem-Solving and Data Analysis (≈20%) Geometry and Trigonometry (≈12.5%)	Algebra (≈35%) Advanced Math (≈35%) Problem-Solving and Data Analysis (≈15%) Geometry and Trigonometry (≈15%)
Math Topics Excluded	Rational and Radical Equations, Trigonometry, Circles, Evaluating Statistical Claims and Making Inferences	Making Inferences from Statistical Samples	None
Section Score Range	120 to 720	160 to 760	200 to 800
Total Score Range	240 to 1440	320 to 1520	400 to 1600

According to College Board, the SAT Suite of Assessments is designed to reflect how prepared you are for college and the working world. By creating a series of tests given over several years, College Board claims to measure a student's progress toward readiness for higher education and beyond. All tests in the Suite use the same vertical scale, meaning that the score you receive on a PSAT 8/9 should be the same score you'd receive on the PSAT or SAT if you took those tests on the same day.

College Board maintains that the best way to prepare for the test is to do the following:

- take challenging courses
- do your homework
- prepare for tests and quizzes
- ask and answer lots of questions

We at The Princeton Review are dubious about these claims, especially in regard to college and career readiness. Moreover, we think the best way to prepare for an exam is to know the content and structure of that exam. By reading this book, you are already on your way to improving your test scores.

WHAT IS THE PRINCETON REVIEW?

The Princeton Review is the nation's leading test-preparation company. In just a few years from our founding in 1981, we became the nation's leader in SAT preparation, primarily because our techniques work. We offer courses and private tutoring for all of the major standardized tests, and we publish a series of books to help in your search for the right school. If you'd like more information about our programs or books, give us a call at 800-2-REVIEW, or check out our website at PrincetonReview.com.

Shortcuts
The Princeton Review's techniques are the closest thing there is to a shortcut to the PSAT. However, there is no shortcut to learning these techniques.

HOW TO USE THIS BOOK

This book is divided into five parts:

- Part I introduces you to the digital PSAT/NMSQT and provides some general strategies for approaching the questions on the test.
- Part II includes Practice Test 1, along with complete answers and explanations for all questions.
- Part III provides a general review of all of the material covered in the test, along with specific methods for approaching the questions and practice drills to hone your skills.
- Part IV provides the answers and explanations for all of the drills in Part III.
- Part V includes two additional practices tests online.

After working through some of the content chapters in Part III and checking your answers and the explanations to the chapter drills in Part IV, take Practice Test 2 online and apply everything you've learned to improve your score. Then work through the remaining content chapters before taking Practice Test 3 online. The "Session-by-Session Study Guide" starting on page 13 provides a plan of attack for these tests and for the rest of the book. There is no single plan that will fit everyone, so be prepared to adapt the plan and use it according to your own needs.

Use our online tools to take your practice tests digitally, or take the test in the book, then enter your answers online. Either way, you'll see your results and a breakdown of the question categories. See page 30 for more info.

Practice Test 1 will give you an idea of your strengths and weaknesses, both of which can be sources of improvement. If you're already good at something, additional practice can make you great at it; if you're not so good at something, what you should do about it depends on how important it is. If the concept is one that frequently appears on the test, you should spend a lot of time on it; if it comes up only once in a while, you should spend very little time working on it and remember that it's something you should either put off until you've completed easier things or skip it entirely.

How do you know what's important? We'll tell you throughout this book, when we discuss techniques like Plugging In, but you can also get an idea of what to focus on simply by observing how this book is laid out. The Reading and Writing Introduction tells you how to jump to the questions you want to work on first. In the Math chapters, the most important concepts appear first. For example, if you're shaky on Reading, you know you'll need to devote some time to Reading questions because there is a total of 25–29 such questions on the test. And if you're not so confident when it comes to geometry, don't panic. Geometry questions appear only in the last math chapter, which tells you that this topic isn't as much of a priority as Plugging In or Math Basics.

One important note: In this book, the sample questions are in numerical order within a chapter. The question number does not indicate where you can expect to see a similar question on the test. As we'll show you later, what really matters is your *Personal* Order of Difficulty.

How Much Should I Prepare for the PSAT?

If you're in that very small percentage of students who are in contention for National Merit recognition, it may be worth your while to put in a good deal of time to prepare for this test. After all, your extra hard work may well put you in a better position for National Merit recognition. Otherwise, you should prepare enough so that you feel more in control of the test and have a better testing experience. (Nothing feels quite as awful as being dragged through a testing experience feeling as if you don't know what you're being tested on or what to expect—except perhaps dental surgery.) The other reason to prepare for the PSAT is that it will give you some testing skills that will help you begin to prepare for the test that actually counts: the SAT.

> **Study**
> If you were preparing to take a biology test, you'd study biology. If you were preparing for a basketball game, you'd practice basketball. So, if you're preparing for the PSAT (and eventually the SAT), study the PSAT. The PSAT can't test everything, so concentrate on learning what it *does* test.

The bottom line is this: The best reason to prepare for the PSAT is that it will help you get an early start on your preparation for the SAT.

Time Management

To manage your PSAT preparation, make use of the study guide on the following pages. This guide breaks down the seemingly daunting task of PSAT prep into bite-sized pieces we call "sessions." We have mapped out tasks for each session to be sure you get the most out of this book. The tests will be the first and last sessions, so you should be sure to plan to have about two-and-a-half hours for these sessions. Most other sessions will last between an hour and two hours, so plan to take a short break in the middle, and if it looks as if the session is going to exceed two hours, feel free to stop and pick up where you left off on the next day.

When You Take a Practice Test

You'll see when to take practice tests in the session outlines. Here are some guidelines for taking these tests:

For more information about how to take and score your practice tests, see page 30.

- If possible, take your practice tests online. Although one test is printed in this book, taking it online instead of on paper will allow you to become more comfortable with the online environment.
- When taking an online test, make sure to practice using the online tools. Use the annotation tool to mark important text in the passages and questions. Use the Answer Eliminator to get rid of the wrong answers. Mark questions you want to return to.
- Take a practice test in one sitting, under conditions similar to those of a proctored test. Sit in a quiet place and remove distractions like phones from the area. You need to build up your endurance for the real test, and you also need an accurate picture of how you will do. However, do take a 10-minute break between the Reading and Writing section and the Math section. On the real test you will have a break, so it's important not to skip it on the practice tests.
- If you take your tests online, you will be able to use the on-screen timer to keep track of the time remaining in each module. If you take the first test in the book instead of online, you can time yourself. Just make sure you do not allow yourself to go over time for any module.
- Whether you take a test online or on paper, write down the things you need in order to answer the question. For the Digital PSAT, you should receive three sheets of scratch paper. Make sure to write down calculations or make notes you need. If you take the test in your book, do not write on the questions or answers themselves, as you will not be able to do so on the Digital PSAT.

Session-by-Session Study Guide

Session Zero You're involved in this session right now. Finish reading this chapter so you'll know what the test is about, how it is used, and what to expect from the rest of the book. This step probably won't take you long, so if you have about two-and-a-half hours after you complete Chapter 1, you can go on to Session One and take the first practice test.

Session One Take Practice Test 1 and score it. You'll use this result to get an idea of your strengths and weaknesses, and the parts of each section you should concentrate on. Note that our explanations refer to concepts discussed elsewhere in this book, so you may want to wait until after Session Four before reviewing this test.

Session Two Work through Chapters 2 and 3 of the Orientation and Chapter 6, Reading and Writing Introduction.

Session Three Work through Chapter 7, Reading: The Fundamentals and the associated reading drill. Then do Chapter 8, Reading: More Question Formats.

Session Four Work through the Math Basics in Chapter 14 and the corresponding drills. Then do Chapter 9, Reading: Mastering the POE.

Session Five Work through the Math Techniques section in Chapter 15 and associated drills. Take a look at Chapter 10, Rules Questions: Introduction. Then, jump right into Chapter 11, Rules Questions: Punctuation.

Session Six Review Advanced Math, Chapter 16. As you work through this chapter, be sure to apply techniques like Plugging In that you learned in Chapter 15. Since these techniques are central to doing well on the Math section, you can never practice them too much. Review Chapter 12, Rules Questions: Grammar.

Session Seven Take Practice Test 2, available online in your student portal. Use the techniques you've been practicing throughout the book.

Session Eight Score Practice Test 2 and go through the explanations, focusing on where you may have missed the opportunity to use a technique and your decisions about whether you should have attempted a question or not, given your pacing goals and Personal Order of Difficulty.

Session Nine Work through Geometry and Trigonometry in Chapter 17. When you finish, read through Chapter 13, Rhetoric Questions. This will complete your work in the content chapters.

Session Ten Take Practice Test 3, also available in your student portal. Score your test and take your time reviewing the explanations.

Some of the terminology in the study guide may be unfamiliar to you now, but don't worry, you'll get to know it soon. Also, you should refer to this study guide after each session to keep yourself on track.

So, what are you waiting for? Go ahead and dive into the Digital PSAT!

Chapter 2
All About the National Merit Scholarships

The NMSQT part of the name PSAT/NMSQT stands for National Merit Scholarship Qualifying Test. That means the PSAT serves as the test that will establish whether you are eligible for National Merit recognition. This chapter will help you figure out what that may mean for you and even other scholarships you may qualify for.

WHAT IS THE NATIONAL MERIT SCHOLARSHIP PROGRAM?

You might think that the PSAT is simply a warm-up for the SAT, but the National Merit Scholarship Program makes the PSAT an important test in its own right.

The mission of National Merit Scholarship Corporation (NMSC) is to recognize and honor the academically talented students of the United States. NMSC accomplishes this mission by conducting nationwide academic scholarship programs. The enduring goals of NMSC's scholarship programs are the following:

- to promote a wider and deeper respect for learning in general and for exceptionally talented individuals in particular
- to shine a spotlight on brilliant students and encourage the pursuit of academic excellence at all levels of education
- to stimulate increased support from organizations that wish to sponsor scholarships for outstanding scholastic talent

The National Merit Scholarship Program is an academic competition for recognition and scholarships that began in 1955. High school students enter the National Merit Program by taking the Preliminary SAT/National Merit Scholarship Qualifying Test (PSAT/NMSQT) and by meeting published program entry and participation requirements.

HOW DO I QUALIFY FOR NATIONAL MERIT?

To participate in the National Merit Scholarship Program, a student must:

1. take the PSAT/NMSQT in the specified year of the high school program and **no later than** the third year in grades 9 through 12, regardless of grade classification or educational pattern;
2. be enrolled as a high school student (traditional or homeschooled), progressing normally toward graduation or completion of high school, and planning to enroll full time in college no later than the fall following completion of high school; and
3. be a citizen of the United States or be a U.S. lawful permanent resident (or have applied for permanent residence, the application for which has not been denied) and intend to become a U.S. citizen at the earliest opportunity allowed by law.

The Index

How does your PSAT score qualify you for National Merit? The National Merit Scholarship Corporation uses a selection index. This number is derived from your Reading-Writing and Math scores and ranges from 48 to 228. Each year, states set a cut-off for National Merit qualification that will likely result in 1% of students who took the test in that state receiving qualification as a semifinalist. Qualifying scores are likely to continue to vary from state to state (generally between 208 and 223), so check with your school counselor as to what the cutoff score is for your school year in your state.

The Awards and the Process

In the fall of their senior year, about 50,000 students will receive one of two letters from NMSC (National Merit Scholarship Corporation): either a Letter of Commendation or a letter stating that they have qualified as semifinalists for National Merit.

Commended Students Roughly two-thirds of these students (about 34,000 total students each year) will receive a Letter of Commendation by virtue of their high scores on the test. This looks great on your college application, so if you have a reasonable chance of getting one, it's definitely worth your time to prepare for the PSAT. Make no mistake, though: these letters are not easy to get. They are awarded to students who score between the 95th and the mid-99th percentiles—that means to the top four to five percent in each state.

If you receive this honorable mention from NMSC, you should be extremely proud of yourself. Even though you won't continue in the process for National Merit scholarships, this commendation does make you eligible for special scholarships sponsored by certain companies and organizations, which vary in their amounts and eligibility requirements.

Semifinalists The other third of these students—those 16,000 students who score in the upper 99th percentile in their states—will be notified that they are National Merit semifinalists. If you qualify, you'll receive a letter announcing your status as a semifinalist, along with information about the requirements for qualification as a finalist. These include maintaining high grades, performing well on your SAT, and getting an endorsement from your principal.

Becoming a National Merit semifinalist is quite impressive, and if you manage it, you should certainly mention it on your college applications.

What does "scoring in the upper 99th percentile in the state" mean? It means that you're essentially competing against the other people in your state for those semifinalist positions. Since some states have higher average scores than others, this means that if you're in states like New York, New Jersey, Maryland, Connecticut, or Massachusetts, you need a higher score to qualify than if you live in other states.

Finalists The majority of semifinalists (more than 90 percent) go on to qualify as finalists. Students who meet all of the eligibility requirements will be notified in February of their senior year that they have qualified as finalists. This means that they are now eligible for scholarship money, though it doesn't necessarily mean that they'll get any. In fact, only about half of National Merit finalists actually win scholarships through NMSC. What determines whether a student gets money or not? There is a final screening process, based on criteria that NMSC doesn't release to the public, to determine who actually gets these scholarships. A total of 2,500 finalists earn $2,500 one-time scholarships from NMSC, and approximately 1,000 more win corporate-sponsored merit scholarships, which are typically given to children of the sponsors' employees, residents of certain communities, and students who plan to study or work in specific fields. The monetary amount of corporate-sponsored scholarships can be anywhere from $500–$10,000, and some are one-time scholarships, while others are given for each year of study. Some students who meet the corporation's qualifications but aren't finalists will also earn Special Scholarships. Approximately an additional 4,000 students will be offered college-sponsored scholarships from the schools they plan to attend. These awards range from $500 to $2,000 and are renewable for four years.

If you're willing to forgo the name-brand recognition of an Ivy, a state school can be an excellent choice—and if it offers you a National Merit scholarship, the trade-off can be more than worth it. Check out *The Best 390 Colleges*, 2025 Edition, for well researched profiles of public and private schools.

Though the amounts of money may not be huge, every little bit helps. One other point to keep in mind is that while most of the scholarships through NMSC are relatively small, many universities seek National Merit finalists because of their academic abilities and (who are we kidding?) because the universities like to brag about how many such students chose them. For this reason, a number of state schools and less elite universities offer significant scholarships to National Merit finalists and sometimes semifinalists as well. Some schools offer full tuition for National Merit finalists, including the University of Alabama, Fordham University, University of Tulsa, University of Mississippi, Washington State University, Texas Tech University, and quite a few others. Many more schools award incomplete but large scholarships to National Merit finalists and semifinalists.

Aside from the possibility of winning a scholarship, the award itself looks great in your portfolio. So, if you think you are in contention for National Merit recognition, practice diligently and smartly! If not, don't sweat it too much, but prepare for the PSAT anyway because it is good practice for the SAT.

But I'm Not a Junior in High School Yet...

If you are not yet a junior, and you're interested in National Merit, you will have to take the test again your junior year in order to qualify.

A certain number of schools give the PSAT to students in their sophomore year—and sometimes even earlier. These schools hope that earlier exposure to these tests will help their students perform better in later years. If you're not yet in your junior year, the PSAT won't count for National Merit scholarship purposes, so it's really just a trial run for you. It's still a good idea to go into the test prepared in order to feel and perform your best. After all, there's nothing more unpleasant than a distressing testing experience, except maybe having a tooth drilled or watching the sad downward spiral of certain pop stars.

What If I'm in a Nonstandard Course of Study?

If you're going to spend only three years in secondary school, you have two options for when to take the PSAT for National Merit purposes: you can take it either in your next-to-last year or in your last year of secondary school. However, our advice is this: if you're in any program other than a usual four-year high school, be sure to talk to your school counselor, who will consult with NMSC and help ensure that you take the PSAT at the right time. This is important, because not taking the PSAT at the right time can disqualify you from National Merit recognition.

What If I Miss the PSAT Administration My Junior Year?

If you aren't concerned about National Merit scholarships, there's no reason to do anything in particular—except, perhaps, to obtain a few PSAT booklets to practice with, just to see what fun you missed.

However, if you want to be eligible for National Merit recognition, then swift action on your part is required. If an emergency arises that prevents you from taking the PSAT, you should write to the National Merit Scholarship Corporation *immediately* to request alternate testing dates. If you know you won't be able to take the PSAT when it is scheduled at your school, make arrangements in advance to take the PSAT on a different day at another school. If you miss the PSAT due to illness or emergency, contact your counselor and/or NMSC right away to see if you can register to take the test on a different date and/or at another school before the testing window ends. If you miss the testing window, contact NMSC as soon as possible, but no later than April 1 following the missed PSAT administration, to inquire about alternative ways to qualify. You'll also need a signature from a school official.

For More Information

If you have any questions or problems, the best person to consult is your school counselor, who can help make sure you're on the right track. If you need further help, contact your local Princeton Review office at 800-2-REVIEW or PrincetonReview.com, or you can contact National Merit directly:

National Merit Scholarship Corporation
1560 Sherman Avenue, Suite 200
Evanston, IL 60201-4897
(847) 866-5100
NationalMerit.org

WHAT OTHER SCHOLARSHIPS CAN I APPLY TO?

In addition to the National Merit Scholarships, you can also apply to College Board's Opportunity Scholarships and their partner scholarships. If you opt in to the free Student Search Service® when you take the PSAT/NMSQT, College Board will further connect you to scholarship partners who offer more than $300 million annually in scholarships to qualifying students!

College Board BigFuture® Scholarships

Beginning with the 2020 class, College Board has offered a scholarship program with $5 million in scholarships each year to qualifying high school juniors in the United States, Puerto Rico, and other U.S. territories. The program consists of six different tasks designed to help students divide the process of applying to college from start to finish. Completing each step gives students the opportunity to enter to win one of the $40,000 scholarships or one of hundreds of $500 scholarships awarded each month. The more tasks a student completes, the more chances that student has to win. The six tasks are as follows:

1. **Build Your College List**
2. **Practice for the SAT**
3. **Explore Scholarships**
4. **Strengthen Your College List**
5. **Complete the FAFSA**
6. **Apply to Colleges**

For information regarding the official rules on how to qualify for these drawings, visit College Board's BigFuture® website: bigfuture.collegeboard.org.

Other Partner Scholarships

Hispanic Scholarship Fund
When to apply: accepting applications from January 1 to March 15 of your junior year
hsf.net/scholarship

United Negro College Fund (UNCF)
When to apply: Anytime
uncf.org/

American Indian Graduate Center
When to apply: Anytime
nativehire.org/american-indian-graduate-center/

Asian Pacific Islander American Scholars
When to apply: September to January of your junior year
apiascholars.org/

Children of Fallen Patriots
When to apply: Anytime
fallenpatriots.org/

Chapter 3
General Strategies

The first step to cracking the PSAT is to know how best to approach the test. The PSAT is not like the tests you've taken in school, so you need to learn to look at it in a different way. This chapter will show test-taking strategies that immediately improve your score. Make sure you fully understand these concepts before moving on to the following chapters. Good luck!

BASIC PRINCIPLES OF CRACKING THE TEST

What College Board Is Good At

The folks at College Board have been writing standardized tests for nearly a century, and they write tests for all sorts of programs. They have administered the test so many times that they know exactly how you will approach it. They know how you'll attack certain questions, what sort of mistakes you'll probably make, and even what answer you'll be most likely to pick. Freaky, isn't it?

However, College Board's strength is also a weakness. Because the test is standardized, the PSAT has to ask the same type of questions over and over again. Sure, the numbers or the words might change, but the basics don't. With enough practice, you can learn to think like the test-writers. But try to use your powers for good, okay?

The PSAT Isn't School

Our job isn't to teach you math or English—leave that to your supersmart schoolteachers. Instead, we're going to teach you what the PSAT is and how to crack the PSAT. You'll soon see that the PSAT involves a very different skill set from the one you use in school.

No Penalty for Incorrect Answers!
You will NOT be penalized on the PSAT for any wrong answers. This means you should always guess, even if this means choosing an answer at random.

Be warned that some of the approaches we're going to show you may seem counterintuitive or unnatural. Some of these strategies may be very different from the way you learned to approach similar questions in school, but trust us! Try tackling the questions using our techniques and keep practicing until they become easier. You'll see a real improvement in your score.

Let's take a look at the questions.

Cracking Multiple-Choice Questions

What's the capital of Azerbaijan?

Give up?

Unless you spend your spare time studying an atlas or live in that part of the world, this may stump you. If this question came up on a test, you'd have to skip it, wouldn't you? Well, maybe not. Let's turn this question into a multiple-choice question—just like all the questions on the PSAT Reading and Writing section, and the majority of questions you'll find on the PSAT Math section—and see if you can figure out the answer anyway.

1 Mark for Review

What is the capital of Azerbaijan?

Ⓐ Washington, D.C.

Ⓑ Paris

Ⓒ London

Ⓓ Baku

The question doesn't seem that hard anymore, does it? Of course, we made our example extremely easy. (By the way, there won't actually be any questions about geography on the PSAT that aren't answered by the accompanying text.) But you'd be surprised by how many people give up on PSAT questions that aren't much more difficult than this one just because they don't know the correct answer right off the top of their heads. "Capital of Azerbaijan? Oh, no! I've never heard of Azerbaijan!"

These students don't stop to think that they might be able to find the correct answer simply by eliminating all of the answer choices they know are wrong.

You Already Know Almost All of the Answers

Most of the questions on the PSAT are multiple-choice questions, and every multiple-choice question has four answer choices. One of those choices, and only one, will be the correct answer to the question. You don't have to come up with the answer from scratch. You just have to identify it.

How will you do that?

It's Not About Finding the Right Answer

The Digital PSAT tools will include an Answer Eliminator, so any wrong answers you find can be crossed off directly on the screen. If you need a more subtle system of rating the answers, write A, B, C, D on your scratch paper to mark them accordingly. Try using the following notations:

- ✔ Put a check mark next to an answer you like.
- ~ Put a squiggle next to an answer you kind of like.
- ? Put a question mark next to an answer you don't understand.
- ~~A~~ Cross out the letter of any answer choice you KNOW is wrong.

You can always come up with your own system. Just make sure you are consistent.

Look for the Wrong Answers Instead of the Right Ones

Why? Because wrong answers are usually easier to find than the right ones. After all, there are more of them! Remember the question about Azerbaijan? Even though you didn't know the answer off the top of your head, you easily figured it out by eliminating the three obviously incorrect choices. You looked for wrong answers first.

In other words, you used the Process of Elimination, which we'll call POE for short. This is an extremely important concept, one we'll come back to again and again. It's one of the keys to improving your PSAT score. When you finish reading this book, you will be able to use POE to answer many questions that you may not understand.

The great artist Michelangelo once said that when he looked at a block of marble, he could see a statue inside. All he had to do to make a sculpture was to chip away everything that wasn't part of it. You should approach difficult PSAT multiple-choice questions in the same way, by chipping away everything that's not correct. By first eliminating the most obviously incorrect choices on difficult questions, you will be able to focus your attention on the few choices that remain.

PROCESS OF ELIMINATION (POE)

There won't be many questions on the PSAT in which incorrect choices will be as easy to eliminate as they were on the Azerbaijan question. But if you read this book carefully, you'll learn how to eliminate at least one choice on almost any PSAT multiple-choice question, if not two or even three choices.

What good is it to eliminate just one or two choices on a four-choice PSAT question?

Plenty. In fact, for most students, it's an important key to earning higher scores. Here's another example:

2 Mark for Review

What is the capital of Qatar?

(A) Paris

(B) Dukhan

(C) Tokyo

(D) Doha

On this question you'll almost certainly be able to eliminate two of the four choices by using POE. That means you're still not sure of the answer. You know that the capital of Qatar has to be either Doha or Dukhan, but you don't know which.

Should you skip the question and go on? Or should you guess?

Close Your Eyes and Point

There is no guessing penalty on the PSAT, so you should enter an answer for every question. If you get down to two answers, just pick one of them. There's no harm in doing so.

You're going to hear a lot of mixed opinions about which answer you should guess or whether you should guess at all. Let's clear up a few misconceptions about guessing.

FALSE: Don't answer a question unless you're absolutely sure of the answer.

> You will almost certainly have teachers and school counselors who tell you this. Don't listen to them! While the SAT used to penalize students for wrong answers prior to 2016, no tests in the current "Suite of Assessments" do this now. Put something down for every question: you might get a freebie.

FALSE: If you have to guess, guess (C).

> While there may be some truth to this on "homemade" tests, standardized tests are exactly that: standardized. Part of the standardization means that over the course of a test each answer choice should show up about the same number of times. While there will be some variation to this, there isn't a single letter that tends to come up more often as the correct answer on the PSAT or SAT. If you have to guess at random, just pick your favorite and move on.

FALSE: Always pick the [fill in the blank].

Be careful with directives that tell you that this or that answer, or type of answer, is always right. It's much safer to learn the rules and to have a solid guessing strategy in place.

As far as guessing is concerned, we do have a small piece of advice. First and foremost, make sure of one thing:

> Answer every question on the PSAT. There's no penalty.

GUESS AND GO

Sometimes you won't be able to eliminate any answers, and other times there will be questions that you won't have time to look at. For those, we have a simple solution. Just Guess and Go! Don't waste time worrying about that question. Fill in an answer, any answer, and move on. You may get a few free points that way.

PACE YOURSELF

Guess and Go should remind us about something very important: there's a very good chance that you won't answer every question on the test. Instead, work at a pace that lets you avoid careless mistakes, and don't stress about the questions you don't get to.

Think about it this way. In each given module, there will be questions that you can tackle quickly and accurately and others that will take you more time and effort. Why should you spend 4 or 5 minutes on one question when you may get two or three questions that are easier for you in the same amount of time?

Another tool you can use on the Digital PSAT to help pace yourself is the Mark for Review tool. If you see a question that looks as if it might be time consuming or that you aren't sure how to solve, but you still want to come back to it if there is time, mark it. You can see the marked questions at a glance both at the end of the section or by opening the section overview at any time. This will allow you to quickly find the ones you want to work after you've done all the questions you know you can do quickly and accurately.

Unless you're currently scoring in the 650+ range on the two sections, you shouldn't be working all the questions.

Slow down, score more. You're not scored on *how many questions you do.* You're scored on *how many questions you answer correctly.* Doing fewer questions can mean more correct answers overall!

EMBRACE YOUR POOD

Embrace your *what* now? POOD! It stands for "Personal Order of Difficulty." The Digital PSAT will put questions in a rough order of difficulty, by content domain on the Reading and Writing section and overall on the Math section. But this Order of Difficulty (OOD) is only what College Board thinks about the question levels, not how you will do on them. So, rather than doing the questions in order, you need to be particularly vigilant about applying your *Personal* Order of Difficulty (POOD).

Think about it this way. There's someone writing the words that you're reading right now. So, what happens if you are asked, *Who is the author of PSAT/NMSQT Prep?* Do you know the answer to that question? Maybe not. Do we know the answer to that question? Absolutely.

So, you can't exactly say that that question is "difficult," but you can say that certain people would have an easier time answering it. Pace yourself. Work carefully on questions you know how to do to make sure you get them right. Mark questions you want to come back to later.

As we've begun to suggest with our Pacing, POE, and Guess and Go strategies, The Princeton Review's strategies are all about making the test your own, to whatever extent that is possible. We call this idea POOD because we believe it is essential that you identify the questions that you find easy or hard and that you work the test in a way most suitable to your goals and strengths.

As you familiarize yourself with the rest of our strategies, keep all of this in mind. You may be surprised to find out how you perform on particular question types and sections. This test may be standardized, but the biggest improvements are usually reserved for those who can treat the test in a personalized, nonstandardized way.

You Can Leave Yourself a Note!

On the PSAT, you can leave yourself a note using a tool within the test called the annotation box. As you work through the test, perhaps you read a question and immediately know something but can't grasp the full answer yet—leave yourself a note in the annotation box, move on, then come back later, and your note will be there.

Summary

- When you don't know the right answer to a multiple-choice question, look for wrong answers instead. They're usually easier to find.
- When you find a wrong answer choice, eliminate it. In other words, use Process of Elimination, or POE.
- There's no penalty for wrong answers, so there's no reason NOT to guess.
- There will likely be at least a few questions you simply don't get to and others for which you find it difficult to eliminate even one answer choice. When this happens, just Guess and Go!
- Pace yourself. Work carefully on questions you know how to do to make sure you get them right. Mark questions you want to come back to later. Guess and Go on any you know are not worth your time or effort or that you know you are unlikely to get right.
- Make the test your own. When you can work the test to suit your strengths (and use our strategies to overcome any weaknesses), you'll be on your way to a higher score.

Part II
Practice Test 1

HOW TO TAKE THE DIGITAL PSAT ON PAPER

The Digital PSAT will be administered online, so it is best if you take your practice tests in the online tools for this book. However, if you prefer to take this test on paper, you can do so by either indicating your answers as described in the directions for print tests included with each module or by entering your answers as you go using the downloadable bubble sheet in your student portal.

On the Digital PSAT, you will get only two modules in each section, and the second module you get in each section will be determined by your performance on the first module in that section. Therefore, for both RW (Reading and Writing) and Math, the following test contains a standard first module and two options for the second module, one easier and one harder. You should take the appropriate second module based on your performance in the first module, as detailed below, but you can feel free to use the other module for extra practice later.

In order to navigate the practice test in this book instead of online, take the following steps.

- ☐ Take Reading and Writing Module 1, allowing yourself 32 minutes to complete it.
- ☐ Go to the answer key on page 92 and determine the number of questions you got correct in RW Module 1.
- ☐ If you get fewer than 15 questions correct, take RW Module 2—Easier, which starts on page 43. If you get 15 or more questions correct, take RW Module 2—Harder, which starts on page 54.
- ☐ Whichever RW Module 2 you take, start it immediately and allow yourself 32 minutes to complete it.
- ☐ Take a 10-minute break between RW Module 2 and Math Module 1.
- ☐ Take Math Module 1, allowing yourself 35 minutes to complete it.
- ☐ Go to the answer key on page 92 and determine the number of questions you got correct in Math Module 1.
- ☐ If you get fewer than 14 questions correct, take Math Module 2—Easier, which starts on page 74. If you get 14 or more questions correct, take Math Module 2—Harder, which starts on page 82.
- ☐ Whichever Math Module you take, start it immediately and allow yourself 35 minutes to complete it.
- ☐ After you finish the test, check your answers to RW Module 2 and Math Module 2.
- ☐ Only after you complete the entire test should you read the explanations for the questions, which start on page 93 and are also available online.
- ☐ Go to your online student tools to see the latest information about scoring and to get your estimated score.

Chapter 4
Practice Test 1

PSAT Prep Test 1—Reading and Writing

Module 1

Turn to Section 1 of your answer sheet to answer the questions in this section.

DIRECTIONS

The questions in this section address a number of important reading and writing skills. Each question includes one or more passages, which may include a table or graph. Read each passage and question carefully, and then choose the best answer to the question based on the passage(s).

All questions in the section are multiple-choice with four answer choices. Each question has a single best answer.

1 Mark for Review

A portmanteau is a single word formed by blending two separate words together. Not only does it contain portions of sounds and spellings from each of the original words, but it also uses the meanings of the original words to create a singular word that represents both the meanings. For instance, the words "breakfast" and "lunch" would be _______ to create the portmanteau word "brunch."

Which choice completes the text with the most logical and precise word or phrase?

Ⓐ defined

Ⓑ combined

Ⓒ explained

Ⓓ separated

2 Mark for Review

Film directors often reference previous works they admire, sometimes even replicating camera angles used in specific scenes. One such example of this occurs in director Darren Aronofsky's film *Requiem for a Dream*, which contains a shot-by-shot _______ of a similar scene from Kon Satoshi's film *Perfect Blue*.

Which choice best completes the text with the most logical and precise word or phrase?

Ⓐ correction

Ⓑ explanation

Ⓒ criticism

Ⓓ reproduction

CONTINUE

3 Mark for Review

In the early twentieth century, city planners in Los Angeles grew frustrated by the inflexibility of the electric rail system. Recognizing the growing popularity of the automobile, they supplanted the rail system with an elevated motorway, an _______ that quickly grew to accommodate thousands of commuters and redefined the city's infrastructure.

Which choice best completes the text with the most logical and precise word or phrase?

Ⓐ expense

Ⓑ inconvenience

Ⓒ appendage

Ⓓ innovation

4 Mark for Review

The increased use of tracking technology, such as the computer vision system Hawk-Eye, has _______ how judgment calls in tennis are made. Formerly, every call was made by a referee, relying only on what that particular referee saw, but now players can appeal those decisions for more precise results.

Which choice best completes the text with the most logical and precise word or phrase?

Ⓐ modified

Ⓑ exhausted

Ⓒ muddled

Ⓓ hampered

5 Mark for Review

A tombstone laid in the American settlement of Jamestown features elaborate carvings in limestone, but little is known of the stone's origin. Researchers believe the stone must have been made for an individual from a _______ family: not only were most tombstones at the time made of wood, a far cheaper material, but analysis has also traced organisms in the stone to Europe, meaning that a great expense was incurred to transport the limestone to the settlement.

Which choice completes the text with the most logical and precise word or phrase?

Ⓐ wasteful

Ⓑ nameless

Ⓒ prosperous

Ⓓ famous

CONTINUE

6 Mark for Review

A study by University of Cambridge researcher Nina Trivedy Rogers and colleagues concluded that a 2016 government program that imposed new taxes on sugary soft drinks helped reduce sugar consumption for adults and children. The study, conducted from 2011 to 2019, relied on responses to a national survey from 8,000 adults and 7,656 children. Assessing the recorded intake of sugars, proteins, and carbohydrates and their respective percentages of daily consumption, the study noted a decrease of 3 grams per day of sugar for both children and adults. Researchers did note, however, that the scope of the study extends before and after the implementation of the government program, so the extent to which the taxes helped reduce sugar usage is difficult to determine.

Which choice best describes the main purpose of the text?

Ⓐ To show a study's conclusion and acknowledge a limitation to that conclusion

Ⓑ To describe an important policy and how results of a study contradict the policy's goals

Ⓒ To argue that researchers were confused by unexpected results from a study

Ⓓ To demonstrate ways to enhance a study's ability to identify societal trends

7 Mark for Review

In 1922, Finnish physician Arvo Ylppö established a pediatric care clinic in Finland and later became a professor of pediatrics. The clinic was the first of its kind in Finland to focus on maternity and child health and developed into a system of clinics. As a research professor, Ylppö discovered that some conditions in prematurely born infants were treatable, and he later became known worldwide for his research on the health and care of premature infants.

Which choice best states the main purpose of the text?

Ⓐ To contrast pediatric physicians with research professors

Ⓑ To emphasis the importance of pediatric care

Ⓒ To describe how physicians treat children

Ⓓ To highlight the contributions and career of an individual

CONTINUE

8 Mark for Review

Text 1

Microbes are known to survive beneath frozen water on Earth where pools of meltwater—water released by the melting of snow or ice—exist and enough sunlight can reach to drive photosynthesis. Some researchers believe that microbes could be found in similar pools of water beneath frozen water on Mars. Most ice on Mars contains particles of dark dust that absorbs sunlight, causing the surrounding ice to melt into liquid water. In a study, the researchers found that sunlight can travel up to depths of nine feet through the dusty ice and in a great enough quantity to support the photosynthetic process.

Text 2

While scientists agree that ice on Mars contains dust particles, some are skeptical about whether meltwater actually exists beneath the surface ice. The thin, dry atmosphere on Mars prevents ice from melting into liquid water, instead turning it directly into gas. While these atmospheric properties may not similarly affect the state of water below the surface, there are also immense quantities of dust particles in Mars's atmosphere that block much of the sunlight that the surface of Mars would otherwise receive.

Based on the texts, how would the author of Text 2 most likely respond to the study findings mentioned in Text 1?

(A) By noting that some dust particles block sunlight to a greater extent than others and therefore, to have any chance at driving photosynthesis, sunlight will need to penetrate more than nine feet below the surface of the ice on Mars

(B) By claiming that since the atmosphere on Mars keeps surface water in a perpetually frozen state, an effort must be made to demonstrate that photosynthesis is achievable on the surface as well beneath the surface ice

(C) By suggesting that the presence of dust particles in the atmosphere of Mars may prevent the necessary amount of sunlight needed for photosynthesis to penetrate the surface ice

(D) By arguing that most scientists would prefer to discover the presence of liquid water on the surface of Mars rather than underneath layers of ice

9 Mark for Review

In the Arctic, greenhouse gases become trapped in ice until the ice melts and releases those gases into the atmosphere. A team of NASA researchers led by Abhishek Chatterjee found that, in recent decades, the Arctic region has become a net contributor to global warming, meaning that the region's ice releases more greenhouse gas than it traps. However, the rate at which the greenhouse gas carbon dioxide is released from the region is far lower than the corresponding rate at which the global temperature is rising. Upon further analysis, the team also found that the greenhouse gas methane, which traps more heat than does carbon dioxide, was also being emitted into the atmosphere from the thawing Arctic ice.

According to the text, what did Chatterjee and his team discover about methane?

(A) It counteracts the effects of carbon dioxide when released into the atmosphere.

(B) It contributes to an increase in the rate of global warming alongside carbon dioxide.

(C) It stays trapped in Arctic ice.

(D) It plays an important role in maintaining a balanced global temperature.

CONTINUE

10 Mark for Review

Recently, archaeologists unearthed a new carving on Easter Island, a volcanic island off the coast of Chile. Easter Island, a UNESCO Heritage Site, contains statues created by a Polynesian tribe more than 500 years ago. The newly discovered statue, of great significance to the native Rapa Nui community, was found in the bed of a lake that may have dried up due to climate change.

Which choice best states the main topic of the text?

Ⓐ The native traditions of the Rapa Nui

Ⓑ Climate change in Chile

Ⓒ A notable discovery on Easter Island

Ⓓ A new way to designate UNESCO Heritage Sites

11 Mark for Review

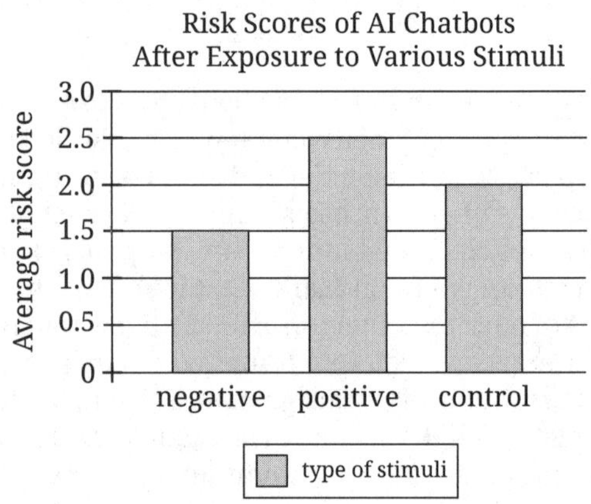

Yukon Zhao and colleagues hypothesized that the behavior and decision-making of artificial intelligence (AI) chatbots could be influenced by exposure to positive and negative inputs. The researchers asked various AI chatbots to make risk assessments of financial questions and graded the bots' responses on a zero to three scale, with low scores indicating an aversion to risk and high scores an acceptance of risk. Prior to being prompted to respond, the bots were primed, or exposed to, images of conventionally positive stimuli (such as an image of a beautiful meadow), conventionally negative stimuli (such as an image of a snake poised to strike), or no stimuli at all. The research team concluded that the experimental group primed with positive stimuli was more inclined to take financial risks than the group primed with negative stimuli.

Which choice best describes data in the graph that support the research team's conclusion?

Ⓐ All three groups of chatbots recommended taking more risk than the researchers expected.

Ⓑ None of the groups had average risk scores of greater than 2.0.

Ⓒ The chatbots in the control group had an average risk score slightly higher than those in the other two groups.

Ⓓ The chatbots exposed to positive stimuli demonstrated a greater likelihood of recommending risk taking than those in the other two groups.

CONTINUE

12 Mark for Review

Severity of Smartphone Overdependence in Adolescents Based on Four Factors, 2024

Factor	No/Minimal	Yes/Severe
Anxiety	18.5%	51.1%
Loneliness	23.3%	41.2%
Depression	22.2%	36.6%
Experience of violent treatment	25.7%	37.1%

Smartphone overdependence—a circumstance in which an individual excessively depends on and is unable to stop using a smart device—is a growing area of concern, especially among psychologists. A 2020 study sought to understand the underlying factors that are commonly associated with overdependence in adolescents, focusing on four primary factors: anxiety, loneliness, depression, and experience of violent treatment. During the study, 54,000 smartphone-overdependent participants were asked to rank how recently and how often they experienced each of the four factors, with possible responses of "yes" and "no" or "severe" and "minimal" depending on the factor. After the responses were recorded, compiled, and analyzed, the factor determined to be most commonly associated with smartphone overdependence was ______

Which choice most effectively uses data from the table to complete the text?

Ⓐ anxiety.

Ⓑ loneliness.

Ⓒ depression.

Ⓓ experience of violent treatment.

13 Mark for Review

The Conscript is an 1831 story by Honoré de Balzac. In the story, the author depicts the character Mme. de Dey as someone whose actions echo her sense of optimism: ______

Which quotation from *The Conscript* most effectively illustrates the claim?

Ⓐ "Every footfall, every sound in the street, raised hopes to be disappointed."

Ⓑ "It was impossible not to read her hopes in the dainty and thoughtful preparations about the room."

Ⓒ "She stared into the darkness, seeing her son in every shadow everywhere; but it was only for a moment."

Ⓓ "She still wavered between the fear that she had lost her son and the hope of seeing him once more."

CONTINUE

14 Mark for Review

Research by Alyssa R. Minton and colleagues examined how a person's age determines how harshly they judge the actions of another person. A group of 225 participants was divided into an 18–30 age group and a 60–79 age group and then shown two realistic simulations—one in which a person intended to harm another person but was not successful and a second in which a person accidentally caused harm to another person without intending to do so. The 60–79 group judged the individual who caused accidental harm much more leniently than did the 18–30 group but the person who intended to cause harm and failed much more harshly than did the 18–30 group. The findings suggest that older participants ______

Which choice most logically completes the text?

Ⓐ were more likely to consider an individual's intent than the participants in the younger age group.

Ⓑ were equally as likely to harshly judge the individual who intended to cause harm but failed as the participants in the younger age group.

Ⓒ may have been more strongly irritated by the recklessness of the individual who caused accidental harm than those in the younger age group were.

Ⓓ may have placed a strong emphasis on the intent of an individual regardless of whether the individual caused harm or not.

15 Mark for Review

A key characteristic of the class of animals known as amphibians is that they live in water until they reach adulthood, at which point they shift to primarily living on land. However, axolotls, a type of amphibian, never complete this metamorphosis and live their entire lives in water. Additionally, axolotls are found only in one location in the world, Lake Xochimilco, a lake in Mexico containing a unique combination of resources. Based on this evidence, a group of researchers has claimed that axolotls have ______

Which choice most logically completes the text?

Ⓐ avoided the dangers posed by land predators by remaining in the water.

Ⓑ forced scientists to re-examine how classes of animals are determined and organized.

Ⓒ adapted to the conditions of their particular habitat and environment.

Ⓓ prospered despite lacking a traditional characteristic of amphibians.

CONTINUE

16 Mark for Review

According to the works of eighteenth-century entomologist Thomas Broun, about one thousand species of beetle can be identified in New Zealand. However, Broun's lists _______ few illustrations and contain a number of duplicate species. The so-called "Broun Effect" explains why New Zealand claims far more beetle species than does Great Britain, despite other insects having comparable numbers of species between the two countries.

Which choice completes the text so that it conforms to the conventions of Standard English?

Ⓐ will have included

Ⓑ include

Ⓒ had included

Ⓓ included

17 Mark for Review

Founded in 1918 on the ideas of politician Albert Schädler, Liechtenstein's Progressive Citizens Party is one of two major political _______ parliament. However, Schädler himself opposed the formation of political parties in Liechtenstein's parliament and identified as an independent throughout his parliamentary career.

Which choice completes the text so that it conforms to the conventions of Standard English?

Ⓐ parties that compose it's

Ⓑ parties' that compose it's

Ⓒ parties that compose its

Ⓓ party's that compose its

18 Mark for Review

In many scientific disciplines, the practice of writing fieldnotes during or after observation in a natural setting is fundamental to research on species and phenomena. To illustrate the appearance of species that they sight, scientists within _______ zoological branch that focuses on the class Aves (birds)—often use sketches that call attention to the birds' specific features in their fieldnotes.

Which choice completes the text so that it conforms to the conventions of Standard English?

Ⓐ ornithology (a

Ⓑ ornithology—a

Ⓒ ornithology, a

Ⓓ ornithology: a

19 Mark for Review

A typical school year in the United States is 180 days, but the number of _______ attend school varies around the world. For example, students in the Netherlands attend school 200 days per year, while students in South Korea are in the classroom 220 days a year.

Which choice completes the text so that it conforms to the conventions of Standard English?

Ⓐ day's students

Ⓑ days students

Ⓒ days student's

Ⓓ day's student's

CONTINUE

20 Mark for Review

Small arachnids found in many homes, dust mites transmit a digestive enzyme that makes _______ a possible cause of asthma- or allergy-induced hives—also known as chronic urticaria—that can be difficult to alleviate.

Which choice completes the text so that it conforms to the conventions of Standard English?

Ⓐ it

Ⓑ one

Ⓒ them

Ⓓ this

21 Mark for Review

Julia Minamata, the creator of the mystery adventure video game *The Crimson Diamond*, set out to develop a game after discovering that new technology made the process more accessible. She began by illustrating an entire house in the style of pixel _______ the mysterious game that takes place inside of the house could take shape.

Which choice completes the text so that it conforms to the conventions of Standard English?

Ⓐ art,

Ⓑ art, then,

Ⓒ art

Ⓓ art; then,

22 Mark for Review

In 1965, Giorgina Reid patented a shoreline protection system she had developed to fortify her New York ocean cottage against storms. Reid volunteered to install her system to protect the Montauk Point Lighthouse from erosion and successfully stabilized the grounds of the lighthouse by 1985, largely at her own expense. _______ in 1996, at the lighthouse's bicentennial celebration, Reid was honored for her work to save the lighthouse.

Which choice completes the text with the most logical transition?

Ⓐ Then,

Ⓑ Previously,

Ⓒ In conclusion,

Ⓓ Similarly,

23 Mark for Review

Over 99% of an atom's mass is in its positively charged nucleus, which consists of protons and neutrons. Neutrons have no electric charge and a relatively large mass. _______ protons are positively charged and have a slightly lower mass.

Which choice completes the text with the most logical transition?

Ⓐ In comparison,

Ⓑ In the end,

Ⓒ For example,

Ⓓ Previously,

CONTINUE

24 Mark for Review

In his 2002 book *The Power of Babel*, American linguist John McWhorter notes that speakers of Danish, Swedish, and Norwegian are able to understand each other more easily than speakers of standard Italian can comprehend those who speak an Italian dialect local to the city of Milan. _______ McWhorter argues that the distinction between a "language" and a "dialect" is relatively meaningless.

Which choice completes the text with the most logical transition?

Ⓐ For this reason,

Ⓑ By contrast,

Ⓒ Conversely,

Ⓓ In other words,

25 Mark for Review

While researching a topic, a student has taken the following notes:

- Dorothy Stanley (1924–1990) was an American educator and activist.
- She was raised in the Miwok culture and fought for Indigenous rights.
- One of the ways she educated people was through demonstrations at festivals and museums.
- She was one of the last speakers of the Miwok languages.

The student wants to introduce Dorothy Stanley to an audience unfamiliar with her career. Which choice most effectively uses relevant information from the notes to accomplish this goal?

Ⓐ American activist Dorothy Stanley fought for Indigenous rights, educated people through demonstrations, and was one of the last speakers of the Miwok languages.

Ⓑ Dorothy Stanley educated people through demonstrations at festivals and museums.

Ⓒ One of the last speakers of the Miwok languages was Dorothy Stanley.

Ⓓ Demonstrations at festivals and museums were one way Dorothy Stanley, who spoke the Miwok languages, educated people.

CONTINUE

26 Mark for Review

While researching a topic, a student has taken the following notes:

- *Peter Pan and Wendy* is a 1911 novel by Scottish writer J. M. Barrie.
- In *Peter Pan and Wendy*, the beginning of the story takes place in London.
- *Peter Pan* is a 2024 musical adaptation of *Peter Pan and Wendy*.
- The beginning of the musical is set in modern-day America.
- It includes references to social media trends.

The student wants to emphasize the setting of the beginning of the musical. Which choice most effectively uses relevant information from the notes to accomplish this goal?

Ⓐ *Peter Pan* includes references to social media trends.

Ⓑ The beginning of *Peter Pan and Wendy* takes place in London.

Ⓒ *Peter Pan and Wendy* is a novel that was adapted into a musical.

Ⓓ The beginning of *Peter Pan*, an adaptation of *Peter Pan and Wendy*, is set in modern-day America.

27 Mark for Review

While researching a topic, a student has taken the following notes:

- The 1939 New York World's Fair contained exhibits grouped into seven zones.
- The exhibits represented nations, US states and territories, and corporations.
- These exhibits introduced fairgoers to cultures from around the world.
- 62 nations participated in the fair.

The student wants to emphasize the number of nations participating in the 1939 New York World's Fair. Which choice most effectively uses relevant information from the notes to accomplish this goal?

Ⓐ Seven zones of exhibits representing nations, US states and territories, and corporations appeared at the fair.

Ⓑ The 1939 New York World's Fair featured 62 nations from around the world.

Ⓒ Exhibits at the New York World's Fair in 1939 introduced fairgoers to cultures from around the world.

Ⓓ The nations participating in the 1939 New York World's Fair were represented by exhibits.

YIELD

Once you've finished (or run out of time for) this section, use the answer key to determine how many questions you got right. If you got fewer than 15 questions right, move on to Module 2—Easier, otherwise move on to Module 2—Harder.

PSAT Prep Test 1—Reading and Writing

Module 2—Easier

Turn to Section 1 of your answer sheet to answer the questions in this section.

DIRECTIONS

The questions in this section address a number of important reading and writing skills. Each question includes one or more passages, which may include a table or graph. Read each passage and question carefully, and then choose the best answer to the question based on the passage(s).

All questions in the section are multiple-choice with four answer choices. Each question has a single best answer.

1 Mark for Review

The following text is adapted from Charles Kingsley's 1865 novel *Hereward: The Last of the English.* Lady Godiva is a noblewoman from England.

> Known to all is Lady Godiva, the most beautiful as well as the most saintly woman of her day; who, "all her life, kept at her own expense thirteen poor folk wherever she went; who, throughout Lent, watched in the church at triple matins, namely, one for the Trinity, one for the Cross, and one for St. Mary; who every day read the Psalter through.

As used in the text, what does the word "kept" most nearly mean?

(A) Held

(B) Prayed

(C) Concealed

(D) Supported

2 Mark for Review

The following text is adapted from John Keats's 1816 poem "Calidore: A Fragment."

> And now the sharp keel of his little boat
> Comes up with ripple, and with easy float,
> And glides into a bed of water-lilies:
> Broad leav'd are they and their white canopies

As used in the text, what does the phrase "comes up" most nearly mean?

(A) Disrupts

(B) Submerges

(C) Approaches

(D) Invents

CONTINUE

3 Mark for Review

Studies show that 3% of adults living in the United States in 2015–2016 had a peanut allergy, compared to less than 1% in 1999. Allergists are specially trained to identify allergens, or allergy triggers, as well as train families to take _______ measures against allergens. Recent research shows that consulting with an allergist can reduce overall health care costs for children with peanut allergies and help families avoid allergy-related expenses.

Which choice completes the text with the most logical and precise word or phrase?

Ⓐ generic

Ⓑ inflammatory

Ⓒ preventative

Ⓓ minimal

4 Mark for Review

Homeowners are often required to provide potential buyers with licensed inspections of their homes' energy efficiency. Studies have shown that this requirement encourages homeowners to invest in energy-saving technology as a means of _______ the probability of a successful sale.

Which choice completes the text with the most logical and precise word or phrase?

Ⓐ exploring

Ⓑ increasing

Ⓒ investigating

Ⓓ diminishing

5 Mark for Review

Fish can both detect and respond to fear in other fish due to oxytocin, a hormone that regulates emotions. <u>When scientists deleted genes used to regulate oxytocin levels in zebrafish, the fish became less able to detect the emotions of other fish</u>. Likewise, when the zebrafish with deleted genes received oxytocin manually, their ability to detect and mimic emotions from other fish was reestablished. The zebrafish also tended to focus more on other fish that had previously exhibited stress.

Which choice best states the purpose of the underlined sentence in the text as a whole?

Ⓐ It contrasts the emotional regulation abilities of zebrafish to other types of fish.

Ⓑ It introduces the hormone oxytocin and its impact on fish.

Ⓒ It indicates a rationale for why zebrafish are able to recognize stress.

Ⓓ It demonstrates an effect that oxytocin regulation can have on zebrafish.

CONTINUE

6 Mark for Review

According to the American Heart Association, cardiovascular health can be measured in terms of diet, physical activity, tobacco use, weight, cholesterol levels, blood sugar levels, and blood pressure. Scientists at the Columbia University Mailman School of Public Health proposed adding an eighth factor: sleep. <u>The scientists believe that both sleep duration and sleep quality are integral components of cardiovascular health and can be predictive of cardiovascular disease and contribute to other risk factors</u>. For example, participants with shorter sleep duration also tended to have irregular sleep patterns and a higher incidence of obesity, high blood pressure, and type 2 diabetes.

Which choice best states the purpose of the underlined sentence in the text as a whole?

Ⓐ It proposes a technique described in the text that should be used for further studies.

Ⓑ It outlines the specific aspects of a factor described in the text that scientists believe contributes to cardiovascular health.

Ⓒ It indicates the context that prompted the study described in the text.

Ⓓ It provides a rationale for why the addition of another cardiovascular health factor described in the text is inevitable.

7 Mark for Review

The Carnaval de Oruro is celebrated in Bolivia. While it originated as a pagan religious festival performed by the indigenous Itu people, the modern Carnaval now also includes a ritual from Christianity honoring the Virgin of Socavón. During the festival, 48 groups of folk dancers perform 18 styles of dance during a pilgrimage that traverses four kilometers. The 18 dance styles represent various groups from Bolivia's diverse cultural heritage. The festival was marked as one of UNESCO's Masterpieces of the Oral and Intangible Heritage of Humanity in 2001.

According to the text, what is one way that the Carnaval de Oruro has shifted from its original context?

Ⓐ It includes elements from multiple religious perspectives.

Ⓑ It focuses on a single ethnic group within Bolivia.

Ⓒ It does not retain any characteristics of its Itu origin.

Ⓓ It remains in a single location for its duration.

CONTINUE

8 Mark for Review

After he was orphaned, Bengali politician Abdul Hamid Khan Bhashani was raised by a preacher at a base in Jaleswar, a region in the Goalpara district of Assam. Jaleswar was situated at a boundary between the Bengal and Assam regions and provided Bhashani with rich exposure to the different languages and religions existing among the Bengali people. His experience living in this area inspired him to become more politically conscious, and he ultimately became an advocate for the lower class and fought for Bangladeshi independence.

Based on the text, what would have been the most likely consequence if Bhashani had not lived in Jaleswar?

Ⓐ He may not have garnered as many supporters for his political causes.

Ⓑ He may have been able to prevent the war fought for Bangladeshi independence.

Ⓒ He may not have been inspired to get involved in politics.

Ⓓ He may have chosen the opposite side during the war for independence.

9 Mark for Review

The following text is from Alexander Pushkin's 1833 short story *The Queen of Spades*. The narrator, Tomsky, is describing Chaplitsky, a man who has suffered losses while gambling.

> Chaplitsky once lost about three hundred thousand roubles. He was in despair. My grandmother took pity. She gave him three cards telling him to play them one after the other, exacting from him a solemn promise that he would never play at cards again as long as he lived. Chaplitsky then went to his victorious opponent, and they began a fresh game. On the first card he staked fifty thousand roubles, and won sonika.

According to the text, what does Chaplitsky do after meeting with Tomsky's grandmother?

Ⓐ He uses Tomsky's grandmother's proposition as an opportunity to make money.

Ⓑ He gave Tomsky's grandmother his promise to avoid cards but immediately broke it.

Ⓒ He expressed concern over his ability to keep his promise to Tomsky's grandmother.

Ⓓ He wins back all of his money and uses it to continue gambling.

CONTINUE

10 Mark for Review

Average Annual Electricity Usage by US Citizens, 1960–2020, in kilowatt hours (kwh)

State	1960	1980	2000	2020
Alabama	1,250	4,100	6,500	6,500
Hawaii	900	1,900	2,250	2,000
New York	750	1,750	2,250	2,750

A high school student in the United States is analyzing the electricity use of different states over a 60-year time span. To help determine where she wants to move, the student is trying to figure out the average electricity used by someone living in Hawaii in 2020. According to the table, the student determines that this amount is ______

Which choice most effectively uses data from the table to complete the statement?

Ⓐ 2,750 kwh.

Ⓑ 2,000 kwh.

Ⓒ 2,250 kwh.

Ⓓ 1,900 kwh.

11 Mark for Review

The European eel has been considered critically endangered since the 1980s. More than a century ago, biologist Johannes Schmidt proposed that this decline was due to the eel's breeding habits, noting that the species undertakes a dangerous journey of 5,000–10,000 kilometers across the Atlantic Ocean to reach the Sargasso Sea to breed. In a study aiming to test this hypothesis, biologist Rosalind Wright and colleagues used satellite tagging to track a group of female eels from rivers in the Azores archipelago near Portugal. Two tags became separated from the eels due to predation, but initial results showed the eels were following a southwesterly trajectory toward the Sargasso Sea.

Which finding from the experiment, if true, would most directly support Schmidt's hypothesis?

Ⓐ Most of the eels were found to end up in a variety of locations with similar conditions to the Sargasso Sea, and they spent the entire breeding window in those locations.

Ⓑ None of the eels migrated to the Sargasso Sea, but they ended up staying in their starting locations and breeding within the confines of their initial habitats with the eels living nearest to them.

Ⓒ Of the eels that were monitored by Wright and her team, more than 30% did not survive the trip to the Sargasso Sea.

Ⓓ Only one eel was found to be located in a specific part of the Sargasso Sea with the conditions most ideal for breeding, and that eel didn't stay for the entire breeding window.

CONTINUE

12 Mark for Review

The Vampyre is an 1819 novel by Jon William Polidori. The narrator describes a young man as feeling a growing sense of dread while conversing with a companion: ______

Which quotation from *The Vampyre* most effectively illustrates the claim?

(A) "Still he found himself more and more attached to the almost fairy form before him."

(B) "She detailed to him the traditional appearance of these monsters, and his horror was increased, by hearing a description of Lord Ruthven."

(C) "But why attempt to describe charms which all feel, but none can appreciate?"

(D) "His oath startled him;—was he then to allow this monster to roam, bearing ruin upon his breath, amidst all he held dear, and not avert its progress?"

13 Mark for Review

The way people wake from sleep and become alert immediately is directly related in part to how they eat in their daily lives. Raphael Vallat and his team conducted a study to explore how a carbohydrate-rich breakfast affects an individual's waking patterns. Participants were provided with muffins high in carbohydrates, shakes high in protein, or granola bars high in fiber. Those who chose to consume muffins had the highest relative alertness score of 0.08, while those who chose to consume protein shakes had the lowest relative alertness score after waking of –0.07. It's appropriate to conclude, then, that ______

Which choice most logically completes the text?

(A) muffins are the only breakfast people should incorporate into their diet if they want to raise their levels of alertness after waking.

(B) people who consume high carbohydrate breakfasts may have a higher level of alertness after waking than those who consume high protein breakfasts.

(C) a combination of high protein and high carbohydrate breakfasts will lead to the highest level of alertness after waking in all ages.

(D) the scientists need to explore the effects of different types of muffins to truly understand how carbohydrate-rich breakfasts affect alertness.

CONTINUE

14 Mark for Review

The precursor to modern polo, chovgan is an Iranian team sport using acrobatic, trained horses. It incorporated storytelling and music and grew popular among the upper classes. After chovgan was brought from India to England in the nineteenth century, many new rules were added, making the sport more complex. Later, in 1900, chovgan was included in the Olympic Games for the first time. Interestingly, there are numerous depictions of the sport in ancient figurines and manuscripts, signifying that ______

Which choice most logically completes the text?

Ⓐ works of art are more significant to Iranian culture and history than athletic activities are.

Ⓑ the new rules added in England improved the game beyond its original status.

Ⓒ the sport held some interest for people well before the nineteenth century.

Ⓓ the Iranian version of the sport was more challenging to participate in.

15 Mark for Review

The first woman to be elected Grand Chief to the Assembly of Manitoba Chiefs was Catherine Ann Merrick. During the two years that she held this position, Merrick ______ unity among the several First Nations in Manitoba.

Which choice completes the text so that it conforms to the conventions of Standard English?

Ⓐ promoted

Ⓑ will promote

Ⓒ to promote

Ⓓ is promoting

16 Mark for Review

On January 20, 2024, 99-year-old Dutch-Canadian swimmer Betty Brussel set three world records on the same day. In April of that year, she earned further acclaim when she ______ record for the 100-to-104 age category.

Which choice completes the text so that it conforms to the conventions of Standard English?

Ⓐ broke another

Ⓑ broke; another

Ⓒ broke. Another

Ⓓ broke, another

CONTINUE

17 Mark for Review

London's National Portrait Gallery opened in 1856 and is one of the most-visited art museums in the world. In 2024, Victoria Siddall _______ appointed as its thirteenth director, the first to be a woman.

Which choice completes the text so that it conforms to the conventions of Standard English?

Ⓐ have been

Ⓑ are

Ⓒ were

Ⓓ was

18 Mark for Review

How valuable are the things you already own? According to research, people tend to value objects they already own more highly than they do other goods of similar worth; this phenomenon _______ known as the endowment effect.

Which choice completes the text so that it conforms to the conventions of Standard English?

Ⓐ were

Ⓑ are

Ⓒ is

Ⓓ have been

19 Mark for Review

At first glance, American artist Bill Braun's pieces look like simple paper projects done by children. Upon closer inspection, however, it becomes evident that he paints in such a realistic _______ that what appear to be paper cutouts are actually cleverly shaded painted shapes.

Which choice completes the text so that it conforms to the conventions of Standard English?

Ⓐ way;

Ⓑ way:

Ⓒ way,

Ⓓ way

20 Mark for Review

One of the paintings housed by the Yale University Art Gallery is Edward Hopper's *Rooms by the* _______ piece that art critic Ken Johnson has called one of Hopper's "strangest" works.

Which choice completes the text so that it conforms to the conventions of Standard English?

Ⓐ *Sea*, while a

Ⓑ *Sea*. A

Ⓒ *Sea*, a

Ⓓ *Sea* a

CONTINUE

21 Mark for Review

Track cyclist Daniela Larreal competed for her home country of Venezuela in five Olympic Games from 1992 to 2012. Later, _______ which criticized the Venezuelan government for corruption, led to her exile from the country.

Which choice completes the text so that it conforms to the conventions of Standard English?

Ⓐ Larreals' outspoken political statements',

Ⓑ Larreal's outspoken political statements,

Ⓒ Larreal's outspoken political statement's,

Ⓓ Larreals outspoken political statements,

22 Mark for Review

When a transmission line in the Feather River Canyon failed during strong winds, the 2018 Camp Fire ignited, burning wildly until it was finally contained after 18 days. _______ it was the most destructive wildfire in the history of California and the most expensive natural disaster that year.

Which choice completes the text with the most logical transition?

Ⓐ Next,

Ⓑ Ultimately,

Ⓒ Specifically,

Ⓓ In other words,

23 Mark for Review

Many people are familiar with the dog Laika, the first animal to orbit the Earth. _______ fewer know the names of Dezik and Tsygan, the first dogs to fly in space six years earlier, in 1951. They experienced four minutes of weightlessness before safely falling back to Earth with the help of a parachute.

Which choice completes the text with the most logical transition?

Ⓐ For instance,

Ⓑ Likewise,

Ⓒ However,

Ⓓ As a result,

24 Mark for Review

The butterfly species *Actinote zikani* is endemic to the Brazilian Atlantic forest. The species was first identified by naturalist Romualdo Ferreira d'Almeida in 1951, but after 1981 it was considered extinct. _______ beginning in 1991, *A. zikani* was observed again and eventually added to a list of the most endangered species in the world.

Which choice completes the text with the most logical transition?

Ⓐ Then,

Ⓑ For example,

Ⓒ In the end,

Ⓓ By comparison,

CONTINUE

25 Mark for Review

While researching a topic, a student has taken the following notes:

- Only a few countries are executively governed by several elected leaders instead of a singular national leader.
- Switzerland's Federal Council consists of seven elected members.
- They collectively serve as the head of state and government.
- Bosnia-Herzegovina's presidency has three elected members.
- They govern the country together and include one Bosniak, one Serb, and one Croat.

The student wants to emphasize the significance of Switzerland's form of government. Which choice most effectively uses relevant information from the notes to accomplish this goal?

Ⓐ Seven elected members serve on Switzerland's Federal Council, and Bosnia-Herzegovina's presidency includes one Bosniak, one Serb, and one Croat.

Ⓑ Both Switzerland and Bosnia-Herzegovina have elected members of government, but Switzerland's Federal Council has more members than Bosnia and Herzegovina's presidency does.

Ⓒ Switzerland has a Federal Council with seven members, and Bosnia-Herzegovina's presidency includes three members.

Ⓓ Switzerland's Federal Council has seven elected members, making Switzerland one of only a few countries not to have a singular national leader.

26 Mark for Review

While researching a topic, a student has taken the following notes:

- The violin is a wooden string instrument that is the smallest in its family.
- The violin family includes the other string instruments viola, cello, and double bass.
- A string quartet is a musical ensemble that consists of two violinists, one violist, and one cellist, with the two violinists playing different parts.
- A string trio consists of three musicians.
- It includes only one violinist, along with the violist and the cellist.

The student wants to contrast how violins are used in string quartets and string trios. Which choice most effectively uses relevant information from the notes to accomplish this goal?

Ⓐ In a string quartet, there are two violinists who play different parts, but in a string trio, there is only one violinist.

Ⓑ A string trio consists of three musicians, one of whom plays the violin, in contrast to the four members of a string quartet.

Ⓒ Both a string trio and a string quartet include musicians who play violin, viola, and cello.

Ⓓ Members of the violin family, such as the violin, appear in both string quartets and string trios.

CONTINUE

27 Mark for Review

While researching a topic, a student has taken the following notes:

- *The Mexican Flyboy* is a 2016 novel by Mexican American author Alfredo Véa.
- It tells the story of a man who uses a time machine to right historical wrongs, such as the execution of Joan of Arc.
- Joan of Arc was a French military leader who refused to conform to gender roles.
- Véa describes his childhood realization that we "could rescue people who had suffered and are now suffering" as inspiration for the book.
- In general, Véa says he "just want[s] justice."

The student wants to use a quotation from Véa to explain his inspiration for the book. Which choice most effectively uses relevant information from the notes to accomplish this goal?

Ⓐ Centering on the idea of righting historical wrongs, *The Mexican Flyboy* was inspired by Véa's childhood realization that we "could rescue people who had suffered and are now suffering."

Ⓑ Véa, whose works include a novel about righting historical wrongs, has stated that justice is important to him.

Ⓒ Véa, the author of *The Mexican Flyboy*, "just want[s] justice."

Ⓓ According to Véa, the execution of Joan of Arc that the main character in his book *The Mexican Flyboy* seeks to prevent is a historical wrong.

STOP

If you finish before time is called, you may check your work on this module only.
Do not turn to any other module in the test.

PSAT Prep Test 1—Reading and Writing

Module 2—Harder

Turn to Section 1 of your answer sheet to answer the questions in this section.

DIRECTIONS

The questions in this section address a number of important reading and writing skills. Each question includes one or more passages, which may include a table or graph. Read each passage and question carefully, and then choose the best answer to the question based on the passage(s).

All questions in the section are multiple-choice with four answer choices. Each question has a single best answer.

1 Mark for Review

Certain species of ants have become quite ______ amidst changes to their physiological features: in a 2024 study by researcher Erik T. Frank, ants that had, through genetics, lost the ability to prevent certain types of infections to one of their limbs learned instead how to perform life-saving amputations on the infected limbs of other ants with the same genetic defect.

Which choice completes the text with the most logical and precise word or phrase?

(A) adaptable

(B) cumbersome

(C) subtle

(D) disorganized

2 Mark for Review

The two Voyager spacecraft launched in 1977 each carried identical golden records that contain selected audio and image files; the audio files included spoken greetings in 55 languages, music, and nature sounds, while the image files included photos of the Solar System, animals, plants, landscapes, food, human anatomy, and human activity. These contents were thus ______ inclusion for their ability to provide insight into many aspects of life on Earth.

Which choice completes the text with the most logical and precise word or phrase?

(A) debarred from

(B) sheltered against

(C) designated for

(D) mandated for

CONTINUE

3 Mark for Review

A study by researcher Asaf Tzachor found that generative artificial intelligence (AI) is likely to vastly increase both e-waste and electricity consumption globally, as AI usage results in a high turnover rate of the hardware used to process its many calculations along with the anatomy, and human activity. These contents were thus _______ amount of energy it takes to produce the generative texts and images.

Which choice completes the text with the most logical and precise word or phrase?

Ⓐ precarious

Ⓑ copious

Ⓒ innocuous

Ⓓ scant

4 Mark for Review

Analysts frequently caution that those funding offshore wind energy projects should allow for flexibility in their project budgets: having excess funds available can help offset the _______ unforeseen costs related to the logistical difficulty of obtaining and building the necessary components needed for such projects to function.

Which choice completes the text with the most logical and precise word or phrase?

Ⓐ motivations for

Ⓑ enhancement of

Ⓒ impediments from

Ⓓ realignments to

5 Mark for Review

The following text is from John Muir's 1915 travelogue *Travels in Alaska*. The narrator is an explorer recounting his journeys.

> An hour or more before sunset the distant mountains, a vast host, seemed more softly ethereal than ever, pale blue, ineffably fine, all angles and harshness melted off in the soft evening light. Even the snow and the grinding, cascading glaciers became divinely tender and fine in this celestial amethystine light.... <u>After my hardtack supper I could have climbed the mountain again and got back before sunrise, but dragging the sled tires me.</u>

Which choice best describes the function of the underlined portion in the text as a whole?

Ⓐ It demonstrates the narrator's affinity for the aesthetics of nature.

Ⓑ It details the narrator's attempt to describe glaciers figuratively.

Ⓒ It offers the rationale behind a choice made by the narrator.

Ⓓ It provides the components of the narrator's dinner.

CONTINUE

6 Mark for Review

The following text is from the 1895 poem "The Meadow" by Archibald Lampman.

> Here when the cloudless April days begin,
> And the quaint crows flock thicker day by day,
> Filling the forests with a pleasant din,
> And the soiled snow creeps secretly away,
> Comes the small busy sparrow, primed with glee,
> First preacher in the naked wilderness,
> Piping an end to all the long distress
> From every fence and every leafless tree.

Which choice best describes the overall structure of the text?

Ⓐ It discusses the behavior of crows, then contrasts it with the behavior of sparrows.

Ⓑ It introduces a month, then lists events associated with that month.

Ⓒ It progressively describes elements of nature becoming livelier.

Ⓓ It presents weather patterns known to be associated with changing seasons.

7 Mark for Review

Blue Note Records was founded by Alfred Lion in 1939, but in the 1950s, Lion sought the services of artist Reid Miles to update the style of album cover that had been produced by the label since its inception. Miles was charged by Lion to include certain features that were becoming more popular—most notably, information about the content of the album and graphics intended to make the album stand out more to potential buyers. Miles, however, knew little about jazz and took direction from descriptions of the music from Lion. The resulting cover art combined asymmetrical letter cases and numerous typefaces, and Miles's Blue Note Records covers became iconic examples of jazz's visual identity.

What does the text most strongly suggest about the jazz art created by Reid Miles?

Ⓐ According to Lion, the art designed by Miles was more visually interesting than those designed by his previous album cover artists.

Ⓑ The album covers have grown in acclaim since Miles first designed them.

Ⓒ There were more albums produced by Blue Note records after Miles's hiring in the 1950s than there were before that time.

Ⓓ There was less of a visual identity for jazz music on the covers of Blue Note Records albums prior to the work produced by Miles.

CONTINUE

8 Mark for Review

The following text is from Thomas Love Peacock's 1818 novel *Nightmare Abbey*. Scythrop lives in his father's mansion, the titular Nightmare Abbey.

> Scythrop had a certain portion of mechanical genius, which his romantic projects tended to develop. He constructed models of cells and recesses, sliding panels and secret passages, that would have baffled the skill of the Parisian police. He took the opportunity of his father's absence to smuggle a dumb carpenter into the Abbey, and between them they gave reality to one of these models in Scythrop's tower. Scythrop foresaw that a great leader of human regeneration would be involved in fearful dilemmas, and determined, for the benefit of mankind in general, to adopt all possible precautions for the preservation of himself.

Which choice best states the main idea of the text?

Ⓐ As is common with other people, Scythrop's belief in his own abilities appears to fluctuate based on his current circumstances.

Ⓑ Left on his own, Scythrop designs and implements a series of safeguards intended to protect himself should the need arise in the future.

Ⓒ Without his father's influences, Scythrop begins to use his mechanical genius for more benevolent purposes.

Ⓓ Like his father, Scythrop takes advantage of the absence of others to further his own goals.

9 Mark for Review

The following text is from William Edmondstoune Aytoun's 1845 short story "The Glenmutchkin Railway." The story takes place in Glenmutchkin, a city in Scotland.

> The population of Glenmutchkin is extremely dense. Its situation on the west coast has afforded it the means of direct communication with America, of which for many years the inhabitants have actively availed themselves. Indeed, the amount of exportation of livestock from this part of the Highlands to the Western continent has more than once attracted the attention of Parliament. The Manufactures are large and comprehensive, and include the most famous distilleries in the world.

What does the text suggest about Parliament?

Ⓐ It is satisfied with the quality of the distilleries in Glenmutchkin.

Ⓑ It has only recently begun to examine the activities in Glenmutchkin.

Ⓒ It has taken note of a particular aspect of Glenmutchkin.

Ⓓ It is as diversely constituted as the population of Glenmutchkin is.

CONTINUE

10 Mark for Review

Orbiting the planet Saturn, Titan is the second-largest moon in our solar system. Despite its relative proximity to Earth and frequent observation by astronomers, many of its features still hold mysteries for scientists to explain: methane is present in its atmosphere, though the chemical should be easily broken down by sunlight; its surface is relatively void of craters, meaning that something is filling in crater impact sites; and it contains liquid water beneath its surface despite Titan being too far from the Sun to receive enough heat to melt ice into water. Dr. Lauren Schurmeier and colleagues believe that methane trapped in crystal-like substances called clathrates provides a solution to these quandaries.

Which statement, if true, would most strongly support the claim made by Schurmeier and colleagues about the presence of methane clathrates on Titan?

Ⓐ Substances trapped in clathrates tend to be released slowly, keeping them present in the atmosphere and creating a warm surface that can both mold over craters and heat water trapped beneath it.

Ⓑ Current models of Titan show a layer of liquid water beneath its surface but do not show evidence of a layer above the water thick enough to provide the number of methane clathrates required to sustain adequate heat levels to be the sole contributor to these effects.

Ⓒ Titan's thick atmosphere and its dark-colored surface help contribute to its ability to trap heat, which may provide too volatile an environment for methane clathrates to sustainably exist in.

Ⓓ The gravitational force exerted on Titan, due to Titan's own mass along with the mass of its host planet, Saturn, provides a supplementary explanation for the absence of impact craters on the moon, while the potential existence of methane clathrates is expected to be further studied in upcoming missions from spacecraft in the near future.

11 Mark for Review

A rare manuscript, known as the Voynich manuscript, has puzzled experts with both its content and origin. The manuscript is written in an unknown language, leading to speculation over whether it was written in a natural or constructed language, as a code, or even as a hoax. While the vellum on which it is written has been carbon-dated to the early fifteenth century, its first known owner was a seventeenth-century alchemist from Prague. The manuscript contains illustrations of plants, plant parts, astronomical figures, flowing water, landscapes, and what appear to be recipes. What is known about the manuscript has led many experts to believe that <u>it is a pharmaceutical guide exploring herbal medicine, recipes to create compound medicines, and medical procedures rooted in astrological beliefs</u>.

Which finding, if true, would most strongly support the underlined explanation?

Ⓐ Modern medical practitioners from Prague often use a type of shorthand writing when prescribing medications, including herbal medicines.

Ⓑ The ink used in the Voynich manuscript is dated to the late fifteenth century instead of the early fifteenth century when the paper is from.

Ⓒ The language used in the Voynich manuscript is discovered in another document, which is dated to the seventeenth century.

Ⓓ A field medicine guide written in a known language is discovered and acknowledges the Voynich manuscript as an inspiration for many of its own treatments.

CONTINUE

12 Mark for Review

Classification of 16 Odors by Study Subjects in Various Emotional States

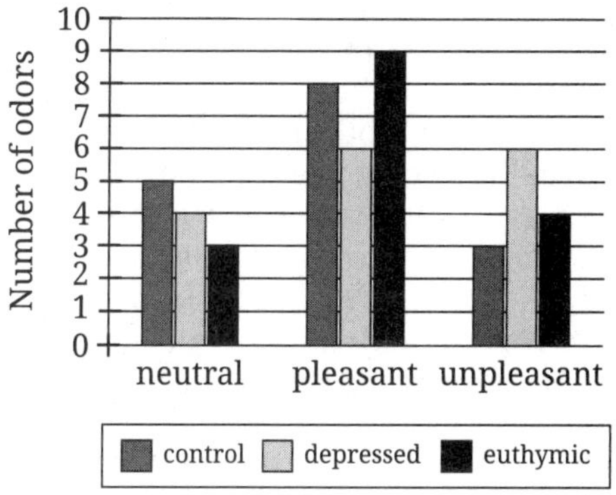

One marker of depression is a "negativity bias," where situations are perceived in a negatively skewed way. To better examine the impact of this bias on the senses, Chantal Henry and Mariana Alonso led a study in which subjects were exposed to 16 various odors and were asked to classify each of the odors as neutral, pleasant, or unpleasant. The subjects were divided into three groups: a control group, a group in which the subjects were experiencing a depressive episode, and a group in which the subjects were in a euthymic state, which is marked by optimism and cheerfulness. Their results illustrate that the brain may be predisposed to classifying more odors as unpleasant than pleasant during depressive episodes and to classifying more odors as pleasant than unpleasant while in a euthymic state: ______

Which choice most effectively uses data from the graph to complete the text?

Ⓐ subjects experiencing a depressive episode classified an equal number of odors as pleasant and unpleasant, while subjects experiencing a euthymic episode were more inclined to classify odors as pleasant than unpleasant.

Ⓑ while control subjects classified more odors as pleasant and fewer odors as unpleasant compared to neutral odors, subjects experiencing a depressive episode classified more odors as either pleasant or unpleasant compared to neutral odors.

Ⓒ while control subjects classified more odors as pleasant and fewer odors as unpleasant compared to neutral odors, subjects experiencing a euthymic state classified more odors as pleasant or unpleasant compared to neutral odors.

Ⓓ subjects experiencing a depressive episode classified odors as pleasant less than either the control group or subjects experiencing a euthymic state did and as unpleasant more than either the control group or subjects experiencing a euthymic state did.

CONTINUE

13 Mark for Review

Joshua Akey led a team of geneticists in mapping the gene flow between two human groups (Neanderthals and modern humans) using genetic data gathered from each of the groups. Previous analysis, based on the presence of Neanderthal-DNA present in modern humans, suggested that modern humans evolved in Africa 250,000 years ago, remained there for about 200,000 years, and then dispersed out of Africa around 50,000 years ago. Additionally, it had been determined that most human-Neanderthal intermingling would have taken place relatively early in this period, from about 200,000 to 250,000 years ago. Akey's team looked for modern-human DNA in the genomes of the Neanderthals instead and found evidence of contact between the groups not just around 200,000 to 250,000 years ago but also around 100,000 years ago and again around 50,000 years ago. Akey and his team concluded that ______ .

Which choice most logically completes the text?

Ⓐ humans from Africa started to interact with Neanderthals around 50,000 years ago.

Ⓑ humans and Neanderthals interacted with each other multiple times over a span of 200,000 years.

Ⓒ Another human group may have had contact with both humans and Neanderthals, which accounts for the intermingled DNA between the groups.

Ⓓ Neanderthals migrated to Africa, where they remained and intermittently interacted with humans.

14 Mark for Review

Riding a bicycle as a method of transportation is known to have many benefits, including improved individual health and reduced damage to the environment. However, this mode of transportation generally has low participation compared to other options. Notable barriers that discourage bike riding include dangerous proximity to motor vehicles, level of physical fitness required, environmental factors (such as weather conditions), and community perceptions of cyclists. Municipalities have begun to construct bike lanes to prevent negative interactions between automobile drivers and bike riders, suggesting that ______

Which choice most logically completes the text?

Ⓐ being aware of traffic is more important for bike riders than it is for drivers of automobiles.

Ⓑ bike riders of all fitness levels should be more wary of automobiles than they should of environmental factors.

Ⓒ more bicycle-friendly infrastructure may alleviate at least some of the concerns regarding bike riding as a form of transportation.

Ⓓ bike riders may attract more positive attention if they became actively involved in their communities' legislatures.

CONTINUE

15 Mark for Review

In 1979's *Chesmac*, one of the first commercial video games published in Finland, the computer could slowly calculate a chess move. This move, an hour-long process in some _______ was indicated with a letter-number combination rather than with an image.

Which choice completes the text so that it conforms to the conventions of Standard English?

Ⓐ cases

Ⓑ cases;

Ⓒ cases:

Ⓓ cases,

16 Mark for Review

In 1916, the best-selling musical genre in the United States was hapa haole, a genre of Hawaiian music that utilizes traditional Hawaiian instruments along with lyrics that are primarily in English. Many of these songs were novelty songs written by non-Hawaiians that have been criticized for their nonsensical _______ the 1930s, the hapa haole "craze" had faded but would be resurrected in the 1970s.

Which choice completes the text so that it conforms to the conventions of Standard English?

Ⓐ lyrics by,

Ⓑ lyrics by

Ⓒ lyrics, by

Ⓓ lyrics. By

17 Mark for Review

Sergei Rachmaninoff's *Piano Concerto No. 2* is a popular yet difficult _______ all of the notes in the chords simultaneously requires large hands, a characteristic of the work's composer that makes Rachmaninoff's own performances of the concerto particularly impressive.

Which choice completes the text so that it conforms to the conventions of Standard English?

Ⓐ piece playing

Ⓑ piece. As playing

Ⓒ piece, playing

Ⓓ piece. Playing

18 Mark for Review

"No net loss" refers to an environmental approach that aims to use mitigation measures to offset the negative environmental effects of development projects. Among various countries and organizations, the idea of preserving wetlands' overall integrity by restoring or enhancing them, allowing some development that would cause wetland losses, _______ some scrutiny.

Which choice completes the text so that it conforms to the conventions of Standard English?

Ⓐ face

Ⓑ have been facing

Ⓒ are facing

Ⓓ faces

CONTINUE

19 Mark for Review

Piano Sonata in E-flat minor, written by American composer Samuel Barber and premiered in 1949, is acknowledged for its difficulty and its fusion of modern and traditional _______ musicologists have noted, specifically, that the piece's formidable finale is particularly impressive.

Which choice completes the text so that it conforms to the conventions of Standard English?

Ⓐ techniques which

Ⓑ techniques

Ⓒ techniques;

Ⓓ techniques,

20 Mark for Review

Some parts of Indonesia use the *noken* system for voting. Unlike the method used by modern democracies, in which each individual votes via secret ballot, the customary *noken* practice is collective and lacks a secret _______ using *noken* bags that represent candidates, people in communities that use this system place their votes in public.

Which choice completes the text so that it conforms to the conventions of Standard English?

Ⓐ ballot:

Ⓑ ballot

Ⓒ ballot, while

Ⓓ ballot while

21 Mark for Review

When Ivan Argüelles was young, his immigrant father, a painter, hoped Ivan would follow the same path. _______ Argüelles took an interest in poetry as a high school student and pursued a career as a poet alongside being a professional librarian. He eventually published over 50 books of poetry between 1978 and 2023.

Which choice completes the text with the most logical transition?

Ⓐ Instead,

Ⓑ For instance,

Ⓒ In addition,

Ⓓ As a result,

22 Mark for Review

As many as half of those who survive tuberculosis are affected by post-tuberculosis lung disease (PTLD), a condition with symptoms such as coughing and breathlessness. Researchers have noted that a second infection of another type may worsen the lung damage from tuberculosis; _______ they recommend vaccination against other diseases as a preventative measure against the effects of PTLD.

Which choice completes the text with the most logical transition?

Ⓐ for example,

Ⓑ in addition,

Ⓒ thus,

Ⓓ by comparison,

CONTINUE

23 Mark for Review

While researching a topic, a student has taken the following notes:

- Cilantro, also known as coriander, is an herb.
- All parts of the plant are edible.
- In Mexican cuisine, cilantro leaves are commonly used.
- They are typically included in salsas and guacamole.
- In Indian cuisine, coriander seeds are commonly used.
- They are typically included in Indian curries.

The student wants to emphasize a difference in how Indian and Mexican cuisines use cilantro, also known as coriander. Which choice most effectively uses relevant information from the notes to accomplish this goal?

Ⓐ Mexican cuisine and Indian cuisine are two examples of culinary traditions that use cilantro.

Ⓑ Indian cuisine commonly uses coriander seeds, and Mexican cuisine commonly includes cilantro leaves.

Ⓒ All parts of the cilantro plant, also known as coriander, are edible.

Ⓓ Unlike Mexican cuisine, which uses cilantro leaves in salsas and guacamole, Indian cuisine uses the seeds of the plant in curries.

24 Mark for Review

While researching a topic, a student has taken the following notes:

- The city of Duluth, Minnesota, flies a flag to represent the city.
- The original flag in 1979 featured a city seal in the center and did not meet modern flag design principles.
- In 2019, the community participated in a competition to design a new flag that would better display the unity of its diverse neighborhoods.
- The new flag features symbols that represent the environment and history of Duluth and is highly rated by flag experts.

The student wants to describe how the flag of Duluth has changed. Which choice most effectively uses relevant information from the notes to accomplish this goal?

Ⓐ Flags designed in 1979 and 2019 featured different designs to represent the city of Duluth.

Ⓑ Duluth, Minnesota, flies a flag to represent the city, with one design featuring a city seal in the center.

Ⓒ Duluth's 1979 flag featured a city seal in the center, while the new flag features symbols that represent the environment and history of the city.

Ⓓ The community of Duluth participated in a competition to design a new flag in 2019, aiming to better display the unity of its diverse neighborhoods.

CONTINUE

25 Mark for Review

While researching a topic, a student has taken the following notes:

- As a college student, Benjamin F. McAdoo became interested in architecture in part because of his belief that housing is a human right.
- In 1946, he became an architect and pursued his goals of making housing accessible and fighting racial discrimination in urban planning.
- One project he is known for is his "House of Merit" design for a 620-square-foot single-family home.
- It was meant to be easy to construct, affordable, and contemporary.
- In the early 1950s, approximately 80 such homes were constructed.

The student wants to begin a narrative about McAdoo's career. Which choice most effectively uses relevant information from the notes to accomplish this goal?

(A) In the early 1950s, approximately 80 620-square-foot single-family homes were constructed according to Benjamin F. McAdoo's "House of Merit" design.

(B) Benjamin F. McAdoo's "House of Merit" was meant to be easy to construct, affordable, and contemporary.

(C) McAdoo's belief that housing is a human right inspired his career as an architect.

(D) Believing that housing is a human right, Benjamin F. McAdoo became an architect and set out to make housing accessible and fight racial discrimination in urban planning.

26 Mark for Review

While researching a topic, a student has taken the following notes:

- A contronym is a word that has two opposite meanings.
- In some cases, the two versions of the word have different etymological origins.
- The English verb "dust" is a contronym.
- It can mean "to add dust" or "to remove dust."
- The English verb "sanction" is a contronym.
- It can mean "to approve" or "to penalize."

The student wants to use one of the examples to illustrate the meaning of "contronym." Which choice most effectively uses relevant information from the notes to accomplish this goal?

(A) As a contronym, "sanction" has two opposite meanings—"to approve" but also "to penalize."

(B) Both "dust" and "sanction" are contronyms.

(C) Some words, such as "sanction," which can mean "to approve" or "to penalize," are contronyms.

(D) The contronym "dust" can mean "to add dust" or "to remove dust."

CONTINUE

27 Mark for Review

While researching a topic, a student has taken the following notes:

- Jennifer Nansubuga Makumbi is a Ugandan British writer.
- She published her novel *Kintu* in 2014 and won several prizes for it.
- This novel focuses on a Ugandan family and incorporates traditional mythology.
- She published her novel *A Girl Is a Body of Water* in 2020 and won a Book of the Year award for it.
- This novel presents a coming-of-age story about women in two different time periods.

The student wants to describe the novel that Makumbi published in 2014. Which choice most effectively uses relevant information from the notes to accomplish this goal?

Ⓐ *Kintu,* a novel that won several prizes, focuses on a Ugandan family and incorporates traditional mythology.

Ⓑ A coming-of-age story about women in two different time periods, *A Girl is a Body of Water* won a Book of the Year award.

Ⓒ While one novel by Jennifer Nansubuga Makumbi focuses on a Ugandan family, another is a coming-of-age story about women in two different time periods.

Ⓓ In both 2014 and 2020, Jennifer Nansubuga Makumbi published novels.

STOP

If you finish before time is called, you may check your work on this module only. Do not turn to any other module in the test.

PSAT Prep Test 1—Math

Module 1

Turn to Section 2 of your answer sheet to answer the questions in this section.

DIRECTIONS

The questions in this section address a number of important math skills.
Use of a calculator is permitted for all questions.

NOTES

Unless otherwise indicated:

- All variables and expressions represent real numbers.
- Figures provided are drawn to scale.
- All figures lie in a plane.
- The domain of a given function f is the set of all real numbers x for which $f(x)$ is a real number.

REFERENCE

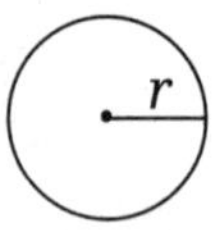

$A = \pi r^2$
$C = 2\pi r$

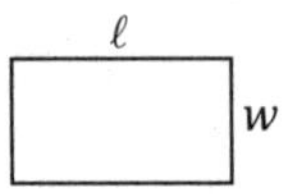

$A = \ell w$

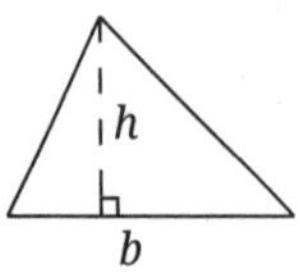

$A = \frac{1}{2}bh$

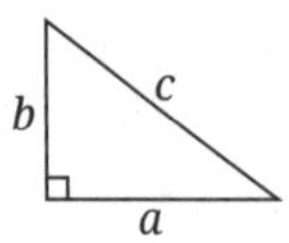

$c^2 = a^2 + b^2$

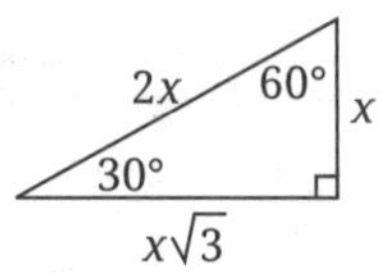

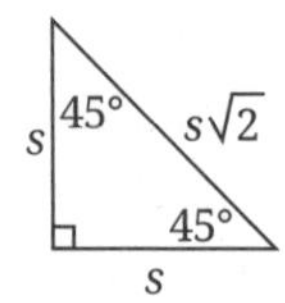

Special Right Triangles

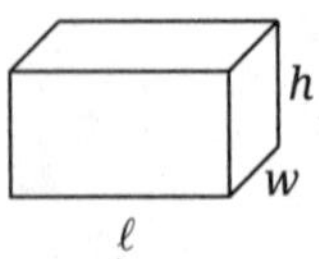

$V = \ell wh$

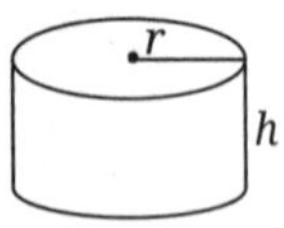

$V = \pi r^2 h$

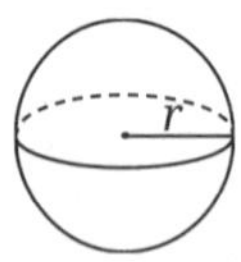

$V = \frac{4}{3}\pi r^3$

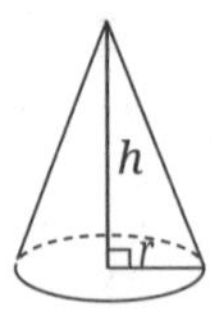

$V = \frac{1}{3}\pi r^2 h$

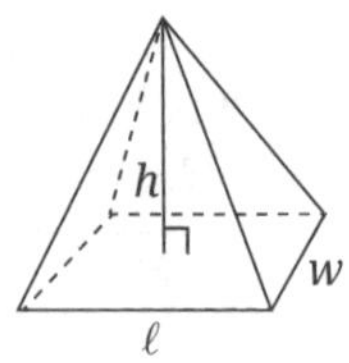

$V = \frac{1}{3}\ell wh$

The number of degrees of arc in a circle is 360.
The number of radians of arc in a circle is 2π.
The sum of the measures in degrees of the angles of a triangle is 180.

CONTINUE

INSTRUCTIONS FOR PRINT TESTS

For multiple-choice questions, solve each problem, choose the correct answer from the choices provided, and then circle your answer in this book. Circle only one answer for each question. If you change your mind, completely erase the circle. You will not get credit for questions with more than one answer circled, or for questions with no answers circled.

For student-produced response directions, solve each problem and write your answer next to or under the question in the test book as described below.

- Once you've written your answer, circle it clearly. You will not receive credit for anything written outside the circle, or for any questions with more than one circled answer.
- If you find **more than one correct answer**, write and circle only one answer.
- Your answer can be up to 5 characters for a **positive** answer and up to 6 characters (including the negative sign) for a **negative** answer, but no more.
- If your answer is a **fraction** that is too long (over 5 characters for positive, 6 characters for negative), write the decimal equivalent.
- If your answer is a **decimal** that is too long (over 5 characters for positive, 6 characters for negative), truncate it or round at the fourth digit.
- If your answer is a **mixed number** (such as $3\frac{1}{2}$), write it as an improper fraction (7/2) or its decimal equivalent (3.5).
- Don't enter **symbols** such as a percent sign, comma, or dollar sign in your circled answer.

CONTINUE

1 Mark for Review

Category	Frequency
string	44
woodwind	14
brass	11
percussion	4

As shown in the frequency table, each of the 73 instruments in an orchestra can be classified as one of four categories. If one instrument from the orchestra is selected at random, what is the probability that the instrument selected is a woodwind?

Ⓐ $\frac{11}{73}$

Ⓑ $\frac{14}{73}$

Ⓒ $\frac{44}{73}$

Ⓓ $\frac{59}{73}$

2 Mark for Review

A shipment of 500 science textbooks contains only chemistry textbooks and physics textbooks. If there are 300 physics textbooks in the shipment, how many chemistry textbooks are in the shipment?

Ⓐ 200

Ⓑ 300

Ⓒ 500

Ⓓ 800

3 Mark for Review

What is the value of $4a + 5$ if $8a - 3 = 45$?

______

4 Mark for Review

How many miles are equivalent to 150 furlongs? (1 mile = 8 furlongs)

______

5 Mark for Review

What is the slope of the graph of $y = -19x - 94$ in the xy-plane?

Ⓐ -94

Ⓑ -19

Ⓒ 19

Ⓓ 94

CONTINUE

6 Mark for Review

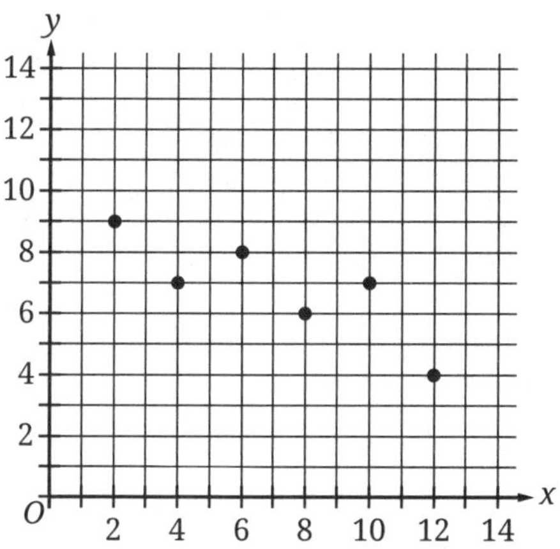

Which of the following equations is the most appropriate linear model for the data shown in the scatterplot?

Ⓐ $y = -0.4x + 9.5$

Ⓑ $y = 0.4x + 9.5$

Ⓒ $y = 0.4x - 9.5$

Ⓓ $y = 0.4x$

7 Mark for Review

What is the circumference, in inches, of a circle with a radius of 18 inches?

Ⓐ 9π

Ⓑ 18π

Ⓒ 36π

Ⓓ 324π

8 Mark for Review

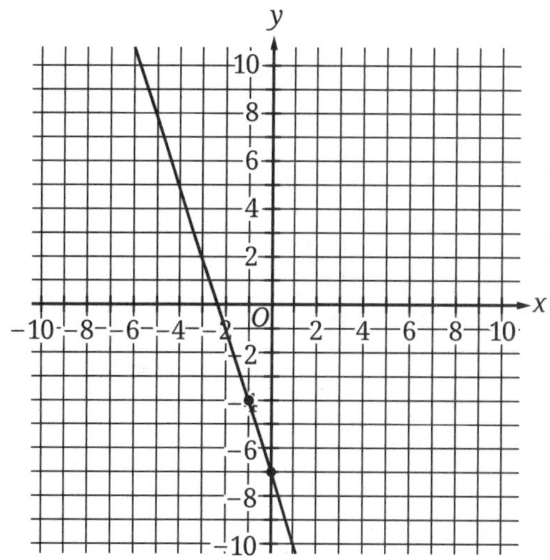

What is the slope of a line that is perpendicular to the line shown in the xy-plane?

CONTINUE

9 Mark for Review

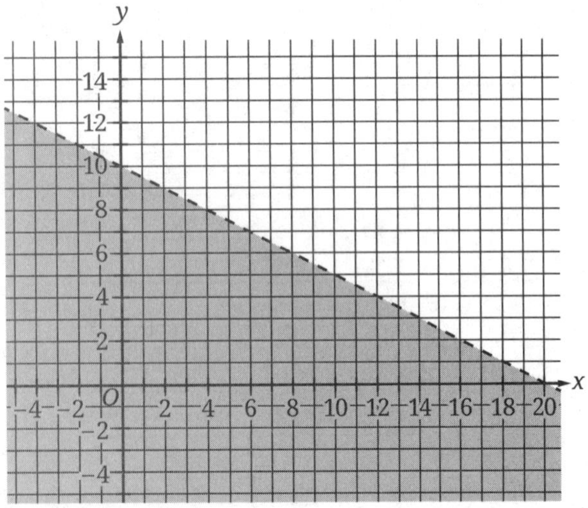

Solutions to which inequality are shown in the shaded region of the graph?

Ⓐ $y < -\frac{1}{2}x - 10$

Ⓑ $y < -\frac{1}{2}x + 10$

Ⓒ $y < -\frac{1}{2}x - 20$

Ⓓ $y < -\frac{1}{2}x + 20$

10 Mark for Review

$$M(d) = 2{,}000(0.93)^d$$

The amount of money, in dollars, remaining in a college student's meal plan d days after the start of the semester is modeled by function M. Given this model, what is the best interpretation of the statement "$M(53)$ is approximately equal to 42.72"?

Ⓐ Approximately \$53 remained in the meal plan at the start of the semester.

Ⓑ Approximately \$53 remained in the meal plan 42.72 days after the start of the semester.

Ⓒ Approximately \$42.72 remained in the meal plan at the start of the semester.

Ⓓ Approximately \$42.72 remained in the meal plan 53 days after the start of the semester.

11 Mark for Review

Over the course of 60 days, the leaves on a certain small tree fall at a constant rate. The equation $L = 300{,}000 - 5{,}000d$ models the predicted number of leaves L on the tree after d days, where $0 \le d \le 60$. What is the predicted number of leaves remaining on the tree 35 days after the leaves start falling?

Ⓐ 125,000

Ⓑ 175,000

Ⓒ 295,000

Ⓓ 300,000

CONTINUE

12 Mark for Review

Sides XY and YZ of triangle XYZ measure 12.08 feet (ft) and 15.23 ft, respectively. Which of the following statements is sufficient to prove that triangle XYZ is an isosceles triangle?

Ⓐ $XZ = 1.523$ ft

Ⓑ $XZ = 12.08$ ft

Ⓒ $XZ = 120.8$ ft

Ⓓ $XZ = 152.3$ ft

13 Mark for Review

The finishing times, in seconds, for 6 runners in the 100-meter dash were as follows:

$$11.3, 12.8, 12.6, 11.9, 12.2, 11.7$$

What was the median time, in seconds, for these 6 runners?

14 Mark for Review

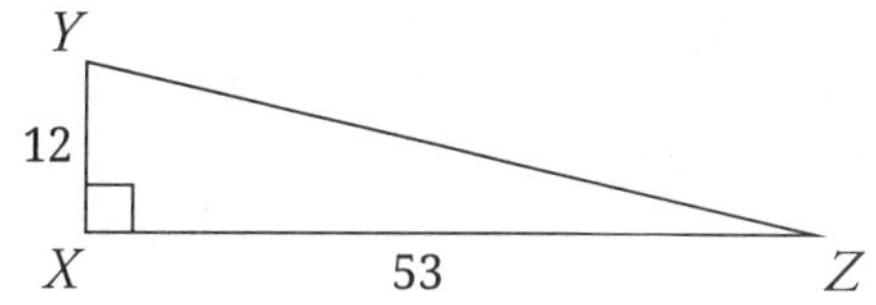

In the triangle shown, what is the value of tan Y?

Ⓐ $\frac{12}{65}$

Ⓑ $\frac{12}{53}$

Ⓒ $\frac{53}{65}$

Ⓓ $\frac{53}{12}$

15 Mark for Review

A graduating class of high school students is split into four groups. The first three groups have the same number of students and account for a total of 87 students. The fourth group is four times the size of each of the first three groups. How many students are in the fourth group?

CONTINUE

16 Mark for Review

A stone with a volume of 378 cubic meters has a density of 3.5 kilograms per cubic meter. What is the approximate mass, in kilograms, of the stone?

Ⓐ 108

Ⓑ 374.5

Ⓒ 381.5

Ⓓ 1,323

17 Mark for Review

The equation $x^2 + 34x + 289 = 0$ has how many distinct real solutions?

Ⓐ Zero

Ⓑ Exactly one

Ⓒ Exactly two

Ⓓ Infinitely many

18 Mark for Review

Which of the following equations defines the linear function f if the graph of $y = f(x)$ in the xy-plane passes through the point (6, 10) and has a slope of -1?

Ⓐ $f(x) = -x - 4$

Ⓑ $f(x) = -x - 1$

Ⓒ $f(x) = -x + 10$

Ⓓ $f(x) = -x + 16$

19 Mark for Review

What is the maximum value of the function g if the equation $g(x) + x^2 = 23$ represents the relationship between the variable x and its corresponding value of $g(x)$?

Ⓐ -529

Ⓑ -23

Ⓒ 23

Ⓓ 529

20 Mark for Review

On October 1, a certain educational archaeology channel on a video streaming platform had 2,975 views. For the next 31 days, the number of views the channel had each day was 9% less than the number of views the channel had the previous day. Which equation gives the number of views, v, the channel had d days after October 1, where $d \leq 31$?

Ⓐ $v = 2{,}975(0.91)^d$

Ⓑ $v = 2{,}975(1.09)^d$

Ⓒ $v = 2{,}975(9)^d$

Ⓓ $v = 2{,}975(9.1)^d$

CONTINUE

21 Mark for Review

Solution A, which is 35% hydrochloric acid by volume, is combined with solution B, which is 70% hydrochloric acid by volume. The combined solution, C, has a total volume of 140 milliliters and is 40% hydrochloric acid by volume. What was the volume, in milliliters, of the hydrochloric acid in solution A?

Ⓐ 14

Ⓑ 20

Ⓒ 42

Ⓓ 120

22 Mark for Review

Which expression represents the result of decreasing a positive value, a, by 24%?

Ⓐ $0.24a$

Ⓑ $2.4a$

Ⓒ $0.76a$

Ⓓ $7.6a$

YIELD

Once you've finished (or run out of time for) this section, use the answer key to determine how many questions you got right. If you got fewer than 15 questions right, move on to Module 2—Easier, otherwise move on to Module 2—Harder.

PSAT Prep Test 1—Math

Module 2—Easier

Turn to Section 2 of your answer sheet to answer the questions in this section.

DIRECTIONS

The questions in this section address a number of important math skills.
Use of a calculator is permitted for all questions.

NOTES

Unless otherwise indicated:

- All variables and expressions represent real numbers.
- Figures provided are drawn to scale.
- All figures lie in a plane.
- The domain of a given function *f* is the set of all real numbers *x* for which *f*(*x*) is a real number.

REFERENCE

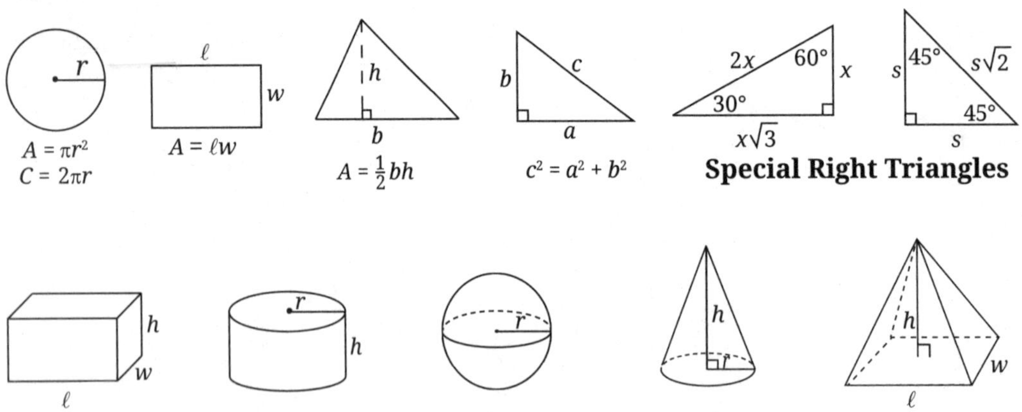

$A = \pi r^2$, $C = 2\pi r$

$A = \ell w$

$A = \frac{1}{2}bh$

$c^2 = a^2 + b^2$

Special Right Triangles

$V = \ell wh$

$V = \pi r^2 h$

$V = \frac{4}{3}\pi r^3$

$V = \frac{1}{3}\pi r^2 h$

$V = \frac{1}{3}\ell wh$

The number of degrees of arc in a circle is 360.
The number of radians of arc in a circle is 2π.
The sum of the measures in degrees of the angles of a triangle is 180.

CONTINUE

INSTRUCTIONS FOR PRINT TESTS

For multiple-choice questions, solve each problem, choose the correct answer from the choices provided, and then circle your answer in this book. Circle only one answer for each question. If you change your mind, completely erase the circle. You will not get credit for questions with more than one answer circled, or for questions with no answers circled.

For student-produced response directions, solve each problem and write your answer next to or under the question in the test book as described below.

- Once you've written your answer, circle it clearly. You will not receive credit for anything written outside the circle, or for any questions with more than one circled answer.
- If you find **more than one correct answer**, write and circle only one answer.
- Your answer can be up to 5 characters for a **positive** answer and up to 6 characters (including the negative sign) for a **negative** answer, but no more.
- If your answer is a **fraction** that is too long (over 5 characters for positive, 6 characters for negative), write the decimal equivalent.
- If your answer is a **decimal** that is too long (over 5 characters for positive, 6 characters for negative), truncate it or round at the fourth digit.
- If your answer is a **mixed number** (such as $3\frac{1}{2}$), write it as an improper fraction (7/2) or its decimal equivalent (3.5).
- Don't enter **symbols** such as a percent sign, comma, or dollar sign in your circled answer.

CONTINUE

1 Mark for Review

A box has 40 game pieces, and 25% of the game pieces are black. How many game pieces in the box are black?

Ⓐ 4

Ⓑ 10

Ⓒ 30

Ⓓ 40

2 Mark for Review

At a local coffee shop, 400 cups of coffee were sold during one 8-hour shift. On average, how many cups of coffee did the coffee shop sell each hour during this shift?

3 Mark for Review

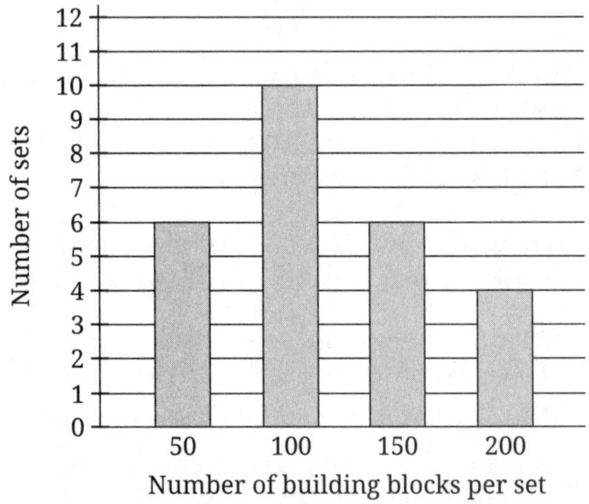

The bar graph shows the number of building blocks per set for 26 sets. How many sets contain 150 building blocks?

Ⓐ 6

Ⓑ 10

Ⓒ 26

Ⓓ 150

4 Mark for Review

What is the negative solution to the equation $|x - 17| = 39$?

Ⓐ –56

Ⓑ –39

Ⓒ –34

Ⓓ –22

CONTINUE

5 Mark for Review

The line graph shows the number of different birds sighted at a certain bird feeder each month during a five-month period.

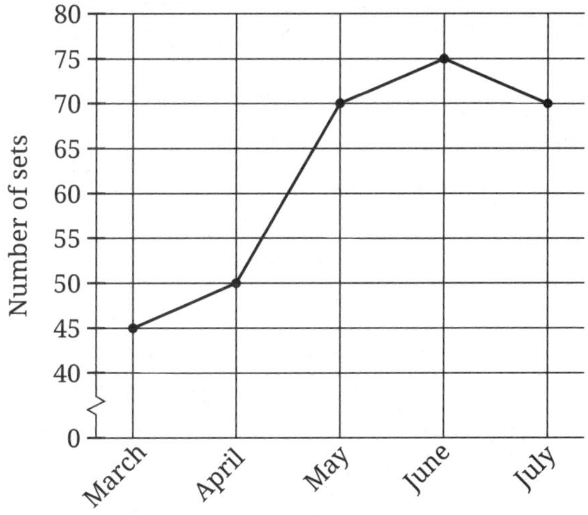

Based on the line graph, during which of these five months were 50 birds sighted at the bird feeder?

Ⓐ March

Ⓑ April

Ⓒ May

Ⓓ June

6 Mark for Review

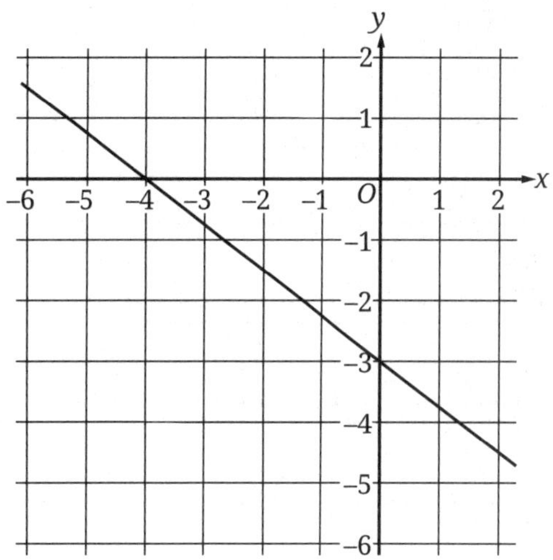

The graph of function g is shown, where $y = g(x)$. What is the x-intercept of the graph?

Ⓐ $(-4, 0)$

Ⓑ $(-3, 0)$

Ⓒ $(0, -4)$

Ⓓ $(0, -3)$

CONTINUE

7 Mark for Review

An organization is gathering signatures for a petition and has already gathered 320 signatures. If the organization gathers 180 more signatures, it will have enough signatures to submit the petition. How many total signatures does the organization need in order to submit the petition?

Ⓐ 140

Ⓑ 180

Ⓒ 250

Ⓓ 500

8 Mark for Review

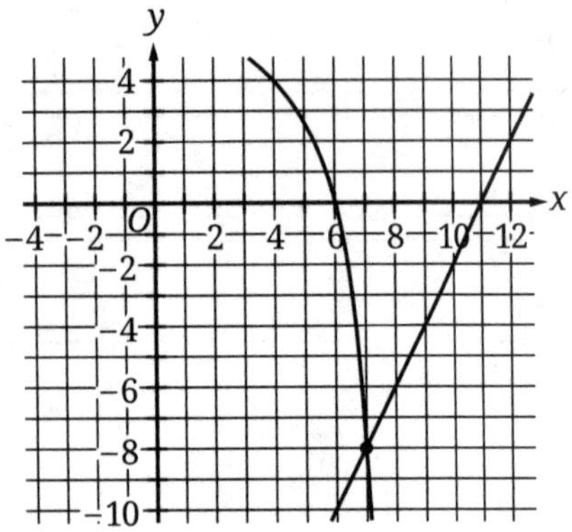

What is the solution (x, y) to the system of one linear equation and one nonlinear equation shown in the graph?

Ⓐ $(-8, 0)$

Ⓑ $(0, 0)$

Ⓒ $(0, 7)$

Ⓓ $(7, -8)$

9 Mark for Review

$$y = -15$$
$$x = y + 22$$

The graphs of the equations in the given system of equations intersect at the point (x, y) in the xy-plane. What is the value of x?

Ⓐ -37

Ⓑ -15

Ⓒ 7

Ⓓ 22

10 Mark for Review

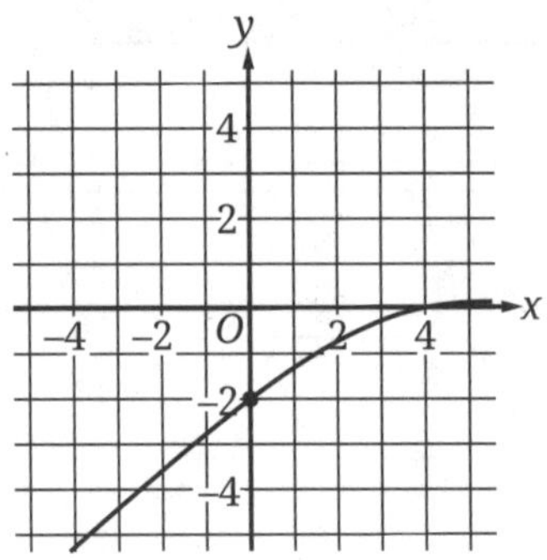

The y-intercept of the graph shown is (x, y). What is the value of y?

______

CONTINUE

11 Mark for Review

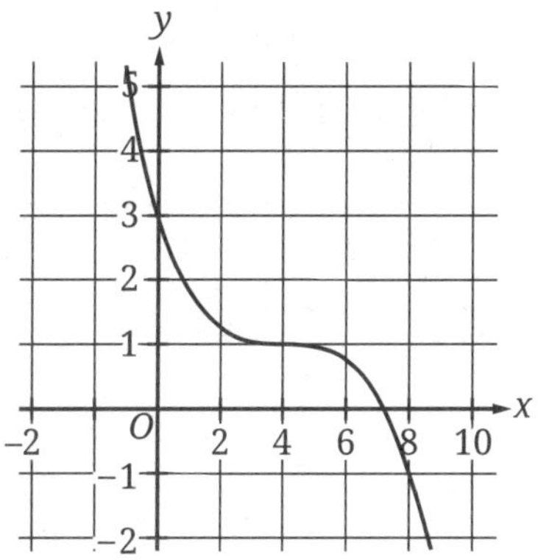

What is the y-coordinate of the y-intercept of the graph shown?

12 Mark for Review

If $5x + 50 = 90 + 4x$, what is the value of x?

13 Mark for Review

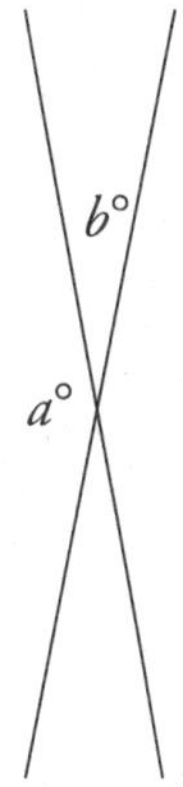

Note: Figure not drawn to scale

Two lines intersect at one point, as shown in the figure. What is the value of b if $a = 158$?

Ⓐ 22

Ⓑ 68

Ⓒ 79

Ⓓ 158

14 Mark for Review

A pump that drains water at a rate of 1,100 gallons each hour is used to drain a pool containing 4,500 gallons of water. Which of the following equations represents this situation, where w is the amount of water, in gallons, remaining in the pool after h hours, when $h \leq 4$?

Ⓐ $w = 1{,}100 - 4{,}500h$

Ⓑ $w = 4{,}500 - 1{,}100h$

Ⓒ $w = 1{,}100 - \frac{h}{4{,}500}$

Ⓓ $w = 4{,}500 - \frac{h}{1{,}100}$

CONTINUE

15 Mark for Review

$$h(x) = 5x - 4$$

The function h is defined by the given equation. What is the value of $h(-6)$?

Ⓐ -34

Ⓑ -26

Ⓒ 1

Ⓓ 26

16 Mark for Review

$$8(y^2 + 21)$$

Which expression is equivalent to the given expression?

Ⓐ $8y^2 + 13$

Ⓑ $8y^2 + 21$

Ⓒ $8y^2 + 29$

Ⓓ $8y^2 + 168$

17 Mark for Review

$$g(x) = 24x^2 - 12$$

The function g is defined by the given equation. What is the value of $g(1)$?

Ⓐ -12

Ⓑ 1

Ⓒ 12

Ⓓ 24

18 Mark for Review

The base of triangle A has a length of 30 centimeters. If the area of triangle A is 120 square centimeters, what is the length, in centimeters, of the height of triangle A?

CONTINUE

19 Mark for Review

Which of the following expressions is equivalent to $12(x^2 - 16xy + 64y^2)$?

Ⓐ $12(x - 8y)(x - 8y)$

Ⓑ $12(x - 4y)(x - 16y)$

Ⓒ $12(x + 4y)(x - 16y)$

Ⓓ $12(x + 8y)(x - 8y)$

20 Mark for Review

$$y = -(x + 6)^2$$
$$x = -4$$

The graphs of the equations in the given system of equations intersect at the point (x, y) in the xy-plane. What is the value of $\frac{y}{x}$?

Ⓐ -2

Ⓑ 1

Ⓒ 10

Ⓓ 16

21 Mark for Review

$$-9x + 15y = -12$$
$$27x - 45y = 36$$

How many solutions does the given system of equations have?

Ⓐ Exactly one

Ⓑ Exactly two

Ⓒ Infinitely many

Ⓓ Zero

22 Mark for Review

One negative integer is 3 less than one-half of another negative integer, and the two integers have a product of 176. What is the greater of the two integers?

STOP

If you finish before time is called, you may check your work on this module only. Do not turn to any other module in the test.

PSAT Prep Test 1—Math
Module 2—Harder

Turn to Section 2 of your answer sheet to answer the questions in this section.

DIRECTIONS

The questions in this section address a number of important math skills.
Use of a calculator is permitted for all questions.

NOTES

Unless otherwise indicated:

- All variables and expressions represent real numbers.
- Figures provided are drawn to scale.
- All figures lie in a plane.
- The domain of a given function f is the set of all real numbers x for which $f(x)$ is a real number.

REFERENCE

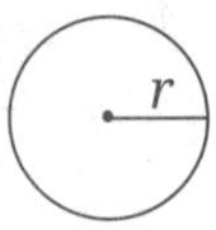

$A = \pi r^2$
$C = 2\pi r$

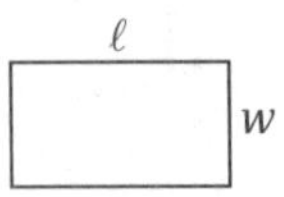

$A = \ell w$

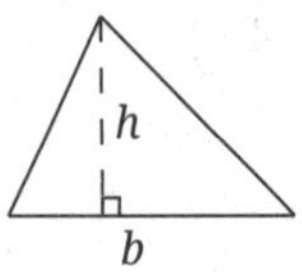

$A = \frac{1}{2}bh$

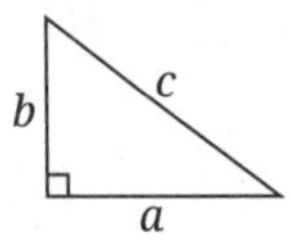

$c^2 = a^2 + b^2$

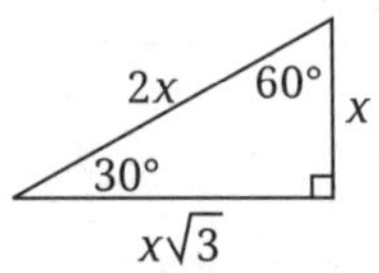

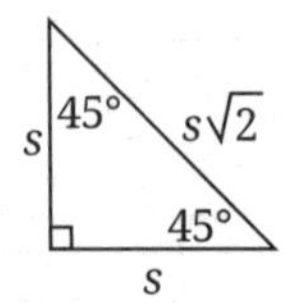

Special Right Triangles

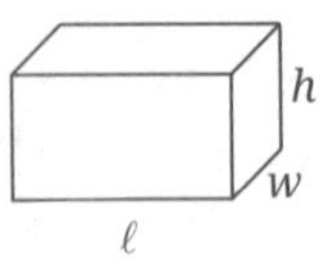

$V = \ell wh$

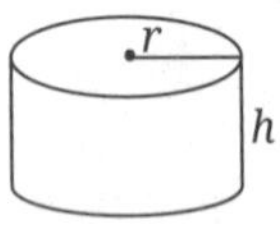

$V = \pi r^2 h$

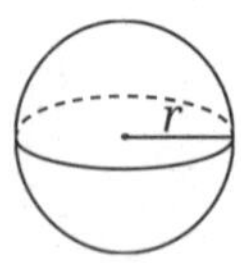

$V = \frac{4}{3}\pi r^3$

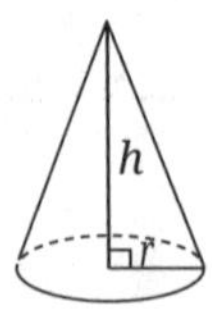

$V = \frac{1}{3}\pi r^2 h$

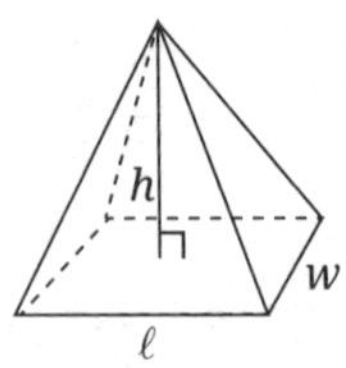

$V = \frac{1}{3}\ell wh$

The number of degrees of arc in a circle is 360.
The number of radians of arc in a circle is 2π.
The sum of the measures in degrees of the angles of a triangle is 180.

CONTINUE

INSTRUCTIONS FOR PRINT TESTS

For multiple-choice questions, solve each problem, choose the correct answer from the choices provided, and then circle your answer in this book. Circle only one answer for each question. If you change your mind, completely erase the circle. You will not get credit for questions with more than one answer circled, or for questions with no answers circled.

For student-produced response directions, solve each problem and write your answer next to or under the question in the test book as described below.

- Once you've written your answer, circle it clearly. You will not receive credit for anything written outside the circle, or for any questions with more than one circled answer.
- If you find **more than one correct answer**, write and circle only one answer.
- Your answer can be up to 5 characters for a **positive** answer and up to 6 characters (including the negative sign) for a **negative** answer, but no more.
- If your answer is a **fraction** that is too long (over 5 characters for positive, 6 characters for negative), write the decimal equivalent.
- If your answer is a **decimal** that is too long (over 5 characters for positive, 6 characters for negative), truncate it or round at the fourth digit.
- If your answer is a **mixed number** (such as $3\frac{1}{2}$), write it as an improper fraction (7/2) or its decimal equivalent (3.5).
- Don't enter **symbols** such as a percent sign, comma, or dollar sign in your circled answer.

CONTINUE

1 Mark for Review

$$f(x) = -\frac{x}{5} + 15$$

Function f is defined by the given equation. What is the value of $f(10)$?

Ⓐ -35

Ⓑ 13

Ⓒ 17

Ⓓ 25

2 Mark for Review

An organization is gathering signatures for a petition and has already gathered 320 signatures. If the organization gathers 180 more signatures, it will have enough signatures to submit the petition. How many total signatures does the organization need in order to submit the petition?

Ⓐ 140

Ⓑ 180

Ⓒ 250

Ⓓ 500

3 Mark for Review

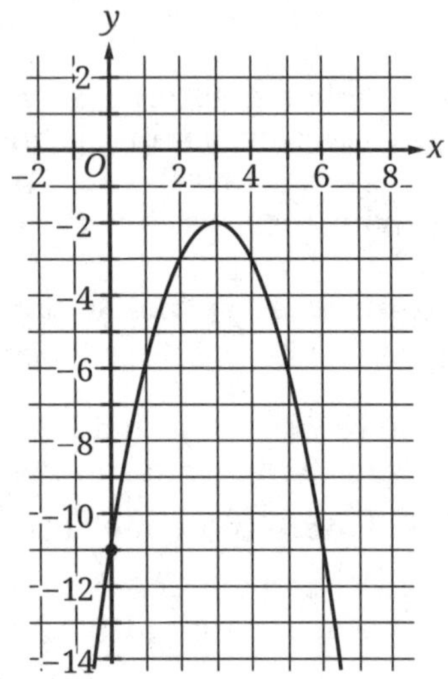

If the y-intercept of the parabola shown has the coordinates (a, b), what is the value of b?

CONTINUE

4 Mark for Review

Linear function h is defined by the equation $h(x) = -10x - 3$. Which of the following tables shows four values of x and their corresponding values of $h(x)$?

Ⓐ

x	2	3	4
$h(x)$	17	7	−3

Ⓑ

x	2	3	4
$h(x)$	−23	−26	−29

Ⓒ

x	2	3	4
$h(x)$	−30	−33	−36

Ⓓ

x	2	3	4
$h(x)$	−23	−33	−43

5 Mark for Review

$$g(x) = 9x^{\frac{1}{2}}$$

The function g is defined by the given equation. What is the value of $g(36)$?

Ⓐ 18

Ⓑ 54

Ⓒ 108

Ⓓ 162

6 Mark for Review

Rectangle $PQRS$ has a perimeter of 22 centimeters. The length of the rectangle is 8 centimeters. What is the width, in centimeters, of the rectangle?

Ⓐ 3

Ⓑ 6

Ⓒ 8

Ⓓ 14

7 Mark for Review

$$x + 5y = -15$$
$$x + \frac{5}{6}y = 10$$

What is the value of y if the solution to the given system of equations is (x, y)?

______

CONTINUE

8 Mark for Review

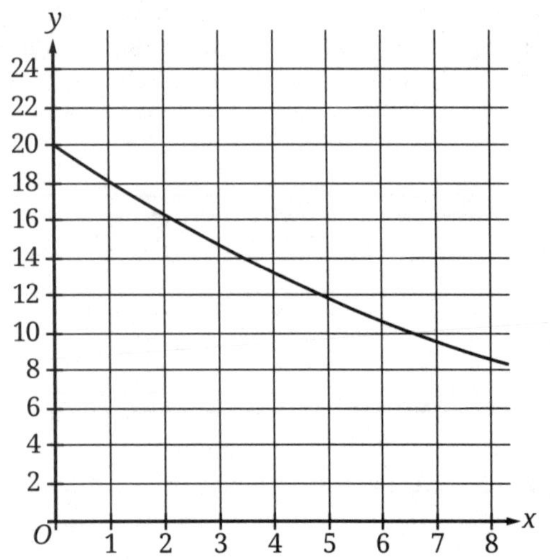

The graph shows the estimated value, in thousands of dollars, of a boat x years after the boat was purchased, where $0 \le x \le 8$. Which of the following is the closest approximation of the change in the value of the boat from $x = 2$ to $x = 5$?

Ⓐ The estimated value of the boat at $x = 5$ is $\frac{2}{5}$ of the estimated value of the boat at $x = 2$.

Ⓑ The estimated value of the boat at $x = 5$ is $\frac{3}{5}$ of the estimated value of the boat at $x = 2$.

Ⓒ The estimated value of the boat at $x = 5$ is $\frac{3}{4}$ of the estimated value of the boat at $x = 2$.

Ⓓ The estimated value of the boat at $x = 5$ is $\frac{4}{3}$ of the estimated value of the boat at $x = 2$.

9 Mark for Review

The scatterplot shows the relationship between the variables x and y. A line of best fit for the data is also shown.

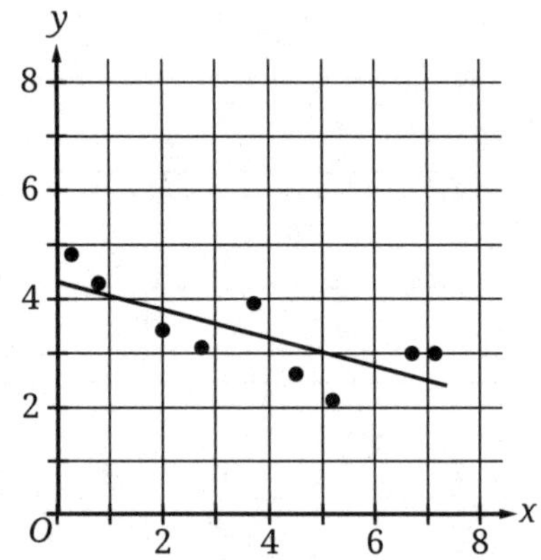

For how many of the 9 data points does the line of best fit predict a smaller y-value than the actual y-value?

10 Mark for Review

The beats per minute (BPM) of the most streamed track by a music producer in November was 125. The BPM of the producer's most streamed track in December was 165. What percent of the BPM of the producer's most streamed track in November was the BPM of the producer's most streamed track in December?

Ⓐ 32

Ⓑ 76

Ⓒ 124

Ⓓ 132

CONTINUE

11 Mark for Review

Linear function p gives the price, in dollars, that a vacation rental company charges to rent accommodations for x nights. The company charges \$410 for 2 nights, and it charges \$650 for 5 nights. Which equation models this situation?

Ⓐ $p(x) = 66x + 80$

Ⓑ $p(x) = 80x + 250$

Ⓒ $p(x) = 130x$

Ⓓ $p(x) = 80x + 210x$

12 Mark for Review

The equation $\frac{k(x-5)}{5} = -3x + 9$, where k is a constant, has no real solutions. What is the value of k?

Ⓐ -15

Ⓑ -5

Ⓒ -3

Ⓓ -1

13 Mark for Review

Which expression is equivalent to the product of the functions defined by the equations $f(x) = 8x + 9$ and $g(x) = \frac{4}{9}x - \frac{5}{8}$?

Ⓐ $\frac{32x^2}{9} - \frac{45}{8}$

Ⓑ $\frac{32x^2}{9} + x - \frac{45}{8}$

Ⓒ $\frac{32x^2}{9} - x - \frac{45}{8}$

Ⓓ $\frac{32x^2}{9} - \frac{4x}{17} - \frac{45}{8}$

14 Mark for Review

$$-14x + y = 0$$
$$x^2 - y + 42 = -7$$

The solution to the given system of equations is (x, y). What is the value of x?

Ⓐ -14

Ⓑ -6

Ⓒ 7

Ⓓ 98

CONTINUE

15 Mark for Review

$$7r(s - 10) = z$$

The given equation relates the distinct positive numbers r, s, and z, where s is not equal to 10. Which equation correctly expresses r in terms of s and z?

Ⓐ $r = \frac{z}{7(s-10)}$

Ⓑ $r = 7z(s - 10)$

Ⓒ $r = \frac{z}{7} - (s - 10)$

Ⓓ $r = \frac{7(s-10)}{z}$

16 Mark for Review

Function h is defined by $h(x) = (x + 4)(x - 6)(x + 1)$. When the graph of h is shifted down 4 units in the xy-plane, where $y = h(x)$, the function f defines the resulting graph. What is the value of the constant k if the graph of $y = f(x)$ crosses through the point $(-2, k)$?

17 Mark for Review

Two machines manufacture widgets at different rates. The second machine works at a rate that is five times the rate of the first machine. The second machine can manufacture $3a$ widgets in b minutes. The amount of time, in minutes, that the first machine takes to manufacture $21a$ widgets can be represented by which of the following expressions?

Ⓐ $7b$

Ⓑ $15b$

Ⓒ $18b$

Ⓓ $35b$

18 Mark for Review

One negative integer is 3 less than one-half of another negative integer, and the two integers have a product of 176. What is the greater of the two integers?

CONTINUE

19 Mark for Review

The function g is defined by $g(x) = 81(3)^x$. Which of the following equations defines function f if $f(x) = g(x + 2)$?

Ⓐ $f(x) = 81(6)^x$

Ⓑ $f(x) = 162(3)^x$

Ⓒ $f(x) = 729(3)^x$

Ⓓ $f(x) = 729(9)^x$

20 Mark for Review

$$x^2 + \frac{1}{16}dc^2$$

In the given expression, c and d are constants, and $c < 0$. If $-x - c$ is a factor of the expression, what is the value of d?

Ⓐ -16

Ⓑ $-\frac{1}{16}$

Ⓒ $\frac{1}{16}$

Ⓓ 16

21 Mark for Review

The equation $17 + x = \sqrt{c + x}$ has no real solutions. If c is an integer, what is the maximum possible value of $8c$?

22 Mark for Review

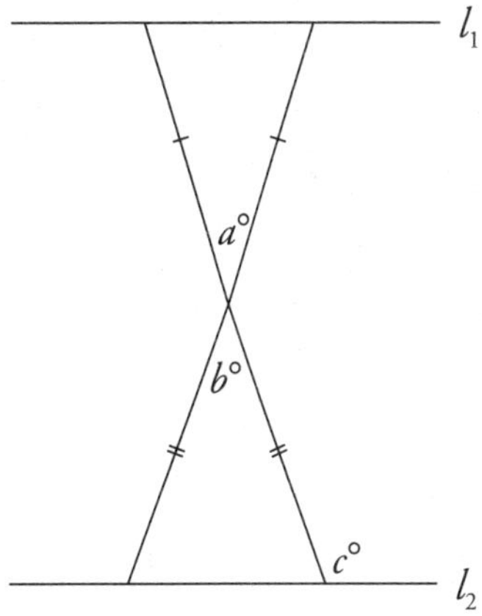

Note: Figure not drawn to scale.

Two isosceles triangles are shown in the figure. If $b = 180 - 4a$ and $a = 35$, what is the value of c?

STOP

If you finish before time is called, you may check your work on this section only. Do not turn to any other section.

Chapter 5
Practice Test 1: Answers and Explanations

PRACTICE TEST 1 ANSWER KEY

Reading and Writing		
Module 1	Module 2 (Easier)	Module 2 (Harder)
1. B	1. D	1. A
2. D	2. C	2. C
3. D	3. C	3. B
4. A	4. B	4. C
5. C	5. D	5. C
6. A	6. B	6. C
7. D	7. A	7. D
8. C	8. C	8. B
9. B	9. A	9. C
10. C	10. B	10. A
11. D	11. C	11. D
12. A	12. B	12. D
13. B	13. B	13. B
14. D	14. C	14. C
15. C	15. A	15. D
16. B	16. A	16. D
17. C	17. D	17. D
18. B	18. C	18. D
19. B	19. D	19. C
20. C	20. C	20. A
21. D	21. B	21. A
22. A	22. B	22. C
23. A	23. C	23. D
24. A	24. A	24. C
25. A	25. D	25. D
26. D	26. A	26. A
27. B	27. A	27. A

Math		
Module 1	Module 2 (Easier)	Module 2 (Harder)
1. B	1. B	1. B
2. A	2. 50	2. D
3. 29	3. A	3. –11
4. 18.75	4. D	4. D
5. B	5. B	5. B
6. A	6. A	6. A
7. C	7. D	7. –6
8. 1/3 or .333	8. D	8. C
9. B	9. C	9. 5
10. D	10. –2	10. D
11. A	11. 3	11. B
12. B	12. 40	12. A
13. 12.05	13. A	13. C
14. D	14. B	14. C
15. 116	15. A	15. A
16. D	16. D	16. 12
17. B	17. C	17. D
18. D	18. 8	18. –11
19. C	19. A	19. C
20. A	20. B	20. A
21. C	21. C	21. 128
22. C	22. –11	22. 110

PRACTICE TEST 1—READING AND WRITING EXPLANATIONS

Module 1

1. **B** This is a Vocabulary question, as it asks for a *logical and precise word or phrase.* The blank describes what action is taken regarding *the words "breakfast" and "lunch,"* so look for and highlight clues in the passage about what should happen to the two words. The passage states that *A portmanteau is a single word formed by blending two separate words together.* Since *breakfast* and *lunch* are being used to make a portmanteau, a good word to enter in the annotation box would be "blended" or "joined."

    - (A) and (C) are wrong because *defined* and *explained* don't match "blended."
    - (B) is correct because *combined* matches "blended."
    - (D) is wrong because *separated* is the **Opposite** of "blended."

2. **D** This is a Vocabulary question, as it asks for a *logical and precise word or phrase.* The blank describes a scene from *Requiem for a Dream* that is in some way related to a similar scene from *Perfect Blue,* so look for and highlight clues in the passage about the relationship between the two scenes. The passage states that *Film directors often reference previous works they admire, sometimes even replicating camera angles used in specific scenes.* Therefore, a good word to enter in the annotation box would be that the *Requiem for a Dream* scene is a "replication" or "copy" of the *Perfect Blue* scene.

    - (A) and (C) are wrong because they are the **Opposite** of the passage—the scene from *Requiem* is not claimed to be a *correction* or *criticism* of a scene that someone thinks is flawed; it's meant to be an example of directors replicating something they *admire.*
    - (B) is wrong because *explanation* doesn't match "replication."
    - (D) is correct because *reproduction* matches "replication."

3. **D** This is a Vocabulary question, as it asks for a *logical and precise word or phrase.* The blank describes the elevated motorway, so look for and highlight clues about the motorway. The passage states that the elevated motorway *supplanted the rail system* and *redefined the city's infrastructure.* Therefore, a good word to enter in the annotation box would be that the elevated motorway was an "improvement" or "modernization" of how the city operated.

    - (A) is wrong because *expense* goes **Beyond the Text**—while building the elevated motorway was likely very costly, no discussion of the project's cost is included in the passage.
    - (B) is wrong because *inconvenience* is the **Opposite** of the passage—the passage describes the *elevated motorway* as a positive improvement over the *electric rail system.*
    - (C) is wrong because *appendage* (addition) doesn't match "improvement" or capture the positive tone with which the elevated motorway is described.
    - (D) is correct because *innovation* matches "improvement."

4. **A** This is a Vocabulary question, as it asks for a *logical and precise word or phrase.* The blank describes how the increased use of tracking technology has affected judgment calls in tennis, so look for and highlight clues about that interaction. The passage states that *Formerly, every call was made a referee, relying only on what that particular referee saw, but now players can appeal those decisions for more precise results.* Therefore, a good word to enter in the annotation box would be "altered" or "changed."

    - (A) is correct because *modified* matches "altered."
    - (B) is wrong because *exhausted* doesn't match "altered."
    - (C) and (D) are wrong because *muddled* (confused) and *hampered* (obstructed) go **Beyond the Text**—while in the real world some people don't like the use of technology in sports, the tracking technology in the passage yields *more precise results* and therefore is only described positively in the passage.

5. **C** This is a Vocabulary question, as it asks for a *logical and precise word or phrase.* The blank describes the type of family the deceased individual may have belonged to, so look for and highlight clues about that family. The passage states most other *tombstones at the time* were *made of wood, a far cheaper material,* and that *a great expense was incurred to transport the limestone to the settlement.* Therefore, a good word to enter in the annotation box would be "wealthy" or "rich."

    - (A) and (D) are wrong because each goes **Beyond the Text**—while wealthy families can be *wasteful* and/or *famous,* neither of these adjectives has support in the passage.
    - (B) is wrong because *nameless* doesn't match "wealthy." This answer also goes **Beyond the Text**—just because *little is known of the stone's origin* does not mean the name of the individual's family is unknown.
    - (C) is correct because *prosperous* (well-off) matches "wealthy."

6. **A** This is a Purpose question, as it asks for the *main purpose of the text.* Read the passage and identify who or what the passage focuses on: the study by Nina Trivedy Rogers and colleagues. Then, highlight the main point made about this focus and any attitude the author expresses toward this focus: the passage states *the study noted a decrease of 3 grams per day of sugar for both children and adults.* Then, the author uses the word *however* to introduce a contrast, stating that *the scope of the study extends before and after the implementation of the government program, so the extent to which the taxes helped reduce sugar usage is difficult to determine.* Therefore, a good main purpose of the passage to enter in the annotation box would be "explain results of study and that it may not account for everything."

    - (A) is correct because it's consistent with the highlighting and annotation.
    - (B) is wrong because the study does not *contradict* the policy's goals: the study is only intended to measure how effective the policy was.
    - (C) is wrong because it's **Extreme Language**—just because the researchers noted that the actual impact that taxes had *is difficult to determine* does not mean they are *confused.*

- (D) is wrong because while the study and its results are given, there is no discussion of how the study could have been enhanced or improved.

7. **D** This is a Purpose question, as it asks for the *main purpose of the text.* Read the passage and identify who or what the passage focuses on: the work of Finnish physician Arvo Ylppö. Then, highlight the main point made about this focus and any attitude the author expresses toward this focus: the passage states that Ylppö's *clinic was the first of its kind in Finland to focus on maternity and child health* and that Ylppö *later became known worldwide for his research.* Therefore, a good main purpose of the passage to enter in the annotation box would be "describe Arvo's work positively."

   - (A) is wrong because it's **Recycled Language**—while Ylppö was both a *pediatric physician* and a *research professor,* no *contrast* between these progressions is made in the passage.
   - (B) is wrong because it goes **Beyond the Text**—the passage describes only one individual's contributions to pediatrics, not the *importance of pediatric care* in general.
   - (C) is wrong because the passage does not discuss how Ylppö or any other physician treats *children.*
   - (D) is correct because it's consistent with the highlighting and annotation.

8. **C** This is a Dual Texts question, as it asks how *the author of Text 2* would *most likely respond to the study findings mentioned in Text 1.* Read Text 1 first and highlight the study findings, which are that *sunlight can travel up to depths of nine feet through the dusty ice and in a great enough quantity to support the photosynthetic process.* Then, read Text 2 and highlight what its author says about the same topic. The author of Text 2 claims that there are *immense quantities of dust particles in Mars's atmosphere that block much of the sunlight that the surface of Mars would otherwise receive.* Enter "Text 2 may disagree – dust may block the sunlight" into the annotation box.

   - (A) is wrong because not only does the author of Text 2 not discuss different types of dust particles, but also the author of Text 2 does not discuss or recommend going even deeper than *nine feet below the surface.*
   - (B) is wrong because it goes **Beyond the Text**—while it's logical that the author of Text 2 would like to see photosynthesis occur anywhere on Mars, the focus of Text 2 is only on the skepticism surrounding the presence of meltwater beneath surface ice, not where photosynthesis needs to be shown to occur.
   - (C) is correct because it's consistent with the highlighting and annotation—Text 2 directly discusses *dust particles in the atmosphere* potentially blocking sunlight, which would be a necessary component for the photosynthesis mentioned in Text 1.
   - (D) is wrong because neither passage claims what *most scientists would prefer* to discover.

9. **B** This is a Retrieval question, as it asks for a detail *According to the text*. Look for and highlight what the passage says about *methane*. The passage states that *the greenhouse gas methane, which traps more heat than does carbon dioxide, was also being emitted into the atmosphere from the thawing Arctic ice.* The correct answer should be as consistent as possible with these details, which offer an additional factor besides *carbon dioxide* that is contributing to the rate at which the global temperature is rising.

- (A) is wrong because it's the **Opposite** of the passage—both *carbon dioxide* and *methane* are greenhouse gases that contribute to global warming, and neither one counteracts the other.
- (B) is correct because it's consistent with the highlighted details regarding methane and how it contributes to global warming, in addition to carbon dioxide's contributions.
- (C) is wrong because it's also the **Opposite** of the passage—the methane does not stay *trapped* in the ice according to the passage; it's *being emitted into the atmosphere from the thawing Arctic ice.*
- (D) is wrong because the passage never discusses *a balanced global temperature*. If anything, this would be an **Opposite** trap as methane is contributing to global warming rather than keeping the temperature *balanced.*

10. **C** This is a Main Idea question, as it asks for the *main topic of the text*. Look for and highlight information that can help identify the main idea. The final sentence claims that *The newly discovered statue, of great significance to the native Rapa Nui community, was found in the bed of a lake that may have dried up due to climate change.* Since the final sentence both mentions the discovery from the first sentence and adds more information as to its importance, the final sentence can serve as the main idea. The correct answer should be as consistent as possible with this portion of the passage.

- (A) is wrong because it's **Recycled Language**—this answer uses *native* and *Rapa Nui* from the passage to create an unsupported main idea about the Rapa Nui's traditions, which are not discussed in the passage.
- (B) is wrong because it's **Right Answer, Wrong Question**—it's implied in the passage that Chile has undergone climate change, but this answer makes no mention of the carving, which is the main focus.
- (C) is correct because it's consistent with the highlighted main idea.
- (D) is wrong because it's also **Recycled Language**—while the passage mentions *UNESCO Heritage Sites*, it does not offer any *new way to designate* them.

11. **D** This is a Charts question, as it asks for *data in the graph that support the research team's conclusion.* Read the title and variables from the graph. Then, read the passage and highlight the research team's conclusion, related to the same information from the table, which is that *the experimental group primed with positive stimuli was more inclined to take financial risks than the group primed with negative stimuli.* The correct answer should offer accurate information from the table that is consistent with the research team's conclusion.

- (A) is wrong because the passage does not discuss the amount of risk the *researchers expected* the chatbots would recommend taking.
- (B) is wrong because it's the **Opposite** of the passage—the positive stimuli group had an average risk score of 2.5.
- (C) is wrong because it's also the **Opposite** of the passage—the control group did have a higher average risk score than did the negative stimuli group, but it had a lower average risk score than did the positive stimuli group.
- (D) is correct because it's consistent with the highlighted conclusion—the positive stimuli group did have the highest average risk score of all three groups.

12. **A** This is a Charts question, as it asks for *data from the table* that will *complete the text.* Read the title and variables from the table. Then, read the passage and highlight the text related to the same information from the table, which is *the factor determined to be most commonly associated with smartphone overdependence.* The correct answer should offer accurate information from the table that completes the text.

    - (A) is correct because it's consistent with the highlighting—if 51.1% of the 54,000 participants ranked *anxiety* as something they've experienced either recently or frequently, it could be more *commonly associated with* smartphone overdependence than the other factors.
    - (B), (C), and (D) are wrong because *loneliness, depression*, and *experience of violent treatment* don't have percentages in the Yes/Severe category that are as high as that of *anxiety.*

13. **B** This is a Claims question, as it asks which choice *most effectively illustrates the claim.* Look for and highlight the claim in the passage, which is that *the author depicts the character Mme. de Dey as someone whose actions echo her sense of optimism.* The correct answer should address and be consistent with each aspect of this claim.

    - (A) and (D) are wrong because they do not mention anything that could be one of Mme. de Dey's *actions* that shows her *optimism.*
    - (B) is correct because it's consistent with the highlighting—*dainty and thoughtful preparations* could be Mme. de Day's *actions*, and *her hopes* could be *her sense of optimism.*
    - (C) is wrong because while *stared* and *seeing* could be actions taken by Mme. de Day, *seeing her son in every shadow everywhere; but it was only for a moment* would be negative (as her hopes keep getting dashed) rather than referencing a *sense of optimism.*

14. **D** This is a Conclusions question, as it asks what *most logically completes the text.* Look for the main focus of the passage, which is *how a person's age determines how harshly one judges the actions of others.* Then, highlight the main points made regarding this focus. First, the two simulations are *one in which a person intended to harm another person but was not successful and a second in which a person accidentally caused harm to another person without intending to do so.* Then, the passage states that the *60–79 group judged the individual who caused accidental harm much more leniently than did the 18–30 group but the person who intended to cause harm and failed much more harshly than did the*

18–30 group. Therefore, a good conclusion regarding the older participants in this passage to enter into the annotation box would be "older folks judged a person more harshly than younger folks did when the person intended to cause harm." The correct answer should be as consistent as possible with this conclusion.

- (A) is wrong because it goes **Beyond the Text**—while the older participants did judge *the individual who intended to cause harm and failed* more harshly than did the younger participants, the level to which each group chose to *consider* an individual's intent is not discussed.
- (B) is wrong because it's the **Opposite** of the passage, which describes a difference in how the two groups judged others rather than stating the two groups judged others *equally.*
- (C) is wrong because it's also the **Opposite** of the passage—the passage states that the older participants judged those *who caused accidental harm much more leniently* than did the younger participants, so the older participants were not likely to be *more strongly irritated* by the accidental harm-causing individuals than the younger participants were.
- (D) is correct because it's consistent with the highlighting and annotation—the older participants were more lenient than the younger participants were when the harm was an accident and more harsh than the younger participants were when the person *intended* to cause harm.

15. **C** This is a Conclusions question, as it asks what *most logically completes the text.* Look for the main focus of the passage, which is the *axolotl, a type of amphibian.* Then, highlight the main points made regarding this focus. First, the passage states that *axolotls...never complete this metamorphosis and live their entire lives in water.* Next, the passage states that *axolotls are found only in...Lake Xochimilco, a lake in Mexico containing a unique combination of resources.* Therefore, a good conclusion for this passage to enter into the annotation box would be "axolotls not completing morph may have to do with location." The correct answer should be as consistent as possible with this conclusion.

    - (A) and (B) are wrong because each goes **Beyond the Text**—while it's normal for animals to want to avoid the *dangers posed by land predators,* nothing to this effect is stated in the passage. Similarly, while it's easy to imagine that scientists would be forced to *re-examine how classes of animals are determined* because the axolotl doesn't fit a key aspect of amphibians, this too is not discussed in the passage itself.
    - (C) is correct because it's consistent with the highlighting and annotation.
    - (D) is wrong because it's **Extreme Language**—while the highlighted sentences support a conclusion that the axolotl may have adapted to survive, there's no evidence in the passage to support that they have actually *prospered*, or thrived.

16. **B** In this Rules question, verbs are changing in the answer choices, so it's testing consistency with verbs. Find and highlight the subject, *lists,* which is plural, so a plural verb is needed. All of the answers work with a plural subject, so look for a clue regarding tense. After the blank, the sentence says ... *and contain,* which is a second verb for the same subject. Thus, the verb in the blank should be consistent with *contain,* which is in present tense. Highlight *contain* and write an annotation that says "present." Eliminate any answer not in present tense or inconsistent with *contain.*

- (A) is wrong because it's in future tense.
- (B) is correct because it's in present tense and is consistent with *contain*.
- (C) and (D) are wrong because they're in past tense.

17. **C** In this Rules question, apostrophes with nouns are changing in the answer choices. Determine whether each word possesses anything. The *parties* do not possess the word *that*, so there should not be an apostrophe on the word *parties*. Eliminate any answer that doesn't match this. Additionally, pronouns and apostrophes are changing in the answer choices, so the question is also testing apostrophes with pronouns. The pronoun is modifying the *parliament* that belongs to *it* (Liechtenstein), so it should be possessive and thus not contain an apostrophe. Eliminate any answer that doesn't match this.

    - (A) and (B) are wrong because *it's* means "it is," which is not correct in this case.
    - (C) is correct because both *parties* and *its* should not have apostrophes.
    - (D) is wrong because *party* should not have an apostrophe.

18. **B** In this Rules question, punctuation is changing in the answer choices. The main meaning of the sentence is *scientists within ornithology often use sketches that call attention to the birds' specific features in their fieldnotes*. The phrase *a zoological branch that focuses on the class Aves (birds)* is a describing phrase that has a long dash after it, so it must have a long dash before to show that it is Extra Information. Eliminate answers that do not have a long dash before the describing phrase.

    - (A), (C), and (D) are wrong because they don't use a long dash.
    - (B) is correct because it uses a long dash before the Extra Information.

19. **B** In this Rules question, apostrophes with nouns are changing in the answer choices. Determine whether each word possesses anything. The *days* do not possess the *students*, and the *students* do not possess *attend*, so there should not be apostrophes on either of the words. Eliminate any answer that doesn't match this.

    - (A), (C), and (D) are wrong because there are apostrophes on at least one of the words.
    - (B) is correct because there is no apostrophe on either word.

20. **C** In this Rules question, pronouns are changing in the answer choices, so it's testing consistency with pronouns. Find and highlight the word the pronoun refers back to, *dust mites*, which is plural, so a plural pronoun is needed. Write an annotation saying "plural." Eliminate any answer that isn't plural.

    - (A), (B), and (D) are wrong because they are singular.
    - (C) is correct because it is plural.

21. **D** In this Rules question, punctuation is changing in the answer choices. Look for independent clauses. The first part of the sentence says *She began by illustrating an entire house in the style of pixel art*, which is an independent clause. The second part of the sentence says *the mysterious game that takes place inside of the house could take shape*, which is also an independent clause. Eliminate any answer that can't correctly connect two independent clauses.

- (A) and (B) are wrong because a comma without a coordinating conjunction (FANBOYS) can't connect two independent clauses, and the second part of the sentence is still an independent clause when *then* is added.
- (C) is wrong because some type of punctuation is needed in order to connect two independent clauses.
- (D) is correct because a semicolon can connect two independent clauses.

22. **A** This is a Transitions question, so follow the basic approach. Highlight ideas that relate to each other. The first sentence states that Reid began her work *In 1965*, the preceding sentence states that she completed work *by 1985*, and this sentence states that she was recognized for her work *in 1996*. These ideas represent a time change, so a time-change transition is needed. Make an annotation that says "time change." Eliminate any answer that doesn't match.

- (A) is correct because it is a time-change transition that accurately presents the events of 1996 as occurring after 1985.
- (B) is wrong because it incorrectly implies that the events of 1996 occurred prior to 1985.
- (C) is wrong because, although this is the last sentence, there is no indication that this is any type of conclusion or ending.
- (D) is wrong because it isn't a time-change transition.

23. **A** This is a Transitions question, so follow the basic approach. Highlight ideas that relate to each other. The preceding sentence says *Neutrons have no electric charge and a relatively large mass*, and this sentence says *protons are positively charged and have a slightly lower mass*. These ideas disagree, so an opposite-direction transition is needed. Make an annotation that says "disagree." Eliminate any answer that doesn't match.

- (A) is correct because *In comparison* is an opposite-direction transition.
- (B) and (C) are wrong because they are same-direction transitions.
- (D) is wrong because no reference to time is made in the passage.

24. **A** This is a Transitions question, so follow the basic approach. Highlight ideas that relate to each other. The preceding sentence states that *speakers of Danish, Swedish, and Norwegian are able to understand each other more easily than speakers of standard Italian can comprehend those who speak an Italian dialect,* and this sentence states that *the distinction between a "language" and a "dialect" is relatively meaningless.* These ideas agree, so a same-direction transition is needed. Make an annotation that says "agree." Eliminate any answer that doesn't match.

- (A) is correct because it is a same-direction transition that accurately expresses that this sentence is a conclusion based on the preceding sentence.
- (B) and (C) are wrong because they are opposite-direction transitions.
- (D) is wrong because this sentence is not restating the same ideas as the preceding sentence.

25. **A** This is a Rhetorical Synthesis question, so follow the basic approach. Highlight the goal(s) stated in the question: *introduce Dorothy Stanley to an audience unfamiliar with her career.* Eliminate any answer that doesn't fulfill this purpose.

- (A) is correct because it introduces Dorothy Stanley as an *American activist* and contains information about her career.
- (B) and (D) are wrong because they contain some information about Dorothy Stanley's career but do not introduce who Dorothy Stanley was.
- (C) is wrong because it does not contain any information about Dorothy Stanley's *career.*

26. **D** This is a Rhetorical Synthesis question, so follow the basic approach. Highlight the goal(s) stated in the question: *emphasize the setting of the beginning of the musical.* Eliminate any answer that doesn't fulfill this purpose.

- (A) and (C) are wrong because they do not contain any information about a setting.
- (B) is wrong because it contains the setting of *Peter Pan and Wendy*, which, according to the notes, is the *novel* and not *the musical.*
- (D) is correct because it contains the setting of *Peter Pan*, which, according to the notes, is *the musical.*

27. **B** This is a Rhetorical Synthesis question, so follow the basic approach. Highlight the goal(s) stated in the question: *emphasize the number of nations participating in the 1939 New York World's Fair.* Eliminate any answer that doesn't fulfill this purpose.

- (A), (C), and (D) are wrong because they do not state *the number of nations participating.*
- (B) is correct because it states *the number of nations participating* (*62*).

Module 2—Easier

1. **D** This is a Vocabulary question, as it asks what "kept" *most nearly means*. Treat "kept" as if it were a blank—the blank describes an action taken by Lady Godiva toward thirteen poor folk, so look for clues regarding that action. The passage describes Lady Godiva as *saintly* and claims that this action was taken *at her own expense*. Therefore, a good word to enter in the annotation box would be "took care of" or "looked after."

    - (A) is wrong because *Held* goes **Beyond the Text**—this is an alternate definition of "kept" that doesn't match "took care of."
    - (B) is wrong because it's **Recycled Language**—it misuses the religious descriptions toward the end of the passage to make an unsupported conclusion regarding Lady Godiva's actions.
    - (C) is wrong because *Concealed* is a negative word that is the **Opposite** tone of the clues in the passage.
    - (D) is correct because *Supported* matches "took care of."

2. **C** This is a Vocabulary question, as it asks what "comes up" *most nearly means*. Treat "comes up" as if it were a blank—the blank describes the movement of the boat, so look for clues about the boat's movement. The passage states that the boat *glides into a bed of water-lilies*. Therefore, a good word to enter in the annotation box would be that the boat "moves gracefully" or "proceeds gently" forward.

    - (A) is wrong because *Disrupts* is a negative word that is the **Opposite** of "moves gracefully."
    - (B) is wrong because *Submerges* doesn't match "moves gracefully."
    - (C) is correct because *Approaches* could match "moves gracefully."
    - (D) is wrong because *Invents* goes **Beyond the Text**—it's another definition of "coming up" with something but doesn't match "moves gracefully."

3. **C** This is a Vocabulary question, as it asks for a *logical and precise word or phrase*. The blank describes the type of measures that allergists train families to take, so look for and highlight clues about those measures. The passage states that allergists can help families *reduce overall health care costs* and *avoid allergy-related expenses*. Therefore, a good word to enter in the annotation box would be "protective" or "pre-emptive."

    - (A) is wrong because *generic* (basic) doesn't match "protective."
    - (B) and (D) are wrong because *inflammatory* (likely to provoke or stir up) and *minimal* are the **Opposite** of "protective" in this context—inflammatory measures may make allergies worse, while minimal measures may not do enough to protect the child from allergies.
    - (C) is correct because *preventative* matches "protective."

4. **B** This is a Vocabulary question, as it asks for a *logical and precise word or phrase*. The blank describes what investing in energy-saving technology might do for the probability of a successful home sale, so look for and highlight clues about that interaction. The passage states that *Homeowners are often required to provide potential buyers with licensed inspections of their homes' energy efficiency*. Therefore, investing in energy-saving technology would likely improve the results from the energy efficiency inspection, thereby "improving" or "enhancing" the probability of a successful home sale for the homeowner, making those words good choices to enter into the annotation box.

    - (A) and (C) are wrong because *exploring* and *investigating* don't match "improving."
    - (B) is correct because *increasing* matches "improving."
    - (D) is wrong because *diminishing* is the **Opposite** of "improving."

5. **D** This is a Purpose question, as it asks for the *function of the underlined sentence in the text as a whole*. Read the text and focus on structural language before and after the underlined sentence to understand its function. The word *When* in the underlined sentence suggests that this part of the passage is an illustration of the opening sentence, which states that *Fish can both detect and respond to fear in other fish due to oxytocin*. The phrase *Likewise* after the underlined sentence means that the author wants to give another example of the main point similar to the example in the underlined sentence. A good function of the underlined sentence to enter into the annotation box would be "explain how oxytocin affects how fish detect and respond to emotions."

    - (A) is wrong because it's **Recycled Language**—the final sentence of the passage does mention *other fish* but does not contrast (or even describe) their *emotional regulation abilities* with those of zebrafish.
    - (B) is wrong because it's **Right Answer, Wrong Question**—this answer describes the role performed by the first sentence rather than the underlined sentence.
    - (C) is wrong because it's also **Right Answer, Wrong Question**—this answer describes the final two sentences, the first of which offers oxytocin as a *rationale* for why zebrafish may be able to *recognize stress*, but neither of those two sentences is the underlined sentence.
    - (D) is correct because it's consistent with the highlighting and annotation—the deletion of the *genes used to regulate oxytocin* affected the ability of the fish to *detect the emotions of other fish*, which supports that oxytocin regulation itself does indeed affect zebrafish.

6. **B** This is a Purpose question, as it asks for the *function of the underlined sentence in the text as a whole*. Read the text and focus on structural language before and after the underlined sentence to understand its function. The phrase *For example* after the underlined sentence indicates that the author wants to further explain how *sleep duration and sleep quality* are factors that affect *cardiovascular health*. A good function of the underlined sentence to enter into the annotation box would be "describe how sleep relates to heart health."

    - (A) is wrong because no *technique* is proposed or described in the underlined sentence.
    - (B) is correct because it's consistent with the highlighting and annotation.

- (C) is wrong because it's **Right Answer, Wrong Question**—the context, or background, that prompted the study is given in the first and second sentences, not the underlined sentence.
- (D) is wrong because it's **Extreme Language**—nothing in the underlined sentence claims that the addition of sleep as the eighth factor was *inevitable*, or destined to happen.

7. **A** This is a Retrieval question, as it asks for a detail *According to the text.* Look for and highlight information about one way that the Carnaval de Oruro has shifted from its original context. The passage states that while the Carnaval *originated as a pagan religious festival performed by the indigenous Itu people, the modern Carnaval now also includes a ritual from Christianity.* The correct answer should be as consistent as possible with this shift.
    - (A) is correct because it's consistent with the highlighted information about how the Carnaval de Oruro now *includes a ritual from Christianity* in addition to its origins as a *pagan religious festival.*
    - (B) and (D) are wrong because they're the **Opposite** of the passage—the festival focuses on *various groups* rather than *a single ethnic group*, and the entire celebration *traverses four kilometers* rather than remaining *in a single location for its duration.*
    - (C) is wrong because it's **Extreme Language**—while the festival has added a ritual from Christianity and expanded its focus, it's not stated in the passage that it does not retain *any* characteristics from its time with the Itu people.

8. **C** This is a Retrieval question, as it asks for a detail *based on the text.* Look for and highlight information about Bhashani living in Jaleswar to understand what may have happened if he hadn't lived there. The passages states that Bhashani's *experience living in this area inspired him to become more politically conscious, and he ultimately became an advocate for the lower class and fought for Bangladeshi independence.* Therefore, had Bhashani not lived in Jaleswar, it's at least possible that he would not have become *more politically conscious.*
    - (A) is wrong because the passage never discusses the number of *supporters* that Bhashani gained, and by extension, never discusses if anything would have affected that number.
    - (B) is wrong because it's the **Opposite** of the passage—if Bhashani didn't live in the area, it's less likely, not more likely, that he would even have been around to *prevent the war fought for Bangladeshi independence.* Additionally, the passage doesn't discuss the topic of prevention either way.
    - (C) is correct because it's consistent with the highlighted information about Bhashani living in Jaleswar.
    - (D) is wrong because it goes **Beyond the Text**—it's not known from the passage that Bhashani would have taken any side in the war at all if it hadn't lived in Jaleswar, much less the *opposite side* of the war.

9. **A** This is a Retrieval question, as it asks for a detail *According to the text.* Look for and highlight information about what Chaplitsky does after meeting with Tomsky's grandmother. The passage states that Tomsky's grandmother *gave him three cards telling him to play them one after the other, exacting from him a solemn promise that he would never play at cards again as long as he lived.* After this, *Chaplitsky then went to his victorious opponent, and they began a fresh game,* which Chaplitsky goes on to win. The correct answer should be as consistent as possible with this sequence of events.

- (A) is correct because it's consistent with the highlighted information about Chaplitsky and Tomsky's grandmother—once he has the three cards after agreeing to Tomsky's grandmother's terms, he immediately goes and wins a game playing the first of those cards.
- (B) is wrong because it goes **Beyond the Text**—as logical as it is to imagine that Chaplitsky might break the promise, he was allowed to play all three cards given to him and had only played one by the conclusion of the passage, so he has not broken the promise.
- (C) is wrong because no *concern* or any other emotion is expressed by Chaplitsky after agreeing to the deal.
- (D) is wrong because it also goes **Beyond the Text**—in the final sentence, it's only known how much he bet, not how much he won. Additionally, it's not stated in the passage that Chaplitsky continued to gamble after that first game, however likely it may seem.

10. **B** This is a Charts question, as it asks for *data from the table* that will *complete the statement.* Read the title, variables, and unit from the table. Then, read the passage and highlight the text related to the same information from the table, which *the student is trying to figure out the average electricity used by someone living in Hawaii in 2020.* The correct answer should offer the correct amount from the table that completes the text.

- (A), (C), and (D) are wrong because these numbers are the electricity usage from New York in 2020, both Hawaii and New York in 2000, and Hawaii in 1980, respectively.
- (B) is correct because it's consistent with the highlighting—in 2020, the average electricity usage from a US citizen in Hawaii was 2,000 kwh.

11. **C** This is a Claims question, as it asks for which detail *would most directly support Schmidt's hypothesis.* Look for and highlight the hypothesis in the text, which is that the *decline* in European eel populations *was due to the eel's breeding habits,* which have it migrating *5,000–10,000 kilometers across the Atlantic Ocean to reach the Sargasso Sea to breed.* The correct answer should be as consistent as possible with this hypothesis.

- (A), (B), and (D) are wrong because each is the **Opposite** of the hypothesis—each of these answers states or implies that none or virtually none of the eels wound up in the Sargasso Sea itself, which Schmidt claimed was their final destination for breeding.
- (C) is correct because it's consistent with the highlighted hypothesis—the eels in this answer do indeed head for the Sargasso Sea, and the fact that *more than 30% did not survive the trip* supports the idea that the journey is *dangerous* and could lead to a decline in eel populations.

12. **B** This is a Claims question, as it asks which choice *most effectively illustrates the claim*. Look for and highlight the claim in the passage, which is the *narrator describes a young man as feeling a growing sense of dread while conversing with a companion*. The correct answer should address and be consistent with each aspect of this claim.

- (A) and (C) are wrong because neither includes anything that could be *dread*, or any other negative emotion for that matter.
- (B) is correct because it's consistent with the highlighting—*his horror was increased* could be a *growing sense of dread* and *She detailed to him* indicates that he is *conversing with a companion*.
- (D) is wrong because although the descriptions of the monster causing *ruin* could mean the narrator feels a sense of dread, nothing in the quotation indicates his dread is *growing*, or increasing. Additionally, there is no evidence that this information is being relayed to the young man as part of a conversation.

13. **B** This is a Conclusions question, as it asks what *most logically completes the text*. Look for the main focus of the passage, which is how eating may affect alertness after waking from sleep. Then, highlight the main points made regarding this focus. First, the passage states that *Participants were provided with muffins high in carbohydrates, shakes high in protein, or granola bars high in fiber*. Next, the passage states that *Those who chose to consume muffins had the highest relative alertness score of 0.08, while those who chose to consume protein shakes had the lowest relative alertness score after waking of –0.07*. Therefore, a good conclusion for this passage to enter into the annotation box would be "carbs may help alertness more than protein." The correct answer should be as consistent as possible with this conclusion.

- (A) is wrong because it's **Extreme Language**—while the muffin helped with alertness more than the protein shake did, the passage does not claim that muffins are the *only* breakfast food that people should incorporate into their diet.
- (B) is correct because it's consistent with the highlighting and annotation—this conclusion is supported by the final full sentence of the passage.
- (C) is wrong because it goes **Beyond the Text**—it's not possible to know from the passage how carbohydrates and protein together would affect someone's alertness, as that scenario is not mentioned.
- (D) is wrong because it's **Extreme Language**—as logical as it is that someone would want to look into *different types of muffins* to understand how carbohydrate-rich breakfasts affect alertness, no such recommendation is made by the author of the passage.

14. **C** This is a Conclusions question, as it asks what *most logically completes the text*. Look for the main focus of the passage, which is the sport chovgan. Then, highlight the main points made regarding this focus. First, the passage states that *chovgan was brought from India to England in the nineteenth century*, and after that *many new rules were added, making the sport more complex*. Next, the passage states that *in 1900, chovgan was included in the Olympic Games for the first time*. Lastly, the passage

notes that *there are numerous depictions of the sport in ancient figurines and manuscripts*. Therefore, a good conclusion for this passage to enter into the annotation box would be "chovgan has been appreciated for a long time." The correct answer should be as consistent as possible with this conclusion.

- (A) is wrong because it goes **Beyond the Text**—while both works of art and an athletic activity are discussed in the passage, neither is described as being more *significant to Iranian culture* than the other.
- (B) is wrong because it also goes **Beyond the Text**—while it's true that *new rules were added* according to the passage, it's not stated that these rules *improved the game*, only that they made it *more complex*.
- (C) is correct because it's consistent with the highlighting and annotation—based on the *ancient figurines and manuscripts*, interest in chovgan seems to predate both the nineteenth century and the 1900 Olympic Games.
- (D) is wrong because it's the **Opposite** of the passage—the English version of the sport is considered *more complex*, so if anything, the English version, not the Iranian version, would be the more *challenging* one.

15. **A** In this Rules question, verbs are changing in the answer choices, so it's testing consistency with verbs. Find and highlight the subject, *Merrick*, which is singular, so a singular verb is needed. All of the answers work with a singular subject, so look for a clue regarding tense. The previous sentence uses the past tense verb *was*, and this sentence begins with the phrase *During the two years that she held this position*, which refers to a time in the past and contains the past tense verb *held*. Highlight these clues and write an annotation that says "past." Eliminate any answer not in past tense.

- (A) is correct because it's in past tense.
- (B), (C), and (D) are wrong because they are not in past tense.

16. **A** In this Rules question, punctuation is changing in the answer choices. Look for independent clauses. The first part of the sentence says *...she earned further acclaim when she broke*, which is not an independent clause because the word *broke* needs what was broken to come directly after it. Therefore, no punctuation should be used between *broke* and *another record*. Eliminate answers with punctuation.

- (A) is correct because no punctuation should be used between *broke* and *another record*.
- (B), (C), and (D) are wrong because they put punctuation between *broke* and the thing that was broken.

17. **D** In this Rules question, verbs are changing in the answer choices, so it's testing consistency with verbs. Find and highlight the subject, *Victoria Siddall*, which is singular, so a singular verb is needed. Write an annotation that says "singular." Eliminate any answer that is not singular.

- (A), (B), and (C) are wrong because they are plural.
- (D) is correct because it's singular.

18. **C** In this Rules question, verbs are changing in the answer choices, so it's testing consistency with verbs. Find and highlight the subject, *phenomenon*, which is singular, so a singular verb is needed. Write an annotation that says "singular." Eliminate any answer that is not singular.

- (A), (B), and (D) are wrong because they are plural.
- (C) is correct because it's singular.

19. **D** In this Rules question, punctuation is changing in the answer choices. The punctuation appears before the word *that*. Phrases beginning with *that* are always Specifying Information, so no punctuation should be used. Eliminate answers that use punctuation.

- (A), (B), and (C) are wrong because no punctuation should be used prior to a phrase beginning with *that*.
- (D) is correct because no punctuation should be used to separate Specifying Information.

20. **C** In this Rules question, punctuation is changing in the answer choices. The first part of the sentence says *One of the paintings housed by the Yale University Art Gallery is Edward Hopper's Rooms by the Sea*, which is an independent clause. The second part of the sentence says *a piece that art critic Ken Johnson has called one of Hopper's "strangest" works*, which is a describing phrase and not an independent clause. Noun phrases beginning with "a" or "an" are always Extra Information and should be set off with commas. Eliminate answers that do not have a comma.

- (A) is wrong because *while* indicates a contrast, and there is no contrast in this sentence.
- (B) is wrong because the second part of the sentence is not an independent clause and can't be its own sentence.
- (C) is correct because it properly separates the Extra Information with a comma.
- (D) is wrong because Extra Information must be separated from the rest of the sentence with punctuation.

21. **B** In this Rules question, apostrophes with nouns are changing in the answer choices. Determine whether each word possesses anything. *Larreal* possesses *outspoken political statements*, so *Larreal* should have an apostrophe. The *statements* don't possess anything, so *statements* should not have an apostrophe. Eliminate any answer that doesn't match this.

- (A) and (C) are wrong because *statements* shouldn't have an apostrophe.
- (B) is correct because *Larreal* has an apostrophe and *statements* does not.
- (D) is wrong because *Larreal* should have an apostrophe.

22. **B** This is a Transitions question, so follow the basic approach. Highlight ideas that relate to each other. The preceding sentence states that *the 2018 Camp Fire ignited, burning wildly until it was finally contained after 18 days*, and this sentence states that *it was the most destructive wildfire*. These ideas agree, so a same-direction transition is needed. Make an annotation that says "agree." Eliminate any answer that doesn't match.

- (A) is wrong because this sentence is describing the same event as the preceding sentence, not an event that takes place afterward.
- (B) is correct because this sentence is describing the eventual outcome of the event in the preceding sentence.
- (C) is wrong because this sentence is not providing specific details about a general claim made in the preceding sentence.
- (D) is wrong because this sentence is not merely a restatement of the preceding sentence.

23. **C** This is a Transitions question, so follow the basic approach. Highlight ideas that relate to each other. The preceding sentence states that *Many people are familiar with the dog Laika*, and this sentence states that *fewer know the names of Dezik and Tsygan*. These ideas disagree, so an opposite-direction transition is needed. Make an annotation that says "disagree." Eliminate any answer that doesn't match.

    - (A), (B), and (D) are wrong because they are same-direction transitions.
    - (C) is correct because it is an opposite-direction transition.

24. **A** This is a Transitions question, so follow the basic approach. Highlight ideas that relate to each other. The first sentence states that Reid began her work *In 1965*, the preceding sentence states that she completed work *by 1985*, and this sentence states that she was recognized for her work *in 1996*. These ideas represent a time change, so a time-change transition is needed. Make an annotation that says "time change." Eliminate any answer that doesn't match.

    - (A) is correct because it is a time-change transition that accurately presents the events of 1996 as occurring after 1985.
    - (B) is wrong because it incorrectly implies that the events of 1996 occurred prior to 1985.
    - (C) is wrong because, although this is the last sentence, there is no indication that this is any type of conclusion or ending.
    - (D) is wrong because it isn't a time-change transition.

25. **D** This is a Rhetorical Synthesis question, so follow the basic approach. Highlight the goal(s) stated in the question: *emphasize the significance of Switzerland's form of government*. Eliminate any answer that doesn't fulfill this purpose.

    - (A), (B), and (C) are wrong because they do not show how Switzerland's form of government is significant.
    - (D) is correct because it shows how Switzerland's form of government is significant by stating that Switzerland is *one of only a few countries* to have a certain form of government.

26. **A** This is a Rhetorical Synthesis question, so follow the basic approach. Highlight the goal(s) stated in the question: *contrast how violins are used in string quartets and string trios.* Eliminate any answer that doesn't fulfill this purpose.

- (A) is correct because it uses the word *but* to show a contrast between the number of violinists in a string quartet and the number of violinists in a string trio.
- (B) is wrong because it contains a contrast between a string trio and a string quartet but not a contrast about *how violins are used* in each.
- (C) and (D) are wrong because they do not contain a contrast.

27. **A** This is a Rhetorical Synthesis question, so follow the basic approach. Highlight the goal(s) stated in the question: *use a quotation from Véa to explain his inspiration for the book.* Eliminate any answer that doesn't fulfill this purpose.

- (A) is correct because it contains a quotation to describe how Véa was *inspired.*
- (B) and (D) are wrong because they do not contain a quotation.
- (C) is wrong because the quotation is not specifically related to Véa's *inspiration for the book.*

Module 2—Harder

1. **A** This is a Vocabulary question, as it asks for a *logical and precise word or phrase.* The blank describes a characteristic of certain species of ants, so look for and highlight clues about a characteristic the ants may possess. The passage states that the ants *learned instead how to perform life-saving amputations on the infected limbs of other ants with the same genetic defect.* Therefore, enter that the ants have become "flexible" or "able to learn" into the annotation box.

- (A) is correct because *adaptable* matches "flexible."
- (B) and (D) are wrong because *cumbersome* and *disorganized* are negative words that are the **Opposite** tone of "flexible."
- (C) is wrong because *subtle* (delicate or fine) doesn't match "flexible."

2. **C** This is a Vocabulary question, as it asks for a *logical and precise word or phrase.* The blank describes an action toward the contents of the golden records, so look for and highlight clues about those contents. The passage states that the records *contain selected audio and image files.* Therefore, the contents of the records were "selected for" or "chosen for" inclusion on the records for some specific reason, making these good phrases to enter into the annotation box.

- (A) and (B) are wrong because *debarred from* (banned) and *shielded against* are the **Opposite** of the passage—either of these would mean the contents described in the passage were not included on the records, when in fact they were.

- (C) is correct because *designated for* matches "selected for."
- (D) is wrong because *mandated for* (required) is **Extreme Language**—it's not known from the passage that any of the audio or image files were required by anyone to be included on the records.

3. **B** This is a Vocabulary question, as it asks for a *logical and precise word or phrase*. The blank describes the amount of energy used by AI, so look for and highlight clues about that amount. The passage states that *artificial intelligence (AI) is likely to vastly increase…electricity consumption globally*. Therefore, a good word to enter in the annotation box would be that more AI use will use a "large" or "substantial" amount of energy.

   - (A) is wrong because *precarious* (hazardous) goes **Beyond the Text**—while using more energy does usually carry increased risk, no such link is mentioned in the passage.
   - (B) is correct because *copious* (vast in quantity) matches "large."
   - (C) is wrong because *innocuous* (harmless) doesn't match "large."
   - (D) is wrong because *scant* (little) is the **Opposite** of "large."

4. **C** This is a Vocabulary question, as it asks for a *logical and precise word or phrase*. The blank describes some aspect of unforeseen costs that having excess funds can offset, so look for and highlight clues about those costs. The passage states that the costs are *related to the logistical difficulty of obtaining and building the necessary components needed for such projects to function*. Therefore, since the clue describes negative things that lead to the costs, enter "complications" or "challenges" into the annotation box.

   - (A) is wrong because *motivations* doesn't match "complications."
   - (B) is wrong because *enhancement* is a positive word that is the **Opposite** tone of "complications."
   - (C) is correct because *impediments* (obstacles) matches "complications."
   - (D) is wrong because *realignments* goes **Beyond the Text**—while it's easy to imagine the components of an energy project needing to be realigned in some way, the passage does not go into any specific aspects of the project besides *obtaining and building* its components.

5. **C** This is a Purpose question, as it asks for the *function of the underlined portion in the text as a whole*. Read the passage and focus on structural language that can help explain the function of the underlined portion. The word *but* in the underlined portion indicates a contradiction between something the narrator *could have* done (*climbed the mountain again and got back before sunrise*) and why he didn't do it (*dragging the sled tires me*). A good function of the underlined portion to enter into the annotation box would be "explain why the narrator didn't climb the mountain again."

   - (A) is wrong because it goes **Beyond the Text**—while the narrator uses descriptive language regarding the aesthetics, or beauty, of nature in the first two sentences, the underlined portion does not specifically claim that he has an *affinity*, or fondness, for those aesthetics.

- (B) is wrong because it's **Right Answer, Wrong Question**—the narrator describes the glaciers using figurative language *(divinely tender and fine)* earlier in the passage, but not in the underlined portion.
- (C) is correct because it's consistent with the highlighting and annotation.
- (D) is wrong because it's also **Right Answer Wrong Question**—though the narrator does describe what he had for supper, *hardtack*, this detail does not capture the entire *function* of the underlined portion, which is about what the narrator could have done and why he didn't do it.

6. **C** This is a Purpose question, as it asks for the *overall structure of the text*. Read the passage and focus on structural language that can help you understand the order of and connections between ideas. The passage begins by describing the scene as *pleasant*, with more and more crows arriving *day by day*, and then describes a sparrow arriving *primed with glee*. Lastly, the sparrow's sounds are described as *Piping an end to all the long distress / From every fence and every leafless tree*. The presence of these increasingly positive words means that the passage is trying to "describe the forest as gradually becoming happier."

    - (A) is wrong because it's **Recycled Language**—while *crows* and a *sparrow* are mentioned in the passage, a specific contrast between their behaviors is not made.
    - (B) is wrong because it's **Right Answer, Wrong Question**—while the passage does introduce the month of April, the author does not claim the events are specifically associated with April, nor is April the main focus of the passage.
    - (C) is correct because it's consistent with the highlighting and annotation—this answer captures the increasingly positive language of the passage by using the words *becoming livelier*.
    - (D) is wrong because it's also **Right Answer, Wrong Question**—this answer focuses only on the snow slowly disappearing, which is not the main focus of the entire passage.

7. **D** This is a Retrieval question, as it asks for what the *text most strongly* suggests. Look for and highlight information about *the jazz art created by Reid Miles*. The passage states that Miles's *cover art combined asymmetrical letter cases and numerous typefaces, and Miles's Blue Note Records covers became iconic examples of jazz's visual identity*. The correct answer should be as consistent as possible with this description of Miles's art and his contributions to the album covers of Blue Note Records.

    - (A) is wrong because it goes **Beyond the Text**—Lion wanted *information about the content of the album and graphics intended to make the album stand out more to potential buyers*, but it's not stated that he actually found what Miles came up with to be *more visually interesting* than what Blue Note Records had before.
    - (B) and (C) are wrong because each goes **Beyond the Text**—people often do tend to appreciate art more over time and great cover art could help a label produce more records, but neither of these claims are made in the passage.

- (D) is correct because it's consistent with the highlighted information—if Lion specifically wanted *graphics intended to make the album stand out more to potential buyers*, it's likely that the albums had less of a visual component before Miles's work. Additionally, Miles's covers became *iconic examples of jazz's visual identity*, indicating that there may not have been as much of a visual identity for jazz on the covers before Miles.

8. **B** This is a Main Idea question, as it asks for the *main idea of the text*. Look for and highlight information that can help identify the main idea. The third sentence states that Scythrop *took the opportunity of his father's absence to smuggle a dumb carpenter into the Abbey, and between them they gave reality to one of these models in Scythrop's tower*. Since the first two sentences explain Scythrop's *models*, and the last sentence offers the reasoning behind making one of the models a *reality*, the third sentence can serve as the main idea. The correct answer should be as consistent as possible with this portion of the passage.

    - (A) is wrong because it goes **Beyond the Text**—Scythrop does think highly of himself based on the final sentence, but his belief in himself is not said to not *fluctuate*, or change, in the passage.
    - (B) is correct because it's consistent with the highlighted main idea—this answer references the design, building, and rationale behind the construction Scythrop did with the carpenter.
    - (C) is wrong because it goes **Beyond the Text**—while Scythrop believes his modifications will help him be around long enough *for the benefit of mankind in general*, it's not stated that Scythrop used his mechanical genius for less benevolent things while his father was present in the tower. Without knowing how Scythrop used his talents before, it's not possible to support he is doing *more benevolent* things with those talents now.
    - (D) is wrong because it's **Half-Right**—Scythrop is using his father's *absence* to *further his own goals*, but it's not stated that this makes him *Like his father*.

9. **C** This is a Retrieval question, as it asks for what *the text* suggests. Look for and highlight information about *Parliament*. The passage states that *the amount of exportation of livestock from this part of the Highlands to the Western continent has more than once attracted the attention of Parliament*. The correct answer should be as consistent as possible with this description of Parliament and its relationship with the city of Glenmutchkin.

    - (A) is wrong because it goes **Beyond the Text**—though the distilleries in Glenmutchkin are *famous*, Parliament's opinion of them is not given in the passage.
    - (B) is wrong because it also goes **Beyond the Text**—it's known from the passage that Parliament has focused on Glenmutchkin before, but not how *recently* Parliament has started examining the city.
    - (C) is correct because it's consistent with the highlighted information—the *particular aspect* would be the *amount of exportation of livestock*.

- (D) is wrong because it's **Recycled Language**—the phrase *population of Glenmutchkin* appears in the passage, but the passage describes neither the population of Parliament nor the makeup of Parliament as *diversely constituted* (meaning the members of either come from varied backgrounds).

10. **A** This is a Claims question, as it asks which detail *would most strongly support the claim made by Schurmeier and colleagues about the presence of methane clathrates on Titan*. Look for and highlight the claim in the text, which is that the *methane trapped in crystal-like substances called clathrates provides a solution to these quandaries*. The presence of the phrase *these quandaries* indicates that the sentence before should be read to determine what these quandaries, or logical difficulties, are. The passage states that the issues are that *methane is present in its atmosphere, though the chemical should be easily broken down by sunlight*, the surface of Titan is *relatively void of craters, meaning that something is filling in crater impact sites*, and that Titan *contains liquid water beneath its surface despite Titan being too far from the Sun to receive enough heat to melt ice into water*. The correct answer should offer an explanation as to how clathrates might solve as many of these issues as possible.

    - (A) is correct because it's consistent with the highlighted claim and related details—this statement regarding clathrates addresses each of the three quandaries in the same order they are discussed in the passage (presence of methane, craters being filled in, and the melting or heating of ice into water.)
    - (B) and (C) are wrong because they're each the **Opposite** of the claim—these answers explain why it would be difficult for methane clathrates to either *sustain adequate heat levels* or even *exist* on Titan, either of which would weaken the claim.
    - (D) is wrong because it would do the **Opposite** of the question task—if an alternate *explanation* for the *absence of impact craters* such as gravitational force is given, this would weaken the idea that the lack of craters is due to the presence of methane clathrates. Additionally, merely stating that the *potential existence of methane clathrates is expected to be studied further* does not support the hypothesis that clathrates are actually present on Titan and explaining the *mysteries* described in the passage.

11. **D** This is a Claims question, as it asks which choice *would most strongly support the underlined explanation*. Look for and highlight the explanation in the passage, which is that the Voynich manuscript *is a pharmaceutical guide exploring herbal medicine, recipes to create compound medicines, and medical procedures rooted in astrological beliefs*. The correct answer should address and be consistent with each aspect of this claim.

    - (A) is wrong because it goes **Beyond the Text**—even if doctors do use a *type of shorthand* to write prescriptions, this fact alone is not enough to claim that the *unknown language* in the Voynich manuscript is also medical shorthand of some kind.
    - (B) and (C) are wrong because they're irrelevant to the claim—the explanation is solely regarding the content of the manuscript, not the dating of its ink, paper, or language.

- (D) is correct because it's consistent with the highlighting—if a *field medical guide* specifically *acknowledges the Voynich manuscript as an inspiration for many of its own treatments*, it's likely that the Voynich manuscript has at least something to do with *herbal medicine* or *recipes to create compound medicines* as the experts believe.

12. **D** This is a Charts question, as it asks for *data from the graph* that will *complete the text*. Read the title, key, and variables from the graph. Then, read the passage and highlight the text related to the same information from the graph, which *the brain may be predisposed to classifying more odors as unpleasant than pleasant during depressive episodes and to classifying more odors as pleasant than unpleasant while in a euthymic state*. The correct answer should offer the correct amount from the graph that both completes this statement and remains consistent with the first part of the statement.

    - (A) is wrong because it's consistent with the graph but the **Opposite** of the claim—those experiencing depressive episodes should classify *more odors as unpleasant than pleasant*, and yet, the two categories are equal for those in a depressed state in both the answer choice and the graph.
    - (B) and (C) are wrong because they're consistent with the graph but irrelevant to the claim—these answers compare the control group to either the group experiencing a depressive episode or the group in a euthymic state, respectively, but the correct answer should compare the group experiencing a depressive episode to the group experiencing a euthymic state.
    - (D) is correct because it's consistent with the highlighting and the graph—although this answer also includes the control group, which is unnecessary for the claim, it is still consistent with the claim by demonstrating the group experiencing a depressive episode finding more odors unpleasant and fewer odors pleasant than did the group experiencing a euthymic state.

13. **B** This is a Conclusions question, as it asks what *most logically completes the text*. Look for the main focus of the passage, which is when and how often genes were transferred between two different groups. Then, highlight the main points made regarding this focus. The word *instead* in the second-to-last sentence indicates there is a contrast between that sentence and the one before it. First, the passage states that *it had been determined that most human-Neanderthal intermingling would have taken place relatively early in this period, from about 200,000 to 250,000 years ago*. Next, the passage states that Akey's team *found evidence of contact between the groups not just around 200,000 to 250,000 years ago but also around 100,000 years ago and again around 50,000 years ago*. Therefore, a good conclusion for this passage to enter into the annotation box would be "humans and Neanderthals interacted more than people thought they did." The correct answer should be as consistent as possible with this conclusion.

    - (A) is wrong because it's the **Opposite** of the passage—both conclusions reached in the passage indicate that the first contact was between 200,000 to 250,000 years ago, not 50,000 years ago. The only point of disagreement is if there was additional contact later than that.
    - (B) is correct because it's consistent with the highlighting and annotation—this conclusion is consistent with what Akey's team found.

- (C) is wrong because it goes **Beyond the Text**—while there could have been a third human group that assisted in the distribution of DNA, no such group is mentioned in the passage.

- (D) is wrong because it also goes **Beyond the Text**—while this answer could be an explanation for the occasional interaction between humans and Neanderthals that Akey's team had, there is no evidence that the Neanderthals *remained* in Africa after their arrival there.

14. **C** This is a Conclusions question, as it asks what *most logically completes the text*. Look for the main focus of the passage, which is the pros and cons of riding a bike as a form of transportation. Then, highlight the main points made regarding this focus. The word *However* early in the passage indicates that the author primarily wants to focus on the negatives of bike riding. The first main point the passage makes after the word *However* is that *Notable barriers that discourage bike riding include dangerous proximity to motor vehicles, level of physical fitness required, environmental factors (such as weather conditions), and community perceptions of cyclists*. Next, the passage states that *Municipalities have begun to construct bike lanes to prevent negative interactions between automobile drivers and bike riders*. Therefore, a good conclusion for this passage to enter into the annotation box would be "municipalities are trying to address some of the barriers to bike riding." The correct answer should be as consistent as possible with this conclusion.

    - (A) is wrong because it goes **Beyond the Text**—as logical as it is that bike riders need to pay more attention to the drivers of automobiles than the reverse, no such statement about who needs to be more careful is made in the passage.

    - (B) is wrong because it also goes **Beyond the Text**—similarly to (A), while it's easy to assume that automobiles may be more dangerous to bike riders than bad weather, the author of the passage makes no such claim.

    - (C) is correct because it's consistent with the highlighting and annotation—bike lanes, if they do *prevent negative interactions between automobile drivers and bike riders* as intended, *may alleviate* both the *dangerous proximity to motor vehicles* and potentially the *community perceptions of cyclists*.

    - (D) is wrong because it's **Extreme Language**—while the passage comments on *community perceptions of cyclists*, the author does not go as far as to recommend anything the bike riders themselves should do.

15. **D** In this Rules question, punctuation is changing in the answers. The main meaning of the sentence is *This move…was indicated with a letter-number combination rather than with an image*. The phrase *an hour-long process in some cases* is a describing phrase that has a comma before it, so it must have a matching comma after to show that it is Extra Information. Eliminate answers that do not have a comma after the describing phrase.

    - (A), (B), and (C) are wrong because they don't use a comma after the phrase.

    - (D) is correct because it uses a comma after the Extra Information.

16. **D** In this Rules question, punctuation is changing in the answers. Look for independent clauses. The first part of the sentence says *Many of these songs were novelty songs written by non-Hawaiians that have been criticized for their nonsensical lyrics*, which is an independent clause. The second part says *by the 1930s, the hapa haole "craze" had faded but would be resurrected in the 1970s*, which is also an independent clause. Eliminate any answer that can't correctly connect two independent clauses.

- (A) and (C) are wrong because a comma without a coordinating conjunction (FANBOYS) can't connect two independent clauses.
- (B) is wrong because some type of punctuation is needed in order to connect two independent clauses.
- (D) is correct because the period makes each independent clause its own sentence, which is fine.

17. **D** In this Rules question, punctuation is changing in the answers. Look for independent clauses. The first part of the sentence says *Sergei Rachmaninoff's Piano Concerto No. 2 is a popular yet difficult piece*, which is an independent clause. The second part says *playing all of the notes in the chords simultaneously requires large hands...*, which is also an independent clause. Eliminate any answer that can't correctly connect two independent clauses.

- (A) is wrong because some type of punctuation is needed in order to connect two independent clauses.
- (B) is wrong because the addition of the word *As* to the beginning of the second part of the sentence makes it a dependent clause, which can't be its own sentence.
- (C) is wrong because a comma without a coordinating conjunction (FANBOYS) can't connect two independent clauses.
- (D) is correct because the period makes each independent clause its own sentence, which is fine.

18. **D** In this Rules question, verbs are changing in the answers, so it's testing consistency with verbs. Find and highlight the subject, *idea*, which is singular, so a singular verb is needed. Write an annotation saying "singular." Eliminate any answer that is not singular.

- (A), (B), and (C) are wrong because they are plural.
- (D) is correct because it's singular.

19. **C** In this Rules question, punctuation is changing in the answer choices. Look for independent clauses. The first part of the sentence says *Piano Sonata in E-flat minor...is acknowledged for its difficulty and its fusion of modern and traditional techniques*, which is an independent clause. The second part says *musicologists have noted...that the piece's formidable finale is particularly impressive*, which is also an independent clause. Eliminate any answer that can't correctly connect two independent clauses.

- (A) is wrong because adding *which* makes the second part into Specifying Information for the word *techniques*, but the second part of the sentence doesn't describe techniques.

- (B) is wrong because some type of punctuation is needed in order to connect two independent clauses.
- (C) is correct because a semicolon can connect two independent clauses.
- (D) is wrong because a comma without a coordinating conjunction (FANBOYS) can't connect two independent clauses.

20. **A** In this Rules question, punctuation is changing in the answers. Look for independent clauses. The first part of the sentence says *Unlike the method used by modern democracies…the customary noken practice is collective and lacks a secret ballot*, which is an independent clause. The second part says *using noken bags that represent candidates, people in communities that use this system place their votes in public*, which is also an independent clause. Eliminate any answer that can't correctly connect two independent clauses.
    - (A) is correct because a colon can connect two independent clauses.
    - (B) is wrong because some type of punctuation is needed in order to connect two independent clauses.
    - (C) and (D) are wrong because the second part is still an independent clause even with the word *while*, and two independent clauses can't be connected with either a comma alone or no punctuation at all.

21. **A** This is a Transitions question, so follow the basic approach. Highlight ideas that relate to each other. The preceding sentence states that *his immigrant father…hoped Ivan would follow the same path* of being a painter, and this sentence states that Argüelles *took an interest in poetry… and pursued a career as a poet*. These ideas disagree, so an opposite-direction transition is needed. Make an annotation that says "disagree." Eliminate any answer that doesn't match.
    - (A) is correct because *Instead* is an opposite-direction transition.
    - (B), (C), and (D) are wrong because they are same-direction transitions.

22. **C** This is a Transitions question, so follow the basic approach. Highlight ideas that relate to each other. The preceding part of the sentence states that *Researchers have noted that a second infection of another type may worsen the lung damage*, and this part of the sentence states that *they recommend vaccination against other diseases*. These ideas agree, so a same-direction transition is needed. Make an annotation that says "agree." Eliminate any answer that doesn't match.
    - (A) is wrong because this part of the sentence is not an example of a claim made in the preceding part of the sentence.
    - (B) is wrong because this part of the sentence is not an additional point for the same argument as the preceding part of the sentence.

- (C) is correct because it logically follows that if a second infection could be harmful, doctors would recommend getting vaccinated to prevent people from getting a second infection.
- (D) is wrong because it is an opposite-direction transition.

23. **D** This is a Rhetorical Synthesis question, so follow the basic approach. Highlight the goal(s) stated in the question: *emphasize a difference in how Indian and Mexican cuisines use cilantro, also known as coriander.* Eliminate any answer that doesn't fulfill this purpose.

    - (A) and (C) are wrong because they do not mention *a difference* in Indian and Mexican cuisines.
    - (B) is wrong because there is no contrast word or phrase that would explicitly indicate a *difference.*
    - (D) is correct because the phrase *Unlike Mexican cuisine* shows a difference between the two cuisines.

24. **C** This is a Rhetorical Synthesis question, so follow the basic approach. Highlight the goal(s) stated in the question: *describe how the flag of Duluth has changed.* Eliminate any answer that doesn't fulfill this purpose.

    - (A) and (D) are wrong because they state that a change in the flag occurred but do not describe *how* the flag of Duluth has changed.
    - (B) is wrong because it does not talk about a change in the flag.
    - (C) is correct because it describes how the flag has changed by describing the old flag and the new flag.

25. **D** This is a Rhetorical Synthesis question, so follow the basic approach. Highlight the goal(s) stated in the question: *begin a narrative about McAdoo's career.* Eliminate any answer that doesn't fulfill this purpose.

    - (A), (B), and (C) are wrong because a *narrative about McAdoo's career* would need to begin by introducing McAdoo and stating what his career was, which these answers don't do.
    - (D) is correct because it describes the belief that led to McAdoo's career as an architect and goes on to describe what McAdoo wanted to do with his career, establishing a narrative.

26. **A** This is a Rhetorical Synthesis question, so follow the basic approach. Highlight the goal(s) stated in the question: *use one of the examples to illustrate the meaning of "contronym."* Eliminate any answer that doesn't fulfill this purpose.

    - (A) is correct because it explains the meaning of "contronym" (*has two opposite meanings*) and uses the word "*sanction*" as an example.
    - (B), (C), and (D) are wrong because the examples do not clearly explain the meaning of "contronym."

27. **A** This is a Rhetorical Synthesis question, so follow the basic approach. Highlight the goal(s) stated in the question: *describe the novel that Makumbi published in 2014.* Eliminate any answer that doesn't fulfill this purpose.

- (A) is correct because it describes the novel *Kintu*, which, according to the notes, is the novel Makumbi published in 2014.
- (B) is wrong because it describes the novel *A Girl is a Body of Water*, which, according to the notes, was published in 2020.
- (C) is wrong because it describes two novels rather than focusing on the 2014 novel *Kintu*.
- (D) is wrong because it does not describe a novel.

PRACTICE TEST 1—MATH EXPLANATIONS

Module 1

1. **B** The question asks for a probability based on data in a frequency table. Probability is defined as $\frac{\text{\# of outcomes that fit requirements}}{\text{total \# of possible outcomes}}$. Read the table carefully to find the numbers to make up the probability. There are 73 instruments, so that is the *total # of possible outcomes.* Of these 73 instruments, 14 are woodwinds, so that is the *# of outcomes that fit requirements.* Therefore, the probability that an instrument chosen at random is a woodwind is $\frac{14}{73}$. The correct answer is (B).

2. **A** The question asks for a value given a specific situation. The question states that there is a *shipment of 500 science textbooks* and that *there are 300 physics textbooks in the shipment.* Find the difference between the total number of textbooks and the number of physics textbooks to determine the number of chemistry textbooks. There are 500 – 300 = 200 chemistry textbooks in the shipment. The correct answer is (A).

3. **29** The question asks for the value of an expression based on an equation. There is not a straightforward way to get from $8a - 3$ to $4a + 5$; however, $8a$ is 2 times $4a$, so start by isolating $8a$ in the equation $8a - 3 = 45$. Add 3 to both sides of the equation to get $8a = 48$. Next, divide both sides of the equation by 2 to get $4a = 24$. Add 5 to both sides of the equation to get $4a + 5 = 24 + 5$, or $4a + 5 = 29$. The correct answer is 29.

4. **18.75** The question asks for a measurement and gives conflicting units. The question provides the conversion that 1 mile = 8 furlongs. Set up a proportion, being sure to match up units. The proportion is $\frac{1 \text{ mile}}{8 \text{ furlongs}} = \frac{x \text{ miles}}{150 \text{ furlongs}}$. Cross-multiply to get $(8)(x) = (1)(150)$, or $8x = 150$. Divide both sides of the equation by 8 to get $x = 18.75$. The correct answer is 18.75.

5. **B** The question asks for the slope of a graph. The equation of the line is in slope-intercept form, $y = mx + b$, in which m is the slope and b is the y-intercept. Since $m = -19$, the slope is –19. The correct answer is (B).

6. **A** The question asks for an equation that represents a graph. One approach is to enter the equation from each answer choice into the built-in calculator and see which graph could be the line of best fit of the scatterplot. Only the graph of the equation in (A) matches the graph in the question, so (A) is correct.

   Another method is to compare features of the graph to the answer choices. The equations in the answer choices are all in slope-intercept form, $y = mx + b$, in which m is the slope and b is the y-intercept. The points descend from left to right, so the line of best fit would have a negative slope. Eliminate (B), (C), and (D) because they have positive slopes. Choice (A) also has a positive y-intercept, which matches the scatterplot, so (A) is correct.

   Using either of these methods, the correct answer is (A).

7. **C** The question asks for the circumference of a geometric figure. Use the geometry basic approach. Start by drawing a circle on the scratch paper and labeling the figure with the given information. Label the radius as 18. Next, write down the formula for the circumference of a circle, either from memory or after looking it up on the reference sheet. The formula is $C = 2\pi r$. Plug in 18 for r to get $C = 2\pi(18)$, which becomes $C = 36\pi$. The correct answer is (C).

8. **1/3 or .3333**

The question asks for the slope of a line that is perpendicular to a line shown by a graph. Perpendicular lines have slopes that are negative reciprocals of each other, so start by finding the slope of the line shown in the graph. Use two points on the line to calculate the slope using the formula $slope = \frac{y_2 - y_1}{x_2 - x_1}$. The line passes through points at (0, –7) and (–1, –4). Plug those values into the slope formula to get $slope = \frac{-4-(-7)}{-1-0}$, which becomes $slope = \frac{-4+7}{-1}$, then $slope = \frac{3}{-1}$, and finally $slope = -3$. The negative reciprocal of –3 is $\frac{1}{3}$, so the slope of a line perpendicular to a line with a slope of –3 is $\frac{1}{3}$. The decimal forms that fill the entire box, .3333 or 0.333, will also be accepted as correct. The correct answer is $\frac{1}{3}$ or an equivalent form.

9. **B** The question asks for an inequality that represents a graph. The most efficient method is to enter the inequality from each answer choice into the built-in calculator and see which graph looks like the graph in the question. The graph of the inequality in (B) matches the graph in the question, so (B) is correct.

Another method is to plug in points from the graph. Start with a point in the shaded area and use the point (0, 0), which is a solution to the inequality and must work in the correct equation. When $x = 0$ and $y = 0$, (A) becomes $0 < -\frac{1}{2}(0) - 10$, then $0 < 0 - 10$, and finally $0 < -10$. This is not true, so eliminate (A). Choice (B) becomes $0 < -\frac{1}{2}(0) + 10$, then $0 < 0 + 10$, and finally $0 < 10$. This is true, so keep (B), but check the remaining answers with the same point. Choice (C) becomes $0 < -\frac{1}{2}(0) - 20$, then $0 < 0 - 20$, and finally $0 < -20$; eliminate (C). Choice (D) becomes $0 < -\frac{1}{2}(0) + 20$, then $0 < 0 + 20$, and finally $0 < 20$; keep (D). Two answers worked with the first point, so try a point that is *not* in the shaded area, such as (0, 11). The point (0, 11) is not a solution to the inequality, so look for an answer that is not true. When $x = 0$ and $y = 11$, (B) becomes $11 < -\frac{1}{2}(0) + 10$, then $11 < 0 + 10$, and finally $11 < 10$. This is not true, so keep (B). Choice (D) becomes $11 < -\frac{1}{2}(0) + 20$, then $11 < 0 + 20$, and finally $11 < 20$. This is true, but a point that is not a solution to the inequality should not result in a true equation, so eliminate (D). Only (B) is left, so it is correct.

Using either of these methods, the correct answer is (B).

10. **D** The question asks for the interpretation of a statement based on a function that represents a situation. It may help to enter the equation into the built-in calculator to see that it is a curve moving downward from left to right. In function notation, the number inside the parentheses is the x-value that goes into the function, or the input, and the value that comes out of the function is the y-value, or the output. In the given function, the input, d, is the number of days after the start of the semester, and the output, M, is the amount of money, in dollars remaining in the meal plan. Thus, in the statement "$M(53)$ is approximately equal to 42.72," 53 is the input and 42.72 is the output, which means that 42.72 is the amount, in dollars, remaining 53 days after the start of the semester. Eliminate (A) and (B) because they describe 53 as a dollar amount, not as a number of days. Eliminate (C) because the start of the semester is 0 days after the start of the semester, not 53 days after the start of the semester. The correct answer is (D).

11. **A** The question asks for a value based on an equation. The question states that the number of leaves on the tree is represented by L and the number of days is represented by d. The question gives the number of days as 35, so plug in 35 for d and solve for L. The equation becomes $L = 300{,}000 - 5{,}000(35)$, then $L = 300{,}000 - 175{,}000$, and finally $L = 125{,}000$. The correct answer is (A).

12. **B** The question asks for information that will provide proof that a triangle is isosceles. An isosceles triangle has two sides with equal lengths. The question gives the lengths of two of the sides as 12.08 feet and 15.23 feet, so the third side must have a length of 12.08 feet or 15.23 feet for the triangle to be isosceles. Choice (B) states that the third side, XZ, has a length of 12.08 feet. The correct answer is (B).

13. **12.05** The question asks for the median of a list of numbers. The median of a list of numbers is the middle number when the numbers are arranged in ascending order. In lists with an even number of numbers, the median is the mean of the two middle numbers. The list has 6 numbers, so the median will be the mean of the two numbers in the middle. First, put the list in ascending order: 11.3, 11.7, 11.9, 12.2, 12.6, 12.8. Next, cross out one number at a time from each end until only the two middle numbers are left, like so: ~~11.3~~, ~~11.7~~, 11.9, 12.2, ~~12.6~~, ~~12.8~~. Add the two middle numbers and divide by 2 to find the mean: $\frac{11.9 + 12.2}{2} = 12.05$. Thus, 12.05 is the median and is correct.

It is also possible to calculate the median of a list of numbers using the built-in calculator. Type *median* into an entry field followed by the list of numbers inside parentheses. The calculator shows a median of 12.05 in the lower right corner of the entry field, so 12.05 is correct.

Using either of these methods, the correct answer is 12.05.

14. **D** The question asks for the value of a trigonometric function. Use the Geometry Basic Approach. Start by redrawing the figure and relabeling the sides and angles. Next, write out SOHCAHTOA to remember the trig functions. The TOA part defines the tangent as $\frac{opposite}{adjacent}$. The side opposite angle

Y is labeled on the figure as 53, and the side adjacent to angle Y is labeled as 12. Plug in these values to get $\tan Y = \frac{53}{12}$. The correct answer is (D).

15. **116** The question asks for a value given a specific situation. Translate the information in Bite-Sized Pieces. The question states that *A graduating class of high school students is split into four groups* and that *The first three groups have the same number of students and account for a total of 87 students.* The question also states that *The fourth group is four times the size of each of the first three groups*, so divide the total of the first three groups by 3 to find the size of one of the first three groups: $\frac{87}{3} = 29$ students in each of the first three groups. Thus, the fourth group has 4(29) = 116 students. The correct answer is 116.

16. **D** The question asks for the mass of a stone. Other information about the stone is given, so use the units to determine where to start. The question asks for the mass in kilograms and gives the density in kilograms per cubic meter and the volume in cubic meters, so density equals mass divided by volume. This happens to be the formula for density, which can be written as $D = \frac{m}{V}$. Plug in the known values to get $3.5 = \frac{m}{378}$. Multiply both sides of the equation by 378 to get $1{,}323 = m$. The correct answer is (D).

17. **B** The question asks for the number of solutions to a quadratic equation. The most efficient approach is to use the built-in calculator. Enter the equation without the "= 0" part to see a parabola, and then scroll and zoom to see how many times, if any, the parabola intersects the x-axis. There is one point of intersection at the vertex, so there is exactly one real solution, and the correct answer is (B).

To determine the number of solutions algebraically, use the discriminant. The discriminant is the part of the quadratic formula under the square root sign and is written as $D = b^2 - 4ac$. When the discriminant is positive, the quadratic has exactly two real solutions; when the discriminant is 0, the quadratic has exactly one real solution; and when the discriminant is negative, the quadratic has no real solutions. This quadratic is given in standard form, $ax^2 + bx + c = 0$, so $a = 1$, $b = 34$, and $c = 289$. The discriminant becomes $D = (34)^2 - 4(1)(289)$, then $D = 1{,}156 - 1{,}156$, and finally $D = 0$. Since the discriminant equals 0, there is exactly one real solution, and (B) is correct.

Using either of these methods, the correct answer is (B).

18. **D** The question asks for the equation of a line. Since $f(x)$ is the same as y, all of the answer choices are linear equations in slope-intercept form, $y = mx + b$, in which m is the slope and b is the y-intercept. All the answer choices have the correct slope of -1, so work with the other piece of information. The question states that the line *passes through the point (6, 10)*. Plug $x = 6$ and y, or $f(x)$, = 10 into each answer choice and eliminate equations that don't work. Choice (A) becomes $10 = -6 - 4$, or $10 = -10$. This is not true, so eliminate (A). Choice (B) becomes $10 = -6 - 1$, or $10 = -7$; eliminate (B). Choice (C) becomes $10 = -6 + 10$, or $10 = 4$; eliminate (C). Choice (D) becomes $10 = -6 + 16$, or $10 = 10$; keep (D). Only (D) worked, so it is correct.

Another method is to enter each equation in the answer choices into the built-in calculator. Enter the point (6, 10) in a separate entry field to see the point marked in the graphing area, and then scroll and zoom as needed to see whether the line passes through the point. Only the graph of the equation in (D) contains the point (6, 10), so (D) is correct.

Using either of these methods, the correct answer is (D).

19. **C** The question asks for the maximum value of a quadratic function. A quadratic graphs a parabola, which reaches its minimum or maximum value at its vertex, so find the vertex. The most efficient method is to enter the equation into the built-in calculator. The calculator does not show a graph, so subtract x^2 from both sides of the equation to get $g(x) = -x^2 + 23$. Now the calculator shows a graph, so scroll and zoom as needed to find the vertex. The vertex is at (0, 23). Read carefully: the question asks for the maximum value of function *g*. The value of a function is the *y*-value, or the output, given a specific *x*-value, or input. In this case, the output is 23 when the input is 0, so (C) is correct.

To solve algebraically, use the shortcut that, when a quadratic is in standard form, $y = ax^2 + bx + c$, the *x*-coordinate of the vertex (*h*, *k*) can be found using the formula $h = -\frac{b}{2a}$. Put the quadratic in standard form by subtracting x^2 from both sides of the equation to get $g(x) = -x^2 + 23$. Thus, $a = -1$ and $b = 0$, so the formula becomes $h = -\frac{0}{2(-1)}$, or $h = 0$. To find the maximum value of the function, plug $x = 0$ into the standard form equation of the function to get $g(0) = -0^2 + 23$, which becomes $g(0) = 23$, and (C) is correct.

Using either of these methods, the correct answer is (C).

20. **A** The question asks for an equation that represents a specific situation. The number of views is decreasing by a certain percent over time, so this question is about exponential decay. Write down the growth and decay formula: *final amount* = (*original amount*)(1 ± *rate*)$^{number\ of\ changes}$. All the answer choices have *v*, 2,975, and *d* in the same place, so focus on the value inside the parentheses. Since this situation involves a decrease, the original amount, 2,975, must be multiplied by (1 – *rate*). The rate given in the question is 9%, or 0.09, so the value inside the parentheses should be 1 – 0.09, or 0.91. Eliminate (B), (C), and (D) because they have a different value inside the parentheses. The correct answer is (A).

21. **C** The question asks for a value given a specific situation. Translate the English to math in Bite-Sized Pieces. One piece of information states that solution A *is 35% hydrochloric acid by volume.* Use *x* to represent the total volume of solution A, and represent 35% of the total volume of solution A as 0.35*x*. Another piece states that solution B *is 70% hydrochloric acid by volume.* Use *y* to represent the total volume of solution B, and represent 70% of the total volume of solution B as 0.70*y*. The question also states that *The combined solution, C, has a total volume of 140 milliliters.* The total volume of solution C is the sum of the total volumes of solutions A and B, so represent this with the equation $x + y = 140$. Finally, the question states that solution C *is 40% hydrochloric acid by volume.* Represent the information about

the percentage of the solutions that are hydrochloric acid with the equation $0.35x + 0.70y = 0.40(140)$, which becomes $0.35x + 0.70y = 56$. Now there are two equations with two variables:

$$x + y = 140$$
$$0.35x + 0.70y = 56$$

Enter both equations into the built-in calculator, and then scroll and zoom as needed to see that the lines intersect at (120, 20). The question asks about solution A, which is represented by x, so the total volume of solution A is 120 milliliters. Read carefully: the question asks for the volume of hydrochloric acid in solution A, which is 35.0% of the total volume of solution A. The volume of hydrochloric acid in solution A is 0.35(120), or 42 milliliters. The correct answer is (C).

22. **C** The question asks for the expression that represents a percent decrease. There are variables in the answer choices, so plug in. Make $a = 100$ because 100 works well with percents. The question states that the value of a is decreased by 24%. *Percent* means out of 100, so translate 24% as $\frac{24}{100}$. Take 24% of 100 to get $\frac{24}{100}(100) = 24$. The value of a is decreased by 24%, so the new value is $100 - 24 = 76$. This is the target value; write it down and circle it. Next, plug $a = 100$ into the answer choices, and eliminate any that do not equal 76. Choice (A) becomes 0.24(100), or 24; eliminate (A). Choice (B) becomes 2.4(100), or 240; eliminate (B). Choice (C) becomes 0.76(100), or 76; keep (C), but check (D) just in case. Choice (D) becomes 7.6(100), or 760; eliminate (D). The correct answer is (C).

Module 2—Easier

1. **B** The question asks for a value based on a percent. Translate the English into math in Bite-Sized Pieces. The question states that 25% of the 40 game pieces in a box are black. *Percent* means out of 100, so translate 25% as $\frac{25}{100}$. Translate *of* as times. Thus, 25% of 40 becomes $\left(\frac{25}{100}\right)(40) = 10$ black game pieces in the box. The correct answer is (B).

2. **50** The question asks for a value given a rate. Begin by reading the question to find information about the rate. The question states that *400 cups of coffee were sold during one 8-hour shift* and asks for the average number of cups of coffee sold each hour. Set up a proportion, being sure to match up the units. The proportion is $\frac{400 \text{ cups}}{8 \text{ hours}} = \frac{x \text{ cups}}{1 \text{ hour}}$. Cross-multiply to get $(8)(x) = (400)(1)$, which becomes $8x = 400$. Divide both sides of the equation by 8 to get $x = 50$. The correct answer is 50.

3. **A** The question asks for a value based on a graph. First, check the units on each axis of the bar graph. The number of building blocks per set is on the x-axis, and the number of sets is on the y-axis. The question asks about sets that contain 150 building blocks, so find 150 on the x-axis. Look at the top of the bar for 150, and then look left to the y-axis, using the mouse pointer or the edge of the scratch paper as a ruler if needed. The top of the bar for 150 building blocks per set is at 6 for the number of sets. Thus, 6 sets contain 150 blocks. The correct answer is (A).

4. **D** The question asks for the negative solution to an equation with an absolute value. One method is to enter the equation into the built-in calculator. When graphed, the points where the two vertical lines cross the x-axis are the solutions. Those points are at $x = 56$ and $x = -22$. The question asks for the negative solution, so (D) is correct.

   To find the negative solution algebraically, recall that with an absolute value, the value inside the absolute value bars can be either positive or negative. To find the solutions, set $x - 17$ equal to both 39 and –39. When $x - 17 = 39$, add 17 to both sides of the equation to get $x = 56$. This is not negative, so find the other solution. When $x - 17 = -39$, add 17 to both sides of the equation to get $x = -22$. This is the negative solution, so (D) is correct.

   Using either of these methods, the correct answer is (D).

5. **B** The question asks for information based on a graph. To find the month during which 50 birds were sighted at the bird feeder, first check the units on each axis of the line graph. The x-axis shows months in order from left to right, and the y-axis shows the number of birds sighted in ascending order from low to high. Find 50 on the y-axis, then move right—using the mouse pointer or the edge of the scratch paper as a ruler as needed—to the point on the graph on the horizontal line for 50, and then move down to the x-axis. The month when 50 birds were sighted is April. The correct answer is (B).

6. **A** The question asks for the coordinates of the x-intercept of a graph in the xy-plane. This is the point at which $y = 0$ on the vertical axis and the line intersects the horizontal x-axis. Look on the graph to find the x-intercept, which is 4 units to the left of the origin, (0, 0), so the coordinates are (–4, 0). The correct answer is (A).

7. **D** The question asks for a total value given a specific situation. The question states that *An organization is gathering signatures for a petition and has already gathered 320 signatures.* It also states that *If the organization gathers 180 more signatures, it will have enough signatures to submit the petition.* Add the number of signatures already gathered and the number of signatures left to gather to get the total. In order to submit the petition, the organization must gather $320 + 180 = 500$ signatures. The correct answer is (D).

8. **D** The question asks for the solution to a system of equations graphed in the xy-plane. This is the point at which the graphs intersect. Look on the graph to see that the point of intersection is marked with a dot 7 units to the right of the origin, (0, 0), and 8 units down from the origin. Coordinates are written in the form (x, y), so the point of intersection is at (7, –8). The correct answer is (D).

9. **C** The question asks for the value of the x-coordinate of the solution to a system of equations. One method is to enter both equations into the built-in calculator, and then scroll and zoom as needed to find the point of intersection. The graph shows one point of intersection at (7, –15). The question asks for the value of x, which is 7, so (C) is correct.

   To solve the system for the y-coordinate algebraically, substitute –15 for y in the second equation to get $x = -15 + 22$, which becomes $x = 7$, making (C) correct.

   Using either of these methods, the correct answer is (C).

10. **–2** The question asks for the value of the y-coordinate of the y-intercept of a graph in the xy-plane. This is the point at which $x = 0$ on the horizontal axis and the graph intersects the vertical y-axis. Look on the graph to find the y-intercept, which is marked by a dot 2 units down from the origin at (0, –2). The correct answer is –2.

11. **3** The question asks for the value of the y-coordinate of the y-intercept of a graph in the xy-plane. This is the point at which $x = 0$ on the horizontal axis and the graph intersects the vertical y-axis. Look on the graph to find the y-intercept, which is 3 units up from the origin at (0, 3). The correct answer is 3.

12. **40** The question asks for the solution to an equation. One method is to use the built-in calculator. Enter the equation as written, and then scroll and zoom as needed to see the solution represented by a vertical line at the point (40, 0), so 40 is correct.

   To solve for the value of x algebraically, isolate x on the left side of the equation. First, subtract $4x$ from both sides of the equation to get $x + 50 = 90$. Next, subtract 50 from both sides of the equation to get $x = 40$.

   Using either of these methods, the correct answer is 40.

13. **A** The question asks for the measure of an angle on a figure. Angle a and angle b form a straight line, and there are 180 degrees in a line. Plug in the value given for angle a and write an equation: $158 + b = 180$. Subtract 158 from both sides of the equation to get $b = 22$. The correct answer is (A).

14. **B** The question asks for an equation that represents a specific situation. Translate the information in Bite-Sized Pieces and eliminate after each piece. One piece of information states that the pump *drains water at a rate of 1,100 gallons each hour*, and another piece states that h represents hours. Multiply the number of hours, h, by the hourly rate of 1,100 gallons to get $1{,}100h$, which represents the total amount of water drained in h hours. Eliminate (A), (C), and (D) because they do not include this term. Choice (B) also correctly translates the starting amount of 4,500 gallons and subtracts $1{,}100h$ from that starting amount. The correct answer is (B).

15. **A** The question asks for the value of a function. In function notation, the number inside the parentheses is the x-value that goes into the function, or the input, and the value that comes out of the function is the y-value, or the output. The question provides an input value of –6, so plug $x = -6$ into the function to get $h(-6) = 5(-6) - 4$, which becomes $h(-6) = -30 - 4$, and then $h(-6) = -34$. The correct answer is (A).

16. **D** The question asks for an equivalent form of an expression. One method is to distribute 8 to get $8y^2 + 168$, making (D) correct.

This question can also be solved using the built-in calculator. Enter the expression from the question into one entry field, and then enter each answer choice expression into another entry field to see which graph matches the graph of the given expression. Only the graph of the expression in (D) matches the graph of the expression in the question, so (D) is correct.

Using either of these methods, the correct answer is (D).

17. **C** The question asks for the value of a function. In function notation, the number inside the parentheses is the x-value that goes into the function, or the input, and the value that comes out of the function is the y-value, or the output. The question provides an input value of 1, so plug $x = 1$ into the function to get $g(1) = 24(1)^2 - 12$, which becomes $g(1) = 24(1) - 12$, then $g(1) = 24 - 12$, and finally $g(1) = 12$. The correct answer is (C).

18. **8** The question asks for a measure on a geometric figure. Use the Geometry Basic Approach. Start by drawing a triangle on the scratch paper. The question does not describe the type of triangle, so keep things simple and make it a right triangle. Next, label the figure with information from the question, and label base as 30. The figure should look something like this:

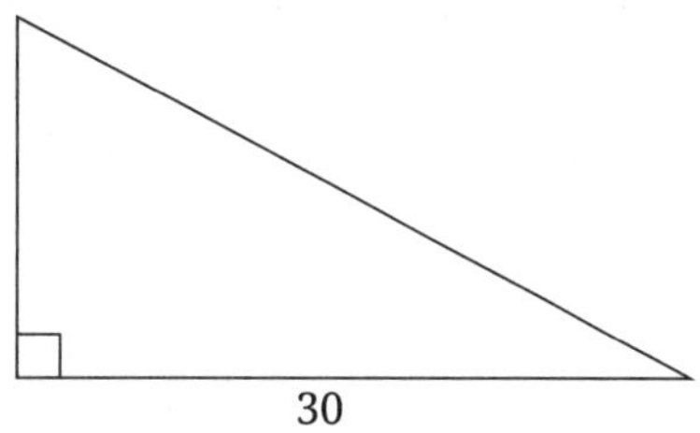

Finally, write down the formula for the area of a triangle, either from memory or after looking it up on the reference sheet. The formula is $A = \frac{1}{2}bh$. Plug in the area and the length of the base to get $120 = \frac{1}{2}(30)(h)$. Simplify the right side of the equation to get $120 = 15h$. Divide both sides of the equation by 15 to get $8 = h$. The correct answer is 8.

19. **A** The question asks for an equivalent form of an expression. One method is to use the built-in calculator. Enter the expression from the question into one entry field, and set it equal to 0 in order to see a graph. Next, enter each answer choice expression into another entry field—again setting it equal to 0—to see which graph looks like the graph in the question. Only the graph of the expression in (A) matches the graph of the expression in the question, so (A) is correct.

It is also possible to find the equivalent expression algebraically. All of the answer choices have 12, so focus on what's inside the parentheses. It is a quadratic in standard form, $ax^2 + bx + c$, so factor the quadratic. Find two terms that multiply to $64y^2$ and add to $-16y$. These are $-8y$ and $-8y$. Thus, the quadratic part of the expression factors into $(x - 8y)(x - 8y)$, and the full expression becomes $12(x - 8y)(x - 8y)$. This matches the expression in (A), so (A) is correct.

Using either of these methods, the correct answer is (A).

20. **B** The question asks for the value of an expression based on the solution to a system of equations. One approach is to enter both equations into the built-in calculator, and then scroll and zoom as needed to find the point of intersection. Click on the gray dot to see that the point is at (–4, –4). Thus, $x = -4$, $y = -4$, and $\frac{y}{x} = \frac{-4}{-4}$, or $\frac{y}{x} = 1$, which is (B).

To solve for $\frac{y}{x}$ algebraically, plug in –4 for x in the first equation to get $y = -(-4 + 6)^2$, which becomes $y = -(2)^2$, and then $y = -4$. Thus, $\frac{y}{x} = \frac{-4}{-4}$, or $\frac{y}{x} = 1$, which is (B).

Using either of these methods, the correct answer is (B).

21. **C** The question asks for the number of solutions to a system of equations. The most efficient method is to use the built-in calculator. Enter both equations into the calculator, and then scroll and zoom to see how many times, if at all, they intersect. Hide one line at a time using the circle icon in the entry field—or use the color coding—to confirm that the same line is graphed twice, making (C) correct.

To determine the number of solutions algebraically, make the two equations look as similar as possible, and then see which terms match up or don't match up. Since 27 is –3 times –9, multiply the entire first equation by –3 to get $27x - 45y = 36$. The two equations are identical, so there are infinitely many solutions, and (C) is correct.

Using either of these methods, the correct answer is (C).

22. **–11** The question asks for a value given a specific situation. Translate the English to math in Bite-Sized Pieces. One piece of information states that *One negative integer is 3 less than one-half of another negative integer.* Use x to represent the first integer and y to represent the second integer. Translate *is* as =, *3 less than* as – 3, and *one-half* as $\frac{1}{2}$. The equation becomes $x = \frac{1}{2}y - 3$. Another piece of information states that *the two integers have a product of 176.* Translate *product* as multiplication, and the equation becomes $xy = 176$. Now enter both equations into the built-in calculator, and then scroll and zoom as needed to see the two points of intersection. These are marked with gray dots at (8, 22) and (–11, –16). The question refers to negative integers, so one integer is –11 and the other is –16. The greater of the two integers is –11. The correct answer is –11.

Module 2—Harder

1. **B** The question asks for the value of a function. In function notation, the number inside the parentheses is the x-value that goes into the function, or the input, and the value that comes out of the function is the y-value, or the output. The question provides an input value of 10, so plug $x = 10$ into the function to get $f(10) = -\frac{10}{5} + 15$, which becomes $f(10) = -2 + 15$, and then $f(10) = 13$. The correct answer is (B).

2. **D** The question asks for a total value given a specific situation. The question states that *An organization is gathering signatures for a petition and has already gathered 320 signatures.* It also states that *If the organization gathers 180 more signatures, it will have enough signatures to submit the petition.* Add the number of signatures already gathered and the number of signatures left to gather to get the total. In order to submit the petition, the organization must gather 320 + 180 = 500 signatures. The correct answer is (D).

3. **–11** The question asks for a value based on a graph in the xy-plane. The y-intercept is the point at which $x = 0$ on the horizontal axis and the line intersects the vertical y-axis. Look on the graph to find the y-intercept, which is 11 units down from the origin, (0, 0), so the coordinates are (0, –11). The question asks for the value of b, which is the y-coordinate, –11. The correct answer is –11.

4. **D** The question asks for the table that contains pairs of input, x, and output, $h(x)$, values for a function. When given an equation and asked for a table of values, plug values from the tables into the equation to see which ones work. Each answer choice table has a different value for $h(x)$ when $x = 4$, so plug 4 into the equation for x to get $h(4) = -10(4) - 3$, which becomes $h(4) = -40 - 3$, and then $h(4) = -43$. Eliminate (A), (B), and (C) because they have an $h(x)$ value other than –43 when $x = 4$. The correct answer is (D).

5. **B** The question asks for the value of a function. In function notation, the number inside the parentheses is the x-value that goes into the function, or the input, and the value that comes out of the function is the y-value, or the output. The question provides an input value of 36, so plug $x = 36$ into the function to get $g(36) = 9(36)^{\frac{1}{2}}$. Use the built-in calculator: enter $9(36)^{\frac{1}{2}}$ into an entry field, and the calculator shows 54 in the lower right corner of the entry field, which means (B) is correct.

   The other way to find the value of $g(36)$ is to know exponent rules. With a fractional exponent, the numerator is the power and the denominator is the root, so the equation $g(36) = 9(36)^{\frac{1}{2}}$ becomes $g(36) = 9\sqrt{36}$. Simplify the right side of the equation to get $g(36) = 9(6)$, and then $g(36) = 54$, making (B) correct.

   Using either of these methods, the correct answer is (B).

6. **A** The question asks for a measurement on a geometric figure. Use the Geometry Basic Approach. Start by drawing a rectangle. Next, label the figure with information from the question: since the opposite sides of a rectangle have the same length, label two sides as 8. The perimeter of a geometric shape is the sum of the lengths of its sides. The question gives the perimeter as 22 centimeters, so subtract the lengths of the two labeled sides to get 22 – 8 – 8 = 6. The remaining two sides have the same length, so the length of each is $\frac{6}{2} = 3$. Thus, the width of the rectangle is 3, and (A) is correct.

   Since the question asks for a specific value and the answers contain numbers in increasing order, another approach is to plug in the answers. Rewrite the answer choices on the scratch paper and label them as "width." Next, start with a number in the middle and try (B), 6. Plug in 6 for the width and 8 for the length. A rectangle has two pairs of sides with equal lengths, so the perimeter is 6 + 8 + 6 + 8 = 28. This does not match the perimeter of 22 given in the question, so eliminate (B). The result was too large, so also eliminate (C) and (D), which leaves (A) as correct.

   Using either of these methods, the correct answer is (A).

7. **–6** The question asks for the value of the y-coordinate of the solution to a system of equations. The most efficient method is to enter both equations into the built-in calculator, and then scroll and zoom as needed to find the point of intersection. The graph shows one point of intersection at (15, –6). The question asks for the value of y, so –6 is correct.

   To solve the system for the y-coordinate algebraically, find a way to make the x-terms disappear when stacking and adding the equations. Multiply the entire first equation by –1 to get the same coefficient with opposite signs on the y-terms. The first equation becomes $-x - 5y = 15$. Now stack and add the two equations.

$$\begin{array}{r} -x - 5y = 15 \\ +\,x + \frac{5}{6}y = 10 \\ \hline 0 - \frac{25}{6}y = 25 \end{array}$$

   Rewrite the resulting equation as $-\frac{25}{6}y = 25$, and then multiply both sides of the equation by 6 to get $-25y = 150$. Divide both sides of the equation by –25 to get $y = -6$.

   Using either of these methods, the correct answer is –6.

8. **C** The question asks for a change in value over time given a graph that models a specific situation. First, find the estimated value of the boat for each x-value. The question states that x is years since the boat was purchased and y is the estimated value, in thousands of dollars, so find 2 on the x-axis and move up to the curve—using the mouse pointer or edge of the scratch paper as a ruler as needed—to see

that the y-value is 16. Do the same for $x = 5$ to find a y-value of 12. The y-values are in thousands, so the estimated value of the boat when $x = 2$ is $16,000 and the estimated value of the boat when $x = 5$ is $12,000. Next, plug in each multiplier from the answer choices to determine which one matches a decrease from $16,000 to $12,000. Eliminate (A) because $\frac{2}{5}$ of $16,000 is $6,400, not $12,000. Eliminate (B) because $\frac{3}{5}$ of $16,000 is $9,600, not $12,000. Keep (C) because $\frac{3}{4}$ of $16,000 is $12,000. Eliminate (D) because $\frac{4}{3}$ of $16,000 will be greater than $12,000. The correct answer is (C).

9. **5** The question asks for a comparison of values shown on a scatterplot. When the line of best fit predicts a smaller y-value than the actual y-value, the line is below the point. When the line of best fit predicts a greater y-value than the actual y-value, the line is above the point. For example, the point at $x = 2$ has an actual y-value of about 3.5, but the line of best fit predicts a greater y-value of about 3.8. The question asks about the line of best fit predicting a smaller y-value, so count the number of points above the line. There are 5 points above the line. The correct answer is 5.

10. **D** The question asks for an increase expressed as a percent. The question asks about a specific value and the answers contain numbers in order, so plug in the answers. Rewrite the answer choices on the scratch paper and label them as "percent." Next, start with a number in the middle and try (B), 76. *Percent* means out of 100, so write 76% as $\frac{76}{100}$. Take 76% of the original BPM of the producer's most streamed track in November, 125, to get $\frac{76}{100}(125) = 95$. This is less than the BPM of the producer's most streamed track in December, so eliminate (B). A larger percent is necessary, so also eliminate (A), and then try (C), 124. Take 124% of the November BPM to get $\frac{124}{100}(125) = 155$. This is still less than the December BPM of 165, so eliminate (C). Only (D) is left, so it must be correct. The correct answer is (D).

11. **B** The question asks for the equation that defines a function representing a situation. There are variables in the answer choices and the question is about the relationship between values, so plug in. The question states that *Linear function p gives the price, in dollars, that a vacation rental company charges to rent accommodations for x nights* and that *The company charges $410 for 2 nights*. Plug in $p(x) = 410$ and $x = 2$, and eliminate answers that don't work. Choice (A) becomes $410 = 66(2) + 80$, then $410 = 132 + 80$, and finally $410 = 212$. This is not true, so eliminate (A). Choice (B) becomes $410 = 80(2) + 250$, then $410 = 160 + 250$, and finally $410 = 410$. This is true, so keep (B), but check the remaining answers with this pair of values. Choice (C) becomes $410 = 130(2)$, and then $410 = 260$; eliminate (C). Choice (D) becomes $410 = 80(2) + 210(2)$, then $410 = 160 + 420$, and finally $410 = 580$; eliminate (D). Only (B) worked with the first pair of values, so stop here. The correct answer is (B).

12. **A** The question asks for a value given an equation. One method is to use the built-in calculator. Entering the full equation does not show the slider or a graph. Instead, enter the expression on the left side and the expression on the right side into separate entry fields. When the equation has no real solutions, the two expressions will graph parallel lines. Click on the slider for k, and then enter each answer choice one at a time until two parallel lines are graphed. This happens when $k = -15$, so (A) is correct.

To solve algebraically, recall that a linear equation with one variable has no real solutions when the x-terms are the same and the constants are different. To find the value of k, make both sides of the equation look the same. First, multiply both sides of the equation by 5 to get $k(x - 5) = -15x + 45$. Next, distribute on the left side of the equation to get $kx - 5k = -15x + 45$. The x-terms must be equal, so $kx = -15x$. Divide both sides of this equation by x to get $k = -15$, which makes (A) correct.

Using either of these methods, the correct answer is (A).

13. **C** The question asks for an expression that is equivalent to the product of two functions. The question asks about an equivalent expression and there are variables in the answer choices, so one option is to plug in. However, that might get messy with two equations and fractions. Another option is to use the built-in calculator. First, enter the equations for $f(x)$ and $g(x)$ into separate entry fields. Next, enter $f(x) * g(x)$ into another entry field. Hide the $f(x)$ and $g(x)$ graphs by clicking the circle icons to the left of those entry fields. Finally, enter the expressions in the answer choices until one of them results in the same graph as the graph of $f(x) * g(x)$. All the answer choices have the same first and last terms, so start with the expression in (A) and then add or change the middle term to match the expressions in (B), (C), and (D). Only the graph of the expression in (C) results in a matching graph, so it is correct.

Another method is to recognize both $f(x)$ and $g(x)$ are binomials and that the answer choices are quadratics in standard form. To see the factored form more clearly, translate *product* as multiplication and rewrite the product of $f(x)$ and $g(x)$ as $(8x + 9)\left(\frac{4}{9}x - \frac{5}{8}\right)$. To expand a factored form quadratic into standard form, use FOIL: First, Outer, Inner, Last. All the answer choices have the same first and last terms, so focus on the OI part of FOIL. Multiply the outer terms to get $(8x)\left(-\frac{5}{8}\right)$, or $-5x$. Multiply the inner terms to get $(9)\left(\frac{4}{9}x\right)$, or $4x$. Add the outer and inner terms to get $-5x + 4x = -x$. Only (C) has the correct middle term, so it is correct.

Using either of these methods, the correct answer is (C).

14. **C** The question asks for the coordinates of the solution to a system of equations. The most efficient method is to enter both equations as written into the built-in calculator, and then scroll and zoom as needed to find the point of intersection. The graphs intersect at (7, 98). The question asks for the value of x, which is 7, so (C) is correct.

To solve algebraically, first combine like terms in the second equation by adding 7 to both sides of the equation to get $x^2 - y + 49 = 0$. The equations have the same y-term with opposite signs, so stack and add the equations to make the y-terms disappear, and then solve for x.

$$\begin{array}{r} -14x + y = 0 \\ + x^2 - y + 49 = 0 \\ \hline x^2 - 14x + 49 = 0 \end{array}$$

The resulting equation is a quadratic in standard form, so factor it. Find two numbers that multiply to 49 and add to –14. These are –7 and –7. Thus, the quadratic has two factors of $(x - 7)$. Set this factor equal to 0 to get $x - 7 = 0$. Add 7 to both sides of the equation to get $x = 7$, making (C) correct.

Using either of these methods, the correct answer is (C).

15. **A** The question asks for an equation in terms of a specific variable. The question asks about the relationship among variables and there are variables in the answer choices, so one option is to plug in. However, that might get messy with three variables. All the answer choices have r by itself, so the other option is to solve for r. To isolate r, first divide both sides of the equation by 7 to get $r(s - 10) = \frac{z}{7}$. Next, divide both sides of the equation by $(s - 10)$ to get $r = \frac{z}{7(s-10)}$. The correct answer is (A).

16. **12** The question asks for the y-coordinate of a point on a graph that has been translated from the graph of a function. In function notation, the number inside the parentheses is the x-value that goes into the function, or the input, and the value that comes out of the function is the y-value, or the output. Together, they represent points on the graph of the function. The question provides an input value, so plug $x = -2$ into function h to get $h(-2) = (-2 + 4)(-2 - 6)(-2 + 1)$, which becomes $h(-2) = (2)(-8)(-1)$, and then $h(-2) = 16$. The question states that the graph of function f is the result of translating the graph of function h down 4 units. This means decreasing the value of y by 4. Decrease 16 by 4 to get 12. Thus, the point (–2, 12) is on the graph of $y = f(x)$, $k = 12$, and 12 is correct.

Another method is to enter the equation for function h into the built-in calculator. Scroll and zoom as needed to find the point at (–2, 16), and then count down 4 units to (–2, 12). Thus, $k = 12$, and 12 is correct.

Using either of these methods, the correct answer is 12.

17. **D** The question asks for an expression that represents a value given a rate. The question is about the relationship among values and there are variables in the answer choices, so plug in. Pick numbers that will work well with the numbers in the question, such as $a = 10$ and $b = 2$. The question states that *The second machine can manufacture 3a widgets in b minutes.* Plug in the chosen numbers to get 3(10) widgets in 2 minutes, or 30 widgets in 2 minutes. This is a rate of 15 widgets per minute for the second machine. The question also states that *The second machine works at a rate that is five times the rate of the first machine.* If the rate of the second machine is 15 widgets per minute, the rate of the first machine is $\frac{15}{5} = 3$ widgets per minute. The question asks for *The amount of time, in minutes,*

that the first machine takes to manufacture 21a widgets. Plug in $a = 10$ to get $21(10) = 210$ widgets. Set up a proportion, being sure to match up units. The proportion becomes $\frac{3 \text{ widgets}}{1 \text{ minute}} = \frac{210 \text{ widgets}}{x \text{ minutes}}$. Cross-multiply to get $(3)(x) = (1)(210)$, or $3x = 210$. Divide both sides of this equation by 3 to get $x = 70$. This is the target value; write it down and circle it. Finally, plug $b = 2$ into the answer choices, and eliminate ones that do not match the target value. Choice (A) becomes $7(2) = 14$. This is not 70, so eliminate (A). Choice (B) becomes $15(2) = 30$; eliminate (B). Choice (C) becomes $18(2) = 36$; eliminate (C). Choice (D) becomes $35(2) = 70$; keep (D). The correct answer is (D).

18. **–11** The question asks for a value given a specific situation. Translate the English to math in Bite-Sized Pieces. One piece of information states that *One negative integer is 3 less than one-half of another negative integer.* Use x to represent the first integer and y to represent the second integer. Translate *is* as =, *3 less than* as – 3, and *one-half* as $\frac{1}{2}$. The equation becomes $x = \frac{1}{2}y - 3$. Another piece of information states that *the two integers have a product of 176.* Translate *product* as multiplication, and the equation becomes $xy = 176$. Now enter both equations into the built-in calculator, and then scroll and zoom as needed to see the two points of intersection. These are marked with gray dots at (8, 22) and (–11, –16). The question refers to negative integers, so one integer is –11 and the other is –16. The greater of the two integers is –11. The correct answer is –11.

19. **C** The question asks for the equation that defines a function. One method is to use the built-in calculator. Enter the equation for $g(x)$ into one entry field, and then enter the $f(x)$ equation into a second entry field. Hide the graph of $g(x)$ by clicking the circle icon to the left. Next, enter each answer choice one at a time to see which equation for $f(x)$ results in the same graph as that of $f(x) = g(x + 2)$. Only the graph of the equation in (C) is the same, so (C) is correct.

There are variables in the answer choices, so another option is to plug in. Make $x = 2$ to keep the numbers small. Since $f(x) = g(x + 2)$, $f(2) = g(2 + 2)$, or $f(2) = g(4)$. Plug $x = 4$ into the g function to get $g(4) = 81(3)^4$, which becomes $g(4) = 81(81)$, and then $g(4) = 6{,}561$. Since $f(2) = g(4)$, $f(2)$ also equals 6,561. This is the target value; write it down and circle it. Now plug $x = 2$ into the answer choices and eliminate any that do not match the target value. Choice (A) becomes $f(2) = 81(6)^2$, then $f(2) = 81(36)$, and finally $f(2) = 2{,}916$. This does not match the target value, so eliminate (A). Choice (B) becomes $f(2) = 162(3)^2$, then $f(2) = 162(9)$, and finally $f(2) = 1{,}458$; eliminate (B). Choice (C) becomes $f(2) = 729(3)^2$, then $f(2) = 729(9)$, and finally $f(2) = 6{,}561$; keep (C), but check (D) just in case. Since (D) is the same as (C) except for a larger number inside the parentheses, the result will be greater than 6,561; eliminate (D). Only (C) matched the target value, so (C) is correct.

Using either of these methods, the correct answer is (C).

20. **A** The question asks for the value of a constant in a quadratic. When given a factor of a quadratic, solve for the solution by setting the factor equal to 0. Set $-x - c = 0$. Add c to both sides of the equation to get $-x = c$. Substitute $-x$ for c in the expression to get $x^2 + \frac{1}{16}d(-x)^2$, which becomes $x^2 + \frac{d}{16}x^2$. To solve the quadratic, set the expression equal to 0 to get $x^2 + \frac{d}{16}x^2 = 0$. Subtract x^2 from both sides of the equation to get $\frac{d}{16}x^2 = -x^2$. Multiply both sides of the equation by 16 to get $dx^2 = -16x^2$. Divide both sides of the equation by x^2 to get $d = -16$. The correct answer is (A).

21. **128** The question asks for the maximum possible value of a term that is related to a constant in a quadratic equation. To determine algebraically when a quadratic equation has no real solutions, use the discriminant. The discriminant is the part of the quadratic formula under the square root sign and is written as $D = b^2 - 4ac$. When the discriminant is positive, the quadratic has exactly two real solutions; when the discriminant is 0, the quadratic has exactly one real solution; and when the discriminant is negative, the quadratic has no real solutions. Thus, the discriminant of this quadratic must be negative. Put the equation in standard form $ax^2 + bx + c = 0$ to determine the values of a, b, and c. Start by squaring both sides of the equation to get $(17 + x)^2 = c + x$. Use FOIL to expand the left side of the equation to get $289 + 34x + x^2 = c + x$. Rearrange the terms on the left side of the equation to get $x^2 + 34x + 289 = c + x$. Now subtract x from both sides of the equation to get $x^2 + 33x + 289 = c$, and then subtract c from both sides of the equation to get $x^2 + 33x + 289 - c = 0$. Now that the quadratic is in standard form, $a = 1$, $b = 33$, and $c = 289 - c$. Plug these into the discriminant formula to get $D = (33)^2 - 4(1)(289 - c)$. The discriminant must be negative, so $(33)^2 - 4(1)(289 - c) < 0$. Simplify to get $1{,}089 - 4(289 - c) < 0$, then $1{,}089 - 1{,}156 + 4c < 0$, and finally $-67 + 4c < 0$. Add 67 to both sides of the inequality to get $4c < 67$. Read carefully: the question asks for the maximum possible value of $8c$, but it also states that c is an integer, so isolate c before solving for $8c$. Divide both sides of the inequality by 4 to get $c < 16.75$. Thus, the greatest possible integer value of c is 16. Multiply this value by 8 to get the greatest possible integer value of $8c$: $(8)(16) = 128$, so 128 is correct.

Another method is to use the built-in calculator, although it takes careful work. Enter the equation as written: type *sqrt* and the calculator will insert the square root symbol. The equation does not show a graph, so move everything to the left side of the equation and enter $17 + x - \sqrt{c + x}$ without the "= 0" part of the equation. Now the calculator shows a graph and the slider option for c. Click on the slider, and then slide it left and right. When an equation has no real solutions, its graph does not intersect the x-axis. Sliding to the right moves the graph closer to the x-axis, so expand the range of the slider and keep moving right. Adjust the slider range and zoom in as needed until the graph touches the x-axis. Click on the equation to see a gray dot and confirm that there is a point at $(-16.5, 0)$ when $c = 16.75$. Keep sliding to see that there is still one solution when c is 17 or greater. Thus, the greatest integer value of c for which the equation has no real solutions is 16. Read carefully: the question asks for the maximum possible value of $8c$, which is $(8)(16) = 128$, so 128 is correct.

Using either of these methods, the correct answer is 128.

22. **110** The question asks for a measurement on a geometric figure. Use the Geometry Basic Approach. Start by redrawing a figure on the scratch paper. It might look like the triangles are formed by two intersecting lines, but the figure is not drawn to scale and it is risky to make assumptions. Instead, label the figure with information from the question. Label angle a as 35°. Since $b = 180 - 4a$, plug in 35 for a to get $b = 180 - 4(35)$, then $b = 180 - 140$, and finally $b = 40$. Label both angle measures on the figure, which now looks like this:

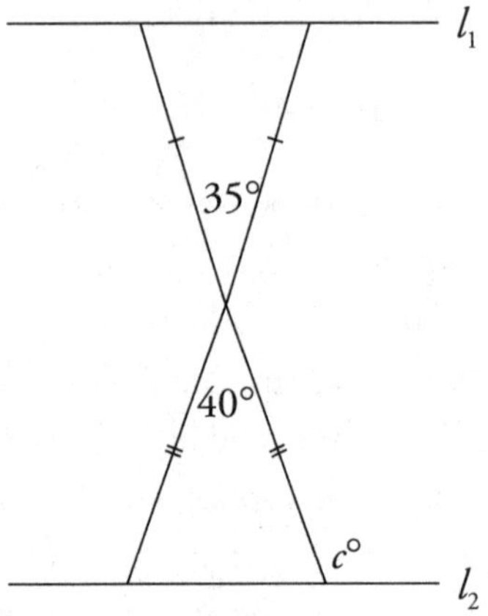

In an isosceles triangle, the two angles opposite the sides with the same length have the same measure. All triangles contain 180°, so the two other angles in the lower triangle have a combined measure of 180° – 40° = 140°. They are equal, so each angle measures $\frac{140°}{2} = 70°$. Label this on the figure, which now looks like this:

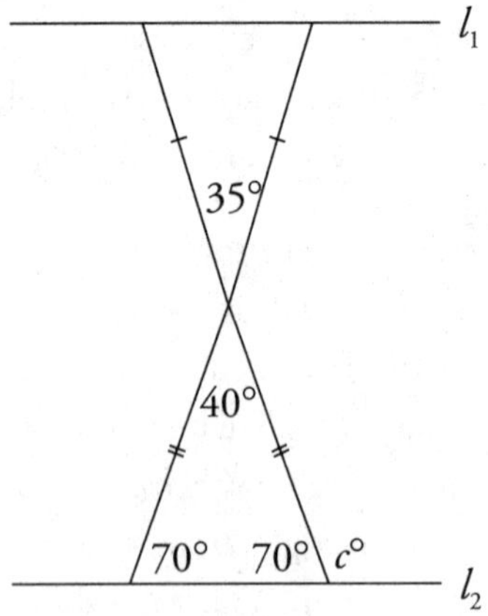

The angle in the lower right and the angle labeled as $c°$ are on a straight line, which contains a total of 180°. Thus, $70 + c = 180$. Subtract 70 from both sides of this equation to get $c = 110$. The correct answer is 110.

Part III PSAT/NMSQT Prep

Chapter 6
Reading and Writing Introduction

Now that you've learned some general strategies for the PSAT and taken and analyzed your first test, it is time to dive into some content chapters. This chapter will introduce you to the Reading and Writing section of the PSAT.

FIND YOUR STRENGTHS AND WEAKNESSES

As you may recall from the Introduction, your PSAT is going to have two Reading and Writing modules, each consisting of 27 questions. Of those 54 total verbal questions, 25–33 will be Reading questions and 19–31 will be Writing questions. You'll have 32 minutes for each module, which gives you a little more than a minute for each question.

While College Board jams the topics of Reading and Writing into the same section, you may have recognized that they really represent two different sets of skills. The Reading questions ask you to either answer a question about a text you have read (such as what its main idea is or why the author included a certain piece of information) or choose an answer that completes the text based on the inferences that can be made. On the other hand, the Writing questions will ask you to choose the best construction of a sentence, based on such aspects as punctuation, grammar, and style. Writing questions will also ask you to connect ideas with transitions or to fit certain rhetorical goals.

This distinction is important because you may find that you are stronger at Reading or stronger at Writing. Recognizing your strengths and weaknesses will help you follow POOD most effectively, and as you practice, it will allow you to identify what areas you need to focus on during your study time.

THE LESSER OF TWO (OR THREE) EVILS

We think you'll find it most helpful to think of each Reading and Writing module as having three parts, displayed visually below.

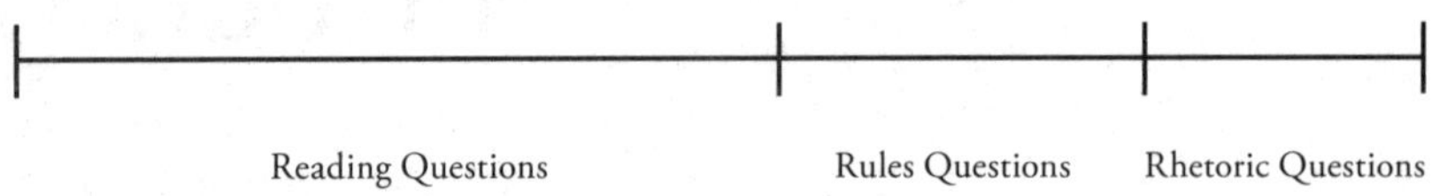

This is the same order and rough proportion of questions you will see in each module. (It's worth keeping in mind that the Reading actually has two parts according to College Board. However, there isn't a strong difference in the types of questions you'll see in both parts, so we don't think you need to notice when the section switches. See the Reading lesson for more on that.) If you are stronger or faster at Writing questions, you may find that it makes more sense for you to start about halfway through the section when those questions start. Of course, if Reading questions are easier for you, it's fine to start at the beginning of the module. Either way, it's helpful to be able to recognize these three categories of questions so that you'll notice when the module switches from one to the next and be able to apply the right set of steps to each question type. Let's take a look at the characteristics of each category.

Reading Questions

Any question with text in the form of a poem or a work of fiction is going to be in the Reading portion. The same is true for dual texts (which have a Text 1 and a Text 2), passages that involve graphs, and questions that ask you to fill in the blank with the most appropriate word. The rest of the Reading questions will generally ask you for the meaning or purpose of some or all of the text.

Rules Questions

It should be easy to spot when the module switches from Reading questions to Rules questions. That's because all Rules questions ask the same thing: *Which choice completes the text so that it conforms to the conventions of Standard English?* Only Rules questions ask this, so if you're planning to start with the Rules questions, you can skip to about the middle of the section and click ahead until you see the first one with that question. It's worth noting that Rules questions will be some of the fastest ones for many students, as you typically need to read only a single sentence and will be tested on basic punctuation and grammar rules, rather than comprehension.

Rhetoric Questions

Once again, it should be easy to spot when the Rules questions end. That's because the rest of the questions, Rhetoric questions, will not ask the standard question you saw above for Rules questions. If you want to start with these questions, go about three-quarters of the way into the section and continue until you stop seeing the question about the conventions of Standard English. Furthermore, Rhetoric questions come in only two formats. The first involves transition words, and the second has bullet points instead of a passage. So, these should be relatively easy to identify by looking for those two unique attributes, but you will learn more about these distinctions in later chapters.

As you prepare for the PSAT, try to identify which of these three categories makes sense for you to begin with. It's best to start with the category in which you will be able to get the questions right quickly and easily.

STARTING OFF ON THE RIGHT SIDE...OF THE SCREEN

As you saw earlier in this introduction, it's the question, rather than the text, that will give you a clue as to what category of question you are dealing with. Once you've established that, you'll be able to execute the appropriate strategy for that specific type of question. To that end, we've developed a basic approach for all Reading and Writing questions:

Reading and Writing Basic Approach

1. Read the question.
2. Identify the question type.
3. Follow the basic approach for that question type.

As we discussed earlier, you are free (and encouraged!) to start with the types of questions at which you excel and to leave for last the ones you struggle with most or that you expect to take the most time. For each question, skip over the text initially and go straight to the question. That will help you to confirm whether it is a Reading question, Rules question, or Rhetoric question. In some cases, such as with most Reading questions, reading the question first will also give you an idea of what you need to find in the text, which will allow you to do double duty as you read: you can already start to look out for what the question will be asking you about as you read the text.

In the chapters that follow, we'll show you our basic approach for each type of question that we expect you to see on the Reading and Writing section. Once you have learned and practiced these approaches, you'll know exactly what to do once you identify the type of question you are looking at. It's worth noting that we have put the verbal chapters in the same order that we expect the questions to be in for both modules of the Reading and Writing section, so you can use them as a guide for approximately where each question type will appear. Let's dive in!

Chapter 7
Reading: The Fundamentals

Reading questions will account for just over half of the 54 RW questions and will always appear before the Writing questions in each module. The Reading questions will ask you to perform a variety of tasks, including selecting the best vocabulary word to fill in a blank, finding the main idea or purpose of a passage, determining which answer would best support an argument, and choosing the most logical conclusion for a passage.

Each passage can contain up to 150 words and will be accompanied by just a single question, so efficiency will be of the essence. The purpose of this chapter is to introduce you to how the Reading and Writing Basic Approach can be adapted to each of the Reading question types. This will help you streamline how you take the test and keep you focused on what information you need in order to answer each question accurately!

PSAT READING: CRACKING THE PASSAGES

Answering Reading questions should be thought of as an open-book test: all of the information you need is right in front of you, so you never have to worry about any history, literature, or chemistry facts that you may (or may not) have learned in school. While you will need to read carefully, your primary goal is to find the information that helps answer the question, NOT to understand every last word of the passage perfectly. What you need is a way to get in and get out of this section with as little stress and as many points as possible.

To put it another way, think of the process you go through when planning a trip. You start by selecting where you most want to visit before you plan anything else, and then you find the best route to your destination. The PSAT Reading questions are the same: for each of them, your first job is to understand the specific question you are answering, then to locate the specific evidence in the passage that either provides a direct answer to the question or offers support as to what the answer to the question should be.

Your Mission

Identify what you are being asked to do for each question and locate the answer or support in the text as efficiently as possible.

Even the instructions given by College Board remind you to stay on task:

DIRECTIONS

The questions in this section address a number of important reading and writing skills. Each question includes one or more passages, which may include a table or graph. Read each passage and question carefully, and then choose the best answer to the question based on the passage(s).

All questions in the section are multiple-choice with four answer choices. Each question has a single best answer.

Notice that the directions clearly state the correct answer is based on the passage(s). This is great news! All College Board cares about is whether you can read a passage and understand it well enough to answer a question about it. Unlike Math or Writing questions, there are no formulas to memorize and no comma rules to learn. You just need to know how to efficiently process the passage, the question, and the answer choices in order to maximize your score.

Your POOD and the Reading Questions

You will see only one question at a time with a passage (or occasionally, with two passages) on screen. While it's tempting to do the questions in the order they appear, all Reading questions are not created equal—some are much harder and much more time-consuming than others. You'll want to skip those questions for now and come back to them once you've answered all of the Reading and Writing questions you definitely know how to do.

Below are some factors that can affect whether a question is within your Personal Order of Difficulty or not:

- **Topic:** You will probably be able to tell from glancing at the passage whether it's about science, social studies, culture, or some other topic area. If you have significant topic-based strengths and weaknesses, use that knowledge to decide your POOD. For example, if you're a science whiz, passages with science topics will likely be easier for you to make sense of quickly.
- **Literature:** All passages sourced from works of fiction such as stories and poems will contain a blurb introducing the author and title. This will help you quickly identify them, and you can decide to do them or skip them based on your level of comfort with literature.
- **Question Type:** In this lesson, you'll learn how to identify the different types of questions as well as the order they come in. Determine which question types you consistently answer quickly and accurately, and start with those.

> On any question you thought was in your POOD but then get stuck on, Mark and Move. Once you've made your initial pass through the entire module, first return to the questions you've marked, and then, if time remains, to the questions you've skipped.

THE READING BASIC APPROACH

To tackle the Reading questions, we'll expand on the Reading and Writing Basic Approach that you learned previously. No matter what type of question you are confronted with, you will follow the same five basic steps. We'll adapt these steps for each question type as we go through this chapter.

Step 1: Read the Question. As with all Reading and Writing questions, you need to first understand what you are being asked to do before you dive into any text.

Step 2: Identify the Question Type. Each question contains specific words and phrases that help you identify what type of question it is. On some question types, it will be helpful in this step to highlight the specific task you were given, which we'll demonstrate throughout the chapter. The question type also affects how you will adapt the rest of the approach and is lastly a chance to apply your POOD. If you've struggled on that question type previously, it will likely be a good one to skip for now, or maybe even **Guess and Go**.

> **Where the Money Is**
> A reporter once asked notorious thief Willie Sutton why he robbed banks. Legend has it that his answer was, "Because that's where the money is." While tackling the Reading questions is safer and slightly more productive than larceny, the same principle applies. Concentrate on the questions and answer choices because that's where the points are. The passage is just a place for College Board to stash facts and details. You'll find them when you need to. Think of the Reading questions as an open-book test. The correct answer is correct because the passage says so, not because of any deep understanding or interpretation of the story.

Step 3: Read the Passage(s). Read efficiently, keeping the question task in mind. Remember that you are looking for an answer to a question, or at the very least, evidence that can help answer the question. You don't need to memorize, or even understand, every detail!

Step 4: Highlight What Can Help (and Annotate if Needed). Within the passage, highlight a phrase or sentence that can help answer the question. It could be a direct answer to the question or a piece of information that the question wants you to do something with. On certain question types, such as Vocabulary or Purpose, you'll also make an annotation that will help you nail the correct answer—more on this shortly!

Step 5: Use POE. Eliminate anything that isn't consistent with your highlighting (and annotation if you made one). Don't necessarily try to find the right answer immediately, because there is a good chance you won't see anything that perfectly matches what you highlighted or annotated. If you can eliminate answers that you know are wrong, though, you'll be closer to the correct answer. If you can't eliminate three wrong answers just based on your highlighting and/or annotation, one or more of the remaining answers are probably trap answers (which we'll talk about next).

Recognizing trap answers is a huge part of POE. You saw earlier in this book how POE, or Process of Elimination, is an effective way to earn points on multiple-choice questions. On Reading, there are very specific types of traps, and if you can learn to catch them during Step 5, your accuracy will improve dramatically!

> **When should you look for trap answers?**
> The best time to look for trap answers is *after* you've already compared the answer choices to your highlighting and annotation but still have more than one answer remaining.

Reading Trap Answers

On many questions, you'll be able to eliminate three of the four answers simply by using your highlighting and annotation. But sometimes, you will be able to get rid of only one or two answers, and then you'll need to consider the remaining answers a little more carefully. If you're left with two answers, for example, and each seems to make sense, you're probably down to the correct answer and a trap answer. Luckily, there are some common traps that College Board will set for you, and knowing them can help you figure out which answer is the trap answer and which is the correct answer. Here are the main types of traps you will see:

- **Opposite** answer choices use a single word or phrase that makes the answer convey a tone, viewpoint, or meaning that is the opposite of what the passage said. This can include using a word such as "not" in the answer or using a negative vocabulary word when the tone of the passage was positive.
- **Recycled Language** choices repeat exact words and phrases from the passage but use those words and phrases incorrectly. The repeated words and phrases can come from a single sentence but often are taken from multiple points within the passage.

- **Extreme Language** choices look just about perfect except for a word or phrase that goes too far beyond what the passage can support. This also includes answers that make too strong of a claim to be supported by the passage.
- **Beyond the Text** answers might initially look good because they make logical sense or are true according to outside reasoning, but they lack support within the passage itself. These answers can also reference ideas that were discussed in the passage but then create a relationship between those ideas that was not discussed.
- **Right Answer, Wrong Question** choices are true based on the passage, but they don't answer the question asked. For example, they could describe the function of another sentence besides the one the question asked you to focus on, or they may accurately describe a detail within a passage rather than its main idea.
- **Half-Right** answers address part but not all of a question task, particularly when the question is about a claim with multiple components. These answers can also accurately describe data from a figure that is irrelevant to a claim within the passage.

The key difference between Extreme Language and Beyond the Text is that Extreme Language traps exaggerate an idea that the passage actually discussed, while Beyond the Text traps reference ideas that were never discussed in the passage at all.

QUESTION TYPES AND FORMATS

Now that you know the steps of the Reading Basic Approach, let's consider the different types of questions you'll be answering. It's not important that you can identify the question types by the names we give them. But it is extremely important that you can read a question and know how to respond. Is the question asking you what a particular word means, why the author included something, what the author says, which answer best supports a claim, etc.? The next section of this chapter will help you decode those question types. Once you know what you are being asked to do, using the Basic Approach will make things as efficient as possible.

There are eight Reading question types, but it's worth noting they don't show up with equal frequency. Some question types, such as Vocabulary, will be present on both of your RW modules, and some question types, such as Dual Texts, may be present on only one. Some question types will show up multiple times within a module, while others will account for only a single question. Luckily, the question types that are present on a given module will typically follow the same set order:

1. **Vocabulary**
2. **Purpose**
3. **Dual Texts**
4. **Retrieval**
5. **Main Idea (Retrieval and Main Idea may be mixed together.)**
6. **Claims**
7. **Charts (Claims and Charts may be mixed together.)**
8. **Conclusions**

The first RW module on an exam could have four Purpose questions, and then the second module could have one or even zero. But when Purpose does appear, it's always after Vocabulary. If there are several of the same type of question in a row, those with lower question numbers will generally be easier than those with higher numbers. Then the difficulty level will reset with the first question of the next type.

Regardless of whether a question type shows up on both modules, one module, multiple times, or one time, you are likely to encounter all eight question types throughout your PSAT, so you need to be prepared for all of them.

Vocabulary is the first of four question types on which we find annotations to be particularly helpful. We'll discuss the others in the sidebars throughout the chapter.

VOCABULARY

The first group of questions you see will ask you to choose an appropriate vocabulary word to fill in a blank or determine what the meaning of a word is in the context of the passage. The PSAT tests vocabulary words of various levels of complexity, but the important thing to remember is that the context of the sentence(s) surrounding the word will provide a clue that you can highlight. This will allow you to annotate, or write down, your own word for the blank, which will help you with POE.

Kuei-Chih Lee's landscape artistry can best be described as ________: his large-format installations make use of raw materials collected on-site in order to blend his created work with the natural environment.

1 Mark for Review

Which choice completes the text with the most logical and precise word or phrase?

Ⓐ beautiful

Ⓑ harmonious

Ⓒ jarring

Ⓓ acclaimed

Throughout these explanations, we will **bold** the steps of the Basic Approach in the order they would be applied. We will *italicize* any parts of the passage that could have been highlighted when working the question. We will put any words that help you identify the question type or any annotation that may have been helpful to have made in "quotes."

Here's How To Crack It

If you **read the question** and see "most logical and precise word or phrase," you can **identify the question type** as a **Vocabulary** question. You don't need to highlight "most logical and precise word or phrase" from the question stem because it doesn't offer any specific information or alter your task in any way.

As you **read the passage,** look for something you can **highlight** to help understand what word should go in the blank. The passage says after the colon that the materials that Kuei-Chih Lee collects are used to *blend his created work with the natural environment.* A good word to write down in your **annotation** box based on the highlighting would be "blended" or "made to fit together."

Use POE! Choice (A), *beautiful,* is a **Beyond the Text** trap answer: while Lee's landscape art may indeed be very beautiful if seen in real life, the author never states how beautiful Lee's art actually is. Eliminate (A). Choice (B), *harmonious,* is a good synonym for "blended," so keep (B). Choice (C), *jarring* (upsettingly out of place), is the **Opposite** of what we annotated, so eliminate (C). Choice (D), *acclaimed,* is another **Beyond the Text** trap: it's very possible Lee is a well-known artist and is celebrated by others, but the passage does not say so one way or the other. Eliminate (D). The correct answer is (B).

PURPOSE

The second group of questions you may see ask you why the author wrote the passage or how a sentence functions in the passage. The PSAT isn't looking for any outside reasoning on these questions, as it's not possible to know why any author does anything without asking that individual! Instead, you're being asked for the *most likely, best supported* reason that the passage or sentence was written or included. Highlight main ideas in the passage or connecting ideas between sentences and make sure to annotate. A good annotation will both contain the main topic of the passage and account for any attitudes expressed toward that idea. Lastly, don't forget the power of using POE—some answers will contain words or phrases that simply don't match what happened in the passage regardless of what the author's purpose was.

Because authors don't usually directly tell you, "Hey, this is why I wrote this passage," we find Purpose to be another question type on which annotations are extremely helpful.

In 1978, British biochemist Sir Philip Cohen was experimenting with a type of enzyme to understand how calcium activated that enzyme. He noticed a faint blue smear occurring at the bottom of the gel used in his experiments but had assumed it to be of little importance. After hearing another scientist's lecture, Cohen realized that calmodulin, a calcium-binding protein, was the source of the blue smear. His next experiments confirmed that calmodulin still appeared in his gels even after the gels had been boiled and was therefore heat stable. He correctly concluded that calmodulin mediated the activity of calcium within the enzyme.

2 Mark for Review

Which choice best states the main purpose of the text?

(A) To explain how misunderstood calmodulin is

(B) To describe Cohen's realization regarding calmodulin

(C) To illustrate how calcium-binding proteins function

(D) To place emphasis on the importance of calcium within enzymes

Here's How To Crack It

If you **read the question** and see "main purpose," you can **identify the question type** as a **Purpose** question. You should highlight *main purpose* in the question stem here—as you'll see in the next chapter, not every Purpose question asks for the same thing!

> Watch for attitudes, and especially shifts in those attitudes, on Purpose questions. Because the passage states that Cohen originally assumed the blue smear to be *of little importance*, you can almost guarantee it's going to wind up being pretty important by the end of the passage. This helps you realize that the purpose of the passage was to describe not just Cohen's work but also specifically his work with calmodulin, the source of the blue smear.

As you **read the passage,** look for something you can **highlight** to help understand why the passage was written. At the end of the passage, Cohen *concluded that calmodulin mediated the activity of the calcium within the enzyme,* which relates back to what Cohen was trying *to understand* at the start of the passage. Write in your **annotation** box that the purpose here is "role of calmodulin in Cohen's work" since both Cohen and calmodulin are the main focuses of the passage.

Use POE! Choice (A) is **Extreme Language**—just because Cohen didn't realize its importance at first, the passage doesn't indicate that the protein is *misunderstood* by Cohen or anyone else. Eliminate (A). Choice (B) is consistent with the annotation, so keep (B). Choice (C) is **Right Answer, Wrong Question.** We do learn a little about how calmodulin, one calcium-binding protein, functions, but this can't be the main purpose because it does not mention Cohen, who is a central figure in the passage. Eliminate (C). Choice (D) is **Recycled Language.** It uses a version of *calcium within the enzyme* from the very end of the passage, but the passage doesn't ever stress exactly how important calcium is to an enzyme, nor does this answer mention calmodulin or Cohen. Eliminate (D). The correct answer is (B).

> On Dual Texts questions, neither author is going to tell you, "Here's exactly what I'd say to that other author!" So, making an annotation on Dual Texts that clearly states the relationship between the passages is a great idea!

DUAL TEXTS

The next question type you may see will offer you two passages rather than one and ask how someone from one of the passages would respond to an idea, person, or group from the other passage. These can seem intimidating at first, but all you are looking for is a single idea mentioned in the original passage that is commented upon by the "responding" passage. It will be pretty obvious when you are faced with a Dual Texts question (after all, there will be two passages rather than one!), so we won't need to **Identify the Question Type.** Instead, you'll slightly modify the Reading Basic Approach to focus on what you need in order to understand the link between these passages!

Dual Texts Basic Approach

1. Read and understand the question.
2. Read the passage that contains the idea asked about in the question and highlight the idea or viewpoint referenced by the question.
3. Read the "responding" passage and highlight what it says about the same information.
4. Annotate the relationship between the passages.
5. Use POE.

Text 1

Anxiety has long been considered a critical area of focus for those involved in both psychological analysis and behavior management. The traditional treatment for anxiety has been prescription medication. But what about situations when medication is ineffective or ill-advised? Psychologists continue to explore possible alternative treatments for anxiety to this day.

Text 2

Professor Spike W. S. Lee and his team have demonstrated a possible link between self-cleansing and anxiety reduction. They conducted a study of 1,150 adults and showed each of them one of three different videos: how to properly wash hands, how to properly peel an egg, and how to properly draw a circle. The subjects were then all exposed to a series of situations meant to induce anxiety. Those individuals who had seen the handwashing video demonstrated consistently lower levels of anxiety than those who had seen either of the other two videos.

3 Mark for Review

Based on the texts, how would Lee and his team (Text 2) most likely respond to the "traditional treatment" discussed in Text 1?

Ⓐ By noting that it may not be the only possible treatment by which an individual may reduce anxiety

Ⓑ By claiming that those who prescribe medication for anxiety completely ignore the emotional benefits of frequent handwashing

Ⓒ By stating that his team's findings help establish handwashing as an alternative treatment to prescribed medication

Ⓓ By calling for other psychologists to focus their own efforts on how handwashing frequency increases with exposure to instructional videos

Here's How To Crack It

As you **read and understand the question,** you can see that it's asking for what Text 1 says about the "traditional treatment" and how Lee in Text 2 would respond to the discussion of that treatment. You should highlight *Lee and his team* and *traditional treatment* from the question stem, so you don't lose sight of what you need to find in Text 1 and whose response you need to find in Text 2.

As you **read Text 1,** look for something you can **highlight** regarding the traditional treatment. The text states that the *traditional treatment for anxiety has been prescription medication.* As you **read Text 2,** look for something you can **highlight** related to treatment, anxiety, or prescription medication. The passage states that there is *a possible link between self-cleansing and anxiety reduction* and that those who watched the handwashing video *demonstrated consistently lower levels of anxiety.* Write in your **annotation** box that Lee and his team would reply by saying "there may be other ways to help reduce anxiety."

Use POE! Choice (A) is consistent with the highlighting and annotation: self-cleansing is mentioned in Text 2 as reducing anxiety levels, so keep (A). Choice (B) is **Extreme Language** because of the phrase *completely ignore.* Lee's team in Text 2 does not comment on whether those who prescribe medication for anxiety are unaware of or ignore the emotional benefits of handwashing. Eliminate (B). Choice (C) is also **Extreme Language**—Lee and his team never state that handwashing is now an *established alternative treatment* to prescription medication, just that it may lower anxiety levels. Eliminate (C). Choice (D) is **Recycled Language.** It misuses *handwashing* and *videos* from Text 2 and establishes a link between them (*increases*) that Text 2 never states. Additionally, Text 2 never calls for any *other psychologists* to research this area. Eliminate (D). The correct answer is (A).

Because Retrieval and Main Idea questions ask mostly about what was directly said in the passage, you'll often be able to go right to the answers after your highlighting. However, you are always encouraged to make an annotation if the passage is particularly complex or if you've found it particularly helpful on the other question types to this point!

RETRIEVAL

The next group of questions will change what you've been asked to focus on. Up until this point in the module, all of the questions will have been about crafting sentences and passage structure—the right vocabulary word for a blank, the reason something was included, how one passage relates to another, etc. However, Retrieval and Main Idea questions are more focused on the actual information and ideas contained in the passage. While these two types often appear mixed together, they ask for slightly different things. Retrieval questions want you to find and highlight what was stated about a person or event, while Main Idea questions ask you to find and highlight the central point made by the author. Since Retrieval questions are a bit more straightforward, we'll start there!

The following is adapted from George Eliot's 1871 novel *Middlemarch.* The author is describing Dorothea Brooke, one of the central characters in the novel.

It had now entered Dorothea's mind that Mr. Casaubon might wish to make her his wife, and the idea that he would do so touched her with a sort of reverential gratitude. How good of him—nay, it would be almost as if a winged messenger had suddenly stood beside her path and held out his hand towards her! For a long while she had been oppressed by the indefiniteness which hung in her mind, like a thick summer haze, over all her desire to make her life greatly effective.

4 Mark for Review

According to the text, what is true about Miss Brooke?

(A) She is skeptical of Mr. Casaubon's career as a messenger.

(B) She wants to know Mr. Casaubon's feelings towards summer.

(C) She is enthused by the prospect of marriage to a particular individual.

(D) She prefers marriage over other types of relationships.

Here's How To Crack It

If you **read the question** and see "according to the text" or "based on the text," you can **identify the question type** as a **Retrieval** question. You should also highlight *Miss Brooke*, as you are being asked for information about a specific character and not for comprehension of the passage overall.

While most of this passage winds up being about Miss Brooke, you wouldn't know that until you've read the passage. Some Retrieval questions ask about incredibly specific things, so get in the habit of always highlighting what specific things are being asked about in the question itself—better safe than sorry!

As you **read the passage,** look for what you can **highlight** about Miss Brooke. The passage states that the idea of Mr. Casaubon wanting to marry her *touched her with a sort of reverential gratitude* and the idea was *almost as if a winged messenger had suddenly stood beside her path and held out his hand towards her.* It also states that *she had been oppressed by the indefiniteness.* When so much of the passage is about one person or idea, you don't know which information about that person or idea the answers will focus on until you see the answers, so highlight anything relevant. Understand that the answers could be consistent with any of your highlighting.

Use POE! Choice (A) is **Recycled Language** as it misuses the word *messenger* from the passage. Eliminate (A). Choice (B) is also **Recycled Language**—the word *summer* is used to describe Miss Brooke's mental state before realizing Mr. Casaubon may propose, not the season. Eliminate (B). Choice (C) is consistent with the positive feelings Miss Brooke expresses in the highlighted text. Keep (C). Choice (D) is a **Beyond the Text** trap—Miss Brooke may indeed prefer marriage over any other types of relationships, but no other types of relationships are mentioned in the passage. Eliminate (D). The correct answer is (C).

One last thing: On a Retrieval question, you could also be asked why something happens in the passage. "Why something happens" is not a Purpose question—it's Retrieval because it's asking for a direct reason the author gave in the passage, instead of the *most likely, best supported* reason the author wrote the passage. You only need to find and highlight the reason given, and then you're ready to go to the answers and use POE. An example of one of these "why" questions is included in the drill for this chapter.

MAIN IDEA

Just as with Retrieval questions, Main Idea questions also ask about what the author said. The difference is that Main Idea questions are looking for the single sentence or idea that is the main focus of the passage rather than a detail about a person or an idea. This main idea should be the sentence or idea that all of the other sentences and ideas are connected to. Many times, this will be the first or last sentence of the paragraph, but College Board can place the main idea anywhere. As you read, ask yourself, "Which sentence do all of the other sentences build to or build off of?"

You shouldn't need to annotate on most Main Idea questions, but sometimes, the passage will be a series of sentences that, when taken together, form a main idea. In these situations, an annotation that acts as a summary of the passage could be helpful!

Fire photography, the practice of taking photographs of firefighting operations, has numerous applications in both occupational safety and criminal investigation. Fire photographers can also work with fire departments directly. Despite their numerous job prospects, all fire photographers must first and foremost undergo rigorous safety training before setting foot into the field.

5 Mark for Review

Which choice best states the main idea of the text?

Ⓐ Advanced cameras can now take pictures from a much safer distance than fire photographers can.

Ⓑ Although there are numerous possible career paths for fire photographers, they must prioritize safety given the nature of their jobs.

Ⓒ While there are many possible career paths, most fire photographers prefer working directly with fire departments.

Ⓓ Fire photographers have been charged with documenting fires for a century.

Here's How To Crack It

If you **read the question** and see "main idea," you can **identify the question type** as a **Main Idea** question. Almost all of these questions use the exact words "main idea" and don't feature any quirks in how they're asked that you'd really need to catch by highlighting in the question stem.

As you **read the passage,** look for a main idea that you can **highlight**. While both sentences 1 and 2 discuss job prospects of fire photographers, sentence 3 mentions that no matter what field they choose, *all fire photographers must first and foremost undergo rigorous safety training.* Notice how this sentence starts with the word *Despite*—that's the author telling you this final sentence will be the most important, regardless of what the other sentences said.

Use POE! Choice (A) goes **Beyond the Text**—while this is probably true in real life, there is no mention of *advanced cameras* in the passage. Eliminate (A). Choice (B) is consistent with the highlighting but written with slightly different words, as College Board will almost always do. Keep (B). Choice (C) is **Half-Right**—there are indeed many possible career paths according to the passage, but the second half of the answer is **Extreme Language.** We don't know that *most* fire photographers prefer any particular field. This half of the answer is also **Recycled Language**: College Board is hoping that you'll see the words *directly, working,* and *with fire departments* and choose them because they match the passage. Eliminate (C). Choice (D) also goes **Beyond the Text**—it's possible the career of fire photography has been around for a century, but we have no proof of that in the passage. Eliminate (D). The correct answer is (B).

One last thing: Main Idea questions, as well as Vocabulary, Purpose, Retrieval, and Claims questions, are the five question types on which you may see an excerpt from a poem. Don't panic when this happens—for the most part, the poem can be treated as if it were a regular paragraph. An example of a Main Idea question with a poem is included in the drill for this chapter.

CLAIMS

The next group of questions you will see ask which answer would best illustrate, support, or weaken a claim made in the passage. Claims questions are often interspersed with the next question type, **Charts**, but luckily, the skills you need for these two question types are similar. Your main job for both question types will be to identify the claim made by the author or someone else in the passage. However, you'll need to perform the exact task required by the question and keep a razor-sharp eye as you use POE: it takes only one word or phrase to make an answer weaken a claim, when your task was actually to support it.

As with Retrieval and Main Idea, you shouldn't need to annotate on most Claims and Charts questions—the claim should be stated in the passage rather directly. However, if a claim is particularly long or dense, an annotation that serves as a paraphrase of the claim may be helpful!

"A Dry Spell" is a 1905 short story by Einar H. Kvaran. In the story, the narrator and his companions wait out an ongoing rain torrent in a store where they work as clerks. In his musings, the narrator expresses a desire for the presence of individuals that he formerly considered an annoyance: ________

6 Mark for Review

Which quotation from the narrator's musings best illustrates the claim?

Ⓐ "We sat there and smoked, staring vacantly at the half-empty shelves, and all but shivering in the damp room."

Ⓑ "We made clever comments to the effect that the farmers were now getting plenty of moisture for the hay-fields, and that it would be a pity if rain should set in now, right at the beginning of the haying season."

Ⓒ "We were tired of the store—indeed, I should like to know who would have enjoyed it."

Ⓓ "We had often cursed their lengthy visits, but now that they had hired themselves out during the haymaking, we suddenly realized that they had often been entertaining."

Here's How To Crack It

If you **read the question** and see words such as "illustrate," "support," or "weaken" along with words like "claim," "hypothesis," or "argument," you can **identify the question type** as a **Claims** question. You should highlight *illustrates the claim* in the question stem—Claims questions have a lot of variety in how they are asked, and you want to make sure you are answering the right question!

Claims questions with the phrase *illustrates the claim* will usually be accompanied by a shorter-than-average passage, but to balance this out, the claim will usually have several components to it, and you need to read carefully and account for all of them in the correct answer.

As you **read the passage,** look to **highlight** the claim, which on this version of a Claims question will come right before the blank—the right answer must show that the narrator *expresses a desire for the presence of individuals he formerly considered an annoyance.*

Use POE! Choice (A) only mentions that the narrator and his companions are miserable in the store and makes no mention of any individuals they now miss, so eliminate (A). Choice (B) is **Half-Right**—the narrator and his companions seem to be poking fun at the farmers by making *clever comments* about them, but the answer does not express any desire to see these farmers back in the store or that the farmers were ever customers in the store in the first place. Eliminate (B). Choice (C) expresses negative emotions toward the store but not toward any individuals, so eliminate (C). Choice (D) is consistent with both halves of the claim: the narrator and his companions have *suddenly realized* the people referred to here *had often been entertaining,* but previously, the narrator and his companions *had often cursed their lengthy visits.* Keep (D). The correct answer is (D).

CHARTS

As mentioned before, Charts questions are often interspersed with Claims questions, and you won't necessarily see both on the same module. The biggest difference here is that you'll be reading some information from a table or graph in addition to the passage. As with Dual Texts questions, it will be pretty clear when you are asked a Charts question, so we'll once again modify the Reading Basic Approach slightly to make sure you catch everything needed to earn these points!

Charts Basic Approach

1. Read and understand the question.
2. Read the title, key/legend, variables, and units from the figure.
3. Read the passage and look for the same information that was referenced in the figure.
4. Highlight the claim or statement made by the passage regarding that information.
5. Use POE.

Approximate Appearance Percentage for Three Blood Types in Four Regions

Region	O+	A+	B+
Asia	37%	28%	25%
Americas	55%	28%	9%
Africa	47%	27%	17%
Oceania	42%	33%	11%

Blood is critical to the function of the human body, as it delivers nutrients to vital organs, exchanges carbon dioxide and oxygen, and moves white blood cells through the circulatory system to fight infections. Blood is often categorized by one of eight blood types, which are referred to first by a letter or letter combination (A, B, AB, or O) and then a positive or negative marker (such as O+ or AB–.) Researcher Anshool Deshmukh compiled blood type data from thousands of individuals and re-organized the data by region to better understand the distribution of the blood types O+, A+, and B+ by region. His research shows that type O+ blood has the highest frequency of occurrence in all four regions researched, while type B+ blood in turn has the lowest frequency of occurrence. For example, whereas the approximate appearance percentage for type O+ blood in Asia was 37%, the approximate appearance percentage for ________

7 Mark for Review

Which choice most effectively uses data from the table to complete the example?

Ⓐ type O+ blood in the Americas was 55%.

Ⓑ type B+ blood in Africa was 17%.

Ⓒ type O+ blood in Oceania was 42%.

Ⓓ type B+ blood in Asia was 25%.

Here's How To Crack It

As you **read and understand the question**, highlight *complete the example*, as Charts questions can ask for different things, which you'll see in the next chapter.

As you **read the title, key/legend, variables, and units** from the table, note that the table shows the approximate appearance percentage for three different blood types in four different regions.

As you **read the passage,** look for a claim the text makes regarding these terms specifically. **Highlight** the second-to-last sentence, which states that *type O+ blood has the highest frequency of occurrence in all four regions researched, while type B+ blood in turn has the lowest frequency of occurrence.* The text should give an example of this, and the first half of the example states that *the average appearance for type O+ blood in Asia was 37%.* So, the correct answer should complete this example while staying consistent with the table and the claim.

Use POE! Choice (A) focuses on the wrong blood type and the wrong region: we want to support the claim that type O+ is the most common of the three types shown, while B+ is the least common. Furthermore, we should focus on the region mentioned in the example, Asia, so that the two percentages discussed in the example have a common link. Eliminate (A) and use this to inform the rest of your POE. Choice (B) is **Half-Right** because it focuses on the correct blood type, B+, but the wrong region. Choice (C), like (A), gets both region and blood type incorrect. Eliminate (C). Choice (D) focuses on the correct blood type, B+, which is contrasted with O+ in the text's claim, as well as the same region, Asia, that the example discusses. Keep (D). The correct answer is (D).

One last thing: Charts questions can feature a bar graph or line graph instead of a table. An example of a Charts question with a bar graph is included in the drill for this chapter, and an example of a Charts question with a line graph is included in Chapter 9.

Conclusions are the fourth and final question type we always recommend making an annotation for. By writing in your own conclusion that you know to be directly supported by the passage, you are far less likely to fall for trap conclusions that sound logical but have zero support!

CONCLUSIONS

The last question type you will see always asks you for the same thing: which of the four answers is the most logical conclusion based on the rest of the passage? Conclusions questions can seem imposing, as it seems like multiple conclusions could be justified as good completions of the passage. However, there will only be one supportable conclusion that's consistent with both the evidence and arguments, and the Basic Approach is your key to selecting the right conclusion.

Western honeybees (*Apis mellifera*) are social insects that live inside rigid colonial nests made from wax, which can make it difficult to observe bee behavior within the colony. Bees typically form colonies with thousands to tens of thousands of bees, the weight of which would seem to place immense strain on the nest structure. Using an X-ray machine, researchers at CU Boulder have observed that swarms of *A. mellifera* inside the nest will form pyramids of bees, with larger numbers of bees at the base of the pyramid and fewer bees in each level as you move up the swarm. These researchers therefore imply that ________

8 Mark for Review

Which choice most logically completes the text?

Ⓐ the pyramids formed by *A. mellifera* swarms may reduce strain on the nest structure.

Ⓑ any individual *A. mellifera* bee can be in danger of suffocation by the rest of the bee swarm.

Ⓒ improving the numbers of *A. mellifera* requires Western intervention.

Ⓓ colonial nests enable *A. mellifera* to produce high quantities of wax.

Here's How To Crack It

If you **read the question** and see "which choice most logically completes the text," you can **identify the question type** as **Conclusions**. That is the prompt you will see on all questions of this type, so you don't need to highlight anything in the question stem.

As you **read the passage,** look for the main focus of the passage. The passage focuses on western honeybees (*Apis mellifera*). You should **highlight** the main points made about these bees: the bees *live in rigid colonial nests,* the bees' *weight would seem to place immense strain on the nest,* and the bees *will form pyramids of bees* inside their nests, *with larger numbers of bees at the base.* Write in your **annotation** box that a good conclusion here would be "larger numbers of bees at the base might help with strain on nest." Notice how this is a synthesis of each main point made about the western honeybee—a good conclusion should serve as a logical ending point to the story told by the passage.

Use POE! Choice (A) is consistent with the main points of the other sentences and references all three ideas. Keep (A). Choice (B) goes **Beyond the Text**—it's logical to think any bee could be *in danger of suffocation* with that many bees in the colony, but the passage never makes this claim. Eliminate (B). Choice (C) is **Recycled Language**—it misuses the words *Western* and the numbers of bees mentioned in the passage. Eliminate (C). Choice (D) also goes **Beyond the Text**—the author says the bees make the nests from wax, not that the nests enable them to make wax. Eliminate (D). The correct answer is (A).

Reading Comprehension Drill

Suggested Time Limit: 8 minutes. This drill contains one of each of the eight question types you've learned in this chapter, in the common order in which they would typically appear on an RW module. Use the Basic Approach the same way you were shown in the chapter, making sure to both highlight and annotate when needed. Answers can be found in Part IV.

1 Mark for Review

Improper drainage of water in pools and spas used for personal recreation has led to widespread contamination that can cause immense environmental damage and even kill plant and animal life. Chemicals in pool water may not ________ local habitats completely but will continue to cause great harm unless disposed of properly.

Which choice completes the text with the most logical and precise word or phrase?

(A) decimate

(B) buttress

(C) overlook

(D) refute

2 Mark for Review

An increasing number of municipality leaders are turning their attention to building eco-friendly parking structures. The city of Palo Alto, California, has devised a parking garage that collects rainwater into a bio-retention pond. The pond acts as a natural filter, ensuring that water runoff from the garage is as clean as possible before reentering the ground. Additionally, energy collected from solar panels on the roof of the garage will be used to add over 90 electric vehicle charging stations to the city. Palo Alto city planners hope that the presence of these charging stations will encourage more residents to switch to electric vehicles, thereby reducing the city's carbon footprint from gas emissions.

Which choice best states the main purpose of the text?

(A) To describe initiatives designed to improve environmental conditions in Palo Alto and compare them to planned initiatives in other municipalities

(B) To discuss a plan designed by the city of Palo Alto to improve environmental conditions and describe some specifics of that plan

(C) To demonstrate that residents of Palo Alto have demanded an increase in the number of electric vehicle charging stations

(D) To claim that eco-friendly parking structures are not the most efficient way to improve environmental conditions

3 Mark for Review

Text 1

Plant species need to be able to ensure their own survival just as animals do. But when a plant species invades a new region and is able to ward off predators, this raises questions as to what could be responsible for such protection. Scientists have been looking into this mostly to discover how to control the spread of invasive plant species and why local animal populations meet with such difficulty in doing so. Though many scientists know of soil microbiota, a type of bacteria found in a plant's root nodule, they believe some other organism must be responsible for the plants' invasiveness and hardiness.

Text 2

Researcher Satu Ramula and her team in Finland planted a mixture of North American and Finnish garden lupines (*lupinus polyphyllus)* into Finnish soil to examine the impact of soil microbiota on the plant's growth and development. One crop was planted into nutrient-poor soil that contained microbiota from local lupine populations while the other crop was planted into nutrient-poor soil that contained no microbiota. Regardless of the country of origin, the crop of garden lupines in the soil containing microbiota not only grew much larger than the other crop's lupines, but also secreted a much stronger scent that is a natural deterrent to snails, the garden lupine's most common predator.

Based on the texts, what would the author of Text 2 most likely say about the scientists' belief regarding soil microbiota from Text 1?

Ⓐ It is overly celebratory given the evidence that Ramula and her team have found to the contrary.

Ⓑ It is understandable given that Ramula and her team have demonstrated that soil microbiota is not linked to plant growth.

Ⓒ It is prematurely dismissive given the experiments run by Ramula and her team.

Ⓓ It is surprising considering that Ramula and her team's research was able to control plant spread.

4 Mark for Review

Once the native language of the region of Cornwall, the Cornish language today has only about 557 practitioners. Cornish can trace its roots back nearly 2,000 years, but the language experienced a sharp decline in users from 1300 to 1800, after which no record of any living user could be found for decades. The efforts of linguists and etymologists over the last hundred years have gone a long way to reviving Cornish, which had its "extinct" status removed by UNESCO in 2010.

According to the text, why was the Cornish language declared extinct?

Ⓐ Its complex syntax discourages any new practitioners.

Ⓑ Its rate of growth slowed down more than linguists expected.

Ⓒ Its active users died or became difficult to verify.

Ⓓ It stopped spreading into new regions because it was surpassed by other languages.

5 Mark for Review

The following text is from Archibald Lampman's 1899 poem "The Mystery of a Year." In this poem, the speaker is describing a woman whom he has known for some time.

A little while, a year agone,
  I knew her for a romping child,
A dimple and a glance that shone
  With idle mischief when she smiled.

To-day she passed me in the press,
  And turning with a quick surprise
I wondered at her stateliness,
  I wondered at her altered eyes.

Which choice best states the main idea of the text?

Ⓐ The speaker is reminiscing about a past romantic relationship with a woman.

Ⓑ The speaker is astonished at the changes within a certain individual.

Ⓒ The speaker is an expert in observing subtle changes in others.

Ⓓ The speaker uses intricate and complex thought processes to impress those around him.

6 Mark for Review

"A Ballad of Evesham" is a 1933 poem by Francis T. Palgrave. The poem demonstrates a character's ignorance of a deception created by his enemy: ______

Which quotation from the poem most effectively illustrates the claim?

Ⓐ "Earl Simon on the Abbey tower / In summer sunshine stood, / While helm and lance o'er Greenhill heights / Come glinting through the wood."

Ⓑ 'My son!' he cried, 'I know his flag / Amongst a thousand glancing':— / Fond father! no!—'tis Edward stern / In royal strength advancing."

Ⓒ "The Prince fell on him like a hawk / At Al'ster yester-eve, / And flaunts his captured banner now / And flaunts but to deceive:—"

Ⓓ "—Look round! for Mortimer is by, / And guards the rearward river:— / The hour that parted sire and son / Has parted them for ever!"

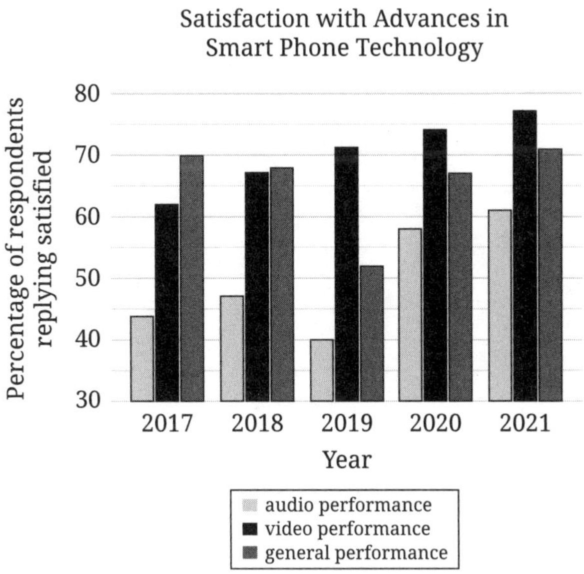

A steep curve of innovation in the domain of smart phone technology can lead to unrealized expectations and unsatisfied consumers, but detailed information regarding consumer satisfaction is not always readily accessible to the public. Recently, a group of researchers from an online technology website released its findings after polling the same tech-savvy smart phone users over the last five years and measuring their general satisfaction with their smart phone performance that year as well as measuring their more specific satisfaction with their phones' audio and video performance. One notable aspect of this publication is that consumer satisfaction with general performance does not necessarily correlate with satisfaction with specific performance areas, as is the case in the group's poll, where general performance satisfaction ______

7 Mark for Review

Which choice most effectively uses data from the graph to complete the example?

Ⓐ was almost equivalent to video performance satisfaction in 2018 and was only slightly below video performance in 2020 and 2021.

Ⓑ was consistently higher than video performance satisfaction each year from 2017 to 2021.

Ⓒ reached its lowest level in 2019, which also had the lowest recorded level of satisfaction in audio performance.

Ⓓ was notably higher than video performance satisfaction in 2017 but significantly lower than video performance satisfaction in 2019.

8 Mark for Review

Barefoot running, the act of running without footwear, has increased in popularity since the year 2000, with exercise enthusiasts looking to reduce the repetitive stress injuries caused by padded running footwear. However, the practice dates back thousands of years, with some long-established Latin American and African groups utilizing barefoot running even up to the present day despite the availability of modern footwear in those regions. This suggests that before the year 2000, ________

Which choice most logically completes the text?

Ⓐ certain practitioners of barefoot running in different regions of the world may have discovered its benefits.

Ⓑ barefoot running has made exercise more accessible to those who cannot afford expensive footwear.

Ⓒ exercise enthusiasts speculated that barefoot running would soon surpass other methods of exercise as awareness of its benefits becomes more prevalent.

Ⓓ footwear manufacturers could increase profits if they created region-specific running shoe designs.

Summary

- The Reading questions on the PSAT make up a little more than 50 percent of the Reading and Writing section.
- Reading questions are presented in order of difficulty (which resets with each question type), but because some question types may appear once, twice, or not at all on each module, it's important to rely on your POOD to know which questions to tackle immediately and which to skip for now.
- Reading is an open-book test! Use that to your advantage by focusing only on the information you need to get the question correct.
- After you read the passage, highlight the sentence or idea that most addresses the question task. Annotate whenever it would be helpful, and you should always annotate on Vocabulary, Purpose, Dual Texts, and Conclusions.
- Make sure to adapt the Reading Basic Approach for Dual Texts and Charts, as discussed in this chapter.
- If you have more than one answer left after you eliminate the ones that don't match what you highlighted and/or annotated, compare the remaining answers to see if any of them are **Opposite**; **Recycled Language**; **Extreme Language**; **Beyond the Text**; **Right Answer, Wrong Question**; or **Half-Right.**
- Practice, practice, practice—with eight question types, most of which have 2–3 different formats, it can feel at first like it's too much to keep track of. But the more you use the Reading Basic Approach and see that it is the same steps every single time, the more comfortable you will be no matter what the PSAT throws at you!
- Remember most of all to not let one single question bog you down. If you find yourself stuck or running low on time, Guess and Go!

Chapter 8
Reading: More Question Formats

In the previous chapter, you learned the eight Reading question types. However, for certain types, College Board has several different ways of formatting the questions. In this chapter, you'll experience the most common variations to the examples from the previous chapter and learn how to apply the Reading Basic Approach to each of them.

Just as you may not see every question type in a module, you may not see every variation of a question type in a module, or even at all. However, since you don't know which variations you will see, it's best to prepare for all of them.

PSAT READING: VARIOUS VARIATIONS

It can sometimes feel in the first half of an RW module that every single question is different. This is because College Board comes up with different ways to ask the same thing or different ways to test the same skills. For example, if College Board wants to assess your ability to understand the structure of a passage, the test-writers could certainly ask for the passage's overall structure, but they could just as easily ask for the function of a single sentence within the passage. You need to account for this shift in the question task, but you also shouldn't allow yourself to be distracted—at the end of the day, you're still being asked to determine the meaning or purpose of some or all of the passage.

The Reading Basic Approach, Revisited

Just because some question types have multiple formats within that type does not mean the Reading Basic Approach doesn't apply. In fact, one of the main strengths of the Basic Approach is how universally it *can* be applied. Here are the steps once more before we dive into the question variations presented in this chapter.

Step 1: Read the Question.
Step 2: Identify the Question Type.
Step 3: Read the Passage(s).
Step 4: Highlight What Can Help (and Annotate if Needed).
Step 5: Use POE.

VOCABULARY: MOST NEARLY MEAN

While most passages you see on the PSAT will be written by College Board, you may have noticed in the previous chapter that there were Retrieval, Main Idea, and Claims questions with passages or answer choices that were sourced from existing works of literature. This can also happen on Vocabulary questions. When it does, instead of being asked to fill in a blank with the *most logical and precise word or phrase*, you will be asked what a given word or phrase most nearly means in the context of the passage. College Board, then, is asking you to define a word in context. Happily, this change doesn't affect your game plan whatsoever. Treat the underlined word as if it were a blank, and use the exact same approach for Vocabulary questions that you saw in the previous chapter.

The following text is adapted from Thomas Love Peacock's 1818 novel *Nightmare Abbey.* Marionetta, a young woman, is reflecting on her relationship with a young man named Scythrop.

> Scythrop grew every day more reserved, mysterious, and distrait; and gradually lengthened the duration of his diurnal seclusions in his tower. Marionetta thought she perceived in all this very manifest symptoms of a warm love cooling.

1 Mark for Review

As used in the text, what does the word "reserved" most nearly mean?

Ⓐ Agreeable

Ⓑ Observant

Ⓒ Withdrawn

Ⓓ Hostile

Here's How To Crack It

If you **read the question** and see "most nearly mean," you can **identify the question type** as a **Vocabulary** question. You don't need to highlight "most nearly mean" from the question stem because it doesn't offer any specific information or alter your task in any way.

As you **read the passage,** treat the word *reserved* as if it were a blank and look for something you can **highlight** to help understand what word should go in the blank. The passage states that Scythrop is lengthening his *seclusions in his tower* and Marionetta feels that a *warm love* is *cooling.* A good word to write down in your **annotation** box based on the highlighting would be that Scythrop is "less available" or "not around as much."

Use POE! Choice (A), *agreeable*, is a positive word that is the **Opposite** tone of "less available," which is negative. Eliminate (A). Choice (B), *observant,* is **Right Answer, Wrong Question**—it's a good synonym for *perceived* later in the passage but not for *reserved*. Eliminate (B). Choice (C), *withdrawn*, is a good synonym for "less available," so keep (C). Choice (D), *hostile*, is an Extreme Language trap. While there is evidence for Scythrop being less warm toward Marionetta, there is no evidence that he has become angry or openly antagonistic toward her, so eliminate (D). The correct answer is (C).

How to Adjust Your Approach:

When a Vocabulary question asks what a word most nearly means, treat the word as if it were a blank, which makes it just like any other Vocabulary question.

PURPOSE: SENTENCE FUNCTION

When you are asked for the function of a sentence rather than the main purpose, the central challenge is the same: just as the author is not going to say, "Hey, here's why I wrote this," they are not going to say "just so you know, this is why I included the second sentence!" You'll need to look beyond the underlined sentence in order to determine why that sentence is there. Usually, there will be structural language, such as a transition, comparing word, contrasting word, or concluding word that will help you understand which other sentence(s) contain information that should be highlighted to understand the function of the underlined sentence. And, as always, make sure to annotate on Purpose questions before going to use POE.

The following text is from Alexandre Dumas's 1850 novel *The Black Tulip*. Cornelius, the main character, is in jail and is guarded by a turnkey, an older word for jailer.

> Cornelius saw nothing but the golden brocade cap, tipped with lace, such as the Frisian girls wore; he heard nothing but someone whispering into the ear of the turnkey. <u>But the latter put his heavy keys into the white hand which was stretched out to receive them, and, descending some steps, sat down on the staircase which was thus guarded above by himself, and below by the dog.</u> The headdress turned round, and Cornelius beheld the face of Rosa, blanched with grief, and her beautiful eyes streaming with tears.

Along with Vocabulary, Retrieval, Main Idea, and Claims, Purpose is the only other question type that could have a literature-based passage.

2 Mark for Review

Which choice best describes the function of the underlined sentence in the text as a whole?

Ⓐ It details the outcome of a conversation mentioned in the previous sentence.

Ⓑ It describes the specifics of the construction of the jailhouse.

Ⓒ It explains that an individual is debating his obligations to duty.

Ⓓ It introduces a claim that the following sentence further explains.

Here's How To Crack It

If you **read the question** and see the word "function," you can **identify the question type** as a **Purpose** question. You should highlight *function of the underlined sentence* in the question stem so you know exactly what your task is.

As you **read the text,** look for something you can **highlight** to help understand why the sentence was included. The underlined sentence includes the word *But*, indicating a contrast with the sentence before it, making the sentence before the most important one for understanding the underlined sentence's function. The sentence before mentions that someone was *whispering into the ear of the turnkey*, or jailer. The turnkey then *put his heavy keys into the white hand* of the other individual and descends the staircase. Write in your **annotation** box that the function of the sentence here is "to describe what happened after the whisper."

Use POE! Choice (A) is consistent with the annotation because it does indeed describe what happens after the whisper, so keep (A). Choice (B) is **Right Answer, Wrong Question.** It's true that we now know something about the layout of this particular part of the jailhouse, but this ignores the question of *why* the sentence was included in the context of the sentences before and after it. Eliminate (B). Choice (C) goes **Beyond the Text**—while we can imagine that a jailer would debate giving his jail keys to someone, we get no insight into any turmoil or debate going on in the jailer's mind. Eliminate (C). Choice (D) is **Half-Right**: the following sentence may further explain what happens next in the story, but no *claim* is introduced in the underlined sentence. Eliminate (D). The correct answer is (A).

How to Adjust Your Approach:

When a Purpose question asks for the function of a sentence, look for structural words such as transitions, comparing and contrasting words, or concluding words in order to determine which sentences most connect to the underlined sentence.

PURPOSE: OVERALL STRUCTURE

We aren't done with Purpose just yet. Instead of asking *why* the passage was written or *why* a sentence was included, College Board can also ask for *how* a passage was structured. You can learn a lot about this variation by looking at the answers to Overall Structure questions: you might notice that all of them are broken into two parts: an "It" part and a "then" part. As in, "it does X, then it does Y." In other words, College Board just wants you to determine what two things the passage focused on, in the right order. If you can find where the shift in the passage occurred from one topic to the other, you can use this to create a helpful annotation.

The following text is adapted from Jane Porter's 1809 novel *The Scottish Chiefs*. The narrator opens the novel by providing the setting within which the action of the story will take place.

> Bright was the summer of 1296. The war which had desolated Scotland was then at an end. Ambition seemed satiated; and the vanquished, after having passed under the yoke of their enemy, concluded they might wear their chains in peace. Such were the hopes of those Scottish noblemen who, early in the preceding spring, had signed the bond of submission to a ruthless conqueror, purchasing life at the price of all that makes life estimable—liberty and honor.

3 Mark for Review

Which choice best describes the overall structure of the text?

Ⓐ It explains one group's strategy for winning a war and then emphasizes the despair that another group feels about not having won the war.

Ⓑ It details the outcome of a war and then explains a group's reasoning for accepting that outcome.

Ⓒ It emphasizes that a group is distraught about the current situation and then speculates as to why allies have yet to assist the group.

Ⓓ It describes one group's concerns about foreign leadership and then specifies the government of that leadership.

Here's How To Crack It

If you **read the question** and see "overall structure," you can **identify the question type** as a **Purpose** question. You should highlight *overall structure* in the question stem to keep track of the specific task you were given.

As you **read the passage,** look for a shift in the passage you can **highlight** to help define the passage's structure. In the middle of the passage, it states that *Such were the hopes of the Scottish noblemen.* Before this point, the passage explains how the Scots hoped to *wear their chains in peace* after losing a war. After this point, the passage explains that the Scots *had signed the bond of submission to a ruthless conqueror, purchasing life at the price of all that makes life estimable—liberty and honor.* Write in your **annotation** box that the structure of this passage is "to describe the Scots' loss and what the Scots hoped for in defeat."

Use POE! Choice (A) is the **Opposite** of the passage—the Scots didn't win the war, and the second half of the passage focuses more on what the Scots *hoped* would happen rather than the *despair* they felt. Eliminate (A). Choice (B) is consistent with the annotation and highlighting. Keep (B). Choice (C) is **Half-Right** at best—the Scots certainly don't seem happy about their loss, but there is no mention of their *allies* in the passage. Eliminate (C). Choice (D) is also **Half-Right**—the Scots are definitely uncertain as to whether they will be allowed to live in peace under the leadership of someone else, but the *government* of that foreign leadership is never discussed in detail. Eliminate (D). The correct answer is (B).

How to Adjust Your Approach:

When a Purpose question asks for the overall structure, look for and highlight where the focus of the passage shifts. From there, you'll be able to create an annotation based on what was discussed before and after that shift.

DUAL TEXTS: POINT OF AGREEMENT

Many Dual Text questions are nice enough, if we can call any PSAT question nice, to directly call out which topic from Text 1 you need to find and who in Text 2 you need to find for a response regarding that topic or vice versa. However, you will sometimes encounter a question asking for a point of agreement between the two passages. Understand this: when College Board writes Dual passages, the two authors rarely agree completely. Instead, there will likely be a smaller detail in both passages that neither author has an issue with.

Text 1

Autism spectrum disorder (ASD), which appears in early childhood, can present wildly differently from person to person. In 2020, scientists Shivani P. Patel and Kritika Nayar examined the effects of ASD on social interaction and communication. They analyzed the rate, rhythm, and intonation of English speech samples from participants with ASD and from a control group composed of individuals without ASD. The scientists found that compared to the control group, the ASD group had markedly slower rates of speech and distinctive tonal patterns.

Text 2

A 2022 experiment led by Joseph C. Y. Lau demonstrated the impact of autism spectrum disorder (ASD) on speech patterns. The team used AI machine learning to trace rhythm and intonation from recorded narrations of both English and Cantonese speakers. The analysis revealed that rhythm—or fluctuations in the timing and volume of one's speech—could reliably differentiate between participants with and without ASD for both language groups. Intonation—or variation in pitch—was a reliable predictor for only the English speakers, not the Cantonese speakers.

4 Mark for Review

Based on the texts, if Patel and Nayar (Text 1) and Lau (Text 2) were aware of the findings of both experiments, they would most likely agree with which statement?

Ⓐ The 2020 experiment most likely did not account for non-English speakers, whose inclusion was a notable aspect of the 2022 experiment.

Ⓑ On average, people with ASD tend to speak more slowly and display more variety in tone, pitch, and rhythm compared to people without ASD.

Ⓒ Controlling for factors such as age and country of origin, English speakers with ASD typically display more predictable speech patterns than their Cantonese-speaking counterparts.

Ⓓ Spectrum disorders like ASD, particularly those presenting in early childhood, impact speech and communication more severely than do other disorders.

Here's How To Crack It

As you **read and understand the question,** you can see that it's asking which idea scientists from both passages would agree on. You should highlight *Patel and Nayar* as well as *Lau*, as it's entirely possible that multiple viewpoints could be present in these passages, and you want to make sure you are focusing on the right people or groups.

As you **read Text 1,** look for a main idea you can **highlight**. The passage states that *the ASD group had markedly slower rates of speech and distinctive tonal patterns.* As you **read Text 2,** look for something you can **highlight** related to the same topic. The passage states that *The analysis revealed that rhythm...could reliably differentiate between participants with and without ASD for both language groups* but that *Intonation...was a reliable predictor for only the English speakers, not the Cantonese speakers.* The two passages don't quite agree, but what was the key detail that caused the difference? The fact that Patel and Nayar looked only at English speech, but Lau looked at both English and Cantonese speakers. Write in your **annotation** box that the point of agreement would be "different languages might affect outcome of experiment."

Use POE! Choice (A) is consistent with the highlighting and annotation—neither author would disagree that one experiment didn't look at non-English speakers and the other did, so keep (A). Choice (B) is **Half-Right**—it's consistent with Text 1, but the author of Text 2 only mentions that Lau found differences, not what those differences actually were. Eliminate (B). Choice (C) is also **Half-Right**—the author of Text 2 would likely agree that English speakers with ASD have *more predictable speech patterns* than their Cantonese-speaking counterparts, but Text 1 doesn't discuss Cantonese speakers at all. Eliminate (C). Choice (D) goes **Beyond the Text**—while ASD may impact speech and communication severely, no *other disorders* are discussed in the passage. Eliminate (D). The correct answer is (A).

How to Adjust Your Approach:

When a Dual Texts question asks for a point of agreement, don't expect the authors to agree on their overall conclusions. Instead, look for a detail or piece of evidence that neither author would have a problem with.

CLAIMS: SUPPORT A CLAIM

A Claims question that asks you to support some claim, argument, theory, or hypothesis is just as likely to appear as one that asks you to illustrate a claim, as seen in the previous chapter. However, supporting a claim and illustrating a claim aren't really that different—whether you want to strengthen a claim or just give an example of it, you need to choose an answer that is as consistent with that claim as possible. The key difference is that passages with questions asking you to support a claim will probably be longer, but the central goal is unchanged: find and highlight the claim, and then proceed to POE.

Claims questions can also ask you to weaken a claim rather than support it. When this happens, you simply want the answer that is most inconsistent with the claim. Make sure to eliminate answers that are irrelevant to the claim entirely. An example of a Weaken the Claim question is provided in the drill for this chapter.

Artificial sweeteners offer an appealing alternative to sugar, but they may carry unintended consequences for the body because of their effect on the gut microbiome. It has been demonstrated that the bacteria that make up the gut microbiome affect glucose tolerance and appetite. Researchers at the Weizmann Institute of Science hypothesize that the consumption of artificial sweeteners such as sucralose can lower glucose tolerance and increase appetite in humans. The researchers conducted a study comparing the glucose tolerance and appetite levels of people who had been fed sucralose against a control group who was not fed sucralose.

5 Mark for Review

Which finding from the researchers' study, if true, would most directly support their hypothesis?

Ⓐ Both the individuals who consumed sucralose and the control group had much higher glucose tolerance levels at the conclusion of the study.

Ⓑ At the conclusion of the study, individuals who consumed sucralose had lower glucose tolerance levels but also lower appetite levels than the control group.

Ⓒ Individuals who consumed sucralose had lower glucose tolerance levels and higher appetite levels at the conclusion of the study than the control group.

Ⓓ When individuals who consumed sucralose were interviewed, they were found to also have consumed large quantities of water, which is known to decrease appetite.

Here's How To Crack It

If you **read the question** and see words such as "illustrate," "support," or "weaken" along with words like "claim," "hypothesis," or "argument," you can **identify the question type** as a **Claims** question. You should highlight *support their hypothesis* in the question stem—that's going to help greatly when you are looking for what to highlight.

If the question refers to a *hypothesis, theory, assertion*, or some other synonym for *claim*, it's likely that the passage will contain some form of that exact word (such as *hypothesized* or *assert*). The word *claim* is generic, however, so it doesn't necessarily indicate the presence of this exact word in the text.

As you **read the passage,** look for and **highlight** the researchers' hypothesis: they hypothesize that *the consumption of artificial sweeteners such as sucralose can lower glucose tolerance and increase appetite.* The right answer should offer a finding that is as consistent with this hypothesis as it possibly can be.

Use POE! Choice (A) is the **Opposite** of the hypothesis, as those who consumed sucralose should have *lower* glucose tolerance levels, not *higher.* Eliminate (A). Choice (B) is **Half-Right**—those who consume sucralose should indeed have *lower glucose tolerance levels* but they should have *higher,* not *lower,* appetite levels than the control group according to the hypothesis. Eliminate (B). Choice (C) is consistent with the hypothesis: it is exactly what the researchers hypothesized should happen in the passage. Keep (C). Choice (D) mentions that those who consumed sucralose also consumed *large quantities of water.* Not only does the researchers' hypothesis not mention the consumption of water, but this answer does not even comment on the whether or not the appetite levels of those who consumed sucralose increased or decreased. Eliminate (D). The correct answer is (C).

How to Adjust Your Approach:

When a Claims question asks you to support or weaken a claim instead of illustrating it, understand that you'll be dealing with a longer passage but your central goal of finding and highlighting the claim remains the same.

CHARTS: SUPPORT A CLAIM

Not only do Charts and Claims questions test the same skills, they can even ask the exact same question. When asked to support a claim, hypothesis, or argument on a Charts question, you still need to find and highlight that claim, hypothesis, or argument in the passage. The most critical thing here is to realize it's not good enough to choose an answer that merely represents the data from the figure accurately. The correct answer must first and foremost be consistent with what you highlighted. In fact, you need to check the data in the figure only if you've eliminated all of the answers that are inconsistent with your claim and still have more than one answer remaining.

It's possible, but rare, for a Charts question to ask you to weaken a claim instead. If this does come up, remember that you should still focus on the claim in the passage first. Eliminate answers that would strengthen the claim or have no relevance to the claim at all; then check the figure for data that would weaken the claim only if more than one answer remains.

Nutritional Information for Skim Cow's Milk and Unsweetened Oat Milk Based on a 1-Cup Serving

Milk type	Skim cow's milk	Unsweetened oat milk
Calories	90	90
Fat (g)	0	1.5
Sodium (mg)	130	120
Sugars (g)	12	4

In the field of nutrition, skim cow's milk and unsweetened oat milk are two popular substitutions for whole milk, which can be too high in fat and cholesterol for some individuals. Each whole milk substitute goes through different processes that affect its final nutritional value. For instance, unsweetened oat milk is made by straining a blend of rolled oats (which have less sugar than cow's milk) and water. A scientist hypothesized that because skim milk is whole milk that has been run through a centrifuge to separate out all of the fat droplets, it would likely have less fat content but higher sugar content than would unsweetened oat milk.

6 Mark for Review

Which choice most effectively uses data from the table that support the scientist's hypothesis?

Ⓐ The skim cow's milk has higher sugar content than fat content, but it also contains more sodium than does unsweetened oat milk.

Ⓑ Both the skim cow's milk and the unsweetened oat milk's sodium contents were over 100 milligrams per cup.

Ⓒ The skim cow's milk and unsweetened oat milk both contain 90 calories in an average 1-cup serving.

Ⓓ The unsweetened oat milk has lower sugar content but higher fat content than does the skim cow's milk.

Here's How To Crack It

As you **read and understand the question**, highlight *support the scientist's hypothesis* so you don't lose track of your specific task.

As you **read the titles, key/legend, variables, and units** from the table, note that the table shows two different milk types, four different nutritional factors (calories, fat, sodium, and sugars), and the units grams and milligrams.

While wrong answers can certainly misrepresent the figure, did you notice that all four answers here represented the table accurately? This is why it's better to compare the answers to the claim or hypothesis first and to the figure second only if necessary—you are more likely to eliminate more answers initially following this order.

As you **read the passage,** look for a hypothesis the scientist puts forth regarding these terms specifically. **Highlight** the last sentence, which states that skim milk *would likely have less fat content but higher sugar content than would unsweetened oat milk.* The answer should be as consistent as possible with this hypothesis.

Use POE! Choice (A) is **Half-Right**—the information might be consistent with the table, but it mentions sodium, which is not related to the sugar and fat content referenced by the hypothesis in the passage. Eliminate (A). Choice (B) is also **Half-Right** for the exact same reason—any mention of sodium is not relevant to the claim. Eliminate (B). Choice (C) is, again, **Half-Right**—it's 100% true but would not support the scientist's hypothesis as the hypothesis does not mention calories. Eliminate (C). Choice (D) is exactly consistent with the scientist's hypothesis as stated in the passage. Keep (D). The correct answer is (D).

How to Adjust Your Approach:

When a Charts question asks you to support a claim rather than complete an example, the only key difference is that the answers will be complete sentences. You should still focus primarily on comparing each answer to the claim you highlighted in the passage, only referring back to the figure if more than one answer remains.

More Question Formats Drill

Suggested Time Limit: 8 minutes. This drill contains six questions with the variations you've learned in this chapter, in the common order in which they would typically appear on an RW module. Continue to use the Basic Approach, and don't forget to highlight in the question stem to keep track of the specific task you were given. Answers can be found in Part IV.

1 Mark for Review

The following text is adapted from Robert Louis Stevenson's 1878 short story "A Lodging for the Night." At the outset of the story, a great blizzard has descended upon the city of Paris.

> High up overhead the snow settled among the tracery of the cathedral towers. Many a niche was drifted full; many a statue wore a long white bonnet on its grotesque or sainted head.

As used in the text, what does the word "settled" most nearly mean?

Ⓐ Resolved

Ⓑ Accumulated

Ⓒ Disappeared

Ⓓ Survived

2 Mark for Review

The Code Girls, women hired by the US Navy to work as cryptographers and cryptanalysts—people who create codes and decipher enemy codes—may finally be receiving their due recognition from World War II historians. During their tenure, the Code Girls successfully intercepted 30,000 messages from the Japanese Navy, leading to the sinking of nearly all Japanese supply ships in the South Pacific. Some historians maintain that the Code Girls' efforts directly shortened the war by two years. Unfortunately, due to the highly secretive nature of their work, the women were discouraged from sharing their stories or identities, so much so that many decades later their efforts have gone unheralded.

Which choice best describes the function of the underlined portion in the text as a whole?

Ⓐ It supplies background information about the institutions that trained many of the women who were cryptographers.

Ⓑ It provides additional perspective to support a claim made earlier in the text about historians' attitudes toward the Code Girls.

Ⓒ It highlights a point about typical roles available to women referenced earlier in the text.

Ⓓ It contrasts the circumstances of the Code Girls with narratives of other heroic women who helped the war effort.

3 Mark for Review

By utilizing advanced imaging techniques in observing the inner ears of guinea pigs, scientists at Oregon Health and Linköping University in Sweden have determined that the cochlea—the spiral-shaped inner ear—contains microscopic hair cells that react to low-frequency sound. Until this discovery, it was believed that individual hair cells reacted independently to set frequencies. A significant outcome of this breakthrough is that patients suffering hearing impairments will benefit from enhanced design of their cochlear implants.

Which choice best describes the overall structure of the text?

(A) It shows how a group of scientists made a major breakthrough, then shows why other scientists in their field are skeptical of the results.

(B) It examines an innovative method used by researchers, then asserts that methods used by previous researchers are superior.

(C) It portrays a research process used for an important discovery, then clarifies one specific outcome of that research.

(D) It presents a hypothesis regarding the inner ears of guinea pigs, then illustrates the steps taken to test that hypothesis.

4 Mark for Review

Text 1

Bill "Bojangles" Robinson's impressive talent for tap dancing can be most understood by examining the multitude of acts with which Robinson was associated. Robinson was featured alongside famous actress Shirley Temple and well-established entertainers such as Fred Astaire and Sammy Davis Jr., and he was even considered a big enough draw to be booked as a solo act. Robinson's versatility made him both adaptable enough to work with others and talented enough to work on his own.

Text 2

Prior to Bill Robinson's rise to prominence, entertainment establishments often prohibited Black performers from appearing onstage alone and stipulated that they could only perform with other Black performers. Despite these restrictions, Robinson was considered so charismatic and skilled a dancer that he was eventually allowed to perform solo and as part of a mixed-race collaboration with white actress Shirley Temple.

Based on the texts, both authors would most likely agree with which statement?

(A) Robinson drew inspiration from several different artists when developing his tap dance routines.

(B) Entertainers who worked with Robinson deeply admired his dedication as a tap dancer.

(C) Robinson's talent was crucial to his success.

(D) The public was largely unaware of the restrictions faced by Robinson.

5 Mark for Review

While grazing on grass, cows suffer immense discomfort from biting flies. Across the world, many societies rely on cows for meat and dairy, yet biting flies account for over $2 billion a year in losses for the US cattle industry alone, as cows succumb to disease or infection caused by the bites. To combat this, a team of Japanese researchers painted zebra stripes onto six Japanese Black cows and then observed the cows for three days. Noting that the number of bites on the zebra-striped cows was far less than those on unpainted cows, the team theorized that the zebra stripes must confuse the biting flies' landing and biting patterns; this, in turn, reduces the number of bites each cow receives.

Which finding, if true, would most directly undermine the team's hypothesis?

Ⓐ For the cows observed in the study, the number of bites caused by insects other than biting flies was not reduced by the presence of the zebra stripes.

Ⓑ For the cows observed in the study, biting flies were more prevalent near cows that did not have the zebra stripes.

Ⓒ For some cows observed in a different study, the presence of zebra stripes reduced the number of bites by biting flies nearly to zero.

Ⓓ For some cows observed in a different study, the number of bites caused by biting flies increased on cows painted with zebra stripes.

6 Mark for Review

Esperanto Speakers by Country

Country	Approximate number of *Esperantujo* (Esperanto speakers)	Estimated % of country's total population
Brazil	7,000	0.003
Japan	1,500	0.001
Togo	200	0.002

As many as 63,000 people worldwide communicate in Esperanto, a language constructed by L. L. Zamenhof in 1887. Esperanto is an international auxiliary language, meaning it's primarily used between speakers who don't share native languages. Esperanto speakers, or *Esperantujo*, are mostly concentrated in Eastern Europe and South America. <u>However, even in countries with the largest communities of Esperanto speakers, *Esperantujo* represent only a tiny fraction of each nation's total population.</u>

Which choice most effectively uses data from the table to support the underlined claim?

Ⓐ Brazil has a much larger number of *Esperantujo* than either Japan or Togo does, but Brazil's 7,000 *Esperantujo* represent just 0.003% of Brazil's population.

Ⓑ An estimated 0.002% of Togo's population is *Esperantujo*, whereas *Esperantujo* account for roughly 0.001% of Japan's population.

Ⓒ Brazil's population, which encompasses 0.003% of the global population, is estimated to have as many as 63,000 *Esperantujo*.

Ⓓ Approximately 0.001% of all *Esperantujo* live in Japan, which has significantly more *Esperantujo* than Togo has but far fewer than Brazil.

Summary

- If a Vocabulary question asks you to define a word in context rather than fill in a blank, treat the word as if it were a blank and use the normal Basic Approach.
- If a Purpose question asks you to determine the function of an underlined sentence, use structural words in the passage to determine which other sentences may help you.
- If a Purpose question asks you to determine the overall structure of the passage, look for shifts in the passage's focus and understand that you want to summarize what comes before and after the shift.
- If a Dual Texts question asks you for a point of agreement, remember that the point of agreement will be a detail or piece of evidence neither author has a problem with rather than any main idea or argument.
- If a Claims question asks you to support or weaken a claim, be prepared for a longer passage, but still focus on highlighting the claim and looking for the answer that's either most consistent or most inconsistent with that claim.
- If a Charts question asks you to support or, rarely, weaken a claim, the answers will be complete sentences rather than incomplete sentences. Still, your goal should be to compare the answers to the claim first, and to the chart only if necessary.

Question Types Review Chart	
Type	**Common Question Phrasing**
Vocabulary	• Which choice completes the text with the most logical or precise word or phrase? • As used in the text, what does the word X most nearly mean?
Purpose	• Which choice best describes the function of the X sentence in the overall structure of the text? • Which choice best states the main purpose of the text? • Which choice best describes the overall structure of the text?
Dual Texts	• Based on the texts, how would X (Text 2) most likely respond to X (Text 1)?
Retrieval	• According to/based on the text, what is true about X? • According to the text, why did X happen? • Based on the text, how does X respond to Y?
Main Idea	• What is the main idea of the text?
Claims	• Which quotation from the poem most effectively illustrates the claim? • Which quotation from X most effectively illustrates X's claim? • Which statement/finding, if true, would most directly/strongly support X's claim/hypothesis/argument/prediction? • Which finding, if true, would most directly weaken/undermine X's claim/hypothesis/argument?
Charts	• Which choice most effectively uses data from the table/graph to complete the text/statement/example? • Which choice most effectively uses data from the table/graph to illustrate the claim? • Which choice best describes data from the table/in the graph that support X's suggestion/claim/hypothesis/conclusion?
Conclusions	• Which choice most logically completes the text?

Chapter 9 Reading: Mastering the POE

Even with a solid Reading Basic Approach, you may still find yourself stuck between two, or even three, answer choices. This chapter is designed to help you understand the different types of Reading trap answers in more detail, so that you'll know what to look for and eliminate once you've already compared the answers back to your highlighting and annotation.

THE BEST LAID PLANS

In this chapter, you'll do a series of exercises designed to deepen your understanding of trap answers before going back to solving regular PSAT-style questions in the chapter drill.

You've probably realized by now that the difficulty of a Reading question on an RW module doesn't necessarily come from the topic of the passage itself: a far greater challenge is the various ways College Board writes the questions and, especially, the answer choices. There will be many times you find yourself down to two or three choices remaining, and they all seem like they could be correct, even if you've highlighted and annotated. This happens because College Board is extremely good at writing attractive-sounding answers that are actually wrong. Learning the different ways an answer could be a trap is critical to making sure you make the right call when down to two or three options.

Before we examine more of this trickery, never forget the most important concept regarding POE:

> The best reason to eliminate an answer on the PSAT is because it's not supported by the passage or not consistent with what you highlighted and annotated.

You look for trap answers when all else fails—not before comparing the answers to your highlighting and annotation!

COMMON TRAP ANSWERS, REVISITED

As a reminder, the six most common trap answers you'll encounter on the PSAT are

- Opposite
- Recycled Language
- Extreme Language
- Beyond the Text
- Right Answer, Wrong Question
- Half-Right

This chapter will take you through these traps, in this order, so you can experience the different ways in which they could appear.

OPPOSITE

An Opposite trap answer uses a single word or phrase that makes the answer convey a tone, viewpoint, or meaning contradictory to what was intended by the author. Since many opposite traps come down to a single opposite word or phrase, they are easy to miss. Furthermore, since many PSAT passages are complex and often discuss both sides of an argument, it can be easy to choose an answer related to one side of the argument, just not the one you were supposed to focus on. So, make sure you highlight the argument as well as any words that speak to a positive or negative tone—this way, you stand less of a chance of going in the opposite direction by accident.

Opposite Traps in Action

> Leonardo da Vinci, renowned as a master artistic innovator, should also be ________ for his scientific forays. For example, he calculated a remarkably close approximation of the gravitational constant centuries before Newton's groundbreaking work in the field.

i. First, determine whether the word to go in the blank should be positive, negative, or neutral.

____

Then, eliminate the two words below that are the opposite **tone** of what should go in the blank:

a. commended
b rebuked
c. disregarded

ii. Eliminate the two statements below that **contradict** a statement made in the passage:

a. Da Vinci was viewed as an amateur artist but a highly regarded scientist.
b. The work of Isaac Newton predated the work of Leonardo da Vinci.
c. Leonardo da Vinci may deserve to be celebrated for accomplishments in more than one field.

Which Answers to Eliminate and Why

i.	*b* and *c* – both of these are negative words when a positive word should go in the blank.
ii.	*a* – da Vinci is described as a master artistic innovator, not an *amateur*. *b* – da Vinci's work comes *centuries before* Newton's, but this answer says Newton's work *predated* that of da Vinci.

RECYCLED LANGUAGE

Recycled Language trap answers repeat exact words and phrases from the passage but use those words and phrases incorrectly. Since time management on the Reading questions is often a struggle, students are looking for any way they can to answer questions quickly. For example, if you were to see a string of words such as *advocates of the Chronological Protection Conjecture* used in the passage and then repeated in an answer, it's easy to be drawn to that answer immediately and actively look to knock out the other three answers, or even fail to consider them at all. It's important to remember that the repetition of a word or phrase doesn't automatically make an answer wrong, but you should still compare usage of repeated words and phrases in the answers with the way those words and phrases were used in the passage.

Recycled Language Traps in Action

For the next two examples, focus entirely on Process of Elimination. Use the descriptions above and the clues given in each prompt to eliminate the two flawed answers.

> The development of theme park attractions has a storied history, and one such attraction, *The Great Movie Ride*, is responsible for the creation of an entire theme park. Historians who study the Walt Disney World resort note that *The Great Movie Ride*, an attraction planned for the existing Epcot theme park, was deemed to represent such a unique and powerful connection to Hollywood and American show business that then-CEO Michael Eisner and President Marty Sklar decided to construct an entire theme park around the ride. Several years later, *The Great Movie Ride* was the centerpiece attraction of the park that would eventually come to be known as Disney's Hollywood Studios.

i. Eliminate the two statements below that contain a **memorable word or phrase** from the passage that is being misused in the statements:

a. American show business has had a major impact on the development of many theme parks.
b. Disney is often lauded for its ability to create unique and powerful connections between characters.
c. The design of a theme park ride had implications beyond the ride's original intent.

ii. Eliminate the two statements below that contain **words out of context** that have been taken from different parts of the passage and combined to make an unsupported statement:

a. The creation of an entire theme park is often the responsibility of the CEO and president of the company building the park.
b. Two individuals saw an opportunity to expand the scope of an upcoming project.
c. It can take several years to learn how to develop theme park attractions responsibly.

Which Answers to Eliminate and Why

i.	*a* – *American show business* is a **memorable phrase** and a common one we hear, but the passage describes it as influencing only one theme park, not *many theme parks*. *b* – *unique and powerful connection* is similarly a **memorable phrase** from the passage but it's used in the passage to describe one ride, not the entirety of the Walt Disney Company.
ii.	*a* – while the words *entire theme park*, *responsible*, *CEO*, and *president* show up at different points in the passage, this answer combines all of these terms to make a claim not present in the passage. *c* – while the words *develop*, *responsible*, and *several years* show up at different points in the passage, this answer combines all of these terms to make a claim not present in the passage.

EXTREME LANGUAGE

Extreme Language trap answers include a word or phrase that takes a stated opinion or viewpoint in the passage too far in a certain direction. Unlike something going Beyond the Text, which means the answer has introduced some completely new idea, most Extreme Language traps are exaggerations in some way of a point the passage or author actually made. The author may approve of an environmental initiative but not be *obsessed* with it. A scientist in a passage may express optimism toward an experiment but not claim that it *proves* anything. So, remember that the correct answers to most PSAT Reading questions are softer and avoid making definitive statements.

Extreme Language Traps in Action

> Born in 1877 in New York City, Rosalia Edge was an environmentalist who sought to improve what she considered to be minimal conservation efforts towards many species, especially avians. Notably, she helped establish the Hawk Mountain Sanctuary, the land of which had been a hawk target shooting and hunting range for decades before Edge's intervention. In an interview regarding her 1962 book *Silent Spring*, scientist Rachel Carson claimed that Edge's work was instrumental in facilitating her own ornithological research, particularly concerning hawks and other birds of prey.

i. Eliminate the two statements below that take an attitude expressed by Edge and turn it into a **judgment** or **recommendation**:

a. Edge would claim that avian conservation efforts could be further expanded.
b. Edge would condemn those who enjoy target shooting and hunting for pleasure.
c. Edge believed that more target shooting ranges should be turned into avian sanctuaries.

ii. Eliminate the two statements below that contain a word that is an **absolute** or a **superlative** (a word ending in *-st*):

a. The work performed by Rosalia Edge seems to have produced several positive results.
b. All hawk species will eventually be protected by sanctuaries such as Hawk Mountain.
c. For ornithologists, the study of birds of prey is the most logical career choice.

Which Answers to Eliminate and Why

i.	*b* – stating that Edge would *condemn those who enjoy shooting and hunting* is a harsh **judgment** not supported by the passage. *c* – in the passage, Edge does not **recommend** that *more target shooting ranges should be turned into avian structures.*
ii.	*a* – *all* is an example of an **absolute** word, and this extreme can't be supported by the passage alone. *c* – *most* is an example of a **superlative** word, and this extreme can't be supported by the passage alone.

BEYOND THE TEXT

Beyond the Text trap answers depend on logical assumptions or outside reasoning but lack actual support in the passage. For some students, these are the most difficult trap answers to catch on the exam. The biggest reason that PSAT Reading can be difficult is that the questions make it sound like an answer can be correct as long as you can justify it. Beyond the Text traps play into this justification—they rely on you, the student, saying an answer "makes sense" or "could very well be true." Even worse, once you get inside of your head trying to justify one of these answers, you will probably spend valuable time on that justification. That's why you absolutely must remember that Reading is an open-book test—an answer is correct only because the author said so, meaning that you found actual evidence for the answer and highlighted it.

Beyond the Text Traps in Action

> The following text is from Thomas Babington Macaulay's 1842 poem "Virginia." The speaker is reciting a song about a military conquest at the request of his audience.
>
> Ye good men of the Commons, with loving hearts and true,
> Who stand by the bold Tribunes that still have stood by you,
> Come, make a circle round me, and mark my tale with care,
> A tale of what Rome once hath borne, of what Rome yet may bear.
> This is no Grecian fable, of fountains running wine,
> Of maids with snaky tresses, or sailors turned to swine.
> Here, in this very Forum, under the noonday sun,
> In sight of all the people, the bloody deed was done.
> Old men still creep among us who saw that fearful day,
> Just seventy years and seven ago, when the wicked Ten bare sway.

i. Eliminate the two statements below that are **too broad** or **too specific** to be supported by the passage:

a. The Romans often commemorated past tragedies through poem and song.
b. The noonday sun provided optimal lighting for the enemy forces to attack the area.
c. Some individuals who witnessed the tragedy referenced in the song were still alive to hear the song.

ii. Eliminate the two statements below that make **predictions of the future** that are not supported by the passage:

a. The area is likely to be attacked again, as it has already proven a vulnerable target.
b. The song is meant to serve as a warning of a fate that could befall Rome again.
c. The bold Tribunes will continue to stand by the good men of the Commons for many years to come.

Which Answers to Eliminate and Why

i.	*a – often commemorated* is **too broad** to be supported here, as we know only this one single tragedy is being commemorated by a poem or song. *b – optimal lighting* is **too specific** to be supported here, as we don't know that's why the battle happened during the noonday sun.
ii.	*a – likely to be attacked again* is a **prediction of the future**, and the passage does not predict the area will likely be attacked again. *c – will continue to stand by...for many years to come* is a **prediction of the future**, and the passage does not predict that one group will continue to stand by the other. (Note that while (*b*) does reference the fate of Rome, it merely mentions a possibility that *could* befall Rome again, making it much more plausible.)

RIGHT ANSWER, WRONG QUESTION

Right Answer, Wrong Question trap answers are actually true based on the passage, but they don't answer the question asked. While most of the other traps are based on misreading or misunderstanding the passage, Right Answer, Wrong Question traps are based on forgetting the question task. These are extremely easy traps to fall into—without the question task, it's going to be nearly impossible to dissuade yourself from an answer that is perfectly consistent with the passage. So, the key to catching these traps is to constantly remind yourself of the question task—all of the reading, highlighting, annotating, and Process of Elimination you do should be singularly focused on completing the very specific job given to you by the question—this is part of why we recommend highlighting the question task so frequently, and why we've included the question stems for this passage.

Right Answer, Wrong Question Traps in Action

> The following text is from Robert Louis Stevenson's 1878 short story "A Lodging for the Night."
>
> It was late in November, 1456. The snow fell over Paris with rigorous, relentless persistence; sometimes the wind made a sally and scattered it in flying vortices; sometimes there was a lull, and flake after flake descended out of the black night air, silent, circuitous, interminable. <u>To poor people, looking up under moist eyebrows, it seemed a wonder where it all came from.</u> Master Francis Villon had propounded an alternative that afternoon, at a tavern window: was it only pagan Jupiter plucking geese upon Olympus? or were the holy angels moulting? He was only a poor Master of Arts, he went on; and as the question somewhat touched upon divinity, he durst not venture to conclude.

Which choice best describes the function of the underlined sentence in the text as a whole?

i. Eliminate the two phrases below that describe the function of the **wrong sentence** from the passage rather than the underlined one:

a. To describe the unfavorable weather conditions in the city of Paris as seemingly unending

b. To characterize a particular group as being astonished regarding the source of precipitation

c. To explain a character's hesitancy at pondering subject matter which he does not feel qualified to examine

Which choice best states the main idea of the text?

ii. Eliminate the two statements below that reference only a **detail** from the passage rather than the **main idea** of the passage:

a. The snowfall in Paris at the time of the story is mostly unceasing, stopping only occasionally and then starting back up again.

b. A character is introduced through the description of a weather phenomenon and an examination into what the source of that phenomenon may be.

c. Master Francis Villon offers some alternative explanations for the relentless snowfall that currently dominates the skies of Paris.

Which Answers to Eliminate and Why

i.	*a* – gives the function of the second sentence rather than the underlined sentence. *c* – gives the function of the last sentence rather than the underlined sentence.
ii.	*a* – accurately describes the second sentence only rather than the main idea. *c* – accurately describes the second-to-last sentence only rather than the main idea.

HALF-RIGHT

Half-Right trap answers address only part of a claim, are consistent with the passage or figure but not both, or are longer answers divided into one supported half and one unsupported half. As with some of the other traps we've discussed, the presence of something that does match the passage correctly can lead one to assume the entire answer is good to go. Be sure to read the entire answer choice, and make sure it addresses every aspect of both the question and the passage that it needs to.

You've already seen Half-Right traps on Charts questions that are consistent with the figure but not the passage, as well as Half-Right traps on Claims questions that don't address each aspect of the claim. This exercise will focus on longer answers that have a seemingly good beginning but lead into a trap as you keep reading.

Half-Right Traps in Action

"The Banshee" is a traditional Irish short story attributed to an unknown author. In the story, the author describes a farmer who is one of the central characters in the story.

> He was rather dark and reserved in his manner, and oftentimes sullen and gloomy in his temper; and this, joined with his well-known disregard of religion, served to render him somewhat unpopular amongst his neighbours and acquaintances. However, he was in general respected, and was never insulted or annoyed. He was considered as an honest, inoffensive man, and as he was well supplied with firearms and ammunition,—in the use of which he was well practised, having, in his early days, served several years in a yeomanry corps,—few liked to disturb him, even had they been so disposed.

When an answer does have one supported half and one unsupported half, the unsupported half will usually contain an **Opposite**, **Recycled Language**, **Extreme Language**, or **Beyond the Text** trap.

i. Eliminate the two statements below that have **only one half** supported by the passage:

a. The farmer is described as having a grave and moody disposition, which has led to a lack of respect for him among his neighbors.

b. The farmer is a firm believer in the virtues of religion, and he conducts himself in an honest and inoffensive manner.

c. The farmer is not sought out by those around him but does not conduct himself in an inappropriate or belligerent manner.

Which Answers to Eliminate and Why

i.	*a – lack of respect* is the **Opposite** of the passage—the farmer was *in general respected.* *b – believer in the virtues of religion* is **Opposite** of the passage—he has a *well-known disregard for religion.*

Mastering the POE Drill

Suggested Time Limit: 10 minutes. This drill contains one each of the eight question types. The answers have been specifically designed here to fall directly into our six trap answer types, so practice efficient POE and don't forget to first eliminate the answers that don't match your highlight or annotation. Answers can be found in Part IV.

1 Mark for Review

In many cultures, dogs and elderly humans share a type of bond known as a true symbiotic relationship: in this positive feedback loop, the dog can help the elderly person complete simple tasks and grants the person a true companion with which to communicate. In return, the person ________ by providing the dog with shelter, food, medical care, and affection, all of which it would respond to warmly based on its natural instincts as a pack animal.

Which choice completes the text with the most logical and precise word or phrase?

Ⓐ diverges

Ⓑ exaggerates

Ⓒ reciprocates

Ⓓ counters

2 Mark for Review

The following text is from Thomas Hardy's 1918 poem "And There Was a Great Calm." It is the final stanza of a poem about the signing of the armistice ending World War I.

> Calm fell. From Heaven distilled a clemency;
> There was peace on earth, and silence in the sky;
> Some could, some could not, shake off misery:
> The Sinister Spirit sneered: 'It had to be!'
> And again the Spirit of Pity whispered, 'Why?'

Which choice best states the main purpose of the text?

Ⓐ To reflect on a conversation the speaker had with a pair of spirits

Ⓑ To contradict the notion that a conflict has truly ended

Ⓒ To describe various emotions regarding the aftermath of a conflict

Ⓓ To lament the passing of those lost in battle

3 Mark for Review

Text 1

In the 1990s, anecdotal evidence was compiled by a group of independent researchers studying animal behavior who announced a surprising conclusion: domesticated felines, commonly known as cats, did not respond when called by their owners. The group concluded that this was most likely due to a cat's more independent natural instincts—because most feral cats are solitary predators, they likely do not see their owners as protectors and therefore may not heed their vocal instructions.

Text 2

A French team of animal behaviorists led by Charlotte de Mouzon has recently investigated how 16 different cats responded to pre-recorded voice samples from their owners versus how the same 16 cats responded to pre-recorded voice samples from strangers. De Mouzon and her team monitored the cats' behaviors as they listened to the audio samples and noted that the cats increased their behavior intensity when directly addressed by the voice on their owners' audio samples but either did not react or decreased their behavior intensity when called by the voice samples of the strangers.

How would the author of Text 2 most likely respond to the underlined claim in Text 1?

(A) By stating that the claim may be inaccurate because the findings of de Mouzon's team imply a stronger link between cats and their owners' voices than the independent researchers do

(B) By strongly concurring with the claim but noting that the connection it assumes conflicts with the findings of the anecdotal analysis run by the independent researchers

(C) By praising the claim for indicating that domesticated cats would have inherited the predator-like nature of their feral feline ancestors

(D) By criticizing the claim for being based on the premise that before being domesticated, cats responded to the human voice

4 Mark for Review

The following text is adapted from Fyodor Dostoevsky's 1880 novel *The Brothers Karamazov*. The description is of Alexei, one of the three brothers.

> He was just a boy who very early in life had come to love his fellow men and if he chose to enter a monastery, it was simply because at one point that course had caught his imagination and he had become convinced that it was the ideal way to escape from the darkness of the wicked world, a way that would lead him toward light and love. This particular way had caught his attention only because he had happened to meet a man who made an overwhelming impression on him—the famous Zosima, the elder of our monastery.

According to the text, why did Alexei become a monk?

(A) He was influenced by another monk and believed it to be the correct path for him.

(B) He did so out of an overwhelming love for his fellow men.

(C) He hoped it would allow him to isolate himself from others.

(D) He believed it to be the only way to battle the forces of darkness and wickedness.

5 Mark for Review

Supposedly depicting a prehistoric animal with plates on its back, "the dinosaur of Ta Prohm" is a sculpture located in a temple-monastery in what is now northern Cambodia. Some theorists cite this sculpture as evidence that humans and dinosaurs, like the plated stegosauruses, may have coexisted in history. However, paleontologists disagree with this claim, arguing that the plates on the animal's back are more akin to ridges similar to those present on the backs of modern chameleons than they are to the features of any dinosaur. Additionally, the temple-monastery of Ta Prohm was dedicated to the worship of several mythical animals, so the "dinosaur" depicted in the sculpture may not have been a real animal at all.

Which choice best states the main idea of the text?

Ⓐ Analyzing ancient sculptures is the best way to determine which organisms lived at the same time in the past.

Ⓑ The sculpture in Ta Prohm proves that dinosaurs and humans lived side-by-side in ancient history.

Ⓒ Paleontologists are certain that the sculpture is depicting a modern organism in an artistic manner.

Ⓓ Despite various theories, the accurate identity of the animal on the Ta Prohm sculpture remains a matter of debate.

6 Mark for Review

Bunraku is a form of Japanese puppetry established in the early seventeenth century that continues to be performed today. The performance typically combines chanting, percussion instruments, and puppeteers into a traditional play. Most *bunraku* performers spend 10 years each mastering the feet, arms, and head movements of a puppet before being recognized as masters of the craft. Some scholars believed that the 30-year training period would have prevented all but the very wealthy from having the resources to master *bunraku* initially, but skeptics claim that the length and rigor of training are more likely to have attracted those in lower classes, as they would be more willing to devote such time to improve their situation.

Which finding, if true, would most directly support the skeptics' claim?

Ⓐ Much of the *bunraku* plays analyzed by scholars contained similar elements regardless of the social status of the author.

Ⓑ Most modern *bunraku* performances are considered affordable by the average Japanese citizen.

Ⓒ The documents available to scholars included many references to *bunraku* using the *shamisen*, believed to be an expensive instrument in early seventeenth century Japan.

Ⓓ Most of the historical records mention that the first performers of *bunraku* were the *kugutsu-mawashi*—a band of wandering performers—who often lived in poverty.

7 Mark for Review

Median Home Prices in US Dollars of Four States, 1950–1990

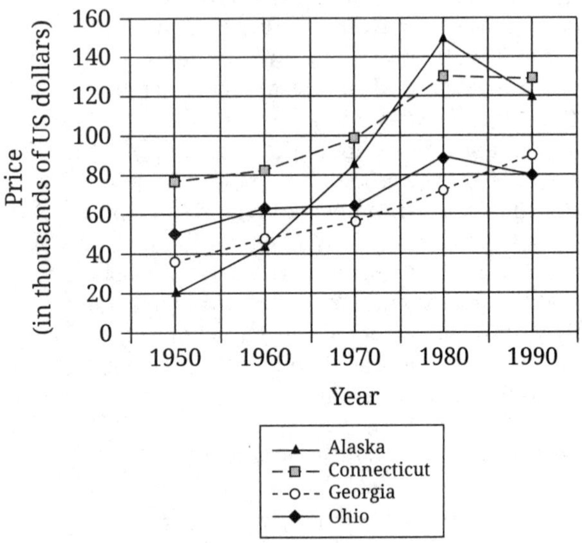

Median home values in the United States grew significantly between 1950 and 1990, but this growth varied by state. For example, in 1950, Connecticut already had a comparatively high median home value of almost $80,000, a threshold Ohio didn't surpass until more than two decades later. The most dramatic growth occurred in states like Alaska, whose median home value went from ________

Which choice most effectively uses data from the graph to complete the assertion?

Ⓐ less than $25,000 in 1950 to around $120,000 in 1990.

Ⓑ around $30,000 in 1950 to over $120,000 in 1990.

Ⓒ around $20,000 in 1950 to over $140,000 in 1990.

Ⓓ less than $50,000 in 1950 to around $80,000 in 1990.

8 Mark for Review

Hobby tunneling, or carving a tunnel by hand, is a form of recreation for individuals wishing to test their physical or emotional fortitude. In a poll of tunnel hobbyists, a large percentage reported that their tunnel started as something useful such as a wine cellar or evacuation route, and then they simply continued digging once the initial job was completed. An even larger percentage of those polled stated that the effort required to make their tunnels seemed disproportionate to the stated purpose. These replies suggest that ________

Which choice most logically completes the text?

Ⓐ many tunnel hobbyists are uncertain of why they started their tunnels.

Ⓑ many tunnel hobbyists believe they should only tunnel on their own properties.

Ⓒ hobby tunneling may be about more than simply accomplishing a goal.

Ⓓ hobby tunneling can improve a practitioner's mental conditioning more than it improves the practitioner's physical conditioning.

Summary

- When you are down to two or more answers after eliminating answers that are not consistent with your highlighting and annotation, ask "Which answers are traps?"
- **Opposite** traps can include words that are the opposite tone as well as contradictory statements.
- **Recycled Language** traps can include memorable words or phrases from the passage and words taken out of context.
- **Extreme Language** traps can include judgments, recommendations, absolutes, and superlatives.
- **Beyond the Text** traps include claims that are too broad or too specific or make predictions of the future.
- **Right Answer, Wrong Question** traps can include wrong sentence functions or incorrect details on a Main Idea question.
- **Half-Right** traps can include answers with only one supported half, answers that address only one part of a claim, or answers that are consistent with a figure but irrelevant to the claim in the passage.
- When a Half-Right answer has only one supported half, the "wrong" half could be Opposite, Recycled Language, Extreme Language, or Beyond the Text.
- Remember: the best reason to eliminate an answer on the PSAT is because it's not supported by the passage or not consistent with what you highlighted. If you know an answer is not supported, eliminate it and don't worry about what specific category the answer falls into!

Chapter 10
Rules Questions: Introduction

After the Reading portion of each RW module, you'll see a set of questions that we call Rules questions. These questions test various punctuation and grammar topics, and rather than being grouped by topic the way the Reading questions are, these are in order of difficulty only. This means you'll see a mix of topics, and you may notice the questions getting harder from the first Rules question to the last one. In this chapter, you'll learn our basic approach for all Rules questions and how to identify when each topic is tested.

KNOW THE RULES TO FOLLOW

You've probably wondered at some point whether people are responsible for following laws that they don't know exist. Couldn't someone go to court and say, "Your Honor, I didn't know it was illegal to sing the national anthem incorrectly in Massachusetts!"? Of course, if we allowed this defense, every troublemaker would simply lie and pretend to be ignorant of whatever law has just been broken. As a result, we're all responsible for knowing the rules of our country, state, and local governments, even the ones that sound a little wacky (don't try to stop anyone from putting up a clothesline in Vermont).

Likewise, when it comes to the PSAT, if you want to score well on the Writing portion of the RW module, you won't be able to plead to College Board that you never learned grammar in school or that you didn't know that commas and semicolons aren't interchangeable. The good news is that the rules that are tested on the PSAT are as good as laws. Learn them, follow them, and you won't metaphorically go to jail (get a low RW score, in this case). You won't be asked to choose an answer that merely seems, feels, or looks right. The right answer will be the one that follows the rules, and the three wrong answers will not.

In the real world, there are dozens or possibly even hundreds of rules that good writers follow (and sometimes break). Although you probably don't have to think about it now, at some point you learned to begin a sentence with a capital letter, end with a period, spell each word correctly, put the words in the correct order, and so on. You might assume that the PSAT could test you on any of the countless writing rules, but in fact, only a small handful of these rules appear on the test. For instance, the PSAT will never test you on capitalization, spelling, frequently confused words (like "effect" and "affect"), or being concise.

Instead of reading each passage and "proofreading" (looking for any possible errors), if you learn the relatively short list of rules that are actually tested, you'll save yourself a great deal of time and effort. In the following chapters, you'll learn every rule that could possibly be tested on the PSAT.

GIVE YOURSELF A HEAD START

Learning the grammar and punctuation rules is only one part (though it's a big one!) of being successful on Rules questions. As we discussed in the RW Introduction, the pacing strategy you use will play a big role in how many questions you are able to get right in the amount of time that you have. In addition, whenever you decide to do the Rules questions (which for most people should be relatively early on), you want to be able to get them right as efficiently as possible. Of course, the more comfortable you are with the punctuation and grammar rules, the faster you'll complete these questions. In addition, though, there's a strategy you can use for all Rules questions that will help you apply those rules more quickly:

> For all Rules questions, look at the answers to see what's changing and determine what topic is being tested.

Remember, you can easily spot Rules questions by their question stem: *Which choice completes the text so that it conforms to the conventions of Standard English?* But this question doesn't tell you whether the topic is verb tense, commas, or any other rule that is tested. Looking at the answers is key in identifying what topic is being tested, and that goes a long way toward getting you the correct answer in the shortest amount of time. If you see pronouns changing in the answer choices, then you know you don't need to waste time thinking about the punctuation and only need to look for the word the pronoun refers back to (more on that later). On the other hand, if only punctuation is changing in the answer choices, then you don't need to consider how the words could be rewritten, because you don't have the option to do that.

Knowing what the question is asking allows you to focus on what you need for Reading questions. In the same way, knowing what's changing in the answers before you read the passage on Rules questions lets you know what you do and do not need to consider as you're reading. In fact, you don't always need to read the entire passage for Rules questions. If the question is testing punctuation within a single sentence, you probably don't need to read the surrounding sentences at all. That's just one more way our strategy helps you save time!

Let's take a look at the basic approach for Rules questions:

Rules Questions Basic Approach

1. Look at the answers to see what's changing.
2. Apply the rules associated with that topic.
3. Use Process of Elimination.

Of course, you haven't learned any of the rules yet (at least not from us). But once you have worked through the next two chapters of this book, you should be able to identify what's being tested on each Rules question based on what's changing in the answers, apply the rules you've learned, and get the correct answer every time.

LET THE ANSWER COME TO YOU

You've already learned about the importance of Process of Elimination several times in this book. It's just as helpful for Rules questions as it is for Reading. Here's why: College Board may not write a sentence the way you'd like to write it. For example, you might think that a period should be used in a certain spot, but College Board might choose to use a semicolon instead. If you are looking for the answer with a period, you could make a mistake (pick an answer with a period without realizing it makes some other type of error) or waste time because what you are looking for doesn't appear in the answers. As you know from your own writing, there are often many different correct ways a sentence can be written and punctuated. Instead of looking for a specific word, phrasing, or punctuation mark, use the on-screen Answer Eliminator to cross off answers that do not follow the rules and choose the remaining answer that doesn't break any rule.

In the following drill, we've put answers to Rules questions without showing you the passage, so you won't actually be able to answer these questions. Try to identify what is changing in the answer choices. Don't worry if your answer isn't very specific—once you learn the punctuation and grammar rules and see more example questions, you'll have a better idea of what rule is being tested in each question.

What's Changing in the Answers Exercise

1 Mark for Review

Ⓐ story, with

Ⓑ story with

Ⓒ story. With

Ⓓ story and with

What's changing in the answers?

____

2 Mark for Review

Ⓐ requires

Ⓑ require

Ⓒ was requiring

Ⓓ has required

What's changing in the answers?

____

3 Mark for Review

Ⓐ their

Ⓑ they're

Ⓒ its

Ⓓ it's

What's changing in the answers?

____

4 Mark for Review

Ⓐ the researchers discovered a surprising anomaly

Ⓑ a surprising anomaly was discovered by the researchers

Ⓒ the researchers' surprising anomaly was discovered

Ⓓ there was an anomaly that surprised the researchers

What's changing in the answers?

____

Answers to What's Changing in the Answers Exercise

1. punctuation
2. verbs
3. pronouns and apostrophes
4. the order of the words, or the subject of the phrase

Summary

- Rules questions are not grouped by topic. They go from easy to hard regardless of topic.
- Rules questions test a specific set of punctuation and grammar topics.
- The topics are based on rules that you can learn and follow.
- When you know you are dealing with a Rules question, look at the answers to see what's changing. This will allow you to get an idea of what topic you're being tested on before you read.
- Use Process of Elimination to remove answers that don't follow the rules, rather than looking for something specific in the answers that may not be there.

Chapter 11
Rules Questions: Punctuation

Many of the Rules questions involve punctuation. In this chapter, you'll learn how punctuation and sentence structure can be tested on the PSAT and the rules that will get you the correct answer every time.

FUN-CTUATION

If you have any feelings about punctuation, we suspect they might be described as confusion, dread, or apathy (a word that here means "not caring about punctuation at all"). We all know about ending a sentence with a period (or in some cases an exclamation mark or a question mark), but what about commas? How do you know whether a comma is needed or not? And what's up with those other weird punctuation marks like semicolons and colons? By the end of this lesson, you'll know the answer to all of these questions and much more. You might even start to find punctuation questions a little…fun! Okay, it's hard to describe anything about the PSAT as "fun," but at the very least, we can say that these questions can become very easy. That's because College Board tests just a handful of rules over and over. As you learned in the Rules Introduction, there is not an unlimited list of topics for College Board to choose from. You need to know only those rules that are actually tested.

In the real world, there are many more ways punctuation is used that aren't tested on the PSAT. In fact, there are plenty of gray areas when it comes to punctuation. Have you ever written an email and debated whether to end a sentence with a period or with an exclamation mark? That's because either one can be acceptable, and the choice is a matter of personal preference as well as the tone you want to convey. In the real world, there are lots of cases like this in which multiple ways of punctuating can be equally correct. The good news is that none of those gray areas are tested on the PSAT. If you find yourself wanting to pick one answer over another because it just *seems* better or *feels* right, you probably haven't learned the rules well enough.

GET ON WITH IT. GET ON WITH IT? GET ON WITH IT!

So, what are those rules? Let's start with how a sentence is constructed, which should be familiar to you. You are probably already aware that "running down the street" is not a complete sentence, but "she runs down the street" is. What's the difference? First off, the second one contains a subject, "she." In the second example, we know who did the running (it's okay that we don't know who "she" is—there's still someone doing the action), whereas in the first one there isn't any subject for the verb.

> Every complete sentence must contain a subject and a verb.

In some cases, a sentence needs more than just a subject and a verb. For instance, "the monkeys are" isn't a complete sentence. It has a subject (*monkeys*) and a verb (*are*), but it's missing the rest of the idea—what exactly the monkeys *are*. That being said, in the vast majority of cases, identifying whether an idea has a subject and a verb will be enough to tell you whether it's a complete sentence.

There's another reason that our first example ("running down the street") isn't a complete sentence. We know that it's missing a subject, but even if we add a subject, it still doesn't work: "she running down the street." That's because although it has a verb (*running*), that verb isn't in the right form to be **the** verb in the sentence—what we would call the main verb. It's tricky to define what a main verb looks like because there are many ways main verbs can appear, but when it comes to the PSAT, all you need to know is what verb forms can't be main verbs. Here's the rule:

> Any verb in the "-ing" or "to" form can't be the main verb in a sentence.

Even if you have never been told this rule before, you may find it quite obvious in the context of a sentence. Here are some examples:

People <u>to listen</u> to music

People <u>listening</u> to music

People <u>listen</u> to music

People <u>will listen</u> to music

People <u>listened</u> to music

The first two examples aren't complete sentences because their verbs aren't in main verb form. The remaining three examples could be complete sentences (just add a period) because each contains a subject and a verb in the correct form.

Now let's see how College Board tests this rule.

Doris Lessing received the Nobel Prize in Literature in 2007 for her literary oeuvre, including her novel *The Golden Notebook*, which ________ the inner life and complexities of the main character, Anna Wulf.

1 Mark for Review

Which choice completes the text so that it conforms to the conventions of Standard English?

Ⓐ exploring

Ⓑ to explore

Ⓒ having explored

Ⓓ explores

Here's How to Crack It

First identify the question category, which is Rules because it has the standard Rules question. Next, look at the answers to see what's being tested. Verbs are changing in the answers, so some verb topic is being tested. Find and highlight the subject of the verb: *which*. Although the blank falls within a part of the sentence that doesn't represent the main point (that's the first part, with the subject *Doris Lessing* and verb *received*), this particular phrase beginning with *which* still needs a main verb in order to state what the novel does. Since the blank needs to provide a main verb, eliminate any answer that isn't in the right form to be a main verb. Choices (A) and (C) are "-ing" verbs, and (B) is a "to" verb. Thus, (D) has to be the correct answer because it's the only one that's in a form that can be a main verb.

When you looked at the answers on the last question, you might have assumed that the question was testing tense. That might be the most obvious verb topic, but it's only one of three verb topics that College Board tests. We'll go over verb tense and another one, subject-verb agreement, in the next chapter. Here, though, the rule being tested is **verb form**. Although this obviously isn't a punctuation topic, it relates to whether something is a complete sentence or not, which affects the punctuation that can be used. It's in this chapter because for verb form you will need the same type of skills that you will need for punctuation questions, since they also relate to the structure of the sentence.

How to Spot Verb Form

The answers will contain verbs, including one or more "-ing" or "to" verbs.

Note that verbs such as "was driving" or "were listening" don't count as *-ing* verbs because the first part of the verb is in main verb form.

When verb form is being tested, the "-ing" or the "to" form can be correct, but only when the sentence already contains a main verb, since these verbs can't be the main verb in a sentence.

If you found the last question pretty easy, you'll be glad to see that the next topic may be just as simple. As you already know, every sentence must end with punctuation, namely a period, a question mark, or an exclamation mark. This next topic tests your understanding of when to use these end-of-sentence symbols.

Researcher Kamran Diba is interested in the formation of long-term memory, and particularly in how interrupting a certain brain signal in rats could disrupt memory. If rats' sleep were interrupted, ________ Diba designed a study to find the answer.

2 Mark for Review

Which choice completes the text so that it conforms to the conventions of Standard English?

Ⓐ would their memory be affected.

Ⓑ their memory would be affected.

Ⓒ would their memory be affected?

Ⓓ their memory would be affected?

Here's How to Crack It

If you know you are looking at a Rules question, then you know to look at the answers to see what's changing. In this case, it's the punctuation at the end of the sentence—periods versus question marks—and some slight variations in the word order at the beginning. The punctuation is likely the easier place to start, so look for a clue in the passage that will let you know whether you are dealing with a question or a statement. The sentence after the blank provides a clue: it says that *Diba designed a study to find the answer*. You would find an answer to a question, so the sentence before must be asking a question and should end in a question mark. Use the Answer Eliminator to cross off (A) and (B). Next, look at the wording in (C) and (D). Choice (D) has a question mark but is written as a statement, so that doesn't work. The answer must be (C).

If you're unsure why (D) doesn't work and (C) does, it's because the word order must be altered for questions. With statements, normally the subject comes before the verb—in this case, the subject is *memory* and the verb is *would be affected*. With questions, the verb—or part of it, in this case—actually comes before the subject.

This topic should be easy to identify:

How to Spot Question versus Statement

The answers will contain phrases that end with periods, question marks, and occasionally an exclamation mark. The order of the words will slightly change as well.

You may be wondering about exclamation marks. Does College Board really test how excited the sentences should sound? The answer is...not really. While we have seen exclamation marks show up on this type of question (very rarely), when they have appeared, the phrase ending with an exclamation mark wasn't phrased correctly, much like (D) in question 2. We don't think you'll be asked to choose solely between a period and an exclamation mark since there isn't a strict rule about when to use one over the other.

For "question versus statement" questions, look for and highlight a clue in the passage that tells you whether the blank needs to be a question or a statement. Keep in mind that a question asks for information, while a statement gives information.

Let's take a look at another, more common way the PSAT can test "end of sentence" punctuation.

English pilot Amy Johnson became famous for being the first woman to fly solo from England to ________ the following years, she set multiple records, including the solo record for a London-to-Cape Town flight.

3 Mark for Review

Which choice completes the text so that it conforms to the conventions of Standard English?

(A) Australia in

(B) Australia. In

(C) Australia, in

(D) Australia and in

Here's How to Crack It

After establishing that this is a Rules question, look to see what's changing in the answers. This time, it's the punctuation between *Australia* and *in*. Notice that (B) gives the option to use a period, separating this into two individual sentences. Read the full passage and determine whether that would work. The first part says *English pilot Amy Johnson became famous for being the first woman to fly solo from England to Australia*. This could be a sentence. The second part says *in the following years, she set multiple records, including the solo record for a London-to-Cape Town flight*. This could also be its own sentence. Therefore, (B) works! Soon you'll learn why (A), (C), and (D) can't work. For now, it's enough to understand that since these are both complete sentences on their own, they can be separated into two sentences. So, (B) is the correct answer.

You will need to read the words in the answers to judge whether something is a complete sentence. Ignore anything that doesn't appear in all four answer choices, like *and* in (D).

Believe it or not, even though the passage from the last question contained two complete sentences, there are other ways to punctuate these words besides making them two separate sentences. Here are some examples, all of which the PSAT considers correctly punctuated and equally acceptable:

> *English pilot Amy Johnson became famous for being the first woman to fly solo from England to* <u>*Australia; in*</u> *the following years, she set multiple records, including the solo record for a London-to-Cape Town flight.*

> *English pilot Amy Johnson became famous for being the first woman to fly solo from England to* <u>*Australia: in*</u> *the following years, she set multiple records, including the solo record for a London-to-Cape Town flight.*

> *English pilot Amy Johnson became famous for being the first woman to fly solo from England to* <u>*Australia, and in*</u> *the following years, she set multiple records, including the solo record for a London-to-Cape Town flight.*

Notice that none of those options appeared in the answer choices in question 3 since College Board decided to use a period and make two separate sentences. That's why your goal should be to eliminate the wrong answers to get the options down to the only one that can work, rather than look for a specific type of punctuation that may not actually appear in the answers.

College Board will NEVER give you two punctuation options that are equally acceptable.

In the examples above, you can see that these two "complete sentences" can actually form a single sentence when they are connected with a semicolon, a colon, or a comma + *and*. In this case, we'll call each part of the sentence an *independent clause*. This is just another way of saying "complete sentence" that makes it less confusing when the two independent clauses are put together into the same sentence. You don't need to know this term for the test, but we'll be using it in the rest of this chapter. It should be pretty easy to remember because "independent" means that the clause can make a complete sentence on its own.

Besides separating the independent clauses into two sentences, both ending with a period, as you saw in question 3, here are some other ways two independent clauses can be punctuated:

Two independent clauses can be joined with...	**Two independent clauses can NEVER be joined with...**
• A semicolon, anytime **;** • A comma plus an appropriate coordinating conjunction (FANBOYS) • A colon, if the second part of the sentence explains the first in some way **:**	• A comma without a coordinating conjunction • A coordinating conjunction without a comma • No punctuation to separate the independent clauses

As this chart implies, a semicolon can always be used to connect two independent clauses, at least when it comes to the PSAT. It functions just like a period, so both halves of the sentence must be independent clauses.

You can also use a comma + FANBOYS to link two independent clauses. FANBOYS stands for **F**or, **A**nd, **N**or, **B**ut, **O**r, **Y**et, **S**o. These are also known as coordinating conjunctions. Let's be clear, though—it's not just the comma or just the FANBOYS word. You must use both a comma and a FANBOYS word to connect two independent clauses. Of course, the specific word matters as well. For example, you can't use *but* if the two halves of the sentence don't contrast with each other. We don't expect this to be tested on the PSAT, however.

Lastly, a colon can be used when there are two independent clauses. A colon always signifies that the part after the colon will explain the first part of the sentence in some way. We'll talk more about colons later, but for now, understand that they represent another valid way to link two independent clauses.

It's just as important to understand how *not* to connect two independent clauses. Most questions with two independent clauses will have one of the options from the left column of the chart as the correct answer and all three of the options from the right column as the three wrong answers. So, if you can recognize these wrong answers, you'll be able to quickly eliminate them as soon as you realize you're dealing with two independent clauses. The rule is that two independent clauses can never be connected with a comma by itself, with a FANBOYS word by itself (remember, you need both!), or without any punctuation at all.

Now that we know the rules, let's see some examples of how this topic is tested.

Ted Ellis, a native of New Orleans and an artist, was examining his mother's home in the wake of Hurricane Katrina when he saw a man repairing the roof of his ______ he was so inspired by this image of hope amidst devastation that he began painting a series of pieces that became the collection *Katrina: The Hope, Healing, and Rebirth of New Orleans*.

4 Mark for Review

Which choice completes the text so that it conforms to the conventions of Standard English?

(A) house,

(B) house;

(C) house

(D) house and

Here's How to Crack It

First, identify from the question that this falls under Rules. In that case, look to see what's changing in the answer choices: punctuation, including a semicolon and a FANBOYS word (*and*). This is a good sign that the question may be testing how to connect two parts of a sentence, so you want to look for independent clauses. Read up until the punctuation (ignore *and* since it's only in one answer choice): *Ted Ellis, a native of New Orleans and an artist, was examining his mother's home in the wake of Hurricane Katrina when he saw a man repairing the roof of his house.* This could be a sentence, so it's an independent clause. The second part of the sentence says *he was so inspired by this image of hope amidst devastation that he began painting a series of pieces that became the collection Katrina: The Hope, Healing, and Rebirth of New Orleans*, which is also an independent clause.

Therefore, the sentence contains two independent clauses. Eliminate any answers that can't connect two independent clauses: (A)—just a comma, (C)—no punctuation at all, and (D)—just the FANBOYS word. Thus, the correct answer has to be (B). Remember, there are other plausible ways of connecting these ideas, but there will be only one answer that follows the rules! Eliminate the wrong ones and you'll be left with the right one.

In 1894, during the first wave of feminism in the Netherlands, Betsy Bakker-Nort joined the Dutch Association for Women's Suffrage and traveled extensively to advocate for women's rights. Women finally gained the right to vote in the 1922 general election. Bakker-Nort's work for women's rights was not ______ she became the first woman to represent the Free-thinking Democratic League political party in the House of Representatives, where she continued to advocate for women's rights around marriage and labor for twenty years.

5 Mark for Review

Which choice completes the text so that it conforms to the conventions of Standard English?

Ⓐ over however

Ⓑ over. However,

Ⓒ over, however,

Ⓓ over, however;

Here's How to Crack It

The question tells you that this is Rules, so look at the answers to see what's changing. In this case, punctuation changes before and after the word *however.* Furthermore, the answers contain a period and a semicolon, so look for independent clauses. Ignore the word *however* since it is not part of the main structure of either part of the sentence. The first part says *Bakker-Nort's work for women's rights was not over*, which is an independent clause. The second part says *she became the first woman to represent the Free-thinking Democratic League political party…*, which is also an independent clause. This means that (A) and (C) can be eliminated because not using punctuation or just using commas wouldn't be an acceptable way to link two independent clauses.

Note that both (B) and (D) separate the independent clauses properly, but there is a difference in where they put the transition word. You'll need to determine where the contrast is. Start by comparing the first half of the sentence to what comes before it. The preceding sentence states that *Women finally gained the right to vote in the 1922 general election*, which does contrast with the first half of this sentence, stating that *Bakker-Nort's work…was not over.* Essentially the text is saying that women got the right to vote, but her work wasn't finished. Since these ideas do contrast, *however* belongs with the first half of the sentence, so (B) doesn't work and the correct answer is (D).

If (B) were the correct answer, this would mean that there is a contrast between the two halves of the sentence with the blank. However, the idea that her work wasn't over and the fact that she continued her work by being a member of the House of Representatives agree with each other, further showing that (B) can't be right.

Fannie Lou Hamer was a leader in the civil rights movement, an activist for voting and women's rights, and a community organizer. In 1962, she attempted to register to vote in ______ she was denied that right due to failing a biased literacy test. This experience led to her increased involvement with the Student Nonviolent Coordinating Committee and years of working on behalf of Black families in Mississippi.

6 Mark for Review

Which choice completes the text so that it conforms to the conventions of Standard English?

Ⓐ Mississippi, but

Ⓑ Mississippi

Ⓒ Mississippi,

Ⓓ Mississippi but

Here's How to Crack It

After identifying from the question that this is Rules, look at the answers to see what's changing. The only punctuation change involves commas, but there are also options with the FANBOYS word *but*, which suggests that this question could involve how to connect ideas. Look for independent clauses. The first part of the sentence says *In 1962, she attempted to register to vote in Mississippi*, which is an independent clause. The second part says *she was denied that right due to failing a biased literacy test*, which is also an independent clause. Therefore, (B), (C), and (D) can all be eliminated because they aren't possible ways to connect independent clauses. See how quick and easy that can be?

Isaac Kerr is a kangaroo paleontologist whose recent work focuses on the discovery of three previously unknown types of ancient kangaroos found at Lake Callabonna in Australia. The three species belong to the *Protemnodon* genus of extinct giant ______ the largest, *Protemnodon viator*, stood eight feet tall and weighed 375 pounds.

7 Mark for Review

Which choice completes the text so that it conforms to the conventions of Standard English?

Ⓐ kangaroos

Ⓑ kangaroos:

Ⓒ kangaroos,

Ⓓ kangaroos while

Here's How to Crack It

You guessed it—confirm that this is Rules and look to see what's changing in the answers. In this case, the only answer that gives a big clue is (B). Colons relate to connecting ideas within a sentence, so that will let you know to look for independent clauses. The first part of the sentence says *The three species belong to the Protemnodon genus of extinct giant kangaroos*, which is an independent clause. The second part says *the largest, Protemnodon viator, stood eight feet tall and weighed 375 pounds*, which is also an independent clause. Therefore, the sentence once again contains two independent clauses, so you can eliminate (A), which has no punctuation, and (C), which has only a comma, because those aren't valid ways to connect two independent clauses. Although we haven't yet gone over words like *while*, you may be able to identify that this is a contrast word. Do the two ideas contrast? No, they agree, so eliminate (D). Thus, (B) is the correct answer.

Many students wouldn't have wanted to pick (B) in question 7. That's why it's so important to know the rules. College Board considers this question to be harder than questions 3, 4, 5, or 6. But if you know the rules from the chart on page 218, this question is equally easy for you, and it can be done quickly as well. Although you may not use many colons in your own writing, it's important to know that a colon is a valid way of connecting two independent clauses when the second one expands on the first, as it does here. As always, though, POE gets us there.

There is one more thing to know about colons. While a colon *can* connect two independent clauses, it doesn't have to. The second part of the sentence doesn't have to be an independent clause: it could be a list or a definition based on the first part of the sentence. Here's the rule:

> The part before the colon must be an independent clause. The part after the colon can be but doesn't have to be.

Let's see another example of a question that involves colons.

A recent study of fossilized dinosaur eggs in the Shanyang Basin in China provides more evidence that dinosaurs were in decline before the extinction event. The 1,000 fossilized eggs studied by researchers belonged to only three dinosaur ______ *Macroolithus yaotunensis, Elongatoolithus elongatus,* and *Stromatoolithus pinglingensis.*

8 Mark for Review

Which choice completes the text so that it conforms to the conventions of Standard English?

Ⓐ species.

Ⓑ species;

Ⓒ species:

Ⓓ species

Here's How to Crack It

This is Rules, based on the question, so look at the answer choices to see that punctuation is changing. Choice (A) puts a period after *species*, so check whether this could be two separate sentences. Right away you might realize that the second part is a list of the three species and thus lacks a verb, so it can't be its own sentence. Eliminate (A). Similarly, (B) uses a semicolon, which is another way of connecting independent clauses. Since the second part isn't an independent clause, (B) doesn't work either.

Next, notice that (C) uses a colon, so see whether that could work. The first part of the sentence then says *The 1,000 fossilized eggs studied by researchers belonged to only three dinosaur species.* That's an independent clause, so this meets one requirement for using a colon. Does the second part of the sentence elaborate on the first? Yes! It lists what the *three dinosaur species* are. Thus, this is an appropriate use of a colon, and the answer is (C).

As for (D), this option doesn't work because some separation is needed between the independent clause and the list. The colon is used to clarify that this list is stating what the three species are.

When you see periods, semicolons, and/or colons in the answers, that's your sign to look for independent clauses to see whether any of these options would work.

How to Spot Connecting Independent Clauses

The answers will contain one or more of the following: a period, a semicolon, a colon, a comma + FANBOYS.

One more related topic has to do with **dependent clauses**. A dependent clause is what it sounds like: a clause that can't stand on its own. It *depends* on an independent clause in order to form a complete sentence. Here are some examples of dependent clauses:

> *while we ate sandwiches*
>
> *because we ran out of peanut butter*
>
> *though I don't like onions*
>
> *when you eat a peanut butter and onion sandwich*

Notice that each of these begins with a transition word, which we've underlined. The rest of the clause, after the underlined word, would be an independent clause since it contains a subject and a verb. So, a dependent clause is like an independent clause but with one of these words tacked onto the front. Let's see how we can make a sentence with these:

> *While we ate sandwiches, we debated whether straws have one hole or two.*
>
> *We had to stop by the store because we ran out of peanut butter.*
>
> *I could eat peanut butter with a spoon, though I don't like onions.*
>
> *When you eat a peanut butter and onion sandwich, you won't be too happy about it.*

As you can see, it's possible for a dependent clause to go either before or after the independent clause. If the dependent clause comes first, it should be followed by a comma. If the dependent clause comes second, a comma should be used if there is a contrast (like the third example above). If there isn't a contrast and the dependent clause comes second in the sentence, there usually isn't a comma (like the second example above), but this is somewhat of a gray area, so we think College Board won't test this.

Shuggie Bain, Scottish-American writer Douglas Stuart's debut novel, tells the story of Shuggie, the youngest of three children. As the novel follows Shuggie as he ages from five to fifteen years ______ explores Shuggie's complicated relationship with his mother, Agnes.

9 Mark for Review

Which choice completes the text so that it conforms to the conventions of Standard English?

Ⓐ old, it

Ⓑ old it

Ⓒ old: it

Ⓓ old. It

Here's How to Crack It

The question tells us that this is Rules, so look to see what's changing in the answers. There is a colon and a period, so look for independent clauses. The first part of the sentence says *As the novel follows Shuggie as he ages from five to fifteen years old.* This isn't an independent clause—it couldn't be its own sentence. That eliminates (D) because (D) makes this its own sentence, as well as (C) because a colon requires the first part to be independent. If you recognize that this is a dependent clause since it begins with *As*, then you can identify that there should be a comma after the dependent clause. Thus, eliminate (B) and choose (A).

If both a semicolon and a period appear in the answers, neither could be correct because they perform the same function.

Dependent clauses aren't tested often, but they occasionally show up on the test. They'll look like the independent clause questions that we just went over, so keep an eye out for dependent clauses in those questions as well.

Before moving on, try the following exercise to review the rules you just learned.

Connecting Clauses Exercise

Instructions: Mark whether each combination is possible or not possible. Answers are on page 236.

	Possible	Not Possible
1. Independent Clause**;** Independent Clause	________	________
2. Independent Clause**,** Independent Clause	________	________
3. Independent Clause**.** Independent Clause	________	________
4. Independent Clause**:** Independent Clause	________	________
5. Independent Clause **and** Independent Clause	________	________
6. Independent Clause Independent Clause	________	________
7. Independent Clause**, but** Independent Clause	________	________
8. Independent Clause**:** List	________	________
9. Non-Independent Clause**:** List	________	________
10. Dependent Clause**,** Independent Clause	________	________
11. Independent Clause**,** Dependent Clause	________	________
12. Independent Clause**;** Dependent Clause	________	________

Next we'll take a look at a few more punctuation topics that could be tested.

EVEN MORE FUN-CTUATION

To illustrate this next rule, we're going to begin with a very basic sentence:

> *Rahul Viswanathan described the book as dull.*

There's nothing wrong with this sentence, but we might have some questions. Who's Rahul, and why should we care about his opinion? And what book are we talking about anyway? Let's add some additional information:

> *Literary critic Rahul Viswanathan described the book, a 500-page explanation of the machines used in early textile factories, as dull.*

Now we know a bit more. The phrase *Literary critic* is a title or label for Rahul (so we now know that his opinion might actually be worth listening to). Notice that we don't put any punctuation before or after his name. You can think of this title or label like an adjective. When you write "the purple sock," you don't put a comma between "purple" and "sock," so don't put any punctuation here either.

> Titles or labels before names don't get punctuation.

We also added a describing phrase set off by commas. This describing phrase tells us a little more about the book. We do need to set it off from the rest of the sentence with punctuation, though—either with two commas, as we did in the example, or with two dashes (two parentheses can also be used in some cases). We call these describing phrases **Extra Information**. They aren't absolutely essential to the meaning of the sentence, so we need to separate them with matching punctuation before and after. Extra Information won't always be in this form, but it's worth noting that describing phrases beginning with *a/an* or *the* are always Extra.

> Extra Information should be separated from the rest of the sentence with either commas or dashes, both before and after.

Obviously, if the Extra phrase comes at the beginning or end of the sentence, it will have only one comma or dash. Let's see an example of how this topic could appear on the test.

Jellyfish Lake, a marine lake located on the island of Eil Malk in Palau, sees millions of golden jellyfish migrate each day. The golden ______ sustain themselves through symbiotic algae and zooplankton.

10 Mark for Review

Which choice completes the text so that it conforms to the conventions of Standard English?

Ⓐ jellyfish, similar to the spotted jellyfish,

Ⓑ jellyfish, similar to the spotted jellyfish

Ⓒ jellyfish similar to the spotted jellyfish,

Ⓓ jellyfish similar to the spotted jellyfish

Here's How to Crack It

Note that this is a Rules question, so look to see what's changing in the answers. In this case, only commas change, and there is no FANBOYS word, so that's a good clue that it's not testing how to connect independent clauses. If only commas change and they appear before and/or after a word or phrase, then the question is likely testing describing phrases. Identify that the subject of the sentence is *The golden jellyfish* and the verb is *sustain*. The phrase in the answer choices, *similar to the spotted jellyfish*, is separating the subject and the verb, and it's a phrase describing *The golden jellyfish*. Right off the bat, you can cross off (B) and (C). You can never have a single punctuation mark between a subject and its verb (you can have two, but not just one). Furthermore, for the describing phrases rule, the phrase either gets two commas (if it's Extra Information) or no commas (if it's Specifying Information).

Next, you need to determine whether the phrase is Specifying or Extra. Try removing it from the sentence. Then the sentence reads *The golden jellyfish...sustain themselves through symbiotic algae and zooplankton*. Does the sentence still work without the phrase? Yes! The phrase isn't specifying anything—it's Extra and not essential to the meaning of the sentence. Thus, (D) can be eliminated and the answer is (A).

Sometimes describing phrases *are* essential to the sentence's meaning. We call these phrases **Specifying Information.** In fact, you saw this in the previous example:

> *Literary critic* *Rahul Viswanathan* *described the book, a 500-page explanation of the machines used in early textile factories, as dull.*

The critic's name is Specifying Information. If we remove his name from the sentence, it reads *Literary critic described the book…*, which doesn't work because *Literary critic* doesn't refer to a specific person and can't be the subject of the sentence. His name specifies which literary critic we're talking about, so that's why it's Specifying Information. Specifying Information isn't separated by any punctuation and is essential to the meaning of the sentence.

If you see this rule tested and you need to determine whether a phrase is Specifying or Extra, try removing the phrase from the sentence. If the sentence still has the same meaning and still works without the phrase, it's Extra and should be set off with punctuation. If the sentence changes its meaning or doesn't work without the phrase, it's Specifying and shouldn't be separated with punctuation.

How to Spot Extra/Specifying Information

One or more answers will contain a dash, or only commas will change in the answers, but they will move around a specific phrase.

Try the following exercise to practice determining whether a phrase is Specifying (and therefore shouldn't have punctuation) or Extra (and should have punctuation). But keep in mind that some questions won't require you to decide because there will be a clue in the sentence.

Describing Phrases Exercise

Instructions: Determine whether the bolded phrase is Specifying or Extra and write your answer on the line. If it's Extra, add punctuation. Answers are on page 236.

1. The ocean liner ***Queen Mary 2*** sails regularly between England and the United States.

   ____

2. A car crashed into the garage door **that had just been repainted**.

   ____

3. **Breaking the awkward silence** one of the students finally answered the teacher's question.

   ____

4. The setting of the TV show **a mysterious remote island** was criticized as clichéd.

   ____

5. Park guests **over seven feet tall** are not allowed on the roller coaster.

   ____

6. Morning light shone into the room **revealing the mess that had been left behind the previous night.**

   ____

The next punctuation topic is Lists. You are most likely familiar with how to write a basic list. Here's an example:

> *My favorite singers are Taylor Swift, Olivia Rodrigo, and SZA.*

Because this is a list of three or more items, the list is separated by commas. Additionally, this type of list needs to have the word *and* or sometimes the word *or* before the last item in the list. If this type of basic list is tested on the PSAT, just follow those simple rules. However, sometimes College Board might throw a more difficult type of list at you. Let's see an example:

> *My favorite singers are Taylor Swift, who was born in Pennsylvania; Olivia Rodrigo, who was born in California; and SZA, who was born in Missouri.*

In this case, we're adding an additional detail about each singer, and that detail is Extra Information, so it needs to be separated with a comma. However, if we were to just add those additional commas, the list could be confusing because it could look like the additional details are part of the list. Instead, we use semicolons to visually separate the list items from each other, and the commas are used within the list items. Remember, semicolons are normally used only when the sentence contains two independent clauses. This is a second, separate use of semicolons. Keep in mind that the semicolons here are being used as a visual separation—they don't perform a structural function as they normally do.

> College Board doesn't test whether there should be a comma before the *and* or *or* near the end of a list.

Let's see how the PSAT could test lists.

American author and MacArthur Fellow Jacqueline Woodson's body of work includes *Brown Girl Dreaming*, her memoir in _______ a picture book about a Black girl and a white girl becoming friends in a segregated town; and *Harbor Me*, a uniquely structured novel that examines the lives and fears of middle school students.

11 Mark for Review

Which choice completes the text so that it conforms to the conventions of Standard English?

Ⓐ verse; *The Other Side*

Ⓑ verse, *The Other Side*:

Ⓒ verse; *The Other Side*,

Ⓓ verse, *The Other Side*,

Here's How to Crack It

The question type tells us that this is Rules, so look for what's changing in the answers. In this case, the answers have commas, colons, and semicolons in different positions. We know that semicolons are usually used to link independent clauses, but if you look toward the end of the sentence, you'll notice that it already has a semicolon, and after the semicolon the phrase starts with the word *and*—it's not an independent clause. This means that the semicolon that's already in the sentence is being used in a different way—for a list.

In that case, you want to highlight a complete list item, such as the last one, which begins after the word *and*. Then, write an annotation of what appears in that item. In this case, there's a title, then a comma, then a description. So, write an annotation saying "title – comma – description." Use this to do Process of Elimination. The word *verse* is the last word of the description for the first book, and it's followed by the beginning of the second list item, which is the title of the second book. Thus, there should be a semicolon after *verse* since it's separating the end of the first item and the beginning of the second. That eliminates (B) and (D). Next, compare (A) and (C). There should be a comma after the title, according to the annotation, so that eliminates (A). The answer must be (C).

As you can see, questions involving complex lists can be tricky. Using this strategy should help a lot. It's worth noting that in some cases the list items may not be parallel. For instance, only one item could contain a comma (in which case the list items are still separated with semicolons). If that happens, you'll just have to use Process of Elimination and be careful.

How to Spot Lists

The answers will likely contain commas and semicolons. The original sentence will have the word *and* or *or* toward the end, especially after a comma or a semicolon.

We have one more punctuation topic to go over, and the good news is, in a way, you already know the rules for it. That's because this last topic is "no punctuation." Sometimes, College Board will give you the option to put punctuation in a place that simply has no reason for punctuation. In that case, pick the answer without punctuation. It's a perfectly legitimate option, but be sure to first go through the rules from this lesson to ensure that there isn't a reason to use punctuation.

If there isn't a reason to use punctuation, don't use any!

People ______ and people with a fear of negative feedback from those around them tend to display a more developed connection between their artistic potential and their actual artistic production.

12 Mark for Review

Which choice completes the text so that it conforms to the conventions of Standard English?

Ⓐ who identify, as creative types,

Ⓑ who identify as creative types,

Ⓒ who identify as creative types

Ⓓ who, identify, as creative types

Here's How to Crack It

Use the question to identify that we're dealing with Rules. That means you need to look at the answers to see what's changing. In this case, only commas change, and there's no FANBOYS word, so look for describing phrases or lists instead of independent clauses. Use Process of Elimination since the commas appear several different ways. Choice (A) sets off *as creative types* in commas, suggesting that it's Extra Information. Try removing it from the sentence: *People who identify and people with a fear....* This doesn't work because the phrase is specifying how these people identify. Eliminate (A). Next, (B) puts a comma before *and*. This could work in a list of three or more things, but there are only two types of people mentioned. A comma with *and* can link two independent clauses, but *People who identify as creative types* isn't an independent clause because there's no main verb. You might also think that it's setting off *and people with a fear of negative feedback from those around them* as an Extra phrase, but there's no comma after that phrase, so this doesn't work. Ultimately, (B) puts a single comma between the subject (the two types of people) and the main verb (*tend*), which is never allowed, so (B) must be eliminated.

Choice (C) doesn't have any punctuation, so skip to (D) to evaluate its use of commas. This is probably one of the more obviously wrong answers, as there is no reason to set *identify* off in commas; removing it from the sentence definitely doesn't work. Thus, the answer must be (C)—there is no reason to use any punctuation here.

Now that you have learned all of the punctuation rules, as you can see, the best way to get the answer is through Process of Elimination. It's often more useful to know what types of punctuation *can't* be used in certain ways than to know what type of punctuation is needed in a sentence, given that there are often multiple correct ones that can be used.

A NOTE ABOUT IDENTIFYING QUESTION TYPES

Throughout this lesson, we have given you some tips for how to identify when each punctuation topic is being tested. Knowing whether you should look for independent clauses, a list, or a describing phrase can make you more efficient at answering these questions. That being said, there are cases in which you may look at the answers and not be sure which punctuation topic is being tested. In that case, just read the sentence to determine what the topic is. The tips in this chapter should help a lot, but they won't cover every single way a question can be tested.

A NOTE ABOUT SCRATCH PAPER AND ONLINE TOOLS

You may have noticed that we aren't advising you to highlight or annotate for many punctuation questions. Remember, you can't highlight in the answer choices, so if you wanted to do something like highlight independent clauses, you wouldn't necessarily be able to do that because you would need one or more words from the answers. That being said, if you find any additional highlighting and annotating to be helpful, we certainly wouldn't discourage you from using those tools. Furthermore, while we aren't promoting the use of scratch paper on RW because we think the online tools are sufficient, if you prefer to use pencil and paper, go right ahead. Learning the rules is nonnegotiable, but do what works for you when it comes to the methods you use to apply them.

CONCLUSION

You have now learned all of the punctuation rules that could be tested on the PSAT (except for apostrophes, which will be covered in the next chapter). On the following drill, see if you can identify the rules being tested based on what you see in the answers. You won't be able to every time, but in many cases you should at least be able to come up with a good guess for what the punctuation topic is when you see punctuation changing in the answer choices. Remember, punctuation on the PSAT is completely rule-based. Make it your goal to master the rules from this chapter and use them every time. When you are eliminating answers or choosing a correct answer, use the rules to determine your reason for doing so.

Punctuation Drill

Suggested Time Limit: 12 minutes. Note that these questions have been placed in order of difficulty, as they will appear on the test, although on the test they will be interspersed with grammar questions. Check your answers in Part IV.

1 Mark for Review

Juan José Soler and his team noticed that the preen oil of spotless starlings changes color as the starlings age. If the chicks have a brighter color oil, ________ Soler and his team designed a study to find out.

Which choice completes the text so that it conforms to the conventions of Standard English?

Ⓐ they could use that color to attract their parents' attention?

Ⓑ could they use that color to attract their parents' attention?

Ⓒ could they use that color to attract their parents' attention.

Ⓓ they could use that color to attract their parents' attention.

2 Mark for Review

In Poland, water filtration plants use freshwater mussels hooked up to a computer ________ the water quality. The mussels close when the water quality is low, indicating a need for the engineers to stop the water flow to investigate for possible pollutants.

Which choice completes the text so that it conforms to the conventions of Standard English?

Ⓐ monitored

Ⓑ monitors

Ⓒ to monitor

Ⓓ is monitoring

3 Mark for Review

Cristina Ibarra's documentary *Las Marthas* follows two girls who are preparing to participate in the Colonial ________ over 100 years the ball in Laredo, Texas, has been part of the celebration of George Washington's birthday.

Which choice completes the text so that it conforms to the conventions of Standard English?

Ⓐ Ball for

Ⓑ Ball and for

Ⓒ Ball, for

Ⓓ Ball. For

4 Mark for Review

The Nobel Prize winners in most categories come from the elite research institutions in the United States and abroad. Not, however, the winners of the Nobel Prize in Literature. These winners share an average age (64) and geographical diversity with those in other ________ they have not attended the same schools—not by a long shot.

Which choice completes the text so that it conforms to the conventions of Standard English?

Ⓐ categories, though

Ⓑ categories; though

Ⓒ categories, though,

Ⓓ categories. Though

5 Mark for Review

A retronym is a phrase that is used to specify the original meaning of a word. For example, diapers were originally made of ________ diapers are mainly disposable now, so the phrase "cloth diaper" is used to describe diapers in their original form.

Which choice completes the text so that it conforms to the conventions of Standard English?

Ⓐ cloth, however;

Ⓑ cloth, however,

Ⓒ cloth however,

Ⓓ cloth; however,

6 Mark for Review

Nearly every player in a standard symphony orchestra reads music using the treble clef or the bass clef, except for ________ violist, who typically reads music using the alto clef.

Which choice completes the text so that it conforms to the conventions of Standard English?

Ⓐ one; the

Ⓑ one: the

Ⓒ one the

Ⓓ one. The

7 Mark for Review

The research of animal ________ has revealed that prairie dog communication may be considered a language. After decades of study, he has found that the prairie dogs' squeaks and yips can communicate specific information, mainly about other animals in the vicinity of the colony.

Which choice completes the text so that it conforms to the conventions of Standard English?

Ⓐ behaviorist, Con Slobodchikoff

Ⓑ behaviorist, Con Slobodchikoff,

Ⓒ behaviorist Con Slobodchikoff

Ⓓ behaviorist Con Slobodchikoff,

8 Mark for Review

Stephanie Kwolek, a Polish American chemist, is credited with inventing ________ while working at the DuPont chemical company during the 1950s and 1960s.

Which choice completes the text so that it conforms to the conventions of Standard English?

Ⓐ Kevlar—a high-strength material used in personal armor, sports equipment, and musical instruments—

Ⓑ Kevlar, a high-strength material used in: personal armor, sports equipment, and musical instruments,

Ⓒ Kevlar—a high-strength material—used in personal armor, sports equipment, and musical instruments,

Ⓓ Kevlar, a high-strength material used in personal armor, sports equipment, and musical instruments

9 Mark for Review

As World War II neared its end, the US government sought to avoid conflict with veterans. Indeed, for many, the goal was not idealistic: the ________ was seen as accelerating the economic collapse of the Great Depression.

Which choice completes the text so that it conforms to the conventions of Standard English?

Ⓐ tremendous unemployment, among World War I veterans,

Ⓑ tremendous unemployment among World War I veterans

Ⓒ tremendous, unemployment among, World War I veterans

Ⓓ tremendous unemployment among World War I veterans,

10 Mark for Review

Hanif Abdurraqib, an American essayist, poet, and cultural critic, published a poetry collection, *The Crown Ain't Worth ________ They Can't Kill Us Until They Kill Us*, in 2017; and a non-fiction book, *Go Ahead in the Rain: Notes on A Tribe Called Quest*, in 2019.

Which choice completes the text so that it conforms to the conventions of Standard English?

Ⓐ *Much*, in 2016, an essay collection,

Ⓑ *Much*, in 2016; an essay collection,

Ⓒ *Much*; in 2016, an essay collection,

Ⓓ *Much*; in 2016; an essay collection;

Answers to Connecting Clauses Exercise

1. **Possible**—a semicolon is used to connect two independent clauses.
2. **Not possible**—a comma by itself can never connect two independent clauses.
3. **Possible**—independent clauses can stand on their own as sentences.
4. **Possible**—a colon can link two independent clauses if the second one elaborates on the first.
5. **Not possible**—a FANBOYS word without a comma can't connect two independent clauses.
6. **Not possible**—it's never allowed to put two independent clauses together without any punctuation.
7. **Possible**—a comma + FANBOYS can connect two independent clauses.
8. **Possible**—a colon can be used when the first part is an independent clause and the second part is a list that expands on that clause.
9. **Not possible**—a colon can be used only when the first part is an independent clause. Plus, every sentence must have at least one independent clause.
10. **Possible**—when a dependent clause comes before an independent clause, a comma should be used.
11. **Possible**—when a dependent clause comes after an independent clause, a comma is often used.
12. **Not possible**—a semicolon links two independent clauses, so it can't be used with a dependent clause.

Answers to Describing Phrases Exercise

1. **Specifying**—without the phrase, the sentence says *The ocean liner sails regularly between England and the United States*, but there isn't just one ocean liner in existence. The name specifies which ocean liner the sentence is talking about.
2. **Specifying**—while the sentence could still work without the phrase in this case, phrases with *that* are always Specifying and never get punctuation. The phrase specifies which garage door the car crashed into.
3. **Extra**—the sentence works without this phrase, and this phrase should be followed by a comma to separate this introductory information from the rest of the sentence so it doesn't sound as if it says "the awkward silence one."
4. **Extra**—this phrase should be separated by commas, dashes, or parentheses on both sides. Phrases starting with *a/an* or *the* are always Extra.
5. **Specifying**—without the phrase, the sentence says *Park guests are not allowed on the roller coaster*, which changes the meaning of the sentence by suggesting that all park guests aren't allowed on, while it means to specify which type of guest isn't allowed on the coaster.
6. **Extra**—the sentence still works without this phrase, and without any punctuation, the phrase looks like it's describing the room. The room isn't what revealed the mess—the light is. Separating this phrase with a comma shows that the phrase describes the whole first part, not just the word right before *revealing*.

Summary

- Punctuation on the PSAT involves a limited range of topics and is based around specific rules that you can learn and use on the test.
- When verb form is tested, find and highlight the subject. Look for a main verb. If there isn't one, the blank must provide the main verb.
- For question versus statement, highlight a clue in the passage that tells you whether the sentence with the blank should be a question (asking for information) or a statement (giving information).
- Two independent clauses can each end with a period and be separate sentences. They can also be in the same sentence if they are connected with a semicolon, a colon, or a comma + FANBOYS.
- FANBOYS stands for For, And, Nor, But, Or, Yet, So.
- Two independent clauses can never be connected with just a comma, just a FANBOYS word, or no punctuation at all.
- For colons, the second part of the sentence doesn't have to be an independent clause, but the first part does.
- A dependent clause has a subject and a verb but starts with a transition word that makes the clause not a complete sentence. Dependent clauses are usually connected to independent clauses with a comma.
- Specifying Information is essential to the meaning of the sentence and isn't separated with punctuation. Extra Information can be removed without changing the meaning of the sentence, and it's set off with commas, dashes, or parentheses.
- A basic list uses commas between the list items. If one or more list items contains a comma within it, then the list items will be separated with semicolons instead. If the items are in a matching pattern, highlight a complete item and annotate what it includes.
- All punctuation on the PSAT is rule-based. Don't pick an answer with punctuation if you don't have a rule-based reason to use that punctuation. The option without punctuation is sometimes correct.

Chapter 12
Rules Questions: Grammar

Besides punctuation, Rules questions also test grammar. In this chapter, you'll learn to recognize and correctly answer all of the types of grammar questions that could appear on the PSAT.

THE WORDS CHANGE, BUT THE SONG REMAINS THE SAME

Remember that the grammar questions and punctuation questions will be mixed up together in the Rules portion, organized from easy to hard.

In the last chapter, we looked at what to do when the PSAT is testing punctuation. In this chapter, we're going to look at what to do when the PSAT is testing the parts of speech—mainly verbs, nouns, and pronouns.

Our basic strategy, however, has remained the same. As we saw in the previous chapter, when faced with a PSAT Rules question, you should always

> Check what's changing in the answer choices and use POE.

As you will notice, throughout this chapter, we talk a lot about certain parts of speech, but we don't really use a lot of grammar terms. That's because we find that on the PSAT grammar questions, there is really one main idea to keep in mind: **consistency**. Correct answers must be consistent with the rest of the sentence and the text as a whole.

Let's look at some examples of how consistency relates to the grammar topics you can expect to see on the test.

VERBS

The circumstances of musician Jimmie Rodgers's birth _______ obscure, but legend has it that he was born in Meridian, Mississippi, in 1897.

1 Mark for Review

Which choice completes the text so that it conforms to the conventions of Standard English?

Ⓐ is

Ⓑ are

Ⓒ has been

Ⓓ was

Here's How to Crack It

First, identify the question type. Since the question mentions Standard English, this is a Rules question. Next, look at the answers to determine the topic. The answers contain verbs, so this question is testing consistency with verbs.

When you see verbs changing in the answer choices, the first thing to check is the subject of the sentence. Look for and highlight the one-word subject—who or what is doing the action. What is *obscure*? The *circumstances* of his birth. Highlight the word *circumstances*, as that is the subject of the sentence.

Because *circumstances* is plural, the verb must also be plural, in order to be consistent. Therefore, (A), (C), and (D) have to be eliminated because they are all singular. So, (B) must be the correct answer.

Thus, when you see verbs changing in the answer choices, check the subject first. Subjects and verbs need to be consistent with each other. You might assume that the question is testing tense when you see verbs, but as with this question, typically only one answer will agree with the subject when the question is testing subject-verb agreement. Therefore, this strategy saves you a lot of time since you don't have to consider tense on this type of question.

Of course, sometimes tense will be tested. Let's see an example.

In 1947, veterans on the G. I. Bill accounted for 49 percent of college admissions. By 1956, of the 16 million World War II veterans, nearly half had used the G.I. Bill for some kind of training. Therefore, by the early 1960s, college training ______ drastically.

2 Mark for Review

Which choice completes the text so that it conforms to the conventions of Standard English?

Ⓐ had changed

Ⓑ changes

Ⓒ will change

Ⓓ has changed

Here's How to Crack It

Identify the question type first. The question reveals that this falls under the Rules category, so look at the answers to see what's changing. Verbs are changing in the answers, so this is a grammar question testing consistency of verbs. The subject is *training*, so highlight that word. All of the answers work with that subject, so this question is testing tense, not subject-verb agreement.

Look for clues in the text to determine whether past, present, or future tense is needed. This sentence is describing what happened by *the early 1960s*, so some form of past tense should be used. Eliminate (B), which is present tense, and (C), which is future tense. The verb in the previous sentence is *had used*, so keep (A) because it is consistent with that verb. Choice (D), *has changed*, is actually a form of present tense, as it would suggest something that has changed going up until right now. However, the text is referring to something that had changed by *the early 1960s*, not going up to the present day. So, eliminate (D) and choose (A), which is the correct answer.

As you can see, verbs are all about consistency.

When you see verbs changing in the answer choices, make sure those verbs are:

- CONSISTENT with their subjects
- CONSISTENT with other verbs in the sentence and surrounding sentences

Let's try one more on a related topic.

It was ultimately not medical science that saved the day during the 1793 Yellow Fever Epidemic in Philadelphia. Doctors tried various treatment approaches, but they were stalled by their inability to figure out both how the disease originated and how it ______ It therefore seemed a godsend when the frost came in November and the number of deaths tapered off. Medical historians now know that the disease was spread by mosquitoes, but this was not verified until nearly a century after the disease had come and gone.

3 Mark for Review

Which choice completes the text so that it conforms to the conventions of Standard English?

Ⓐ was spreading.

Ⓑ spread.

Ⓒ had been spread.

Ⓓ spreads.

Here's How to Crack It

Identify the category, which is Rules. Then, look to the answers to see what's changing: the form of the verbs. This lets you know that the question is testing consistency of verbs. Look at the rest of the context to determine what this verb needs to be consistent with.

In this case, the verb is part of a list of two things that doctors had an *inability to figure out.* The first thing is *how the disease originated,* so this verb should be in the same tense. Highlight *originated.* The verb *originated* is in past tense, so eliminate (D) because it's in present tense. Next, eliminate any other past tense verbs that aren't in the correct form. Choices (A) and (C) are not in the same type of past tense as *originated* (the simple past), so they must be eliminated. Choice (B), *spread,* is consistent with *originated.* Therefore, (B) is the correct answer.

Consistency applies across the grammar questions. Let's see another topic in which the idea of Consistency might help us.

PRONOUNS

What are pronouns? Pronouns are words that stand in for nouns. They make writing less repetitive, because they prevent us from having to use the same nouns over and over. On the PSAT, you'll be tested on which pronoun agrees with the noun (or sometimes another pronoun) that it is referring back to. Let's see an example.

A traditional form of Japanese theater, Nōgaku involves masks, costumes, and props. Although its popularity peaked in the fourteenth and fifteenth centuries, ______ actually originated in the eighth century.

4 Mark for Review

Which choice completes the text so that it conforms to the conventions of Standard English?

(A) they

(B) one

(C) those

(D) it

Here's How to Crack It

Start by identifying the question type: Rules. Next, look at the answers to determine what topic is being tested. Since pronouns are changing in the answer choices, the question is testing consistency with pronouns.

Since a pronoun refers back to a noun or another pronoun, determine who or what *actually originated in the eighth century.* The sentence is talking about *its popularity,* referring to that of Nōgaku. Highlight the existing pronoun, *its.* Since the blank refers to the same thing, the pronoun that is needed is *it.* Eliminate (A), (B), and (C). The correct answer is (D).

That one may have seemed pretty easy. Let's take a look at a tougher way pronouns can be tested.

The fact that winners of the Nobel Prize in Literature have come from diverse educational backgrounds should remind us that creativity can strike anywhere. One of the Nobel committee's great merits is that ______ been willing to identify great talent outside of the typical places.

5 Mark for Review

Which choice completes the text so that it conforms to the conventions of Standard English?

(A) they have

(B) we have

(C) it has

(D) you have

Here's How to Crack It

Begin by identifying the category of question. Since it mentions Standard English, this is a Rules question. Next, look to see what's changing in the answers: pronouns. Therefore, this question is testing consistency of pronouns.

Identify who or what the pronoun refers back to. The sentence discusses one of the *merits* of *the Nobel committee*. Therefore, the blank refers to the *committee* being willing to do something. Highlight that word and be careful! The word *committee* is singular, which you can note with an annotation. Therefore, a singular pronoun is needed. Eliminate (A) and (B) because *they* and *we* are plural. Keep (C) because *it* is singular. While *you* can be singular, it isn't appropriate to describe the *committee* as *you* because this isn't directed toward the committee. Eliminate (D). The correct answer is (C).

As you can see, you may not be able to use your ear for all of these questions. We may think of a committee as a "they," since it is composed of multiple people, but the word itself is singular and thus must be referred to with a singular pronoun. Think about it this way—you would say "the committee is," not "the committee are." So, that shows that the noun is singular. You can also think about the fact that "committees" is plural, so "committee" must be singular.

Another, less common way pronouns can be tested is with apostrophes. Nouns with apostrophes can also be tested. Let's take a look at what rules you'll need to know in order to get these questions right.

YOUR GOING TO BE TESTED ON APOSTROPHE'S (AND INTERNET SPELLING IS A TERRIBLE GUIDE!)

As with commas, apostrophes have only a very limited set of applications. Apostrophes are a little trickier, though, because you can't really hear them in speech, so people misuse them all the time in their writing. Think about the header of this section. The apostrophes are wrong there. Here's the correct way of punctuating it: *You're going to be tested on apostrophes.* Can you hear the difference? Neither can we.

Therefore, as with all punctuation,

> If you can't cite a reason to use an apostrophe, *don't use one.*
>
> On the PSAT, there are only two reasons to use an apostrophe:
>
> - possessive nouns (NOT pronouns)
> - contractions

Here are some examples.

While many humans and animals have influenced the history of the United States and Canadian border, one _______ has been as significant as it is overlooked. Although Michigan eventually became a powerhouse in the later part of the Industrial Revolution, it was initially attractive to settlers who wanted to cash in on the fur trade, and beaver pelts were some of the hottest commodities.

6 Mark for Review

Which choice completes the text so that it conforms to the conventions of Standard English?

(A) animals influence, the beavers

(B) animal influence, the beavers,

(C) animals' influence, the beaver's,

(D) animal's influence, the beaver's,

Here's How to Crack It

Start by identifying the category, which is Rules, and then the specific topic, punctuation. Even more specific than that, apostrophes are changing in the answers. The apostrophes are on nouns, so consider whether those nouns should be possessive.

Does something belong to the *animal* or *animals*? Yes, it's the *influence* of the *animal(s)*, so eliminate (A) because it lacks an apostrophe in *animals*. Next, consider whether something belongs to the *beaver* or *beavers*. The sentence is referring also to the *influence* of the *beaver(s)*, so there does need to be an apostrophe there. Eliminate (B) because it says *beavers* with no apostrophe.

Next, compare (C) and (D). The difference is that (C) means *animals*, plural, while (D) is *animal*, singular. The part before the blank says *one*, so the word should be singular. Eliminate (C) and choose (D).

Let's see another example of how the PSAT tests apostrophes.

In the absence of light, people report seeing a dark gray background color that has been called *Eigengrau*, which means "intrinsic gray." Scientists have suggested that different people have ______ own perceptions of Eigengrau, however.

7 Mark for Review

Which choice completes the text so that it conforms to the conventions of Standard English?

Ⓐ they're

Ⓑ their

Ⓒ it's

Ⓓ its

Here's How to Crack It

Start by identifying the category as Rules. Then, look at the answers to determine that the topic is punctuation, and specifically apostrophes. Here, the apostrophes appear on pronouns, which would signify a contraction—in this case "they are" or "it is." The other options are possessive pronouns, which have no apostrophes.

Start by determining whether a form of "they" or a form of "it" is needed. In this case, the perceptions belong to the *people*, which is a plural noun. Eliminate (C) and (D) because any form of *it* is singular. Next, do you want to say, "they are own perceptions?" No, so eliminate (A). Since this is the perception of the people, a possessive pronoun is needed, and *their* is the correct spelling. The correct answer, therefore, is (B).

Phew! These apostrophes can get a little tricky, so let's try a few more. On these (as on many parts of the PSAT), you'll find that using your ear, sounding things out, doesn't really help all that much.

Circle the option that works. The big question is this: apostrophes or no apostrophes?

1. *Salims/Salim's* teacher said *hes/he's* allowed to miss next *Tuesdays/Tuesday's* exam.
2. *Its/It's* really not going to hurt my feelings if you don't want to go to *they're/their* party with me.
3. Whatever the *justification's/justifications* for *your/you're* attitude, *there/they're* is no reason to be so obnoxious about it.
4. *Were/We're* going to get back to you as soon as your *application's/applications* are processed.
5. *They're/Their they're/their* nachos, but they *wont/won't* share any unless *its/it's* absolutely necessary or we share *ours/our's*.

Answers are on page 249.

MODIFIERS

Let's take a look at a type of question that students often have difficulty with.

A recent study helps explain why animals continue to live after they are no longer able to reproduce. After watching over 750 hours of video and observing the behavior of pods of whales, _______ The older female whales were the most likely to lead younger whales to salmon feeding grounds, particularly in the periods where the usually plentiful salmon were sparse. This knowledge is particularly useful for whale pods because the abundance of salmon is typically what determines whale life cycles, both reproduction and mortality.

8 Mark for Review

Which choice completes the text so that it conforms to the conventions of Standard English?

Ⓐ whale grandmothers were observed to have teaching behaviors by the scientists.

Ⓑ scientists observed that many of the teaching behaviors were performed by whale grandmothers.

Ⓒ whale grandmothers were the most likely to exhibit teaching behaviors.

Ⓓ teaching behaviors were observed from whale grandmothers that were shown to scientists.

Here's How to Crack It

Look at the question to determine the category: Rules. Next, look at the answers to see what's changing. You'll probably notice right away that the beginnings of the answer choices (which you could call the subjects) are changing. This is a big clue that the question could be testing modifiers. Look for a describing phrase, which often comes at the beginning of a sentence, followed by a comma.

Did you spot it? We have the describing phrase, known as a modifier, at the beginning: *After watching over 750 hours of video and observing the behavior of pods of whales.* Highlight that phrase. Whom is that describing? Take a look at the subjects in the answers and use POE.

It can't be the *whale grandmothers* who were watching the videos, so eliminate (A) and (C). The *scientists* could have watched the videos, so keep (B). As for (D), it doesn't make sense that *teaching behaviors* could have watched videos, so eliminate that answer. Therefore, the answer must be (B). You don't even need to read the rest of the answer choice.

For modifier questions, the toughest part is identifying the error. Once you've spotted it, all you need to do is eliminate answers that don't match with what the phrase is intended to describe.

Let's have a look at some more of these modifiers. Rewrite each sentence below so the modifier and what it is referring to are *consistent.*

1. Given all its logical twists and turns, many people struggle with philosophy.
2. Readers in different times tend to gravitate toward different philosophers and places.
3. Once cracked, you can find incredible guidance and solace in philosophy.
4. I first learned about Pragmatism from a professor in college at 20.
5. Boring and uninteresting, Jack didn't care much for the work of William James.

Answers are on page 249.

Consistency

- When verbs are changing in the answer choices, make sure those verbs are consistent with their subjects and with other verbs.
- When pronouns are changing in the answer choices, make sure those pronouns are consistent with the nouns or other pronouns that they refer back to.
- When the subjects are changing in the answer choices, look for a modifier. The modifier must come as close as possible to the person or thing it's describing.

As we have seen in this chapter, when the PSAT is testing grammar (i.e., anytime the words are changing in the answer choices), make sure that those words are **consistent** with the rest of the sentence and text.

Answers to Questions on Page 247:

1. Salim's, he's, Tuesday's
2. It's, their
3. justifications, your, there
4. We're, applications
5. They're, their, won't, it's, ours

Answers to Questions on Page 248:

1. Many people struggle with philosophy given all its logical twists and turns.
2. Readers in different times and places tend to gravitate toward different philosophers.
3. Once cracked, philosophy can provide incredible guidance and solace.
4. I first learned about Pragmatism from a college professor when I was 20 years old.
5. Jack didn't care much for the work of William James, which he found boring and uninteresting.

Note: these are just examples of ways to fix the modifier errors. It's fine if you rewrote the sentence differently, as long as your version makes the intended meaning clear.

Grammar Drill

Suggested Time Limit: 14 minutes. Note that these questions have been placed in order of difficulty, as they will appear on the test, although on the test they will be interspersed with punctuation questions. Check your answers in Part IV.

1 Mark for Review

Co-commissioned by the Metropolitan Opera and the Los Angeles Opera, *Eurydice* had its world premiere in 2020. Its co-writers, composer Matthew Aucoin and librettist Sarah Ruhl, ________ multiple significant awards.

Which choice completes the text so that it conforms to the conventions of Standard English?

Ⓐ has won

Ⓑ was winning

Ⓒ has been winning

Ⓓ have won

2 Mark for Review

Ugandan writer Doreen Baingana earned a law degree from Makerere University before she studied creative writing and ________ her MFA in that subject. Afterward, she became the writer-in-residence at the Jiménez-Porter Writers House and published quite a few short stories, novels, and works of non-fiction.

Which choice completes the text so that it conforms to the conventions of Standard English?

Ⓐ obtained

Ⓑ obtaining

Ⓒ to obtain

Ⓓ having obtained

3 Mark for Review

Hikaye is a Turkish narrative genre, performed by a singer-poet, which is primarily prose but interspersed with poems that the artist will sing. A hikaye centers around the performer's romantic exploits, and ________ the poems to express the performer's emotions.

Which choice completes the text so that it conforms to the conventions of Standard English?

Ⓐ they use

Ⓑ it uses

Ⓒ one uses

Ⓓ you use

4 Mark for Review

The Servicemen's Readjustment Act was signed into law in 1944. More than twenty years earlier, after the conclusion of World War I, the veterans of the bloodiest war on record were more or less forgotten by the US government. Many of them were given little more than a $60 allowance and a train ticket home. While ________ was some talk of military bonuses, those bonuses were not easily obtained.

Which choice completes the text so that it conforms to the conventions of Standard English?

Ⓐ they're

Ⓑ it

Ⓒ their

Ⓓ there

5 Mark for Review

Trịnh Xuân Thuận, a Vietnamese American astrophysicist, has focused his research on compact blue dwarf galaxies, the chemical composition of the universe, and the evolution of galaxies. He is a professor at the University of Virginia and ________ astronomy there since 1976.

Which choice completes the text so that it conforms to the conventions of Standard English?

Ⓐ has taught

Ⓑ had taught

Ⓒ taught

Ⓓ teaches

6 Mark for Review

The nutrient-poor soil and extremely salty water have posed a challenge to the possibility that one day people might work or even live on Mars. A study led by then-high school student Pooja Kasiviswanathan has demonstrated that alfalfa, a plant that is often used for hay to feed cattle, could grow well in Mars's soil and even ________ vegetables such as radishes, lettuces, and turnips to help them survive.

Which choice completes the text so that it conforms to the conventions of Standard English?

Ⓐ fertilizing

Ⓑ fertilize

Ⓒ fertilized

Ⓓ fertilizes

7 Mark for Review

Maintaining the public face of a company has created a new job: Chief Listening Officer (CLO). While a Social Media Manager might be in charge of a ________ on social media websites, a Chief Listening Officer is on the other side. A CLO scours review sites as well as social media to make sure that a company's public image is under control.

Which choice completes the text so that it conforms to the conventions of Standard English?

Ⓐ companies posts

Ⓑ companies' posts

Ⓒ company's posts

Ⓓ company's post's

8 Mark for Review

Navajo Nation member Annie Dodge Wauneka became the second woman elected to the Tribal Council, after she saw the poverty and lack of medical care around the reservation and vowed to do what she could to address these problems. Wauneka worked to eradicate tuberculosis within her nation and authored a dictionary that translated English medical terms into the Navajo language. Her interest in public health ________ in part inspired by her experience as a child caring for other students during the 1918 influenza epidemic.

Which choice completes the text so that it conforms to the conventions of Standard English?

Ⓐ is

Ⓑ will be

Ⓒ was

Ⓓ has been

9 Mark for Review

The long, stiff plumes known as flight feathers primarily assist in generating thrust and lift, enabling birds to fly. In addition, some birds use their flight feathers to present ________ as potential mates as part of a courtship ritual.

Which choice completes the text so that it conforms to the conventions of Standard English?

Ⓐ them

Ⓑ it

Ⓒ itself

Ⓓ themselves

10 Mark for Review

Beaver skins were once popular in stylish clothes of the 1700s, particularly hats. Although silks had become more popular than animal skins in the early 1800s, by that time the beaver had been hunted to the point that ________ nearly eliminated from the region altogether.

Which choice completes the text so that it conforms to the conventions of Standard English?

Ⓐ it was

Ⓑ this was

Ⓒ they were

Ⓓ one was

11 Mark for Review

Work in economics, medicine, or the sciences ________ a vibrant, collaborative atmosphere, with the best minds in the field working together toward solutions.

Which choice completes the text so that it conforms to the conventions of Standard English?

Ⓐ requires

Ⓑ require

Ⓒ do require

Ⓓ have required

12 Mark for Review

A global team of 49 researchers wanted to determine the evolution of the donkey. Where and when was it domesticated? Analyzing the genomes of existing populations and fossil DNA, ________ came from Africa about 7,000 years ago and quickly spread into Europe and Asia.

Which choice completes the text so that it conforms to the conventions of Standard English?

Ⓐ donkeys

Ⓑ the research demonstrated that donkeys

Ⓒ the scientists determined that donkeys

Ⓓ the genetic information revealed that donkeys

Summary

- Grammar questions are all about consistency.
- When verbs are changing in the answer choices, highlight the subject and annotate whether it's singular or plural. Eliminate answers that don't agree.
- If the question isn't testing verb form or subject-verb agreement, it's testing tense. Look for clues about whether past, present, or future tense is needed and make an annotation; then use POE.
- When pronouns are changing in the answer choices, highlight the word the pronoun refers back to and annotate whether it's singular or plural; then use POE.
- When apostrophes with nouns are changing in the answers, consider whether each noun possesses anything and use POE.
- When the order of the words or the subjects change in the answers, the question is testing modifiers.
- Look for and highlight a modifying phrase; then eliminate answers that start with something the modifying phrase cannot describe.

Chapter 13 Rhetoric Questions

After all of the Rules questions, you'll see the last category of RW questions, which we call Rhetoric. You'll see Transitions questions, from easy to hard, and then Rhetorical Synthesis questions, from easy to hard. In this lesson, you'll learn how to approach both types of questions that fall into this category.

The last portion of each Reading and Writing module will include two types of questions: Transitions and Rhetorical Synthesis, in that order. We call these Rhetoric questions because they relate to the purpose or quality of the writing. These questions will not test your understanding of the rule-based punctuation and grammar topics. In fact, for these questions, all four answer choices will be or will produce complete sentences that are grammatically correct. Instead, you will need to consider the *content* of the writing and how the answers fulfill certain meaning-related or rhetorical goals. Let's take a look at the first type of question in this category.

A SMOOTH TRANSITION

Transition questions will be easy to spot. Let's look at an example.

Pragmatism may be rooted in the German philosophers Immanuel Kant and Georg Friedrich Hegel, but it has found more popularity in Anglo-American communities than in German or French ones. ______ the term "Pragmatism" was first used by Americans—philosophers William James and Charles Sanders Peirce.

1 Mark for Review

Which choice completes the text with the most logical transition?

Ⓐ However,

Ⓑ In fact,

Ⓒ Likewise,

Ⓓ Therefore,

Like the question above, all transition questions will ask you the same thing: *Which choice completes the text with the most logical transition?* As soon as you see that question, you'll know you're dealing with a transition question. Let's take a look at the basic approach for transition questions and apply it to this one.

Transition Questions Basic Approach

1. Read the text and highlight any ideas that support or contradict each other.
2. Make an annotation indicating whether the ideas surrounding the blank agree or disagree, or whether they represent a time change.
3. Eliminate any answers that go the wrong direction. Then, use POE on any remaining options.

Here's How to Crack It

Highlight anything that is the same in both sentences. The first sentence mentions that Pragmatism *has found more popularity in Anglo-American communities than in German or French ones.* The second sentence repeats a word, *American,* so highlight the phrase in that sentence: *the term "Pragmatism" was first used by Americans.* These two ideas agree, so make an annotation that says "agree." Then, eliminate any opposite-direction transitions, since we need a same-direction transition here. Eliminate (A).

Now, compare the remaining answers. *In fact* can be used to support the previous idea, so keep (B). *Likewise* is used to compare two different things that have something in common. In this case, there isn't a separate thing being compared to the previous sentence, so eliminate (C). Eliminate (D) because *therefore* comes before a conclusion, and this sentence doesn't draw a conclusion from previously stated evidence. Therefore, (see what we did there?) the correct answer is (B).

Let's try another example.

Camille Henrot's installation *The Pale Fox* is a collection of objects that at first glance appears to be random. For example, a sculpture of Buddha props up a copy of a modern magazine. There is an organization, ______ that is revealed as the audience spends time in the space.

2 Mark for Review

Which choice completes the text with the most logical transition?

Ⓐ likewise,

Ⓑ specifically,

Ⓒ though,

Ⓓ rather,

Here's How to Crack It

Start by highlighting ideas that relate to each other. The first sentence says that the collection *at first glance appears to be random.* The third sentence says *There is an organization.* These ideas disagree, so write that in an annotation. Next, eliminate any same-direction transitions: (A) and (B). Compare (C) and (D). *Though* works well, so keep (C). While *rather* is an opposite-direction transition, it means something more like "instead," so it doesn't fit correctly in this sentence. The correct answer is (C).

Let's try one more.

Sandra Welner, a medical professor, wanted to make medical care more accessible for patients with disabilities. ______ she invented an examination table that could be lowered for easier access to and from a wheelchair and called it the Universally Accessible Examination Table.

3 Mark for Review

Which choice completes the text with the most logical transition?

Ⓐ To that end,

Ⓑ Additionally,

Ⓒ Not surprisingly,

Ⓓ Rather,

Here's How to Crack It

First, highlight any phrases that draw a connection. The first sentence states that Welner *wanted to make medical care more accessible for patients with disabilities.* The second sentence says she *invented* the *Universally Accessible Examination Table.* These ideas agree, so make an annotation saying "agree" and eliminate any opposite-direction transitions. In this case, (D) can be eliminated.

Next, consider the link between the highlighted phrases. The first sentence states Welner's goal, while the second sentence states what she did. Use POE. Choice (A) is a good match because an *end* is a goal, and this transition essentially means "with that goal in mind." Keep (A). Eliminate (B) because *additionally* is used to add on to the previous point, but this would suggest that the sentences are two separate things, when instead the second sentence explains what she did in pursuit of her goal. Eliminate (C) because there is no evidence that her invention was *not surprising*; one could be surprised or not that she was able to accomplish her goal. The correct answer is (A).

READY, SET... SYNTHESIZE

Now, let's move on to the other type of question in the Rhetoric category, the one that will appear at the very end of each verbal module: Rhetorical Synthesis. The word *synthesize* means "put together," so these questions are asking you to put together two or more bullet points in order to fulfill a certain rhetorical goal. Let's see an example.

While researching a topic, a student has taken the following notes:

- Robin Wall Kimmerer is a writer, educator, and scientist working in the field of biocultural restoration.
- She is also a member of the Citizen Potawatomi Nation.
- Her first book, *Gathering Moss*, published in 2003, contained a series of essays about mosses that mixed scientific writing and personal reflection together.
- In her second book, *Braiding Sweetgrass*, Kimmerer's writing weaves together different types of knowledge: the Western scientific tradition, Traditional Ecological Knowledge, and lessons that plants themselves can teach.

4 Mark for Review

The student wants to emphasize a similarity between the two books Kimmerer wrote. Which choice most effectively uses relevant information from the notes to accomplish this goal?

(A) *Gathering Moss* is about moss, and *Braiding Sweetgrass* is about lessons from plants.

(B) *Gathering Moss* and *Braiding Sweetgrass* both include scientific writing.

(C) *Gathering Moss* combines science and personal reflection, while *Braiding Sweetgrass* combines three different types of knowledge.

(D) Published in 2003, *Gathering Moss* was written by Robin Wall Kimmerer, who has worked in the field of biocultural restoration.

Here's How to Crack It

First, identify the type of question. Rhetorical Synthesis questions are extremely easy to identify: they are the only question type to use bullet points instead of text in the form of a paragraph. Then, just as you did with all Reading and Writing questions, determine what the question is asking. Rhetorical Synthesis questions always contain the same question: *Which choice most effectively uses relevant information from the notes to accomplish this goal?* The key part to notice is *this goal.* You MUST read the sentence before the question to determine what the goal is.

Here, the stated goal is to *emphasize a similarity between the two books.* Now, your impulse might be to read the bullet points and identify a similarity. However, we've found that you probably don't need to do this. Instead, highlight the task or tasks of the question and then go straight to the answer choices and eliminate anything that doesn't completely fulfill the task. In this case, highlight *similarity* and *two books*. Any answer that does not mention *two books* or draw a comparison can be eliminated. Let's go to POE.

Choice (A) mentions the two books, and *moss* and *plants* are somewhat similar, so keep (A). Choice (B) mentions the two books and uses the word *both* to state a similarity. Keep (B). Choice (C) mentions both books, but the word *while* and the types of content in the books indicate a contrast, not a *similarity*. Eliminate (C). Choice (D) mentions only one of the books, so eliminate it because the question asked about *two books*.

Finally, compare (A) and (B). Choice (A) does not clearly state that this is a similarity between the two; it merely presents information about the content of both books. Eliminate (A). On the other hand, (B) clearly states that there is a similarity between the two books: both contain *scientific writing*. Therefore, the correct answer is (B).

Of course, we can also confirm that this information is in the bullet points: the third bullet point states that *Gathering Moss* contains *scientific writing*, and the fourth bullet point mentions that the *Western scientific tradition* is part of the book's content, which clearly indicates that *scientific writing* is a component of the book.

Here's the basic approach for these questions:

Rhetorical Synthesis Basic Approach

1. Read the question and highlight each goal that is mentioned.
2. Eliminate any answer choice that does not completely fulfill the goal or goals.
3. Read the bullet points to confirm the answer if needed.

If the question asks for a generalization or a summary, or if more than one answer could possibly fulfill the goal, be sure to read the bullets.

It's unlikely that you will see an answer choice that is inconsistent with what is stated in the bullet points, though it does happen once in a while. That is, you won't often see the kind of wrong answers that you will see on the Reading questions—ones that could be arrived at through misreading or making assumptions. Instead, most wrong answers will simply not completely fulfill the goal or goals stated in the question. This is why you can save yourself some time by not reading the bullet points first; you generally won't need to prove that the information is supported. However, be sure to carefully read all four answers, since it's possible that two answers may fulfill the goal but one of them isn't consistent with the information in the notes, in which case you'll have to look at the notes to confirm. It's also worth remembering that these questions do NOT test you on punctuation, grammar, style, being concise, or any other Rules topics. Focus on the content of the sentence in each answer choice and how well it does or does not fulfill the goal or goals.

Let's try another one.

While researching a topic, a student has taken the following notes:

- Large animals known as megafauna have substantial impacts on their environments.
- However, many native megafauna are extinct, so their effects on the ecosystem are unknown.
- Bison are a type of megafauna that used to be dominant in the United States.
- Reintroducing bison to their native environments doubled plant diversity.
- The presence of cattle, a domesticated megafauna, in the same environments produced a significantly lower increase in plant diversity.

5 Mark for Review

The student wants to present one impact that native megafauna have on their environments. Which choice most effectively uses relevant information from the notes to accomplish this goal?

(A) Bison, a type of native megafauna, doubled plant diversity in their native environments.

(B) Bison and cattle are two types of megafauna that live in the United States.

(C) Although many native megafauna are extinct, bison were reintroduced to their native environment.

(D) Native and domesticated megafauna can have impacts on their environments.

Here's How to Crack It

Once you've established that you're dealing with a Rhetorical Synthesis question, highlight the goal or goals in the question. Here, you should highlight *one impact that native megafauna have on their environments*. The correct answer should relate to *native megafauna* and a specific environmental *impact*. Move on to POE.

Choice (A) mentions *a type of native megafauna* and describes an environmental *impact* (*doubled plant diversity*), so keep (A). Choice (B) mentions *megafauna*, but there's no environmental impact. Eliminate (B). Choice (C) mentions *native megafauna* but does not say the *impact* of reintroducing bison; eliminate it. Choice (D) mentions *impacts* but does not *present one impact*; it's not specific about what that impact might be. Eliminate (D). The correct answer is (A).

Let's try one more.

While researching a topic, a student has taken the following notes:

- R. Murray Schafer was a Canadian composer, writer, and environmentalist.
- Schafer created many soundscapes during his career.
- Soundscapes are the sounds that arise from a location.
- Soundscapes include animal sounds, natural sounds such as weather, and human-created sounds.
- Schafer wrote *The Tuning of the World* and *The Soundscape*, which are books on soundscapes.

6 Mark for Review

The student wants to introduce soundscapes to an audience familiar with Schafer. Which choice most effectively uses relevant information from the notes to accomplish this goal?

Ⓐ Canadian composer, writer, and environmentalist R. Murray Schafer created and wrote about the collections of animal sounds, natural sounds such as weather, and human-created sounds known as soundscapes.

Ⓑ *The Tuning of the World* and *The Soundscape* were written by R. Murray Schafer, a Canadian composer, writer, and environmentalist.

Ⓒ R. Murray Schafer, a Canadian composer, writer, and environmentalist, created many soundscapes during his career.

Ⓓ Schafer wrote about and created soundscapes, which are sounds that arise from a location, including animal sounds, natural sounds such as weather, and human-created sounds.

Here's How to Crack It

Identify that this is a Rhetorical Synthesis question, and then highlight the goal or goals in the question. In this case, you should highlight *introduce soundscapes* and *audience familiar with Schafer*. It's common for Rhetorical Synthesis questions to specify whether the audience is familiar or unfamiliar with something. If the audience is unfamiliar, the answer should explain who or what the person or thing is; however, if the audience is familiar, the answer should not include an explanation. Let's go to POE.

Eliminate (A) because it describes Schafer—the audience is *familiar* with Schafer, so he should not be introduced. Eliminate (B) and (C) for the same reason. No description of Schafer is needed if the audience is familiar. Check (D). This answer does not describe Schafer, but it does *introduce soundscapes* by defining what they are. Therefore, this answer fulfills all parts of the question. The correct answer is (D).

CONCLUSION

While the term *Rhetoric* might have sounded scary initially, we hope you're feeling more confident now that you know how to approach the two types of questions in this category. Remember, you choose the order of questions—practice Rhetoric questions on the following drill and use the results to help determine when to attempt them.

Take a Breather
You've made it through the entire Reading and Writing section! Next up is Math, so feel free to take a break before diving in. Grab a snack, relax with a book, go for a walk—anything that will help you refresh before reviewing more content. Remember that study breaks can make you more productive, so don't deprive yourself of some needed relaxation time.

Rhetoric Questions Drill

Suggested Time Limit: 12 minutes. Note that these questions have been placed in order of difficulty for each of the two question types, as they will appear on the test. Check your answers in Part IV.

1 Mark for Review

The popular board game *Monopoly* rewards players who compete with each other, act aggressively, and acquire as much money as possible. ________ the original version of *Monopoly*, *The Landlord's Game*, had a much different objective. *The Landlord's Game*, created by Lizzie Magie in 1903, was designed to demonstrate the negative effects of monopolies and included a second set of rules, called Prosperity, in which players were encouraged to cooperate with each other.

Which choice completes the text with the most logical transition?

(A) Likewise,

(B) Regardless,

(C) By contrast,

(D) In effect,

2 Mark for Review

The play *The 7 Stages of Grieving*, written by Wesley Enoch and Deborah Mailman, was directed by Enoch and performed by Mailman for the first time in 1995. The title of the play references seven phases of Aboriginal history in Australia as well as the stages of grieving as developed by Elisabeth Kübler-Ross. Since then, the play has gone on to become a classic of Australian theater and has been updated with each production. ________ the current version added an epilogue that introduces seven actions of healing for the audience to engage in.

Which choice completes the text with the most logical transition?

(A) For instance,

(B) Moreover,

(C) Similarly,

(D) Subsequently,

3 Mark for Review

Researchers interested in how nanoplastics can move up the food chain planted lettuce in soil contaminated with nanoplastics. They fed some of the lettuce to black soldier fly larvae and then fed some of the larvae to an insectivorous fish. When the researchers examined the larvae, they found nanoplastics in the mouths and guts of the larvae. ________ when they examined the fish, they also found nanoplastics in different parts of the fish.

Which choice completes the text with the most logical transition?

- Ⓐ To that end,
- Ⓑ Specifically,
- Ⓒ Similarly,
- Ⓓ Nevertheless,

4 Mark for Review

Dugongs, a species of marine mammal similar to manatees, may be extinct in China. Dugongs rely on seagrass, a type of habitat that is particularly vulnerable to pollution. Although conservation efforts have been enacted, it may be too late. ________ hope is not lost, as there are populations of dugongs in other parts of the world.

Which choice completes the text with the most logical transition?

- Ⓐ Therefore,
- Ⓑ Still,
- Ⓒ Instead,
- Ⓓ For example,

5 Mark for Review

Located in Millennium Park in Chicago, Illinois, *Cloud Gate* is a sculpture by Anish Kapoor. The sculpture is constructed of stainless steel plates and has a 12-foot-high arch in the middle, making it look like a large, silver bean. ________ the sculpture has been nicknamed "The Bean," a name that Kapoor initially disliked.

Which choice completes the text with the most logical transition?

Ⓐ Though,

Ⓑ Indeed,

Ⓒ In conclusion,

Ⓓ Nonetheless,

6 Mark for Review

While researching a topic, a student has taken the following notes:

- Researchers in the Ugandan rainforest have found that wild chimpanzees drum on tree roots to communicate.
- Each chimpanzee has a distinct drumming pattern that scientists could use to identify and locate the chimp.
- The drumming could help explain why scientists observed chimpanzees greeting each other when meeting but not "saying goodbye" when they parted.
- The chimpanzees may not "say goodbye" because they can still communicate with each other over long distances.

The student wants to present a possible explanation for chimpanzees not "saying goodbye." Which choice most effectively uses relevant information from the notes to accomplish this goal?

Ⓐ Chimpanzees have distinct drumming patterns that they use to greet each other when meeting, but they do not "say goodbye."

Ⓑ Chimpanzees may not "say goodbye" because they can use their distinct drumming patterns to communicate with each other over long distances.

Ⓒ Scientists can use the distinct drumming patterns to identify and locate chimps even if the chimpanzees may not "say goodbye."

Ⓓ Chimpanzees drum on tree roots to communicate their identity and location.

7 Mark for Review

While researching a topic, a student has taken the following notes:

- Louise Erdrich is an American novelist and an enrolled member of the Turtle Mountain Band of Chippewa.
- She frequently writes stories about the contemporary Native American experience and is recognized as one of the writers in the second wave of the Native American Renaissance.
- Her early novels, including *Love Medicine* and *Four Souls*, tell the story of the same three families who live in and around a reservation in North Dakota.
- Her novel *The Round House*, published in 2012, won the National Book Award for Fiction.
- Another one of her novels, *The Night Watchman*, won her the Pulitzer Prize for Fiction in 2021.

The student wants to highlight the various literary accolades that Erdrich has received. Which choice most effectively uses relevant information from the notes to accomplish this goal?

Ⓐ Erdrich received a Pulitzer Prize for her novel *The Night Watchman.*

Ⓑ Erdrich has written many stories about the contemporary Native American experience, including *Love Medicine*, *Four Souls*, *The Round House*, and *The Night Watchman.*

Ⓒ Erdrich received a National Book Award for *The Round House* and a Pulitzer Prize for *The Night Watchman.*

Ⓓ Erdrich is part of the second wave of the Native American Renaissance and has won the National Book Award.

8 Mark for Review

While researching a topic, a student has taken the following notes:

- Crème brûlée is a custard-based dessert.
- Typically, crème brûlée is made with heavy cream, eggs, sugar, and vanilla.
- These ingredients are mixed together, baked, and then cooled.
- A defining feature of crème brûlée is a caramelized sugar surface.
- Caramelization is the use of heat to change the chemical structure of sugar.
- Caramelized sugar is darker in color and nuttier in flavor than white sugar.

The student wants to introduce crème brûlée to an audience familiar with caramelization. Which choice most effectively uses relevant information from the notes to accomplish this goal?

Ⓐ Caramelization, which is the use of heat to change the chemical structure of sugar, is a defining feature of the custard-based dessert crème brûlée.

Ⓑ Crème brûlée is a custard-based dessert featuring a caramelized sugar surface.

Ⓒ Crème brûlée is made with heavy cream, eggs, sugar, and vanilla, ingredients that are mixed together, baked, and then cooled.

Ⓓ Sugar that is darker in color and nuttier in flavor can be made by caramelization, a process that uses heat to change the chemical structure of sugar.

9 Mark for Review

While researching a topic, a student has taken the following notes:

- Many place names in the US have French origins.
- Some city names are French words or phrases, such as Detroit and Baton Rouge.
- Some city names are translations of French phrases, such as Little Rock and Green Bay.
- Some state names are French words, such as Louisiana and Vermont.
- Some state names are French interpretations of Native American words, such as Illinois and Wisconsin.

The student wants to introduce the main point to an audience unfamiliar with US city and state names. Which choice most effectively uses relevant information from the notes to accomplish this goal?

(A) Many place names in the US, from Little Rock to Wisconsin, have French origins.

(B) From cities such as Detroit and Green Bay to states such as Illinois and Wisconsin, many places in the US have names with French origins.

(C) Many cities in the US, such as Baton Rouge and Little Rock, have names with French origins.

(D) Many states in the US, such as Louisiana and Wisconsin, have names with French origins.

10 Mark for Review

While researching a topic, a student has taken the following notes:

- Green spaces in urban areas can help support biodiversity.
- However, the maintenance and mowing of lawns in urban areas can negatively affect arthropods (animals such as insects and spiders).
- Researchers analyzed a group of studies that looked at the impact of reduced mowing on arthropods.
- The analysis showed that reduced mowing was connected to an increase in the abundance of arthropods.
- The analysis also showed that reduced mowing was connected to an increase in the taxa richness (or diversity) of arthropods.

The student wants to emphasize the two results of the study. Which choice most effectively uses relevant information from the notes to accomplish this goal?

(A) Green spaces in urban areas can help support biodiversity, but mowing lawns can negatively affect arthropods.

(B) Reduced mowing was connected to an increase in taxa richness.

(C) Researchers analyzed studies about arthropod abundance and taxa richness.

(D) Reduced mowing was connected to an increase in abundance and diversity of arthropods.

Summary

- Rhetoric questions relate to the meaning of the passage and the answer choice. They don't test punctuation or grammar.
- Transition questions are organized from easy to hard.
- Highlight ideas in the passage that relate to each other, specifically near the blank and in the surrounding sentences (usually the sentence just before the one with the blank).
- Annotate whether those ideas agree, disagree, or involve a time change.
- Eliminate based on the direction of the answers and then use POE for anything that remains.
- Rhetorical Synthesis questions are organized from easy to hard.
- Don't read the bullet points unless you need to.
- Highlight the goal(s) stated in the question and go straight to POE.
- Eliminate any answer that doesn't completely fulfill the goal(s). Don't consider the construction of the answer choice—all that matters is whether it fulfills the goal(s).

Chapter 14
Math Basics

The PSAT tests some mathematical concepts that you probably learned in middle school or even earlier. If you're a little rusty, this chapter is for you. Read on for a review of the math basics you'll need to know.

HOW TO CONQUER PSAT MATH

So, what do you need to do? There are four important steps:

1. **Know the basic content.** To perform well, you do need to know the basics of arithmetic and algebra. We'll cover what you need to know in this chapter.
2. **Learn some PSAT-specific problem-solving skills.** Since these basic concepts appear in ways you're probably not used to from math class, you need to prepare yourself with a set of test-specific problem-solving skills designed to help you answer PSAT Math questions. We'll cover the most important ones in the next chapter.
3. **Use the built-in calculator.** Even for basic algebra, the calculator that is built into the testing app can be a big help.
4. **Have a sound overall testing strategy.** This means knowing what to do with difficult questions and having a plan to pace yourself to get the maximum number of correct answers in the time allotted. Be sure to read carefully the material in Chapter 3 to make sure you're using the strategy that will get you the greatest number of correct answers in the time you have.

KNOW THE STRUCTURE

The Math section of the Digital PSAT is split into two modules. Each module contains 22 questions, of which 16 or 17 are multiple-choice questions and the rest are student-produced response questions (SPR), or fill-ins, meaning that you fill in your own answer instead of choosing from four answers. Questions on the second module are, on average, easier or harder based on performance on the first module. Each module has two "pre-test" questions that do not count toward your score, but they are not identified, so treat every question as if it counts.

The Math section is further broken down by question type and content area, as follows.

By Question Type	
70% Problem Solving	15–16 questions per module
30% Word Problems	6–7 questions per module

By Content Area	
35% Algebra	7–8 questions per module
32.5% Advanced Math	7–8 questions per module
20% Problem-Solving & Data Analysis	4–5 questions per module
12.5% Geometry and Trigonometry	2–3 questions per module

(PERSONAL) ORDER OF DIFFICULTY

The questions on each module in the Math section of the Digital PSAT have a loose order of difficulty. You may notice the questions becoming harder as the section progresses. More important than any question format, math content, or official order of difficulty is your own Personal Order of Difficulty. Though the last questions of each module are likely to be the hardest, use your own personal strengths and weaknesses to decide which questions to do and which to skip.

USING THE ONLINE TOOLS AND SCRATCH PAPER

Online Tools

Several of the on-screen features of the PSAT will be useful on the Math section.

- Mark for review tool to mark questions to come back to later
- Built-in calculator, which can be accessed at any time
- Reference sheet with common math formulas, which can be accessed at any time
- The annotate tool is NOT available on the Math section, so you will not be able to underline or highlight parts of the question.

Scratch Paper

The proctor at the test center should hand out three sheets of scratch paper, although this might vary from place to place, and you can use your own pen or pencil. Plan ahead about how to use the scratch paper in combination with what's on the screen.

Use the Tools Effectively!

Online Tools

- Eliminate wrong answers
- Work steps on the calculator
- Look up geometry information

Scratch Paper

- Rewrite key parts of the question
- Write out every calculation
- Redraw geometric figures and label them
- Rewrite answer choices as needed

USING YOUR CALCULATOR

The Calculator Guide in your Online Student Tools will show you how to get the most out of the built-in calculator. Refer to it as you work through the Math chapters in this book.

You are allowed to use a calculator on all Math questions on the PSAT, and you should definitely do so. You can use any graphing, scientific, or plain old four-function calculator, **provided that it doesn't have a keyboard**.

There is a built-in Desmos calculator that you can click open on the screen at any time. To practice with it, download the Bluebook app from College Board's website, where you can do untimed practice to get used to the built-in calculator.

Not sure whether your calculator is acceptable? Check College Board's website for a list of approved calculators.

The built-in calculator will make many questions, especially ones dealing with functions and graphs, easier than they would be by hand. Even if you have a high-powered graphing calculator that you're accustomed to using, learn everything you can about the built-in calculator and practice with it. It has many useful features and a larger display area, so you may find yourself using a handheld calculator for basic operations and the built-in calculator for everything else.

Drill 1

DEFINITIONS

One of the reasons that good math students often don't get the credit they deserve on the PSAT is that they've forgotten one or more of these definitions—or they read too fast and skip over these "little" words. Be sure you know them cold and watch out for them!

Match the words with their definitions, and then come up with some examples. Answers can be found in Part IV.

1. integers
2. positive numbers
3. negative numbers
4. even numbers
5. odd numbers
6. factors
7. multiples
8. prime numbers
9. distinct
10. digit

a. numbers that a certain number can be divided by, leaving no remainder
Examples: ____________________

b. integers that cannot be divided evenly by 2
Examples: ____________________

c. numbers that have no fractional or decimal parts
Examples: ____________________

d. numbers that are greater than zero
Examples: ____________________

e. having a different value
Examples: ____________________

f. integers that can be divided by 2 evenly (with no remainder)
Examples: ____________________

g. numbers that are less than zero
Examples: ____________________

h. numbers that have exactly two distinct factors: themselves and 1
Examples: ____________________

i. numbers that can be divided by a certain number with no remainder
Examples: ____________________

j. a numerical symbol from 0 through 9 that fills a place in a number
Examples: ____________________

Drill 2

Match the words with their definitions, and then come up with some examples. Answers can be found in Part IV.

11. consecutive numbers
12. divisible
13. remainder
14. sum
15. product
16. difference
17. quotient
18. absolute value

k. the result of addition
Examples: ____________________

l. a whole number left over after division
Examples: ____________________

m. the result of subtraction
Examples:____________________

n. can be divided with no remainder
Examples: ____________________

o. a number's distance from zero; always a positive value or 0
Examples: ____________________

p. numbers in sequential order
Examples: ____________________

q. the result of division
Examples: ____________________

r. the result of multiplication
Examples: ____________________

EQUATIONS AND INEQUALITIES

An **equation** is a statement that contains an equals sign, such as $3x + 5 = 17$.

To solve an equation, you must get the variable x alone on one side of the equals sign and everything else on the other side.

The first step is to put all of the variables on one side of the equation and all of the numbers on the other side, using addition and subtraction. As long as you perform the same operation on both sides of the equals sign, you aren't changing the value of the variable.

Then you can divide both sides of the equation by the *coefficient,* which is the number in front of the variable. If that number is a fraction, you can multiply everything by its reciprocal.

For example,

$$\begin{array}{rcrl} 3x+5 & = & 17 & \\ -5 & & -5 & \text{Subtract 5 from each side.} \\ \hline 3x & = & 12 & \\ \div 3 & & \div 3 & \text{Divide each side by 3.} \\ \hline x & = & 4 & \end{array}$$

Always remember this rule of equations:

> Whatever you do to one side of the equation, you must also do to the other side.

The built-in calculator can also solve many algebra questions. Be aware that it works only with x and y, so sometimes it will be necessary to change the letter that represents the variable. Simply enter the equation into an entry field either by typing in the field in the upper left or by clicking the icon for the keypad in the lower left and using the keypad.

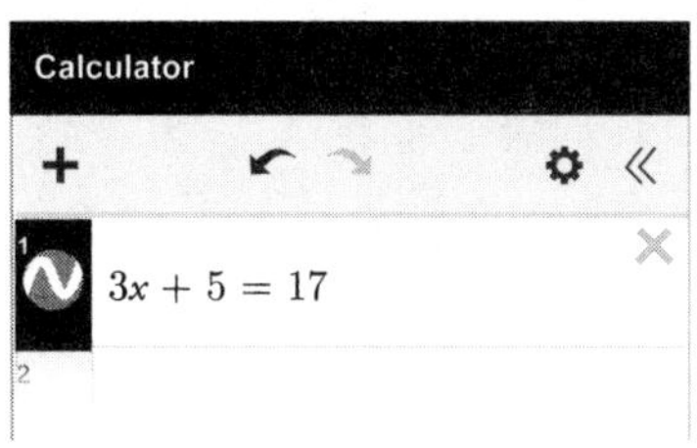

Look in the graphing area to the right, and scroll and zoom as needed to see where the vertical line crosses the x-axis; that is the solution to the equation. Click on the gray dot to see that the coordinates are (4, 0), which means $x = 4$.

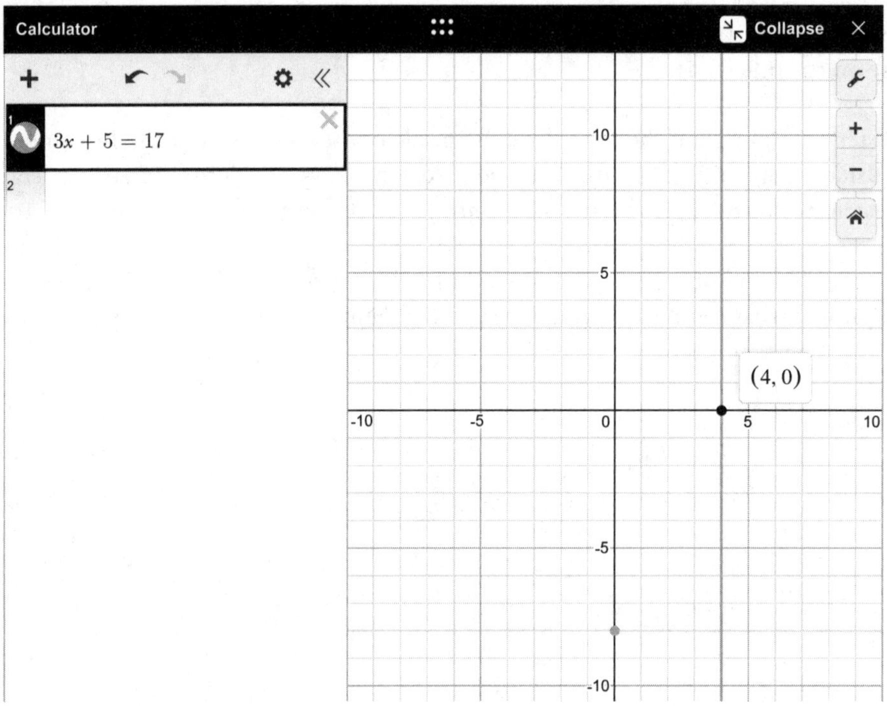

The example above was fairly simple. The PSAT may test this idea with more complex equations and formulas, though. Just keep trying to isolate the variable in question by undoing the operations that have been done to it. Use the built-in calculator as much as possible, but there will be questions for which it doesn't work. Here's an example.

1 Mark for Review

$$K = \frac{L + 3M}{22}$$

The given equation relates the distinct positive numbers K, L, and M. Which equation correctly expresses L in terms of K and M?

Ⓐ $L = 22K - 3M$

Ⓑ $L = 22K + 3M$

Ⓒ $L = (K - 3M)(22)$

Ⓓ $L = (K + 3M)(22)$

Here's How to Crack It

The question asks for an equation in terms of a specific variable. The built-in calculator won't work this time because there are three variables. All of the answer choices have L by itself, so use algebra to isolate L. Multiply both sides of the equation by 22 to get $22K = L + 3M$. Subtract $3M$ from both sides of the equation to get $22K - 3M = L$. Reverse the two sides of the equation to get $L = 22K - 3M$. The correct answer is (A).

An **inequality** is any statement with one of these signs:

$<$	(less than)
$>$	(greater than)
$\leq$	(less than or equal to)
$\geq$	(greater than or equal to)

You can solve inequalities in the same way you solve equations, with one exception: whenever you multiply or divide an inequality by a negative value, you must change the direction of the sign: for example, $>$ becomes $<$, and $\leq$ becomes $\geq$.

For example,

$$\begin{array}{lcl} 3x+5 & > & 17 \\ \quad -5 & & -5 \\ \hline 3x & > & 12 \\ \div 3 & & \div 3 \\ \hline x & > & 4 \end{array}$$

Subtract 5 from each side.

Divide each side by 3.

In this case, we didn't multiply or divide by a negative value, so the direction of the sign didn't change. However, if we were to divide by a negative value, we would need to change the direction of the sign.

$$\begin{array}{lcl} -4x+3 & > & 15 \\ \quad -3 & & -3 \\ \hline -4x & > & 12 \\ \div -4 & & \div -4 \\ \hline x & < & -3 \end{array}$$

Subtract 3 from each side.

Divide each side by −4.

When graphing an inequality in the built-in calculator, the solutions are represented by a shaded region. A dashed line represents < or > while a solid line represents ≤ or ≥.

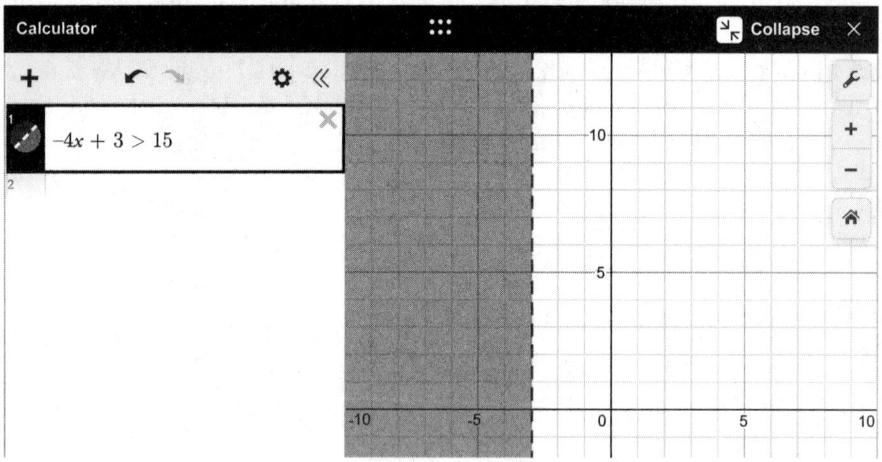

2 Mark for Review

$$4(7x - 6) < 32$$

Which inequality is equivalent to the given inequality?

(A) $7x - 24 < 36$

(B) $7x - 24 < 32$

(C) $7x - 6 < 28$

(D) $7x - 6 < 8$

Here's How to Crack It

The question asks for an equivalent form of an inequality. The expression $7x - 6$ is in the question and two of the answer choices, so isolate that expression. Divide both sides of the inequality in the question by 4 to get $7x - 6 < 8$. This matches (D), so (D) is the correct answer.

To answer this question with the built-in calculator, first enter the inequality from the question into an entry field. Next, enter each answer choice inequality one at a time in another entry field, and eliminate ones that do not show the same graph. Only the inequality in (D) results in the same graph, so (D) is correct.

Using either of these methods, the correct answer is (D).

PSAT Smoke and Mirrors
When you're asked to solve an equation involving an absolute value, it is very likely that the correct answer will be the negative result. Why? Because the test-writers know that you are less likely to think about the negative result!

ABSOLUTE VALUES

Absolute value is a measure of the distance between a number and 0. Since distances are always positive, the absolute value of a number is also always positive. The absolute value of a number is written as $|x|$.

When solving for the value of a variable inside the absolute value bars, it is important to remember that variable could be either positive or negative. For example, if $|x| = 2$, then $x = 2$ or $x = -2$ since both 2 and -2 are a distance of 2 from 0.

Here's an example.

3 Mark for Review

$$|x + 3| = 6$$

The value of one solution to the given equation is 3. What is the value of the other solution?

Here's How to Crack It

The question asks for a solution to an equation with an absolute value. Since the value inside the absolute value bars can be positive or negative, set that value equal to 6 and -6 to find both solutions. When $x + 3 = 6$, $x = 3$. This solution was already given, so try the other one. When $x + 3 = -6$, $x = -9$, which is correct.

To avoid potential confusion about signs or the definition of absolute value, use the built-in calculator. Enter the equation as written into an entry field, and then scroll and zoom as needed to see that the solutions are represented by vertical lines at -9 and 3. The solution of 3 was given in the question, so the answer is -9.

Using either of these methods, the correct answer is -9.

SYSTEMS OF EQUATIONS

A system of equations contains two or more equations with the same variable or variables. In school, you learned how to substitute and solve or to stack the equations and then add or subtract to make one variable disappear. On the PSAT, you can almost always answer these questions with the built-in calculator.

4 Mark for Review

$$x + 2y = 12$$
$$2x + y = 9$$

The solution to the given system of equations is (x, y). What is the value of $x + y$?

Ⓐ 3

Ⓑ 7

Ⓒ $\frac{21}{2}$

Ⓓ 21

Here's How to Crack It

The question asks for the value of an expression given a system of equations. Enter each equation into its own entry field in the built-in calculator, and then scroll and zoom as needed to see the point of intersection, which is represented by a gray dot. Click on the dot to see that the coordinates are (2, 5). The question asks for the value of $x + y$, which is $2 + 5 = 7$. The correct answer is (B).

WRITING YOUR OWN EQUATIONS

For the most part, we've been looking at solving equations given to you in questions. Sometimes, however, you will be required to create one of your own. The PSAT Math section tests not only your math skills but also, and possibly even more important to your score improvement, your reading skills. On word problems, it is imperative that you read the questions carefully and translate the words in the question into math.

ENGLISH	MATH EQUIVALENTS
is, are, were, did, does, costs	=
what (or any unknown value)	*any variable* (x, y, b)
more, sum	+
less, difference	–
of, times, product	× (*multiply*)
ratio, quotient, out of	÷ (*divide*)

Sometimes you'll be asked to take a word problem and create equations or inequalities from that information. Usually, they will not ask you to solve these equations/inequalities, so if you are able to locate and translate the information in the question, you have a good shot at getting the correct answer. Always start with the most straightforward piece of information. What is the most straightforward piece of information? Well, that's up to you to decide. Consider the following question.

5 Mark for Review

Elom joined a gym that charges a monthly fee of \$35. A one-time enrollment fee of \$40 is charged when he joins. Which of the following represents the total amount of fees that Elom has paid to his gym after m months, in dollars?

Ⓐ $35m + 40$

Ⓑ $35 + 40m$

Ⓒ $35m - 40$

Ⓓ $(35 + 40)m$

Here's How to Crack It

The question asks for an expression that represents a situation. Read the question carefully and translate the information. The question states that there is a monthly fee of $35 and that the variable m represents the number of months. Therefore, the correct answer should include $35m$, so you can eliminate (B). The one-time enrollment fee of $40 has nothing to do with the number of months, so the 40 should be by itself. Eliminate (D), which multiplies the 40 by m. The fee should be added, not subtracted, so the correct answer is (A).

Use Your Tools!

We showed you in the introduction how important it is to utilize the online tools and scratch paper frequently and effectively. This question is a great example. You worked the question one piece at a time and eliminated answers as you went. Use your scratch paper to rewrite parts of the question and translate them into math, and then use the Answer Eliminator tool to eliminate answers that don't match that piece. Take a look below at an example of what your screen and scratch paper should look like at the end of a question like this.

6 Mark for Review

Elom joined a gym that charges a monthly fee of $35. A one-time enrollment fee of $40 is charged when he joins. Which of the following represents the total amount of fees that Elom has paid to his gym after m months, in dollars?

A) $35m + 40$ ~~(A)~~

~~B) $35 + 40m$~~ Undo

~~C) $35m - 40$~~ Undo

~~D) $(35 + 40)m$~~ Undo

6)

monthly fee of $35
35m

$40 NOT monthly
so not × m

There might be similar questions with inequalities instead of equations. Follow the same approach: translate one piece at a time and eliminate incorrect answer choices after each step. Here's an example.

7 Mark for Review

Students in a chemistry class recorded the densities of several common fluids at room temperature. The minimum density recorded was 0.85 grams per cubic centimeter and the maximum density recorded was 1.26 grams per cubic centimeter. Which inequality is true for all values of d, where d represents a density, in grams per cubic centimeter, recorded by the students?

(A) $0 \leq d \leq 0.85$

(B) $0.85 \leq d \leq 1.26$

(C) $d \leq 0.41$

(D) $d \leq 1.26$

Here's How to Crack It

The question asks for an inequality that models a specific situation. Translate the information one piece at a time, and eliminate incorrect answers after each piece. One piece of information says that *d represents a density...recorded by the students*. The question provides a minimum value and a maximum value for d, so the correct inequality must include d and two other values. Eliminate (C) and (D) because they include d and only one other value. Another piece of information says that *the maximum density recorded was 1.26 grams per cubic centimeter*. Translate *maximum* as less than or equal to, or ≤. Thus, the correct inequality must include $d \leq 1.26$. Eliminate (A) because it shows 0.85 instead of 1.26 as the maximum value. This leaves (B), which also correctly translates *the minimum density recorded was 0.85 grams per cubic centimeter* as $0.85 \leq d$. The correct answer is (B).

Drill 3

Suggested Time Limit: 15 minutes. Answers can be found in Part IV.

1 Mark for Review

The number a is 2 more than one-fourth of the number b. Which of the following represents the relationship between a and b?

Ⓐ $a = \frac{1}{4}b - 2$

Ⓑ $a = \frac{1}{4}b + 2$

Ⓒ $a = 4b - 2$

Ⓓ $a = 4b + 2$

2 Mark for Review

Which of the following is equivalent to $-12 \leq 3x + 3$?

Ⓐ $-7 \leq x$

Ⓑ $-5 \leq x$

Ⓒ $-4 \leq x$

Ⓓ $-3 \leq x$

3 Mark for Review

A ski resort is renting skis for \$30 and snowboards for \$20 over a three-day weekend. Over the three days combined, 180 total skis and snowboards were rented, and the resort collected \$4,600 in total rental fees. Solving which of the following systems of equations yields the number of skis, s, and the number of snowboards, b, that were rented over the three-day weekend?

Ⓐ $s + b = 50$
$30s + 20b = 180$

Ⓑ $s + b = 180$
$30s + 20b = 460$

Ⓒ $s + b = 180$
$30s + 20b = 4{,}600$

Ⓓ $s + b = 4{,}600$
$30s + 20b = 180$

4 Mark for Review

$$-3|x + 5| = -4|x + 5| + 14$$

What is the negative solution to the given equation?

5 Mark for Review

$$10(3x + 4) = 2(15x + 4k)$$

In the given equation, k is a constant. If the equation has infinitely many solutions, what is the value of k?

Ⓐ 1

Ⓑ 5

Ⓒ 10

Ⓓ 20

6 Mark for Review

If a certain number is 3 more than 7 times itself, what is the number?

Ⓐ -3

Ⓑ $-\frac{3}{2}$

Ⓒ $-\frac{1}{2}$

Ⓓ $-\frac{3}{8}$

7 Mark for Review

Ann is writing a book that will include no more than 98 recipes. She currently has 32 main dish recipes and 18 dessert recipes. If r represents the number of additional recipes that Ann could include in her book, which of the following inequalities represents all possible values of r?

Ⓐ $r - 50 \geq 98$

Ⓑ $r - 50 \leq 98$

Ⓒ $48 + r \leq 0$

Ⓓ $48 - r \geq 0$

8 Mark for Review

A carpenter at a toy factory makes sets of wooden blocks and tops. The carpenter uses a total of 28 planks of wood to make b identical sets of blocks and t identical sets of tops. The carpenter uses 2.1 planks of wood to create one set of blocks and 0.7 planks of wood to create one set of tops. Which of the following equations best represents this situation?

Ⓐ $b + t = 28$

Ⓑ $0.7b + 2.1t = 28$

Ⓒ $2.1b + 0.7t = 28$

Ⓓ $40b + 13.3t = 28$

9 Mark for Review

$$2x - 6 = y + 8$$
$$2x + 15 = -2y + 8$$

If the solution to the given system of equations is (x, y), what is the value of $3y$?

Ⓐ -21

Ⓑ -7

Ⓒ 3.5

Ⓓ 10.5

10 Mark for Review

A baker has a recipe for cake that calls for both eggs and cups of flour. The baker can purchase five eggs and four cups of flour for $\$5.50$ and nine eggs and eight cups of flour for $\$10.50$. Based on these costs, what is the cost of the ten eggs that the baker will need for her recipe?

Ⓐ $\$5.00$

Ⓑ $\$5.50$

Ⓒ $\$7.50$

Ⓓ $\$10.50$

EXPONENTS AND SQUARE ROOTS

Exponents are just shorthand for multiplication. Instead of writing 3 × 3 × 3 × 3, you can write 3^4. Thus, you can handle exponents by expanding them out if necessary.

$$y^2 \times y^3 = y \times y \times y \times y \times y = y^5$$

$$\frac{y^4}{y^2} = \frac{y \times y \times y \times y}{y \times y} = \frac{\not{y} \times \not{y} \times y \times y}{\not{y} \times \not{y}} = y^2$$

$$(y^2)^3 = (y \times y)^3 = (y \times y)\,(y \times y)\,(y \times y) = y^6$$

However, you can also multiply and divide exponents that have the same base using a shortcut called MADSPM. MADSPM also helps you remember how to deal with raising exponents to another power. Let's see the breakdown:

- **MA** means when you see a Multiplication sign between like bases, Add the exponents. So, $y^2 \times y^3 = y^{2+3} = y^5$.
- **DS** means when you see a Division sign (or fraction), Subtract the exponents. So, $\frac{y^5}{y^2} = y^{5-2} = y^3$.
- **PM** means when you see a base with an exponent raised to a Power, Multiply the exponents. So, $(y^2)^3 = y^{2\times 3} = y^6$. (This is really easy to confuse with multiplication, so watch out!)

Here are some additional rules to remember about exponents:

Warning
The rules for multiplying and dividing exponents do not apply to addition or subtraction:
$2^2 + 2^3 = 12$
$(2 \times 2) + (2 \times 2 \times 2) = 12$
It does not equal 2^5 or 32.

- Anything to the zero power equals 1: $3^0 = 1$. Mathematicians argue about whether 0^0 is 1 or is undefined, but that won't come up on the PSAT.
- Anything to the first power equals itself: $3^1 = 3$.
- 1 to any power equals 1: $1^{3876} = 1$.
- A **negative exponent** means to take the reciprocal of what would be the result as if the negative weren't there: $2^{-2} = \frac{1}{2^2} = \frac{1}{4}$.
- A **fractional exponent** has two parts (like any other fraction): the numerator is the power the base is raised to, and the denominator is the root of the base. For example, $8^{\frac{2}{3}} = \sqrt[3]{8^2} = \sqrt[3]{64} = 4$.

Apply several of these rules on the following question.

8 Mark for Review

Which of the following is equivalent to the expression $x^6y^{-3}z^{\frac{1}{2}}$?

(A) $\dfrac{x^6\sqrt{z}}{3y}$

(B) $\dfrac{x^6\sqrt{2z}}{y^3}$

(C) $\dfrac{6x\sqrt{z}}{y^3}$

(D) $\dfrac{x^6\sqrt{z}}{y^3}$

Here's How To Crack It

The question asks for an equivalent form of an expression. Apply the exponent rules to each part of the expression, and eliminate answers after each step. Since x^6 doesn't change form, eliminate (C). A negative exponent means to take the reciprocal of what would be the result if the negative weren't there. Therefore, y^{-3} can be rewritten as $\dfrac{1}{y^3}$; eliminate (A). In a fractional exponent, the numerator is the power the base is raised to, and the denominator is the root of the base. Therefore, $z^{\frac{1}{2}}$ can be rewritten as $\sqrt{z}$; eliminate (B). The correct answer is (D).

Remember that in calculating the value of a root, you're looking for what number multiplied by itself results in the number under the radical. For example, $\sqrt[3]{64} = 4$ because $4 \times 4 \times 4 = 64$.

When you see the square root sign, that means to take the positive root only. So, $\sqrt{9} = 3$, but not –3.

Try a PSAT question with a square root.

---

9 Mark for Review

$$\sqrt{x^2 + 39} = 8$$

Which of the following is a possible solution to the given equation?

Ⓐ 3

Ⓑ 4

Ⓒ 5

Ⓓ 6

Here's How To Crack It

The question asks for a solution to an equation. Before solving algebraically using your knowledge of roots, keep in mind that the built-in calculator can solve many basic algebra questions. Enter the equation into the built-in calculator. To enter the square root symbol, either use the on-screen keypad in the lower left or type "sqrt" and let the calculator convert it to the symbol. Scroll and zoom as needed to see that the solutions are indicated by vertical lines that cross the x-axis at –5 and 5. Only 5 is an answer choice, so it is correct.

To solve algebraically, square both sides of the equation to get $x^2 + 39 = 64$. Subtract 39 from both sides of the equation to get $x^2 = 25$. Take the square root of both sides of the equation to get $x = \pm 5$. Only 5 is an answer choice, so it is correct.

Using either the built-in calculator or solving algebraically, the correct answer is (C).

Drill 4

Answers can be found in Part IV.

a. $3^3 \times 3^2 =$ ________

b. $\frac{3^3}{3^2} =$ ________

c. $\left(3^3\right)^2 =$ ________

d. $x^6 \times x^2 =$ ________

e. $\frac{x^6}{x^2} =$ ________

f. $\left(x^6\right)^2 =$ ________

g. $\sqrt{8} =$ ________

h. $\sqrt[3]{-64} =$ ________

THE COORDINATE PLANE

You will definitely see some questions on the coordinate plane, or *xy*-plane, on the PSAT. Let's start by covering the basics here. You'll see more advanced concepts in the Advanced Math chapter. So, let's just review:

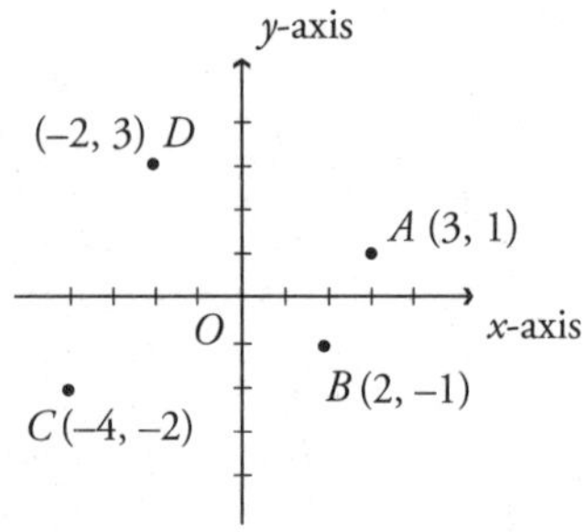

The *x*-axis is the horizontal axis, and the *y*-axis is the vertical axis. Points are given on the coordinate plane with the *x*-coordinate first. Positive *x*-values go to the right, and negative ones go to the left; positive *y*-values go up, and negative ones go down. So, point *A* (3, 1) is 3 points to the right on the *x*-axis and 1 point up from the *y*-axis. Point *B* (2, –1) is 2 points to the right on the *x*-axis and 1 point down from the *y*-axis.

Slope is a measure of the steepness of a line on the coordinate plane. On some slope questions, you need to recognize only whether the slope is positive, negative, or zero. A line that goes up and to the right has positive slope; a line that goes down and to the right has negative slope, and a flat horizontal line has zero slope. In the figure below, ℓ_1 has positive slope, ℓ_2 has zero slope, and ℓ_3 has negative slope.

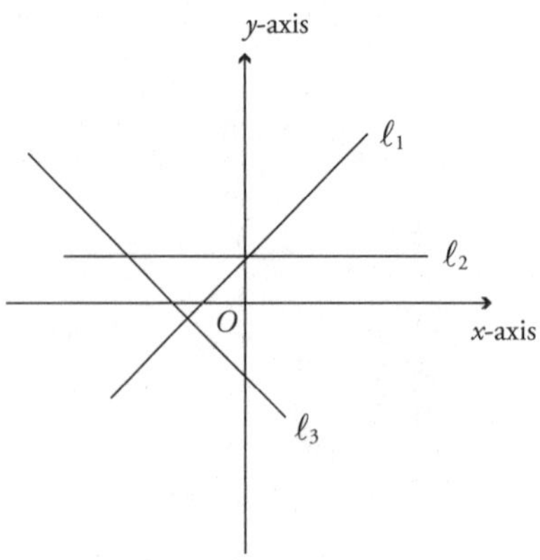

If you do need to calculate the slope, and the graph is drawn for you, here's how: slope = $\frac{y_2 - y_1}{x_2 - x_1}$. The *slope* of a line is equal to $\frac{rise}{run}$. To find the slope, take any two points on the line and count off or calculate the distance you need to get from one of these points to the other.

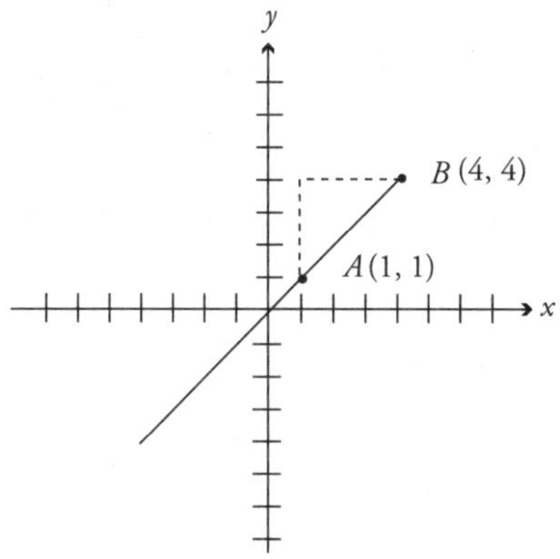

In the graph above, to get from point A to point B, we count up (rise) 3 units and count over (run) 3 units. Therefore, the slope is $\frac{rise}{run} = \frac{3}{3} = 1$. Always remember to check whether the slope is positive or negative when you use slope $= \frac{rise}{run}$.

If you're not given a figure and you can't draw one easily using the points given, you can find the slope by plugging the coordinates you know into the slope formula. Just remember to plug the numbers into the formula carefully!

Here's an example.

10 Mark for Review

Line l contains the points $\left(-3, \frac{7}{3}\right)$ and $\left(2, -\frac{5}{3}\right)$. What is the slope of line l?

Here's How to Crack It

The question asks for the slope of a line and gives two points. Use $\frac{rise}{run}$ to find the slope, being careful to start with the same point for both A and B. The equation slope $= \frac{y_2 - y_1}{x_2 - x_1}$ becomes slope $= \frac{-\frac{5}{3} - \frac{7}{3}}{2-(-3)}$, which simplifies to slope $= \frac{-\frac{12}{3}}{5}$ and then slope $= \frac{-4}{5}$. This can be entered as –4/5 or in decimal form as –0.8.

The equation of a line can take multiple forms. One is known as the **standard form**. In this form, $Ax + By = C$, the slope is $-\frac{A}{B}$ and the y-intercept is $\frac{C}{B}$. Knowing these shortcuts can help you avoid having to convert a linear equation into the more common form known as the **slope-intercept form**. A slope-intercept equation takes the form $y = mx + b$, where m is the slope and b is the y-intercept.

Knowing how to find the slope is useful for solving questions about perpendicular and parallel lines. **Perpendicular lines** have slopes that are negative reciprocals of one another. **Parallel lines** have the same slope and no solutions. You may also be given two equations that have infinitely many solutions.

Take a look at an example.

To Infinity...and Beyond!
When given two equations with infinitely many solutions, find a way to make them equal. The equations represent the same line.

11 Mark for Review

$$gx - hy = 78$$
$$4x + 3y = 13$$

In the given system of equations, g and h are constants. If the system has infinitely many solutions, what is the value of $\frac{g}{h}$?

Ⓐ $-\frac{4}{3}$

Ⓑ $-\frac{3}{4}$

Ⓒ $\frac{3}{4}$

Ⓓ $\frac{4}{3}$

Here's How to Crack It

The question asks for the value of a fraction given a system of equations. This question may have you scratching your head and moving on to the next question, but you may be surprised by how easy it is to solve.

When equations have infinitely many solutions, it means they are the same equation, or one is a multiple of the other. In other words, these two equations represent the same line. If it's the same line, it has the same slope. Both equations are in standard form, $Ax + By = C$, in which the slope is $-\frac{A}{B}$. In the first equation, $A = g$ and $B = -h$, so the slope is $-\frac{g}{-h}$, or $\frac{g}{h}$. In the second equation, $A = 4$ and $B = 3$, so the slope is $-\frac{4}{3}$. Set the two slopes equal to get $\frac{g}{h} = -\frac{4}{3}$. Knowing how to work with different forms of linear equations made this much simpler than it would have been with simultaneous equations. The correct answer is (A).

The previous question asked about two lines with infinitely many solutions. Here's one about two lines with exactly one real solution.

---

12 Mark for Review

$$8x - 32y = -28$$

A system of two linear equations has exactly one real solution. If the given equation is one of the equations in the system of equations, which of the following could be the second equation in the system?

Ⓐ $6x - 24y = -21$

Ⓑ $6x - 24y = 21$

Ⓒ $12x - 48y = 21$

Ⓓ $24x - 6y = -21$

Here's How to Crack It

The question asks for the equation that makes a system of equations have exactly one real solution. The most efficient method is to use the built-in calculator to graph the first equation and the equations in the answer choices and eliminate answer choices that don't generate a system of equations with exactly one solution. The graph of (A) is the same line as the graph of the equation given in the question, so a system with the original equation and the equation in (A) would have infinitely many solutions; eliminate (A). The graphs of (B) and (C) are parallel to the line graphed by the equation given in the question, so a system with the original equation and the equation in (B) or (C) would have no solutions; eliminate (B) and (C). The graph of (D) has a different slope from the graph of the original equation, and the two lines intersect at exactly one point, so they have exactly one solution and (D) is correct.

Another method is to use the slope. A system of linear equations in two variables has exactly one solution when the equations have different slopes and intersect at a single point on the coordinate plane. Compare the slopes of the equations. All of the equations are linear equations in standard form, $Ax + By = C$. In this form, the slope is $-\frac{A}{B}$, so the slope of the line graphed by the equation in the question is $-\frac{8}{-32}$, or $\frac{1}{4}$. The slopes of the lines graphed by the equations in (A) and (B) are $-\frac{6}{-24}$, or $\frac{1}{4}$. This is the same slope, so the lines are the same or parallel. Either way, the system does not have exactly one solution; eliminate (A) and (B). The slope of the line graphed by the equation in (C) is $-\frac{12}{-48}$, or $\frac{1}{4}$; eliminate (C) for the same reason as (A) and (B). The slope of the line graphed by the equation in (D) is $-\frac{24}{-6}$, or 4. This is a different slope than that of the given equation, so the lines will intersect once, making (D) correct.

Using either of these methods, the correct answer is (D).

Sometimes, it's a little trickier. Let's look at a difficult question that combines several of the previous concepts. Keep in mind that the built-in calculator is often the best option for questions about graphs in the coordinate plane.

13 Mark for Review

Line 1 contains the points (4, 7) and (1, –2), and line 2 contains the points (–2, 9) and (10, –3). What is the y-coordinate of the point of intersection of lines 1 and 2?

Ⓐ –1

Ⓑ 3

Ⓒ 4

Ⓓ 7

Here's How to Crack It

The question asks for the y-coordinate of a point of intersection. The most efficient method is to use the built-in calculator. It might feel complicated at first, so be sure to practice. Click the plus sign in the upper left, and then select Table. Enter the two points for line 1 into the table, and then click **and hold** the icon to open additional options. Click on the toggle for Lines, and the graphing area will show a line connecting the two points. Do the same thing with the points for line 2 in a separate entry field to see both lines in the graphing area.

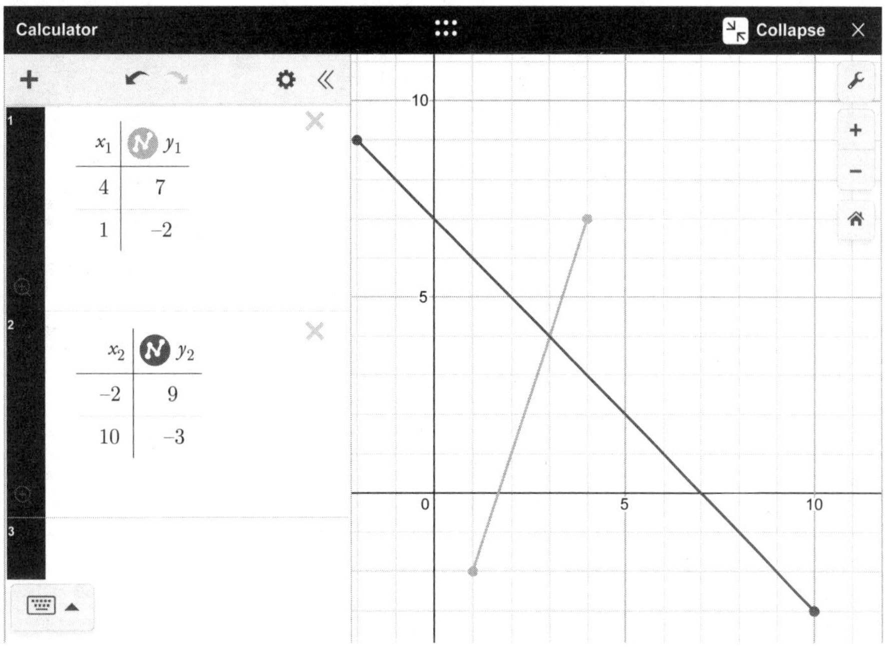

Scroll and zoom as needed to find that the coordinates of the point of intersection are (3, 4). The question asks for the y-coordinate, so (C) is correct.

To solve algebraically, first find the equations of the two lines. Given two points on a line, you can find the slope using $\frac{rise}{run}$, or $\frac{y_2 - y_1}{x_2 - x_1}$. The slope of line 1 is $\frac{-2-7}{1-4}$, which becomes $\frac{-9}{-3}$, or 3. Plug this and the coordinates of the point (4, 7) into slope-intercept form, $y = mx + b$, to find the value of b. The equation for line 1 becomes $7 = 3(4) + b$, or $7 = 12 + b$. Subtract 12 from both sides of the equation to get $-5 = b$. The equation for line 1 is now $y = 3x - 5$. Do the same for line 2: the slope of line 2 is $\frac{-3-9}{10-(-2)}$, which becomes $\frac{-12}{12}$, or –1. Plug this and the coordinates of the point (–2, 9) into the slope-intercept equation to get $9 = (-1)(-2) + b$, or $9 = 2 + b$. Subtract 2 from both sides of the equation to get $7 = b$. The equation for line 2 is now $y = -x + 7$. Next, set the right sides of the two slope-intercept equations equal to each other, and solve for x: $3x - 5 = -x + 7$. Add x to both sides of the equation to get $4x - 5 = 7$. Add 5 to both sides of the equation to get $4x = 12$. Divide both sides of the equation by 4 to get $x = 3$. Finally, plug $x = 3$ into one of the equations, and solve for y. Using the equation of line 1, $y = 3(3) - 5$, which becomes $y = 9 - 5$, and then $y = 4$, so (C) is correct.

Using either of these methods, the correct answer is (C).

Although the calculator method for the previous question was complicated, it was still much simpler than solving algebraically. Look for more chances to use the built-in calculator in the following drill.

Drill 5

Suggested Time Limit for Questions 1 through 8: 13 minutes. Answers can be found in Part IV.

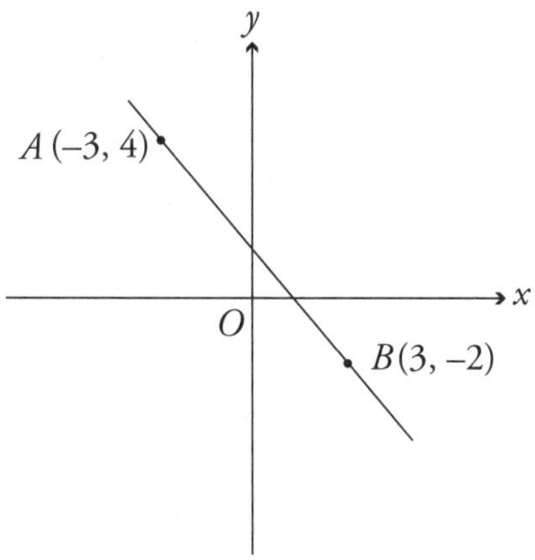

a. What is the change in y (rise)?

____

b. What is the change in x (run)?

____

c. What is the slope of the line above?

____

(Remember, the line is going down to the right, so it must have a negative slope.)

d. What would be the slope of a line parallel to AB? __________

e. What would be the slope of a line perpendicular to AB? __________

1 Mark for Review

A line defined by the equation $y = 6x + 3$ is perpendicular to a line defined by the equation $y = cx + 3$. What is the value of c?

Ⓐ -6

Ⓑ $-\frac{1}{6}$

Ⓒ $\frac{1}{6}$

Ⓓ 6

2 Mark for Review

What is the y-intercept of the line with equation $2x + 3y = 12$?

Ⓐ $\frac{1}{4}$

Ⓑ 2

Ⓒ 3

Ⓓ 4

3 Mark for Review

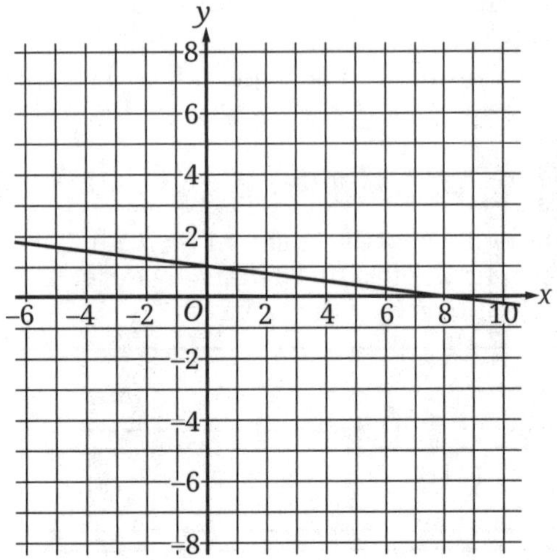

Which of the following could be the equation of the line in the graph shown?

Ⓐ $2y - x = -8$

Ⓑ $4y + x = -8$

Ⓒ $8y - 3x = 8$

Ⓓ $8y + x = 8$

4 Mark for Review

$$y = 4x^2 - 6x + 4$$
$$y = 2x + 4$$

In the xy-plane, the graphs of the given equations intersect at two points. What is the sum of the x-coordinates of the two points of intersection?

5 Mark for Review

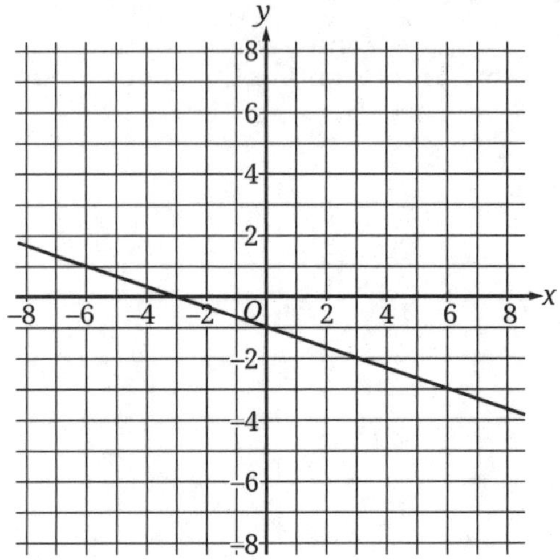

Line l is shown graphed in the xy-plane. If line m is parallel to line l, which of the following could be the equation of line m?

Ⓐ $y = -3x - 1$

Ⓑ $y = -\frac{1}{3}x + 2$

Ⓒ $y = \frac{1}{3}x - 3$

Ⓓ $y = 3x + 2$

6 Mark for Review

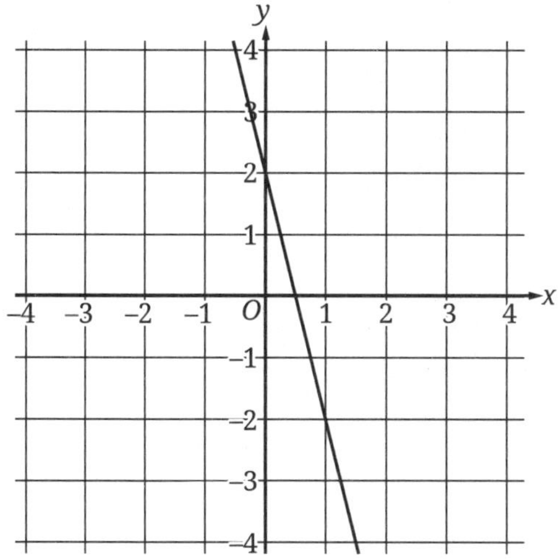

What is the slope of the line shown in the xy-plane?

Ⓐ -4

Ⓑ $-\frac{1}{4}$

Ⓒ $\frac{1}{4}$

Ⓓ 4

7 Mark for Review

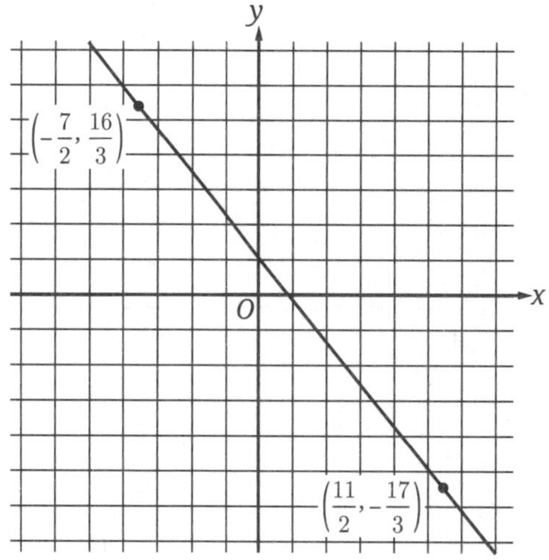

Which of the following is the slope of the line in the graph shown?

Ⓐ $-\frac{11}{6}$

Ⓑ $-\frac{11}{9}$

Ⓒ $-\frac{9}{8}$

Ⓓ $-\frac{9}{11}$

8 Mark for Review

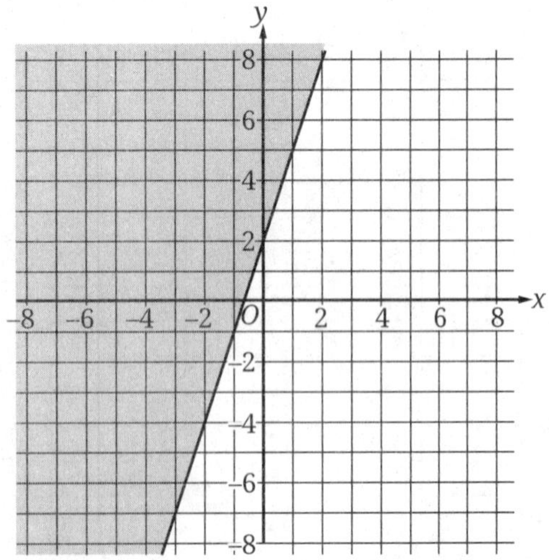

The solutions to which of the following inequalities are represented by the shaded region of the graph shown?

Ⓐ $y \geq -3x + 2$

Ⓑ $y \leq -3x + 2$

Ⓒ $y \geq 3x + 2$

Ⓓ $y \leq 3x + 2$

CHARTS AND GRAPHS

Another basic math skill you will need for the PSAT is the ability to read charts and graphs. Let's look at the types you may encounter and the skills you'll need to be familiar with when you work with charts and graphs.

The Scatterplot

A scatterplot is a graph with distinct data points, each representing one piece of information. On the scatterplot below, each dot represents the number of televisions sold at a certain price point.

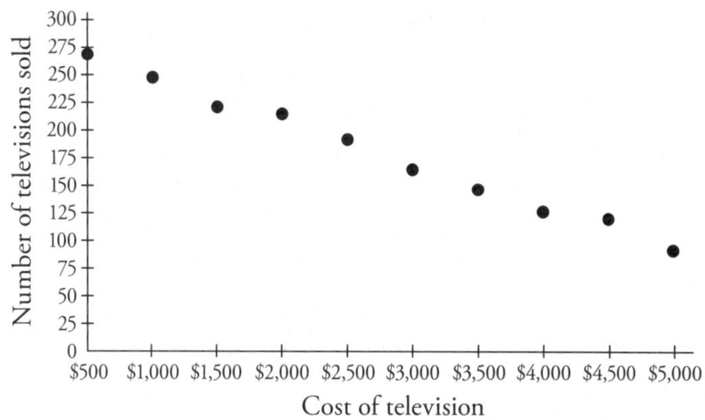

Finding the Best Fit
Scatterplots will sometimes contain a line that approximates the data. This is called a line of best fit.

Here's How to Read It

To find the cost of a television when a certain number of televisions are sold, start at the number of televisions sold on the vertical axis and imagine a horizontal line to the right until you hit a data point. You can't draw on the figures on the PSAT, but you can move the mouse pointer to the right starting from the number on the vertical axis. Once you hit a point, trace with the mouse pointer a straight line down from it to the horizontal axis and read the number the line hits. To determine the number of televisions sold when they cost a certain amount, reverse the steps—start at the bottom, trace up until you hit a point, and then move left until you intersect the vertical axis. You can also hold your scratch paper up to the screen and use it as a ruler.

The Line Graph

A line graph is similar to a scatterplot in that it shows different data points that relate the two variables. The difference with a line graph, though, is that the points have been connected to create a continuous line.

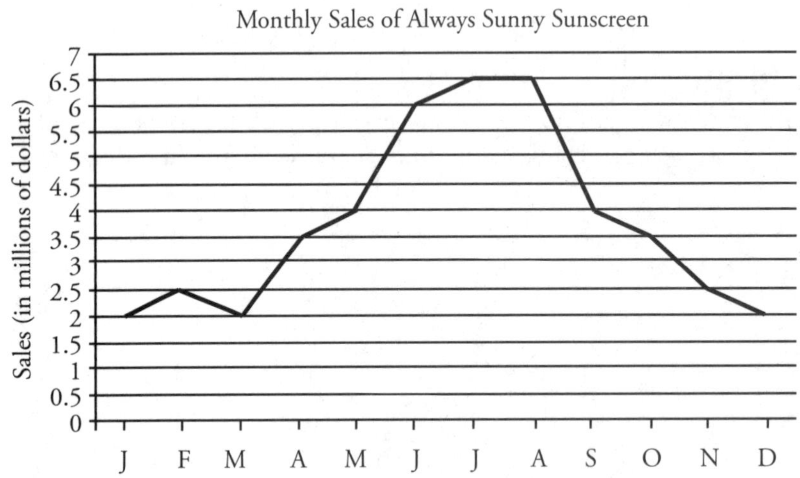

Here's How to Read It

Reading a line graph is very similar to reading a scatterplot. Start at the axis that represents the data given and trace a straight line with the mouse pointer up or to the right until you intersect the graph line. Then move left or down until you hit the other axis. For example, in February, indicated by an F on the horizontal axis, Always Sunny Sunscreen had 2.5 million in sales. Make sure to notice the units on each axis. If February sales were only \$2.50, rather than \$2.5 million, then this company wouldn't be doing very well!

The Bar Graph (or Histogram)

Instead of showing a variety of different data points, a bar graph will show how many items belong to a particular category. If the variable at the bottom is given in ranges, instead of distinct items, the graph is called a histogram, but you read it the same way.

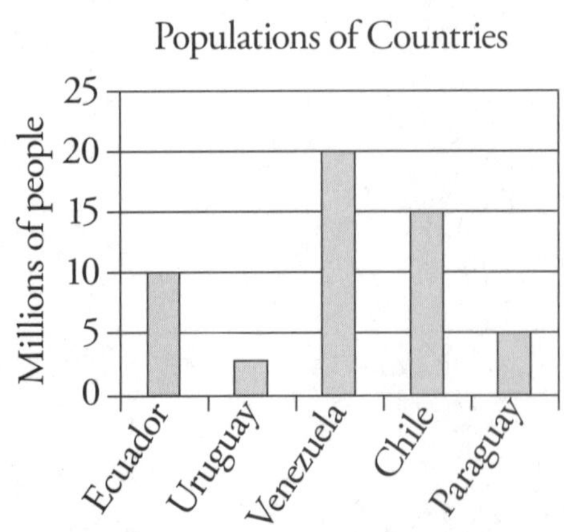

Here's How to Read It

The height of each bar corresponds to a value on the vertical axis. In this case, the bar above Chile hits the line that intersects with 15 on the vertical axis, so there are 15 million people in Chile. Again, watch the units to make sure you know what the numbers on the axes represent. On this graph, horizontal lines are drawn at 5-unit intervals, making the graph easier to read. If the bar isn't exactly at a line—or if the graph doesn't have horizontal lines at all—use your scratch paper as a ruler.

The Two-Way Table

A two-way table is a way to represent data without actually graphing it. Instead of having the variables represented on the vertical and horizontal axes, the data will be arranged in rows and columns. The top row will give the headings for each column, and the left-most column will give the headings for each row. The numbers in each box indicate the data for the category represented by the row and the column the box is in.

	Computer Production	
	Morning Shift	**Afternoon Shift**
Monday	200	375
Tuesday	245	330
Wednesday	255	340
Thursday	250	315
Friday	225	360

Here's How to Read It

If you wanted to see the number of computers produced on Tuesday morning, you could start in the Morning Shift column and look down until you found the number in the row that says "Tuesday," or you could start in the row for Tuesday and look to the right until you found the Morning Shift column. Either way, the result is 245. Some tables will give you totals in the bottom row and/or the right-most column, but sometimes you will need to find the totals yourself by adding up all the numbers in each row or in each column.

The Box Plot

A box plot shows data broken into quartiles, as follows:

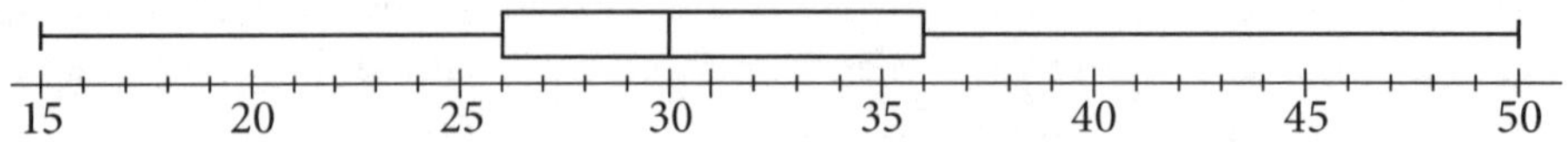

Here's How to Read It

Here is what all the parts of the box plot represent.

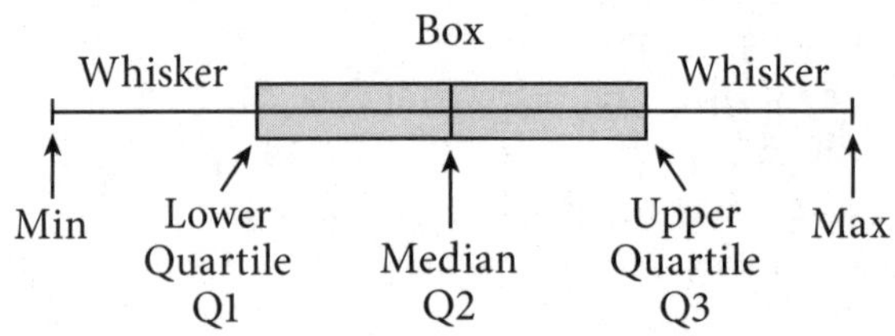

The line in the middle of the box shows the median value of the data, which is 30 in the example above. The "whiskers," which give this figure the alternate name "box-and-whisker plot," represent the highest value on the list with the end of the whisker on the right and the lowest value with the end of the whisker on the left. Thus, the minimum value of this data set is 15, and the maximum is 50. Then the data between the median and these minimum and maximum values is broken into two parts on each side, creating four "quartiles." The median of the lower half of the data is the Q1 value on the left side of the box, at about 26, and the median of the upper half of the data is the Q3 value on the right side of the box, at about 36. The PSAT is unlikely to test the lower and upper quartiles, so focus on the minimum, maximum, and median.

The Stem-and-Leaf Plot

A stem-and-leaf plot shows data according to a common first digit.

2 | 0 1 7
3 | 2 2 4
4 | 0 1 5 7 7 8
5 | 1 1 4 5 5 7 9
6 | 2 5 8 8 9
7 | 0

A book club took a survey of the age, in years, of its members. The data is shown in the stem-and-leaf plot above.

Here's How to Read It

The numbers on the left of the vertical line are the initial digit of each age, and the numbers to the right of the vertical line are the following digits corresponding to the given first digit. This means that the ages of the members of the book club are 20, 21, 27, 32, 32, 34, etc. Questions using stem-and-leaf plots often ask for things like the range of the data, the median of the data, or the probability of selecting a certain number. We will look at all those statistical measures in the Math Techniques chapter.

Figure Facts

Every time you encounter a figure or graphic on the PSAT, you should make sure you understand how to read it by checking the following things:

- What are the variables for each axis or the headings for the table?
- What units are used for each variable?
- Use the mouse pointer or the edge of your scratch paper to make sure you are locating the correct data in the graph.

FILL-INS: THE BASICS

You will see 10–12 questions in the Math section of the PSAT that ask you to enter your own numerical answer in a box, rather than answer a multiple-choice question. The test-writers call these Student-Produced Response questions, but we're going to keep things simple and call them fill-ins.

The only difficulty with fill-ins is getting used to the way in which you are asked to answer the question. For each fill-in question, you will have a box like this:

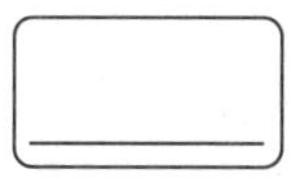

To enter your answer, click inside the box and start typing. The numbers you enter will automatically appear left to right, and the computer will show a preview of your answer, so you can make sure it looks right.

The fill-in instructions appear on the left side of the screen for every fill-in question. You can click in the center and drag left to shrink the fill-in instructions and focus on the question.

You don't want to have to spend time rereading the instructions every time, so here is some additional information about entering a fill-in answer:

1. There is space to enter 5 characters if the answer is positive and 6 characters—including the negative sign—if the answer is negative.
2. You can enter your answer as either a fraction or a decimal. For example, both 1/2 and .5 are acceptable answers. Use the forward slash for fractions. Leave out the leading zero for decimals between 0 and 1, as you cannot enter a zero as the first number.
3. If your answer is a fraction, it must fit within the space. Do not try to enter something like $\frac{200}{500}$ as a fraction: either reduce it or convert it to a decimal.
4. Fractions do not need to be in the lowest reduced form. As long as it fits, it's fine.

5. You cannot fill in mixed numbers. Convert all mixed numbers to ordinary fractions or decimals. If your answer is $2\frac{1}{2}$, you must convert it to 5/2 or 2.5. If you enter 21/2, the computer will read your answer as $\frac{21}{2}$.

6. You do not need to type the comma for numbers longer than three digits, such as 4,200. In fact, the computer will not allow it.

7. The computer also will not allow symbols such as %, \$, or π. Additionally, square roots, units, and variables cannot be entered.

8. If your answer is a decimal that will not fit in the space provided, either enter as many digits as will fit or round the last digit. The fraction $-\frac{2}{3}$ can be entered in decimal form as –0.666, –0.667, –.6666, or –.6667.

9. Some questions will have more than one right answer. Any correct answer you enter will count as correct; do not try to enter multiple answers.

Drill 6

Suggested Time Limit: 9 minutes. Answers can be found in Part IV.

1 Mark for Review

If $5x^2 = 125$, and $x < 0$, what is the value of $5x^3$?

______

2 Mark for Review

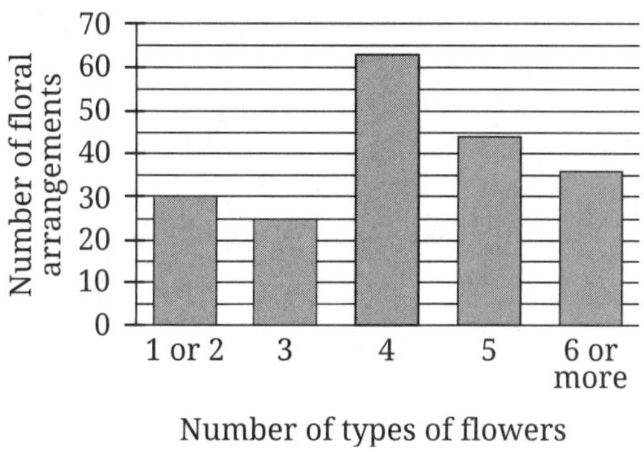

A florist recorded how many different types of flowers were included in each floral arrangement sold last week. The results are shown in the bar graph above. How many floral arrangements included exactly four different types of flowers?

Ⓐ 30

Ⓑ 44

Ⓒ 63

Ⓓ 70

3 Mark for Review

If $3x + 2y = 37$ and $7x + 4y = 85$, what is the value of y?

______

4 Mark for Review

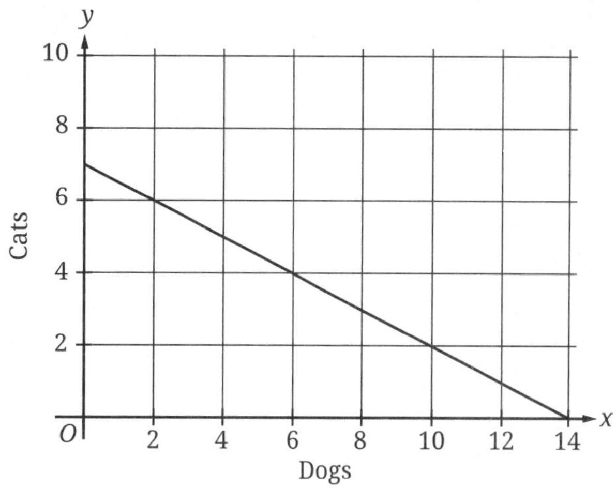

The graph shows the combinations of cats and dogs that a veterinarian can vaccinate in 90 minutes. On Tuesday, the veterinarian vaccinated 6 cats and d dogs in 90 minutes. What is the value of d?

Ⓐ 2

Ⓑ 4

Ⓒ 15

Ⓓ 54

5 Mark for Review

If $5-\sqrt{x}=\sqrt{x-5}$, what is the value of x?

______

6 Mark for Review

$$y = x^2 - 27$$

$$y = 6x$$

One solution to the given system of equations can be expressed as (x, y). If $x < 0$, what is the value of x?

______

Summary

- Each Math module is arranged in a loose Order of Difficulty, which can make it easier to spot the less difficult questions. However, remember that the test-writers' idea of "easier" questions is not necessarily the same as your idea. Let your Personal Order of Difficulty be your guide.
- Write on your scratch paper to set up your work, and then use your calculator or the built-in calculator to figure out solutions. And remember to type carefully—a calculator won't check for mistakes.
- The built-in calculator is an extremely powerful tool. Learn and practice new ways to use it as you work through this book.
- Review basic definitions again before the test to make sure you don't get stuck on the "little words."
- To solve equations for a variable, isolate the variable. Make sure you perform the same operations on both sides of the equation. The built-in calculator is a good option for many algebra questions.
- Inequalities can be worked just like equations until you have to multiply or divide by a negative number. Then you need to flip the inequality sign. You can also graph inequalities in the built-in calculator.
- The absolute value of a number is the positive distance from zero, or practically, making the thing inside the | | sign positive. Everything inside the | | is equal to the positive and the negative value of the expression to which it is equal. The built-in calculator works for most absolute value questions.
- When you have to manipulate exponents, remember the MADSPM rules.
- When a question is testing systems of equations, make the built-in calculator your first option.
- When writing a system of equations or inequalities based on words in the question, start with the most straightforward piece of information.
- You can also use the equations or inequalities in the answer choices to help you narrow down the possibilities. Eliminate any answers in which an equation or inequality doesn't match a piece of information in the question.

- Parallel lines have the same slope and no solutions. If two lines have the same slope and infinitely many solutions, they are actually the same line. Perpendicular lines have slopes that are negative reciprocals of each other.
- When you encounter charts, carefully check the chart for information you should note, and use the mouse pointer or edge of your scratch paper to locate information.
- When answering fill-in questions, don't bother reducing fractions or rounding decimals if they fit in the allotted space. Check the answer preview on the screen before moving on.

Chapter 15
Math Techniques

In the previous chapter, we mentioned that one of the keys to doing well on the PSAT is to have a set of test-specific problem-solving skills. This chapter discusses some powerful strategies, which—though you may not use them in school—are specifically designed to get you points on the PSAT. Learn them well!

PLUGGING IN

One of the most powerful problem-solving skills on the PSAT is a technique we call Plugging In. Plugging In will turn nasty algebra questions into simple arithmetic and help you through the particularly twisted problems that you'll often see on the PSAT. There are several varieties of Plugging In, each suited to a different kind of question.

Plugging In Your Own Numbers

The problem with doing algebra is that it's just too easy to make a mistake.

Whenever you see a question with variables in the answer choices, think Plugging In.

Start by picking a number for the variable in the question (or for more than one variable, if necessary), solve the problem using your number, and then see which answer choice gives you the correct answer.

Take a look at the following question.

1 Mark for Review

$$(x^2 - 9)^2 - (x + 7)(x - 7)$$

Which of the following is equivalent to the given expression?

Ⓐ $x^4 - 32x^2 + 81$

Ⓑ $x^4 - 19x^2 - 32$

Ⓒ $x^4 - 19x^2 + 130$

Ⓓ $x^4 + 4x^2 + 60$

When to Plug In

- phrases like "in terms of" or "equivalent form" in the question
- variables in the question and/or answer choices

Here's How to Crack It

The question asks for an equivalent form of an expression. Solving algebraically would be messy, and one small mistake could lead directly to one of the trap answers. Instead, plug in. With exponents involved, there's a chance that 0 or 1 would make two answers work, so make $x = 2$. Plug this into the expression in the question to get $(2^2 - 9)^2 - (2 + 7)(2 - 7)$. Solve by hand or with the built-in calculator to get $(4 - 9)^2 - (9)(-5)$, which becomes $(-5)^2 - (-45)$, then $25 + 45$, and finally 70. This is the target value; write it down and circle it. Now plug $x = 2$ into the answer choices, and eliminate any that do not match the target value. The built-in calculator or your own hand-held calculator can help with the math.

A) $(2)^4 - 32(2)^2 + 81 = -31$	Not 70; eliminate!
B) $(2)^4 - 19(2)^2 - 32 = -92$	Not 70; eliminate!
C) $(2)^4 - 19(2)^2 + 130 = 70$	Is 70; keep!
D) $(2)^4 + 4(2)^2 + 60 = 92$	Not 70; eliminate!

The wrong answers are all the result of making algebra mistakes, including errors with signs such as forgetting that a negative value squared becomes positive. When you use real numbers instead of variables, you're much less likely to make that kind of mistake. Here, you turned algebra into arithmetic and got (C) as the correct answer.

As you learned in the previous chapter, the built-in calculator is also a good option for questions about solving. In this case, you could enter the expression from the question in an entry field, and then enter each answer choice expression one at a time in another entry field. Scroll and zoom as needed to see the graphs, and eliminate graphs that are not the same as the initial graph. Only the expression in (C) results in the same graph, so (C) is correct.

As you can see, Plugging In can turn messy algebra questions into more straightforward arithmetic questions. Here are the steps to follow.

Plugging In

1. When you see *in terms of* or *equivalent* and there are variables in the answer choices, you can Plug In.
2. Pick your own number(s) for the variable(s) in the question.
3. Do the necessary math to find the answer to the question, which is the target number. Circle the target number.
4. Use POE to eliminate every answer that doesn't match the target number.

Plugging In is also a powerful technique when a word problem asks about the relationship among numbers or variables. Here's an example.

2 Mark for Review

The ratio of pink socks to white socks in a drawer is 2 to 15. If there are x pink socks in the drawer, which of the following expressions represents the number of white socks in the drawer?

Ⓐ $15x - 2$

Ⓑ $30x$

Ⓒ $\frac{2}{15}x$

Ⓓ $\frac{15}{2}x$

Here's How to Crack It

Once again, algebra is possible but could lead to a trap answer if you aren't extremely careful. Avoid that by turning algebra into arithmetic. To make the math simple, double the number of pink socks to get $x = (2)(2)$, or $x = 4$. Since there are twice as many pink socks, there must also be twice as many white socks: (2)(15), or 30. This is the target value: write it down and circle it. Next, plug $x = 4$ into the answer choices, and then eliminate any that do not match the target value.

A) $15(4) - 2 = 58$	Not 30; eliminate!
B) $30(4) = 120$	Not 30; eliminate!
C) $\frac{2}{15}(4) = \frac{8}{15}$	Not 30; eliminate!
D) $\frac{15}{2}(4) = 30$	Is 30; keep!

Once again, algebra and the potential mistakes that come along with it are gone, Plugging In saves the day, and the correct answer is (D).

Use Your Tools!

Plugging In offers a fantastic opportunity to make full use of the online tools and your scratch paper. See all those notes above that helped find the target value and check each answer choice? Those go on your scratch paper. Instead of writing down "eliminate," use the Answer Eliminator tool on the screen.

Plugging In is such a great technique because it turns hard algebra questions into medium and sometimes even easy arithmetic questions. Remember this when you're thinking of your POOD and looking for questions to do among the hard ones; if you see variables in the answers, there's a good chance it's one to try.

Don't worry too much about what numbers you choose to plug in; just plug in easy numbers (small numbers like 2, 5, or 10 or numbers that make the arithmetic easy, like 100 if you're looking for a percent). Also, be sure your numbers fit the conditions of the questions (for example, if they say $x \leq 11$, don't plug in 12).

Also, be sure to check all four answers. Once in a while, the numbers you plug in work for more than one answer. In those cases, pick a new number or numbers, get a new target value, and plug into the remaining answers until you are down to one.

What If There's No Variable?

Sometimes you'll see a question that doesn't contain an x, y, or z, but which contains a hidden variable. If your answers are percents or fractional parts of some unknown quantity (total number of marbles in a jar, total miles to travel in a trip), try Plugging In.

3 Mark for Review

Ratio of Students in a Club

	Male	Female	Total
Junior	18%	27%	45%
Senior	24%	31%	55%
Total	42%	58%	100%

We'll cover probability in more detail later in this chapter.

The two-way table shows the percentages of male students and female students and juniors and seniors in a particular club. If a male student is chosen at random, what is the probability that he will be a junior?

Ⓐ $\frac{9}{50}$

Ⓑ $\frac{3}{7}$

Ⓒ $\frac{27}{58}$

Ⓓ $\frac{3}{4}$

Here's How to Crack It

The question asks for the probability that a male student chosen at random will be a junior. The total percentage of students is 100%, so plug in for the total number of students. Make the number of students 100. To find the number of students in each category, you only need to remove the percent sign. For example, 18% of 100 is 18. This gives you the following:

	Male	Female	Total
Junior	18	27	45
Senior	24	31	55
Total	42	58	100

You're asked to find the probability of choosing a junior if you choose from the male students. Probability is $\frac{\textit{number of outcomes you want}}{\textit{number of possible outcomes}}$. There are 18 male juniors and 42 total male students, making the probability of choosing a junior from the male students $\frac{18}{42}$, which reduces to $\frac{3}{7}$. This matches (B).

Drill 1

Suggested Time Limit: 10 minutes. Answers can be found in Part IV.

1 Mark for Review

The expression $-2x - (3x - 8x)$ is equivalent to which of the following?

Ⓐ $-13x$

Ⓑ $-7x$

Ⓒ $3x$

Ⓓ $9x$

2 Mark for Review

x	y
0	7
1	−1
2	−9
3	−17

There is a linear relationship between x and y. The table shows four values of x and their corresponding values of y. Which equation represents this relationship?

Ⓐ $y = 8 - 9x$

Ⓑ $y = 8 - x$

Ⓒ $y = 7 - x$

Ⓓ $y = 7 - 8x$

3 Mark for Review

A certain standardized test has 50 questions. A student receives 1 point for each correct answer and loses $\frac{1}{4}$ of a point for each incorrect answer. Which of the following equations best models the net score, S, in points, for a student who completes all 50 questions and answers c of the questions correctly?

Ⓐ $S = 50 - 0.25c$

Ⓑ $S = 50 - 0.75c$

Ⓒ $S = c - 0.25(50 - c)$

Ⓓ $S = c - 0.75(50 - c)$

4 Mark for Review

David acquired a data plan for his smart phone. Every month he pays a flat rate of \$25 and an additional \$0.05 for every megabyte he goes over his monthly limit. Which of the following represents David's monthly data bill when he goes over his limit by m megabytes?

Ⓐ $25 + 1.05m$

Ⓑ $25 + 0.05m$

Ⓒ $0.05(25 + m)$

Ⓓ $1.05(25 + m)$

5 Mark for Review

The expression $x^2 + 4x - 4$ is written in the equivalent form $(x + 2)^2 - a$. What is the value of a?

Ⓐ -2

Ⓑ 2

Ⓒ 4

Ⓓ 8

6 Mark for Review

The population of a resort area decreased by 37% from the end of August to the end of November and then increased by 112% from the end of November to the end of February. What was the net percentage increase in the population of the resort area from the end of August to the end of February?

Ⓐ 29.44%

Ⓑ 33.56%

Ⓒ 41.44%

Ⓓ 70.56%

PLUGGING IN THE ANSWERS (PITA)

You can also plug in when the answer provided to a question is an actual value, such as 2, 4, 10, or 20. Why would you want to do a lot of complicated algebra to solve a question when the answer is right there on the screen? All you have to do is figure out *which* choice it is.

How can you tell which is the correct answer? Try every choice *until you find the one that works.* Even if this means you have to try all four choices, PITA is still a fast and reliable means of getting the right answer.

If you work strategically, however, you almost never need to try all four answers. If the question asks for either the greatest or the least answer, start there. Otherwise, start with one of the middle answer choices. If that answer works, you're done. If the answer you started with was too big, try a smaller answer. If the answer you started with was too small, try a bigger answer. You can almost always find the answer in two or three tries this way. Let's try PITA on the following question.

4 Mark for Review

A chef makes 519 ounces of a soup base by mixing together 15-ounce cans of chicken broth and 32-ounce cans of vegetable broth. If the chef uses 9 cans of chicken broth, and the soup base contains no other ingredients, how many cans of vegetable broth does the chef use to make the soup base?

(A) 9

(B) 12

(C) 15

(D) 32

PITA = Plugging In the Answers
Don't try to solve problems like this by writing equations and solving for *x* or *y*. Plugging In the Answers lets you use arithmetic instead of algebra, so you're less likely to make errors.

Here's How to Crack It

Notice how the question is asking for a specific value and the answer choices are only numbers? That means that one of those numbers must be the number of cans of vegetable broth. This is a great chance to use PITA. First, rewrite the answer choices on your scratch paper and label them "cans of vegetable broth" or an abbreviation that will make sense to you.

cans VB
A) 9
B) 12
C) 15
D) 32

Next, pick one of the numbers in the middle and start with (B), 12. Plug in 12 for the cans of vegetable broth and see what else you can determine from the question. Each can of vegetable broth contains 32 ounces, so the total number of ounces of vegetable broth is (12)(32) = 384. Add a column for this information:

# cans VB	# ounces VB
A) 9	
B) 12	384
C) 15	
D) 32	

The question also states that the chef uses 9 cans of chicken broth that contain 15 ounces each, so there are (9)(15) = 135 total ounces of chicken broth.

# cans VB	# ounces VB	# ounces CB
A) 9		
B) 12	384	135
C) 15		
D) 32		

Add the total ounces of each type of broth to see whether the grand total matches the total given in the question:

# cans VB	# ounces VB	# ounces CB	Total ounces
A) 9			
B) 12	384	135	384 + 135 = 519
C) 15			
D) 32			

The totals do match, so there are 12 cans of vegetable broth. The correct answer is (B).

Neat, huh? The previous question asked for a specific value and had numbers in the answer choices. Those are both good signs that PITA will work, no matter what the question format and math topic are.

Try this one about the graph of an equation.

5 Mark for Review

$$16x^2 + 8x - c = 0$$

For which of the following values of c will the given equation have exactly one real solution?

Ⓐ $-\frac{1}{4}$

Ⓑ -1

Ⓒ 0

Ⓓ 1

Here's How to Crack It

If you remember questions like this from school, you might be having flashbacks to the discriminant or completing the square. On the PSAT, a combination of PITA and the built-in calculator makes this much easier. Open the built-in calculator, and enter the equation into an entry field. The calculator will give you an option to add a slider for c. Click on the slider to see that the default value is $c = 1$. The graphing area shows a parabola that intercepts the x-axis twice, so it has two solutions, not one. Eliminate (D).

Next, either move the slider to $-\frac{1}{4}$, -1, and 0 or enter those values for c. When $c = -1$, the parabola intercepts the x-axis once.

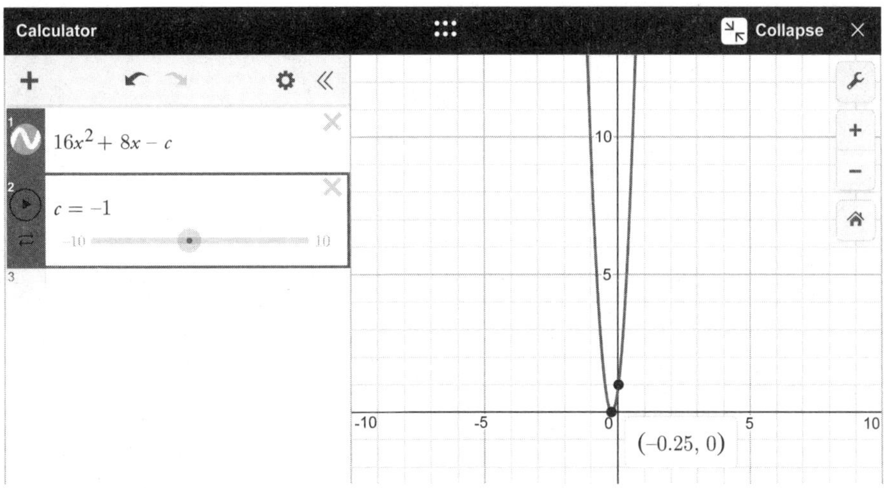

Be careful! The vertex of the parabola is at (–0.25, 0), which might make you think that (A) is the correct answer. However, the question asked for the value of c when the equation has exactly one real solution, and this happens when $c = -1$. The correct answer is (B).

Use Your Tools!

Be sure to let your scratch paper and the Answer Eliminator tool help on PITA questions. Rewrite the answers in order to try them out one by one. Label what the answers represent: one of them is the answer to the question. Then label each step along the way and check whether the result matches the information in the question. If it doesn't, cross out that answer on the screen.

When to Use PITA

- When the question asks for a specific amount
- When there are numbers in the answer choices
- When you are tempted to write your own equation

PITA Pointers

- Keep your work neatly organized on your scratch paper.
- Start with one of the middle values and work through the problem.
- Eliminate answers that are too big or too small.
- When one answer works, stop! That's the correct answer.

Drill 2

Suggested Time Limit: 11 minutes. Answers can be found in Part IV.

1 Mark for Review

$$2(n + 5) = 3(n - 2) + 8$$

In the given equation, what is the value of n?

Ⓐ 1

Ⓑ 3

Ⓒ 4

Ⓓ 8

2 Mark for Review

$$2x - y > -3$$
$$4x + y < 5$$

Which of the following points is in the solution set of the given system of inequalities?

Ⓐ (−4, −1)

Ⓑ (−3, −2)

Ⓒ (−1, −1)

Ⓓ (3, −5)

3 Mark for Review

Which table shows three values of x and their corresponding values of y for the equation $y = -x + 9$?

Ⓐ

x	y
0	0
2	2
4	4

Ⓑ

x	y
0	4
2	2
4	0

Ⓒ

x	y
0	9
2	7
4	5

Ⓓ

x	y
0	5
2	7
4	9

4 Mark for Review

If the mean of 8 and x is equal to the mean of 5, 9, and x, what is the value of x?

Ⓐ 1

Ⓑ 2

Ⓒ 4

Ⓓ 8

5 Mark for Review

One employee of a catering company took an inventory of the company's supplies and determined that the company had 4 times as many dinner plates as coffee mugs. A second employee took an inventory of the same supplies and found that the company had 450 more dinner plates than coffee mugs. Assuming that both employees counted correctly, how many dinner plates were in the catering company's inventory?

Ⓐ 150

Ⓑ 450

Ⓒ 600

Ⓓ $1,800$

6 Mark for Review

The system of inequalities $x < 21$ and $x - 7y \geq -12$ is graphed in the xy-plane. If $(8, y)$ is a point in the graph of the system, what is one possible value of y?

Ⓐ 2

Ⓑ 5

Ⓒ 12

Ⓓ 44

7 Mark for Review

In a certain game, enchanted items are worth 15 points each and normal items are worth 4 points each. If a player has 9 items worth 102 points, how many enchanted items does the player have?

Ⓐ 3

Ⓑ 4

Ⓒ 5

Ⓓ 6

DATA ANALYSIS

The PSAT has questions that ask you to work with concepts such as means, percentages, and unit conversions. Luckily, The Princeton Review has you covered! The rest of this chapter will give you techniques and strategies to help you tackle these questions.

Means and $T = AN$

You probably remember the average formula from math class, which says **mean** (or **average**) $= \frac{\text{total}}{\text{\# of things}}$. Of the three parts of this equation—the mean, the total, and the number of things—a PSAT question will often give you the mean and the number of things, and you'll need to use the total to answer the question. Whenever you see a question about means, therefore, write down $T = AN$, which stands for Total = Average × Number of things. Plug the information into the formula and solve.

Let's try this example.

6 Mark for Review

The mean of 3 numbers is 22 and the smallest of these numbers is 2. If the remaining two numbers are equal, what are their values?

Ⓐ 22

Ⓑ 32

Ⓒ 40

Ⓓ 64

Total

When calculating means, always find the total. It's the one piece of information that the PSAT loves to withhold.

Here's How to Crack It

The question gives the value of one number and the mean of all three numbers and asks for the value of the two remaining numbers. Use $T = AN$. The average, or mean, is 22, and there are 3 numbers. Therefore, $T = (22)(3)$, so $T = 66$. If the smallest number is 2, the remaining two numbers equal $66 - 2 = 64$. Finally, the remaining two numbers are equal, so divide: $64 \div 2 = 32$. The correct answer is (B).

The built-in calculator can also calculate the mean of a list of numbers. Simply type the word *mean* followed by the list of numbers inside parentheses, and the mean will appear in the lower right corner of the entry field. Try the previous question this way: plug in 2 for the first value and each answer choice for the remaining two values, and see which group of three numbers results in a mean of 22.

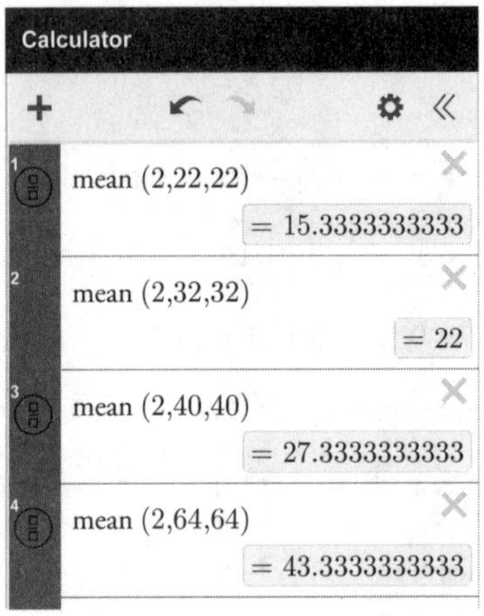

Only (B) works, so it is correct.

Median and Range

Two more terms that are often tested along with mean are median and range.

The **median** of a group of numbers is the number in the middle, just as the "median" is the large divider in the middle of a road. To find the median, here's what you do:

Finding a Median
To find the median of a set containing an even number of items, take the mean of the two middle numbers after putting the numbers in numerical order from least to greatest.

- First, put the elements in the group in numerical order from lowest to highest.
- If the number of elements in the group is *odd*, find the number in the middle. That's the median.
- If you have an *even* number of elements in the group, find the two numbers in the middle and calculate their mean.

Try this on the following question.

7 Mark for Review

If the 5 students in a math class scored 91, 83, 84, 90, and 85 on their final exams, what is the median score for the class on the final exam?

(A) 84

(B) 85

(C) 86

(D) 88

Here's How to Crack It

First, let's place these numbers in order from least to greatest: 83, 84, 85, 90, 91. There are an odd number of elements in the group, and the number in the middle is 85, so the median of this group is 85 and the answer is (B).

Just like with mean, the built-in calculator can make short work of questions about median. Type the word *median* followed by the list of numbers inside parentheses, and the median will appear in the lower right corner of the entry field. This is often better than determining the median by hand because you don't need to put the list of numbers in order: the calculator takes care of that for you! Here's how the previous question looks in the built-in calculator:

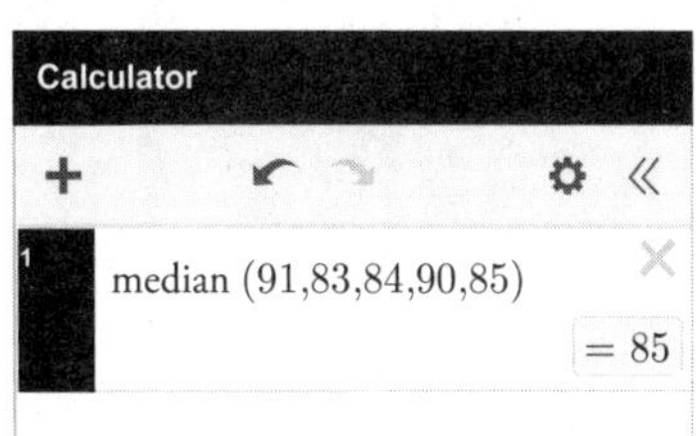

Without the calculator, it's easy to forget about putting the list in order and pick trap answer (A). With the calculator, however, you're guaranteed to get the correct answer, (B), as long as you enter the numbers accurately.

The **range** of a list of numbers is the difference between the greatest number on the list and the least number on the list. For the list 4, 5, 5, 6, 7, 8, 9, 10, 20, the greatest number is 20 and the least is 4, so the range is 20 – 4 = 16.

Let's look at a question.

8 Mark for Review

184	176	181	157	168
154	148	165	190	162

A group of patients is recruited for a clinical trial. Their heights, recorded in centimeters, are listed in the table. Two more patients are recruited to the study. After these patients join, the range of the heights is 42 cm. Which of the following could NOT be the heights of the two new patients?

Ⓐ 154 cm and 186 cm

Ⓑ 146 cm and 179 cm

Ⓒ 150 cm and 188 cm

Ⓓ 148 cm and 185 cm

Here's How to Crack It

The question asks for the values that cannot be the heights of two new patients given information about the range of the data. To determine the current range, take the difference of the greatest and least values: 190 – 148 = 42 cm. If the range is to remain 42 cm, then the new patients' heights cannot be greater than 190 cm or less than 148 cm tall. Choice (B) violates this restriction. Because the question wants what could NOT be the heights of the new patients, the answer is (B).

PROBABILITY

Probability refers to the chance that an event will happen, and it is given as a percent or a fractional value between 0 and 1, inclusive. A probability of 0 means that the event will never happen; a probability of 1 means that it is certain to happen.

$$\text{Probability} = \frac{\text{number of outcomes you want}}{\text{number of possible outcomes}}$$

For instance, if you have a die with faces numbered 1 to 6, what is the chance of rolling a 2? There is one face with the number 2 on it, out of 6 total faces. Therefore, the probability of rolling a 2 is $\frac{1}{6}$.

What is the chance of rolling an even number on one roll of this die? There are 3 faces of the die with an even number (the sides numbered 2, 4, and 6) out of a total of 6 faces. Therefore, the probability of rolling an even number is $\frac{3}{6}$, or $\frac{1}{2}$.

Let's look at how this concept will be tested on the PSAT.

9 Mark for Review

A child randomly selects one toy out of a toy box that contains 24 toy soldiers, 13 toy cars, 8 dolls, and 5 puzzles. What is the probability that the child selects a toy that is not a doll or a puzzle?

Ⓐ $\frac{13}{50}$

Ⓑ $\frac{8}{13}$

Ⓒ $\frac{37}{50}$

Ⓓ $\frac{13}{37}$

Here's How to Crack It

The question asks for a probability based on a situation. Probability is defined as $\frac{\text{number of outcomes you want}}{\text{number of possible outcomes}}$. Read carefully to find the numbers that make up the probability. First, find the total number of toys by adding up the numbers of each toy. There are $24 + 13 + 8 + 5 = 50$ toys, so 50 is the *number of possible outcomes.* To find the *number of outcomes you want*, subtract the number of dolls and puzzles from the total number of toys to get $50 - 8 - 5 = 37$. Thus, there are 37 toys that are not a doll or a puzzle. Therefore, the probability of selecting a toy that is not a doll or a puzzle is $\frac{37}{50}$. The correct answer is (C).

RATES

Rate is a concept related to mean, or average. Cars travel at an average speed. Work gets done at an average rate. PSAT questions will often ask you to express a rate in different units.

Let's look at an example of a PSAT rate question.

10 Mark for Review

A machine produces 100 screws per minute. How many seconds will it take the machine to produce 450 screws?

Here's How to Crack It

The question asks for time in seconds but gives the rate in screws per minute. First, determine how many minutes it will take for the machine to produce 450 screws by setting up a proportion: $\frac{100 \text{ screws}}{1 \text{ minute}} = \frac{450 \text{ screws}}{x \text{ minutes}}$. Cross-multiply to get $(100)(x) = (1)(450)$, which becomes $100x = 450$. Divide both sides of this equation by 100 to get $x = 4.5$ minutes to produce 450 screws. Next, convert minutes to seconds with another proportion. There are 60 seconds in 1 minute, so the proportion becomes $\frac{60 \text{ seconds}}{1 \text{ minute}} = \frac{x \text{ seconds}}{4.5 \text{ minutes}}$. Cross-multiply to get $(1)(x) = (60)(4.5)$, which becomes $x = 270$ seconds to produce 450 screws. It is also possible to convert the rate to screws per second before figuring out how long in seconds it will take to make 450 screws. No matter which order you do the steps in, write out everything to make sure you keep the units straight. The correct answer is 270.

PERCENTS

Percent just means "divided by 100." So, 20 percent = $\frac{20}{100} = \frac{1}{5}$, or 0.2.

Likewise, 400 percent = $\frac{400}{100} = \frac{4}{1} = 4$.

Any percent question can be translated into algebra—just use the following rules:

percent	÷ 100
of	×
what	x (or any variable)
is, are, equals	=

Take a look at some examples of phrases you might have to translate on the PSAT:

8 percent of 10	becomes	$\frac{8}{100}(10) = 0.8$
10 percent of 80		$\frac{10}{100}(80) = 8$
5 is what percent of 80?		$5 = \frac{x}{100} \times 80$
5 is 80 percent of what number?		$5 = \frac{80}{100}x$
What percent of 5 is 80?		$\frac{x}{100} \times 5 = 80$

11 Mark for Review

A shop owner fills a display case with 28 wheels of cheese. How many wheels of cheese are cheddar if 25% of the wheels of cheese are cheddar?

Here's How to Crack It

The question asks for a value based on a percent. Since *percent* means out of 100, translate 25% as $\frac{25}{100}$. Translate *of* as times to get $\frac{25}{100}(28) = 7$ wheels of cheddar.

It is also possible to use the built-in calculator to find 25% of the total of 28 wheels of cheese. The built-in calculator automatically adds "of" after the percent sign, so enter "25% 28" and the calculator will display "25% of 28" and will show "= 7" in the lower right corner of the entry field. Thus, 7 wheels of cheese are cheddar.

Using either of these methods, the correct answer is 7.

GROWTH AND DECAY

Another aspect of percent questions may relate to things that increase or decrease by a certain percent over time. This is known as "growth and decay." Real-world examples include population growth, radioactive decay, and credit payments, to name a few. While Plugging In can help on these, it is also useful to know the growth and decay formula.

When the growth or decay rate is a percent of the total:

$$\textit{final amount} = \textit{original amount}\ (1 \pm \textit{rate})^{\textit{number of changes}}$$

When the growth or decay is a multiple of the total:

$$\textit{final amount} = \textit{original amount}\ (\textit{multiplier})^{\textit{number of changes}}$$

Let's see how this formula can make quick work of an otherwise tedious question.

12 Mark for Review

The population of a certain city is currently 61,000 and is growing at a rate of 2.5% every three months. If the city's population, P, is a function of time in years, t, which of the following functions represents the city's population growth?

Ⓐ $P(t) = 61{,}000(1.025)^t$

Ⓑ $P(t) = 61{,}000(1.1)^t$

Ⓒ $P(t) = 61{,}000(1.025)^{4t}$

Ⓓ $P(t) = 61{,}000(1.1)^{3t}$

Here's How to Crack It

The question asks for a function to represent population growth over time. Carefully translate the information in the question in bite-sized pieces. Because the rate of growth is 2.5%, you need to add 0.025 (2.5% in decimal form) to 1 within the parentheses. This would be 1 + 0.025 = 1.025. Eliminate (B) and (D) because they do not have this piece. The only difference between (A) and (C) is the exponent, which represents the number of changes. Here, t is in years, but the population increases every 3 months, which is 4 times a year. This means you want 4 changes when $t = 1$; this gives you (C) as your answer.

RATIOS AND PROPORTIONS

Some questions will ask about ratios and proportions. With the strategies that you'll learn on the next few pages, you'll be well prepared to tackle these concepts on the PSAT.

$$\text{Fraction} = \frac{\text{part}}{\text{whole}}$$

$$\text{Ratio} = \frac{\text{part}}{\text{part}}$$

Ratios

Ratios are about relationships between numbers. Whereas a fraction is a relationship between a part and a whole, a ratio is about the relationship between parts. So, for example, if there were 3 boys and 7 girls in a room, the fraction of boys in the room would be $\frac{3}{10}$. But the ratio of boys to girls would be 3:7 or $\frac{3}{7}$. Notice that if you add up the parts, you get the whole: 7 + 3 = 10.

Filling In
A ratio is usually expressed as 2:3 or 2 to 3, but on a fill-in question, enter it as 2/3.

Ratio questions usually aren't difficult to identify. The question will tell you that there is a "ratio" of one thing to another, such as a 2:3 ratio of boys to girls in a club. Sometimes, a PSAT question will ask you to compare different ratios or to find the greatest or least ratio. To do so, divide the first part of the ratio by the second and compare the resulting values.

Try this one.

13 Mark for Review

The ratio a to b is equivalent to the ratio k to 15. In terms of k, what is the value of a when $b = 210$?

Ⓐ $225k$

Ⓑ $195k$

Ⓒ $15k$

Ⓓ $14k$

Here's How to Crack It

The question asks for the value of one variable in terms of another. The question asks about the relationship among variables and there is a variable in the answer choices, so one option is to plug in. However, that might get messy with three variables. The question gives the value of b, so the other option is to work with the ratios and solve for a. A ratio can be written as a fraction, so translate *the ratio a to b* as $\frac{a}{b}$, and translate *the ratio k to 15* as $\frac{k}{15}$. The question states that the two ratios are equivalent, so set the two fractions equal to each other: $\frac{a}{b} = \frac{k}{15}$. Next, plug in 210 for b, and the equation becomes $\frac{a}{210} = \frac{k}{15}$. Cross-multiply to get $(210)(k) = (a)(15)$, or $210k = 15a$. Divide both sides of the equation by 15 to get $14k = a$. The correct answer is (D).

Proportions

You have already used proportions to answer questions about rates and ratios. **Proportions** occur when two variables increase together or decrease together. These questions generally ask you to make a conversion (such as from ounces to pounds) or to compare two sets of information and find a missing piece. For example, a proportion question may ask you to figure out the amount of time it will take to travel 300 miles at a rate of 50 miles per hour.

> To answer proportion questions, just set up two equal fractions. One will have all the information you know, and the other will have a missing piece that you're trying to figure out.

$$\frac{50\text{ miles}}{1\text{ hour}} = \frac{300\text{ miles}}{x\text{ hours}}$$

Be sure to label the parts of your proportion so you'll know you have the right information in the right place; the same units should be in the numerator on both sides of the equals sign and the same units should be in the denominator on both sides of the equals sign. Notice how using a setup like this helps you keep track of the information you have and to find the information you're looking for.

Now you can cross-multiply and then solve for x: $50x = 300$, so $x = 6$ hours.

> **Formula for Proportions**
>
> $$\frac{x_1}{y_1} = \frac{x_2}{y_2}$$

Let's try the following question.

14 Mark for Review

John receives $2.50 for every 4 pounds of berries he picks. How much money will he receive if he picks 90 pounds of berries?

(A) $36.00

(B) $42.25

(C) $48.50

(D) $56.25

Here's How to Crack It

The question gives a relationship between two variables and asks for a value based on that relationship. To solve this, set up a proportion. Label the units to keep everything organized.

$$\frac{\$2.50}{4\text{ pounds}} = \frac{x}{90\text{ pounds}}$$

Now you can cross-multiply: $4x = 2.50 \times 90$, so $4x = 225$, and $x = 56.25$. The correct answer is (D).

Drill 3

Suggested Time Limit for Questions 1 through 8: 13 minutes. Answers can be found in Part IV.

a. If a student scores 70, 90, 95, and 105, what is the mean score for these tests? ________

b. If a student has a mean score of 80 on 4 tests, what is the total of the scores received on those tests? ________

c. If a student has a mean score of 60 on tests, with a total of 360, how many tests has the student taken? ________

d. If the mean of 2, 8, and x is 6, what is the value of x? ________

2, 3, 3, 4, 6, 8, 10, 12

e. What is the median of the group of numbers above? ______

f. What is the range of the group of numbers above? ________

g. What percent of 5 is 6? ________

h. 60 percent of 90 is the same as 50 percent of what number? ________

The amount of money in a savings account after m months is modeled by the function $f(m) = 1{,}000(1.01)^m$.

i. What was the original amount in the bank account? ________

j. By what percent does the amount in the account increase each month? ________

k. In a certain bag of marbles, the ratio of red marbles to green marbles is 7:5. If the bag contains 96 marbles, how many green marbles are in the bag? ________

l. One hogshead is equal to 64 gallons. How many hogsheads are equal to 96 gallons? ________

1 Mark for Review

If 10 pecks are equivalent to 2.5 bushels, then 4 bushels are equivalent to how many pecks?

Ⓐ 4

Ⓑ 10

Ⓒ 12.5

Ⓓ 16

2 Mark for Review

A forest fire is burning an area of forest that is 10 square miles. An air squad is able to reduce the size of the fire by 7% every hour. If $F(t)$ is the area being burned by the fire, which function represents the area of forest still on fire after t hours?

Ⓐ $F(t) = 0.07(10)^t$

Ⓑ $F(t) = 0.93(10)^t$

Ⓒ $F(t) = 10(0.07)^t$

Ⓓ $F(t) = 10(0.93)^t$

3 Mark for Review

A student took five tests. He scored a mean of 80 on the first three tests and a mean of 90 on the other two. What was the student's mean score on all five tests?

____

4 Mark for Review

Esther is paying off her student loans. She currently owes $\$20,000$, and she will reduce the amount due by $\frac{1}{2}$ every 5 years. How much will she owe after 20 years?

Ⓐ $\$625$

Ⓑ $\$1,000$

Ⓒ $\$1,250$

Ⓓ $\$5,000$

5 Mark for Review

A certain solution has a concentration of 125 milligrams of solute per cubic centimeter. If a syringe filled with this solution contains $1{,}000$ milligrams of solute, what is the volume of the syringe, in cubic centimeters?

Ⓐ 8

Ⓑ 64

Ⓒ 200

Ⓓ $1{,}125$

6 Mark for Review

When Everett drives home from college to visit his parents, he drives at an average speed of 66 miles per hour. When his parents go to visit him, they drive at an average speed of 54 miles per hour. If each trip is 594 miles long, approximately how much less time, in hours, does Everett spend driving than his parents spend driving?

Ⓐ 2

Ⓑ 9

Ⓒ 11

Ⓓ 12

7 Mark for Review

Estimated Numbers of Cell Phone Users by Type (in millions)

	Prepaid users	Contracted users	Total
2022	45	225	270
2023	75	250	325
Total	120	475	595

If a cell phone user from 2022 is selected at random, what is the probability that the user is a contracted user?

8 Mark for Review

How many gallons is equivalent to a volume of 768 fluid ounces?

(1 gallon $= 8$ pints and 1 pint $= 16$ fluid ounces)

Summary

- The test is full of opportunities to use arithmetic instead of algebra—just look for your chances to use Plugging In and Plugging In the Answers (PITA).
- If a question has *in terms of* or variables in the answer choices, it's a Plugging In question. Plug in your own number, do the math, find the target number, and use POE to get down to one correct answer.
- If a question doesn't have variables but asks for a fraction or a percent of an unknown number, you can also plug in. Just substitute your own number for the unknown and take the rest of the question step by step.
- If a question has an unknown and asks for a specific amount, making you feel as if you have to write an equation, try PITA instead.
- When a question asks about a mean or average, use $T = AN$, plug in the values given in the question, and solve for what you need. The built-in calculator can also calculate the mean of a list of numbers.
- The median is the middle value in a list of numbers in consecutive order from least to greatest. If there is an even number of elements, the median is the average of the two middle values. The built-in calculator can also calculate the median of a list of numbers.
- The range is the difference between the greatest and least values in a list of numbers.
- Probability is a fractional value between 0 and 1 (inclusive), and it is equal to the number of outcomes the question is asking for divided by the total number of possible outcomes. It can also be expressed as a percent.
- Percent simply means "per 100." Many percent questions can be tackled by translating English to math.

- Growth and decay are given by the formulas *final amount* = *original amount*(1 ± *rate*)$^{number\ of\ changes}$ and *final amount* = *original amount* (*multiplier*)$^{number\ of\ changes}$.
- Set up ratios like fractions. Take care to put the first term of the ratio in the numerator and the second term in the denominator.
- A proportion means as one value goes up, the other goes up. The formula is $\frac{x_1}{y_1} = \frac{x_2}{y_2}$.

Chapter 16
Advanced Math

There will be 7 or 8 questions on each Math module of the PSAT that test what College Board calls "Advanced Math," which is mostly nonlinear algebra. This category includes topics such as functions and quadratics. The algebra and calculator skills you learned in the Math Basics chapter and the test-taking tactics you learned in the Math Techniques chapter will all come in handy.

FUNCTIONS

In the Math Basics chapter, we looked at some concepts related to the *xy*-plane. Here, we will look at some more topics involving functions and graphs. The functions on the PSAT mostly look like this:

$$f(x) = x^2 + 6x + 24$$

Just Follow the Instructions
Functions are like recipes. Each one is just a set of directions for you to follow. College Board provides the ingredients and you work your magic.

Some questions of this type will give you a specific value to plug in for x and then ask you to find the value of the function. Each function is just a set of instructions that tells you what to do to x, the input, in order to find the corresponding value for $f(x)$ (a fancy name for y), the output. Just plug your information into that equation and follow the instructions.

Let's try an easy one.

---

1 Mark for Review

If $f(x) = x^2 + 3x - 3$, what is the value of $f(7)$?

Ⓐ 14

Ⓑ 20

Ⓒ 32

Ⓓ 67

Fundamental facts about functions
$f(x) = y$
x is the input
y is the output

Here's How to Crack It

The question asks for the value of $f(7)$ given the definition of $f(x)$. Function questions are just trying to see if you can follow the directions, so follow them! The instructions, in this case, are in the equation. The question gives an input value of 7, so plug 7 into the equation and it should look like this: $f(7) = (7)^2 + 3(7) - 3$. Do the math and $f(7) = 67$. Therefore, the answer is (D).

Sometimes you'll get more complicated questions. As long as you know that when you put in x, your function will spit out another number, you'll be fine. Try this next one.

2 Mark for Review

$$f(x) = 5x^3$$

The function f is defined by the given equation. If $f(x) = 135$, what is the value of x?

Ⓐ 3

Ⓑ 5

Ⓒ 27

Ⓓ 125

Here's How to Crack It

The question asks for a value given a function. If you remember your functions basics, you know that x is the value that goes into the function, or the input, and y is the value that comes out of the function, or the output. The question gives an output value of 135 and asks which input, or x, will produce that value. It must be one of the answer choices, so plug in the answers!

Start with one of the middle values and try (B), 5. Plug $x = 5$ into the function to get $f(5) = 5(5)^3$. Simplify the right side of the equation to get $f(5) = 5(125)$, and then $f(5) = 625$. This is too big, so eliminate (B).

Since (C) and (D) will also be too big, the answer has to be (A), but try it just in case. Plug $x = 3$ into the function to get $f(3) = 5(3)^3$. Simplify the right side of the equation to get $f(3) = 5(27)$, and then $f(3) = 135$. This matches the output value given in the question, so stop here. The correct answer is (A).

The PSAT will also relate points and functions by using tables, and plugging in will be useful once again. If the question has a table and the answers have functions, plug pairs of values from the table into the answer choices and eliminate functions that don't work. If the question has a function and the answers have tables of values, plug in x-values from the answers and eliminate answers that have the wrong y-value. The built-in calculator will often help you visualize what's going on.

Here's an example.

3 Mark for Review

Linear function g is defined by the equation $g(x) = 25$. Which table gives three values of x with their corresponding values of $g(x)$?

Ⓐ

x	$g(x)$
1	0
2	0
3	0

Ⓑ

x	$g(x)$
1	25
2	50
3	75

Ⓒ

x	$g(x)$
1	−25
2	0
3	25

Ⓓ

x	$g(x)$
1	25
2	25
3	25

Here's How to Crack It

The question asks for the table that contains values that are solutions to a function. In function notation, $g(x) = y$, so $y = 25$. This will be true for all values of x, which makes (D) correct. To check, enter the equation into the built-in calculator, either as $g(x) = 25$ or as $y = 25$. Scroll and zoom as needed to see that the graph is a straight horizontal line at $y = 25$. Whether $x = 1$, $x = 2$, or $x = 3$, the value of y is always 25. The correct answer is (D).

Sometimes the PSAT will use a word problem to describe a function, and then ask you to "build a function" that describes that real-world situation.

Try one of those.

4 Mark for Review

A scientist noted that the rate of growth of a tree which he had been observing is directly proportional to time. The scientist first measured the height of the tree to be 20 feet; two years later, the tree was 21 feet tall. If the tree continues to grow at a constant rate, which of the following represents the height of the tree in feet, $f(x)$, as a function of time, x, in years since the scientist's first measurement?

Ⓐ $f(x) = 0.5x + 20$

Ⓑ $f(x) = 21x + 20$

Ⓒ $f(x) = x + 20$

Ⓓ $f(x) = 20x + 21$

Here's How to Crack It

The question asks for the function that represents the height of the tree over time. Instead of trying to write your own equation, use the ones in the answer choices. According to the question, 2 years after the first measurement, the tree was 21 feet tall. Therefore, when $x = 2, f(x) = 21$. Plug these values into the answers to see which answer works. Choice (A) becomes $21 = 0.5(2) + 20$. Solve the right side of the equation to get $21 = 1 + 20$, or $21 = 21$. The correct function must work for all of the input and output values, so check the remaining answers just in case. Choice (B) becomes $21 = 21(2) + 20$, then $21 = 42 + 20$, and finally $21 = 62$. This is not true, so eliminate (B). Choice (C) becomes $21 = 2 + 20$, or $21 = 22$; eliminate (C). Choice (D) becomes $21 = 20(2) + 21$, then $21 = 40 + 21$, and finally $21 = 61$; eliminate (D). Only (A) worked, so it is the correct function. The correct answer is (A).

Types of Functions

Some PSAT questions will ask you to describe the type of function based on a scenario. The answer choices will be combinations of increasing/decreasing and linear/exponential, so use the information in the question—and perhaps the built-in calculator—to eliminate answer choices.

Here's an example.

5 Mark for Review

The function g is defined by the statement "$g(x)$ is 30% of $-x$" for $x < 0$. Which of the following could describe this function?

Ⓐ Decreasing exponential

Ⓑ Decreasing linear

Ⓒ Increasing exponential

Ⓓ Increasing linear

Here's How to Crack It

It may be tempting to assume that % means exponential and the negative sign in front of x means decreasing and pick (A), but use all of the tools at your disposal and check with the built-in calculator. Translate *is* as =. The built-in calculator automatically adds "of" after the percent sign, so enter "$g(x) = 30\% -x$" and the calculator will display "$g(x) = 30\%$ of $-x$."

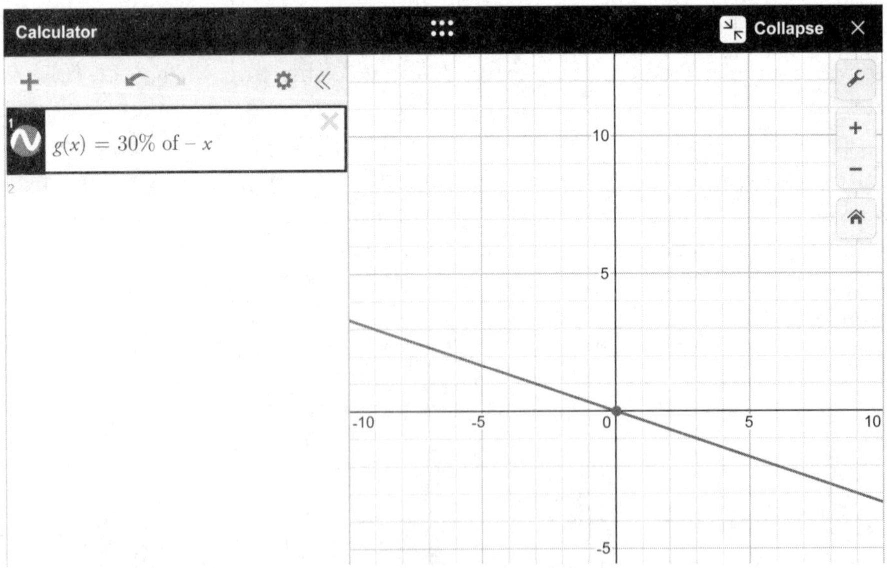

Look in the graphing area to see a straight line descending from left to right, which means the function is linear and decreasing. The "obvious" answer, (A), was half-right, but that's still wrong! The correct answer is (B).

Drill 1

Suggested Time Limit: 9 minutes. Answers can be found in Part IV.

1 Mark for Review

$$h(a) = 5a^4$$

The function h is defined by the given equation. What is the value of a when $h(a)$ equals 405?

Ⓐ $\frac{1}{81}$

Ⓑ 3

Ⓒ $\frac{81}{4}$

Ⓓ 81

2 Mark for Review

A car dealership leases a new truck for a down payment of \$3,200 plus monthly payments of \$380 per month for 36 months. Which of the following functions, f, represents the total amount paid, in dollars, after m months, where $0 \leq m \leq 36$?

Ⓐ $f(m) = 380 + 3{,}200m$

Ⓑ $f(m) = 3{,}200 + 36m$

Ⓒ $f(m) = 3{,}200 + 380m$

Ⓓ $f(m) = 10{,}480 - 380m$

3 Mark for Review

The number of bonus points, $B(p)$, that a credit card holder receives is given by the function $B(p) = ap + 7$, where p represents the number of purchases made and a is a constant. If the number of purchases is increased by 4, the number of bonus points increases by 25. What is the value of a?

Ⓐ 4

Ⓑ 4.5

Ⓒ 6.25

Ⓓ 11

4 Mark for Review

x	-1	c	3
$f(x)$	-2	c	4

The table shows selected values for the linear function $f(x)$. What is the value of c?

Ⓐ $\frac{2}{3}$

Ⓑ 1

Ⓒ $\frac{3}{2}$

Ⓓ 2

5 Mark for Review

A certain sandwich shop sells sandwiches every day from Monday through Friday. Each day throughout a given week, the shop sells twice as many sandwiches as the day before. Which type of function best models the relationship between the number of sandwiches sold and the day of the week?

Ⓐ Decreasing exponential

Ⓑ Decreasing linear

Ⓒ Increasing exponential

Ⓓ Increasing linear

6 Mark for Review

Which of the following could be the equation of linear function f if $f(2) = -5$, and $f(4) = 15$?

Ⓐ $f(x) = 5x - 25$

Ⓑ $f(x) = 10x - 25$

Ⓒ $f(x) = 10x - 5$

Ⓓ $f(x) = 10x$

QUADRATIC EQUATIONS

Ah, quadratics. You're likely to see several questions on the PSAT that require you to expand, factor, or solve quadratics. You may even need to find the vertex of a parabola or the points of intersection of a quadratic and a line. We'll review the basics, but keep in mind that the built-in calculator is often the best way to answer questions about quadratics, parabolas, and systems of equations.

Expanding

The first basic operation you might need to perform with a quadratic is to expand an expression simply by multiplying it out. When working with an expression of the form $(x + 3)(x + 4)$, multiply it out using the following rule:

FOIL = First Outer Inner Last

Start with the *first* figure in each set of parentheses: $x \times x = x^2$.

Now do the two *outer* figures: $x \times 4 = 4x$.

Next, the two *inner* figures: $3 \times x = 3x$.

Finally, the *last* figure in each set of parentheses: $3 \times 4 = 12$.

Add them all together, and we get $x^2 + 4x + 3x + 12$, or $x^2 + 7x + 12$.

Factoring

The reverse of expanding is factoring. If you ever see an expression of the form $x^2 + 7x + 12$ on the PSAT, there is a good chance that factoring it will be the key to cracking it.

The key to factoring is figuring out what pair of numbers will multiply to give you the constant term (12, in this case) and add up to the coefficient of the x term (7, in this case).

Let's try an example:

$$x^2 + 7x + 12$$

Step 1: Draw two sets of parentheses next to each other and fill an x into the left side of each. That's what gives us our x^2 term.

$$(x \quad)(x \quad)$$

Step 2: 12 can be factored a number of ways: 1×12, 2×6, and 3×4. Which of these adds up to 7? It's 3 and 4, so place a 3 on the right side of one set of parentheses and a 4 in the other.

$$(x \quad 3)(x \quad 4)$$

Step 3: Now we need to figure out what the correct signs should be. They should both be positive in this case, because that will sum to 7 and multiply to 12, so fill plus signs into each parentheses.

$$(x + 3)(x + 4)$$

A quick way to compare different forms of a quadratic is to graph both forms in the built-in calculator to see whether the resulting graphs are the same. For example, enter the expanded and factored forms from the previous examples:

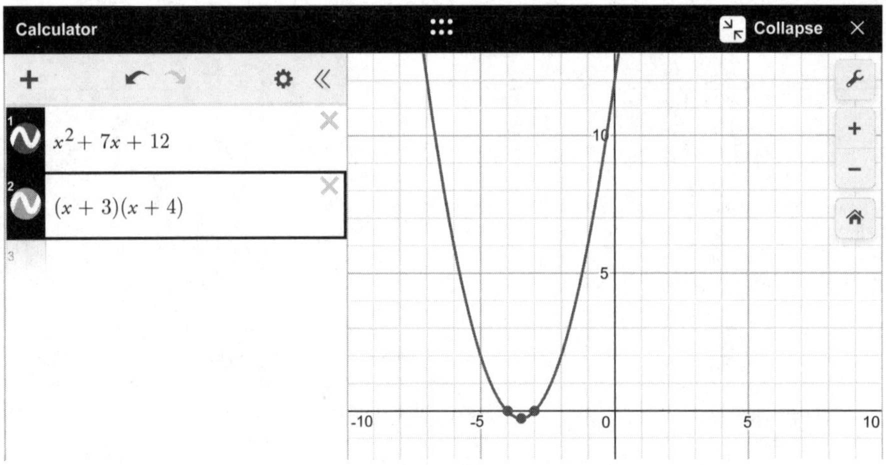

To confirm that the graphs are the same, you can click on one equation after the other to see the same parabola change color, compare the coordinates marked by gray dots, or click on one of the symbols to hide that graph and see the other.

Now try the following question.

6 Mark for Review

$$324a^2 - 484$$

Which of the following is equivalent to the given expression?

Ⓐ $(18a - 22)(18a + 22)$

Ⓑ $(18a - 22)(18a - 22)$

Ⓒ $(9a - 11)(9a + 11)$

Ⓓ $(9a - 11)(9a - 11)$

You can also plug in on a question like this. The question has the word *equivalent*, and there are variables in the answers.

Here's How to Crack It

The question asks for an equivalent form of an expression. The first and second terms are perfect squares and are being subtracted, so one approach is to factor the perfect squares to get $(18a + 22)(18a - 22)$. Check that (A) is correct by using FOIL—First, Outer, Inner, Last—to expand factored form into standard form: $(18a + 22)(18a - 22) = 324a^2 - 396a + 396a - 484$, which becomes $324a^2 - 484$. Thus, $(18a + 22)(18a - 22)$ is an equivalent form of $324a^2 - 484$, and (A) is correct.

Another method is to use the built-in calculator. Change every a to x in order to see a graph. Enter the expression from the question in the first entry field, and then enter the expression for (A) in the second entry field. The graph is the same, so (A) is an equivalent form. If (A) didn't work, you could change numbers and signs to test the expressions in the remaining answer choices until one of them worked.

Using either of these methods—or Plugging In—the correct answer is (A).

Solutions

Sometimes you'll want to factor to solve an equation. In this case, there will be two possible values for x, which you might know as roots or zeros but are usually called solutions on the PSAT. You can solve for the solutions by hand using algebra, but the built-in calculator is usually easier and faster. To solve for x algebraically, use the following steps:

Step 1: Make sure that the equation is set equal to zero.
Step 2: Factor the equation.
Step 3: Set each parenthetical expression equal to zero. So, if you have $(x + 2)(x - 7) = 0$, you get $(x + 2) = 0$ and $(x - 7) = 0$. When you solve for each, you get $x = -2$ and $x = 7$. Therefore, –2 and 7 are the solutions or roots of the equation.

Try the following question.

7 Mark for Review

If $x^2 + 2x - 8 = 0$, and $x < 0$, what is the value of x?

Ⓐ –6

Ⓑ –4

Ⓒ –2

Ⓓ 0

Here's How to Crack It

The question asks for the value of x in a quadratic equation. The question states that $x < 0$, so it is asking for the negative solution. Enter the equation into the built-in calculator, and you will see two vertical lines. You might have expected to see a parabola, and if you delete the "=0" part of the equation, you will. However, it's better to get used to the vertical lines because they show the solutions no matter what form the quadratic is in. Click on the gray dots to see that the solutions are at (–4, 0) and (2, 0). The question asks for the negative value of x, which is –4, so (B) is correct.

To solve algebraically, start by using Process of Elimination. Since the question states that $x < 0$, eliminate (D). Now follow the steps:

1. The equation is already set equal to zero.
2. You can now factor the left side of the equation to get $(x + 4)(x - 2) = 0$.
3. When you set each parenthetical expression equal to zero, you get $x = -4$ and $x = 2$. Since $x < 0$, the answer is –4, or (B).

Using either of these methods, the correct answer is (B).

Sometimes, a PSAT question will ask about the solution(s) to a system of one quadratic equation and one linear equation. As before, start with the calculator and fall back on algebra only if it's absolutely necessary.

Let's try one.

8 Mark for Review

$$x - 5 = 2$$

$$y = x^2 - 12x + 35$$

The given system of equations has the solution (x, y). What is the value of y?

Here's How to Crack It

The question asks for the value of the y-coordinate of the solution to a system of equations. Try the built-in calculator before doing anything else. Enter each equation into an entry field, and then scroll and zoom as needed to find the point of intersection. That point is (7, 0). Be careful! The question asks for the y-coordinate, so 0 is correct.

To solve the system for the y-coordinate algebraically, first isolate x in the first equation. Add 5 to both sides of the equation to get $x = 7$. Now, plug in 7 for x in the second equation to get $y = 7^2 - 12(7) + 35$. Simplify the right side of the equation to get $y = 49 - 84 + 35$, which becomes $y = 0$.

Using either of these methods, the correct answer is 0.

Forms of Quadratics

When graphed in the xy-plane, quadratics form a parabola. The PSAT will ask questions using three different forms of the equation for a parabola.

> The **standard form** of a parabola equation is as follows:
>
> $$y = ax^2 + bx + c$$

In the standard form of a parabola, the value of a tells whether a parabola opens upward or downward (if a is positive, the parabola opens upward, and if a is negative, the parabola opens downward).

There are two useful shortcuts to know when a quadratic is in standard form.

The sum of the solutions is $-\frac{b}{a}$.

The product of the solutions is $\frac{c}{a}$.

We discussed factoring quadratics a few pages back. The result of factoring a parabolic equation is the factored form.

> The **factored form** of a parabola equation is as follows:
>
> $$y = a(x - s)(x - t)$$
>
> In the factored form, s and t are the x-intercepts.

The final form you might see is called vertex form.

> The **vertex form** of a parabola equation is as follows:
>
> $$y = a(x - h)^2 + k$$
>
> In the vertex form, the point (h, k) is the vertex of the parabola.

9 Mark for Review

$$x^2 + 60x + 15 = 0$$

What is the product of the solutions to the given equation?

(A) -60

(B) -15

(C) 15

(D) 60

Here's How to Crack It

The question asks for the product of the solutions to a quadratic equation. Rather than trying to factor the quadratic—which will not be easy in this case—use the shortcut that the product of the solutions is $\frac{c}{a}$ when a quadratic equation is in standard form, $ax^2 + bx + c = 0$. In this quadratic, $c = 15$ and $a = 1$, so the product of the solutions is $\frac{15}{1}$, or 15, making (C) correct.

If you forget the shortcut, or simply prefer using the calculator, enter the equation into the built-in calculator. The solutions are shown by gray dots at (–59.749, 0) and (–0.251, 0). Multiply the two x-values to get $(-59.749)(-0.251) \approx 14.997$. This is almost 15, so (C) is correct.

Using either of these methods, the correct answer is (C).

The vertex form is great for answering questions about the minimum or maximum value a parabolic function will reach or the x-value that results in that minimum or maximum y-value. So, another good thing to know is the method for turning a quadratic in the standard form into the vertex form. One way is to complete the square, but it is often simpler to use the formula

$$h = -\frac{b}{2a}$$

This solves for h, the x-coordinate of the vertex, using the values of a and b in standard form. Then plug the value of h into the standard form equation to find k, the y-coordinate of the vertex.

Say you were given the equation $x^2 - 4x - 12$. The equation for the x-coordinate of the vertex becomes $h = -\frac{-4}{2(1)}$, or $h = 2$. Plug that into the standard form quadratic to get $2^2 - 4(2) - 12$, which becomes $4 - 8 - 12 = -16$. The vertex is (2, –16), and the vertex form of the equation is $y = (x - 2)^2 - 16$.

You can also find the vertex quickly by using the built-in calculator. Carefully enter the equation of the parabola. The graph will mark the vertex and intercepts with gray dots. Hover over or click on the dot at the vertex, and it will show the coordinates. Your screen will look like this:

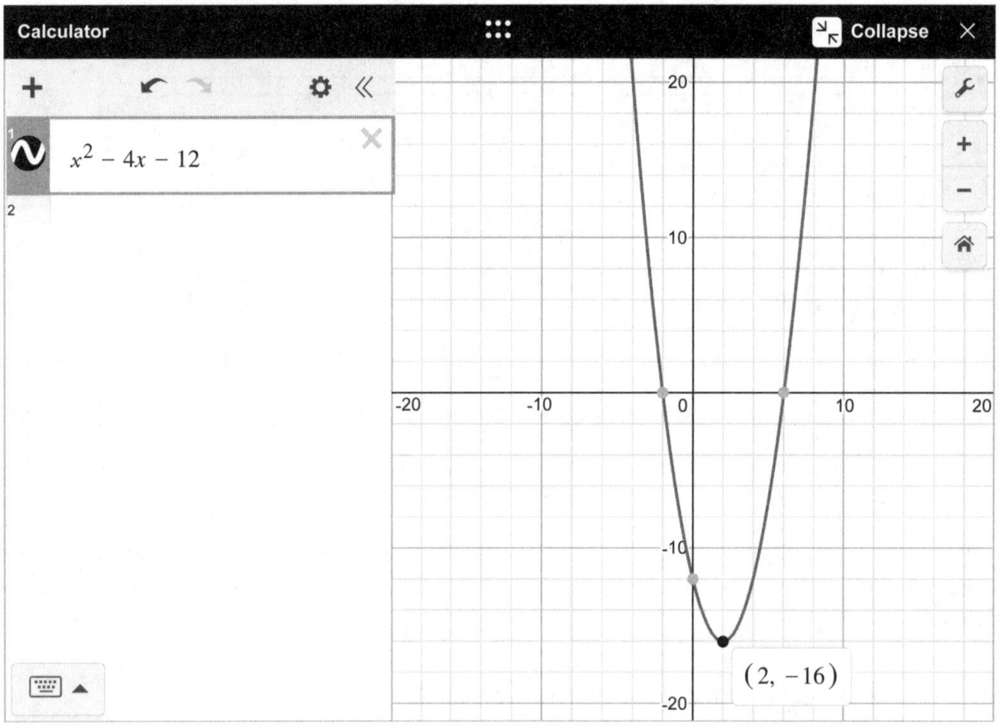

Your Friend the Calculator

As you have seen, the built-in calculator can be a game changer on some questions, especially ones dealing with functions and graphs. Here's how to become familiar with everything it can do so you're ready to take full advantage on test day.

1. Read the *Digital PSAT Calculator Guide* in your online student tools.
2. Practice with the calculator in the testing app. When you open the Bluebook app, click on Test Preview and advance to the math section. This way, you can experiment with the built-in calculator without being timed or scored.
3. Use it while working through this book, practice tests, and any other prep that you do.

Other Quadratic Questions

Sometimes, quadratic equations will be tested with word problems or charts. Let's look at these types of questions.

10 Mark for Review

The profit that a donut shop makes can be modeled by the equation $P = -4x^2 + 24x + 1{,}964$, where x is the price per donut sold, in dollars. What price, in dollars, should the donut shop charge per donut in order to maximize its profit?

Here's How to Crack It

If you look past the words, this question gives you a quadratic in standard form, $ax^2 + bx + c$, and asks for the maximum, which is the vertex. Enter the equation into the built-in calculator, and then scroll and zoom to see the vertex. Click on the gray dot to see that the coordinates of the vertex are (3, 2,000). The question asks for the price, in dollars, per donut, which is x. Thus, the company should charge $3.00 per donut in order to maximize its profit. The correct answer is 3.

Now look at an example of a chart-based quadratic question.

11 Mark for Review

Trajectory of a Dolphin's Jump

Horizontal distance (feet)	Vertical height (feet)
0	0
1	2.7
2	4.8
3	6.3
4	7.2
5	7.5
6	7.2
7	6.3
8	4.8
9	2.7
10	0

The table shows the horizontal distance and vertical height, both in feet, of a typical dolphin jumping out of the water (a height of 0 represents the surface of the water). If d represents the horizontal distance and h represents the vertical height, which of the following equations would best represent the trajectory of the dolphin's jump?

Ⓐ $h = -0.3d^2 + 3d$

Ⓑ $h = -0.4d^2 + 4d$

Ⓒ $h = -0.5d^2 + 5d$

Ⓓ $h = -0.6d^2 + 6d$

Here's How to Crack It

The question asks for an equation to model the trajectory of a dolphin's jump based on a table of values. This is a similar task to "building a function" that we discussed earlier in this chapter. You should plug values from the table into the equations in the answer choices to see which equation works. According to the table, when $d = 1$, $h = 2.7$. Plug these values into (A) to get $2.7 = -0.3(1^2) + 3(1)$. Solve the right side of the equation to get $2.7 = -0.3 + 3$ or $2.7 = 2.7$.

Keep (A), but check the remaining answers just in case. Choice (B) becomes $2.7 = -0.4(1^2) + 4(1)$. Solve the right side of the equation to get $2.7 = -0.4 + 4$ or $2.7 = 3.6$. This is not true, so eliminate (B). Choice (C) becomes $2.7 = -0.5(1^2) + 5(1)$. Solve the right side of the equation to get $2.7 = -0.5 + 5$ or $2.7 = 4.5$. Eliminate (C). Choice (D) becomes $2.7 = -0.6(1^2) + 6(1)$. Solve the right side of the equation to get $2.7 = -0.6 + 6$ or $2.7 = 5.4$. Eliminate (D). The correct answer is (A).

Other word problems will ask you to interpret part of a linear or nonlinear function or equation. For these, label parts of the equation one at a time, and use that information to eliminate answer choices.

12 Mark for Review

Two groups spend the morning cleaning windows, and each person takes the same amount of time per window cleaned. Group A cleans p windows per person, and group B cleans q windows per person. At the end of the morning, the two groups have cleaned a total of 122 windows. If the situation can be represented by the equation $5p + 11q = 122$, what is the best interpretation of the number 11 in this context?

Ⓐ Group A cleans 11 windows per person.

Ⓑ Group B cleans 11 windows per person.

Ⓒ Group A has 11 people in it.

Ⓓ Group B has 11 people in it.

Here's How to Crack It

The question asks for the meaning of a number in context. Start by reading the final question, which asks for the meaning of the number 11. Then label the parts of the equation with the information given. The question states that *Group A cleans p windows per person, and group B cleans q windows per person*. There's no way for two parts of the equation to represent the same thing, so 11 cannot be the number of windows cleaned by one of the groups. Eliminate (A) and (B).

Since q represents the number of windows washed by each person in group B, the number multiplied by q must have something to do with group B. Eliminate (C). If 5 and 11 represent the number of people in group A and group B, respectively, that would mean that 5 times the number of windows washed per person in group A plus 11 times the number of windows washed per person in group B equals the total number of windows washed, so the equation makes sense. You didn't really need to figure that out, though, because labeling and using Process of Elimination got you the right answer, which is (D).

Drill 2

Suggested Time Limit: 16 minutes. Answers can be found in Part IV.

1 Mark for Review

If $12 - (x + 2)^2 = 3$, which of the following could be the value of x?

Ⓐ −9

Ⓑ −5

Ⓒ 5

Ⓓ 7

2 Mark for Review

The function g is defined by the equation $g(x) = (x - 14)^2 - 6$. For what value of x does $g(x)$ reach its minimum?

______

3 Mark for Review

Which of the following equations has a vertex of $(-5, -2)$?

Ⓐ $y = x^2 - 10x - 23$

Ⓑ $y = x^2 - 10x + 23$

Ⓒ $y = x^2 + 10x - 23$

Ⓓ $y = x^2 + 10x + 23$

4 Mark for Review

The function $f(x) = 35{,}000(0.82)^x$ predicts the amount of a certain car's value, in dollars, x years after the car is purchased new, where $0 < x \leq 15$. What is the best interpretation of the statement "$f(7)$ is approximately equal to $8{,}725$" in this context?

Ⓐ When the car's predicted value is approximately $8{,}725$ dollars, it is 7% greater than the predicted value for the following year.

Ⓑ When the car's predicted value is approximately $8{,}725$ dollars, it is 7 times the predicted value for the following year.

Ⓒ 7 years after the car is purchased, its predicted value will have decreased by a total of $8{,}725$ dollars.

Ⓓ 7 years after the car is purchased, its predicted value is approximately $8{,}725$ dollars.

5 Mark for Review

The height in feet (h) of a certain projectile t seconds after being launched can be expressed using the function $h(t) = -5t^2 + 20t + 45$. Which of the following represents the initial height of the projectile, in feet?

Ⓐ -5

Ⓑ 20

Ⓒ 45

Ⓓ 65

6 Mark for Review

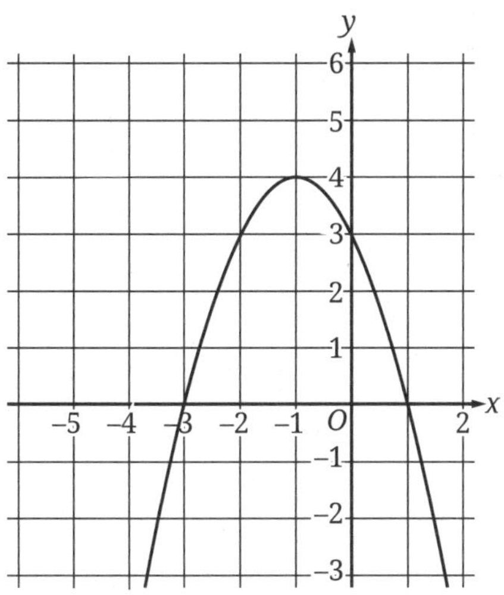

Which of the following equations is shown graphed in the xy-plane?

Ⓐ $y = -(x - 3)(x + 1)$

Ⓑ $y = -(x + 3)(x - 1)$

Ⓒ $y = -(x + 3)(x + 4)$

Ⓓ $y = -(x - 1)(x + 4)$

7 Mark for Review

If $f(x) = x^2 - x + 4$, a is non-negative, and $f(a) = 10$, what is the value of a?

8 Mark for Review

In the equation $x^2 + 24x + c = (x + 9)(x + p)$, c and p are constants. If the equation is true for all values of x, what is the value of c?

Ⓐ 33

Ⓑ 135

Ⓒ 144

Ⓓ 216

9 Mark for Review

The stream of water that shoots out of a certain fountain takes the form of a parabola. The water shoots from a spout that is 8 feet above the ground and reaches a maximum height of 39.25 feet. If y represents the height of the water, in feet, and x represents the time, in seconds, which of the following equations could describe the trajectory of the stream of water?

Ⓐ $y = -x^2 + 15$

Ⓑ $y = -5x^2 + 25x + 8$

Ⓒ $y = 2x^2 + 32x + 8$

Ⓓ $y = 8x + 39.25$

10 Mark for Review

$$g(x) = -\frac{c+7}{x} - 2$$

Function g is defined by the given equation, where c is a constant. The graph of function h in the xy-plane, where $y = h(x)$, is the result of translating the graph of $y = g(x)$ to the left 2 units and up 5 units. Which equation defines function h?

Ⓐ $h(x) = -\frac{c+12}{x-2} - 2$

Ⓑ $h(x) = -\frac{c+12}{x+2} - 2$

Ⓒ $h(x) = -\frac{c+7}{x-2} + 3$

Ⓓ $h(x) = -\frac{c+7}{x+2} + 3$

Summary

- Don't be intimidated by "Advanced Math" topics. Keep using your test-taking skills (such as Plugging In and POE), the built-in calculator, and your knowledge of algebra.
- Given a function, you put an x-value in and get an $f(x)$ or y-value out.
- Look for ways to use Plugging In and PITA on function questions.
- For questions about the graphs of functions, remember that $f(x) = y$.
- If the graph contains a labeled point or the question gives you a point, plug it into the equations in the answers and eliminate any that aren't true.
- To find a point of intersection, either graph the equations using the built-in calculator, set the equations equal, or plug a given point into both equations to see if it works.
- When solving quadratic equations, you may need to FOIL or factor to get the equation into the easiest form for the question task.
- The standard form of a quadratic equation is $ax^2 + bx + c = 0$. In this form, the sum of the solutions is $-\frac{b}{a}$, and the product of the solutions is $\frac{c}{a}$.
- The factored form of a quadratic equation is $y = a(x - s)(x - t)$, where s and t are the x-intercepts.
- Use the built-in calculator for questions about the solutions or number of solutions to a quadratic or a system of equations.
- The vertex form of a parabola equation is $y = a(x - h)^2 + k$, where (h, k) is the vertex. To get a parabola in the standard form into vertex form, use the equation $h = -\frac{b}{2a}$. To find the vertex, use the built-in calculator.

Chapter 17
Geometry and Trigonometry

Approximately 12.5% of the questions on the PSAT Math section will be about geometry and trigonometry. While there are many topics in these categories that could be tested, each one will appear only once or twice on the test. Everything you've learned so far, such as Plugging In and POE, will often work on geometry and trig questions. Spend time on this chapter only after you have mastered the topics and techniques in the previous three chapters.

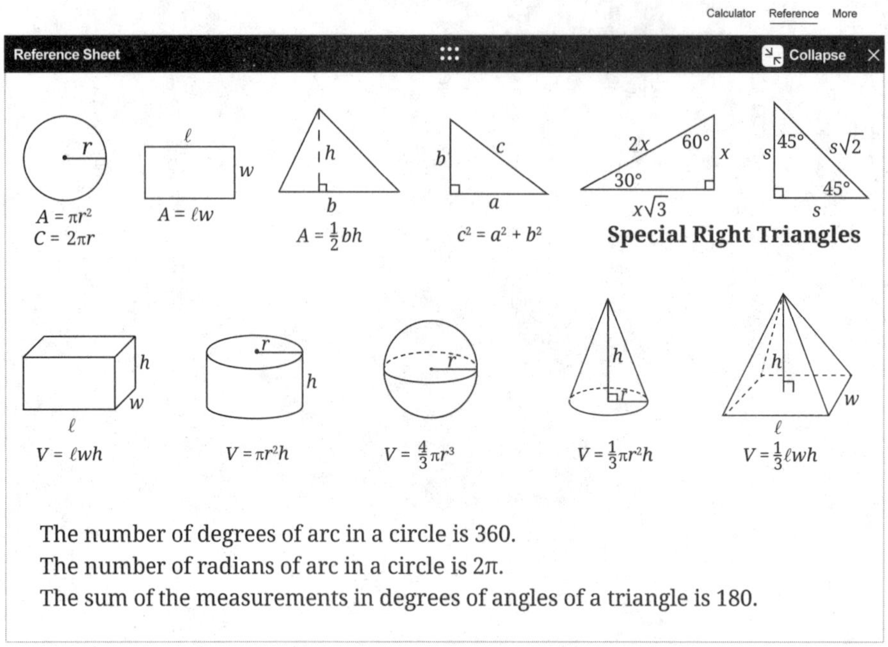

You can access the reference sheet above at any point during the Math section by clicking **Reference** in the upper right corner of the screen. Once you look up the information you need, click the **X** to return to the question. You can also click **Collapse** to shrink the reference window in order to see the formulas and the question at the same time or **Expand** to make it full size.

GEOMETRY

Lines and Angles

Common sense might tell you what a line is, but for this test you are going to have to learn the particulars of a line, a ray, and a line segment.

A **line** continues on in each direction forever. You need only two points to form a line, but that line does not end at those points. A straight line has 180 degrees on each side.

A **ray** is a line with one distinct endpoint. Again, you need only two points to designate a ray, but one of those points is where it stops—it continues on forever in the other direction. A ray has 180 degrees as well.

A **line segment** is a line with two distinct endpoints. It requires two points, and it is the length from one point to the other. A line segment has 180 degrees.

Whenever you have angles on a line, remember *the rule of 180*: The angles on any line must add up to 180. These angles are called *supplementary angles.* In the figure below, what is the value of x? We know that $2x + x$ must add up to 180, so we know that $3x = 180$. This makes $x = 60$.

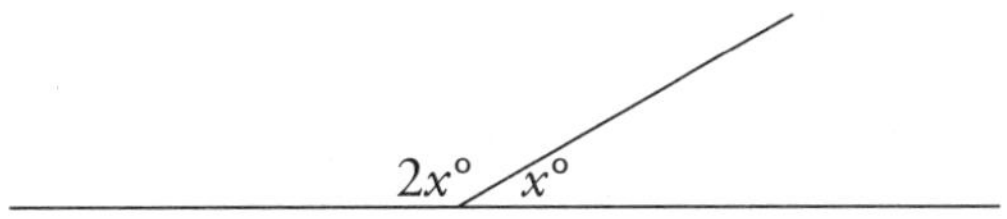

Note: Figure not drawn to scale.

If two lines cross each other, they make *vertical angles*—that is, angles opposite each other when two lines intersect. These angles will always have the same measure. In the figure below, z and x are vertical angles, and y and the 130° angle are vertical angles. Also, we know that z must equal 50, since $130 + z$ must equal 180. We know that y is 130, since it is across from the 130° angle. We also know that x is 50, since it is across from z.

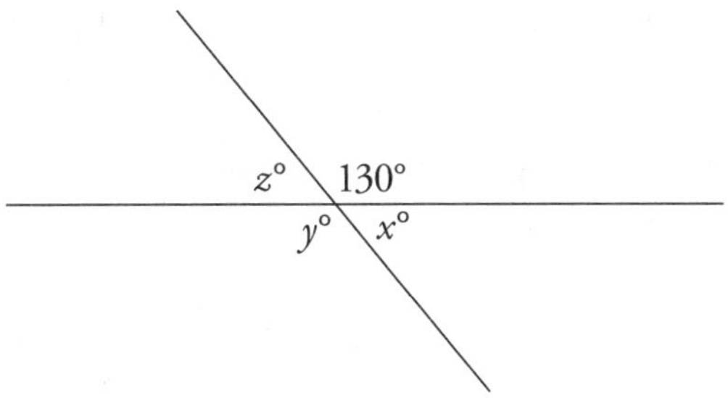

Any time you have two parallel lines and a line that crosses them, you have two kinds of angles: big angles and small angles. All of the big angles have the same measure, and all of the small angles have the same measure. In the following figure, angles a, d, e, and h all have the same measure; angles b, c, f, and g also all have the same measure. The sum of the measure of any big angle plus any small angle equals 180 degrees.

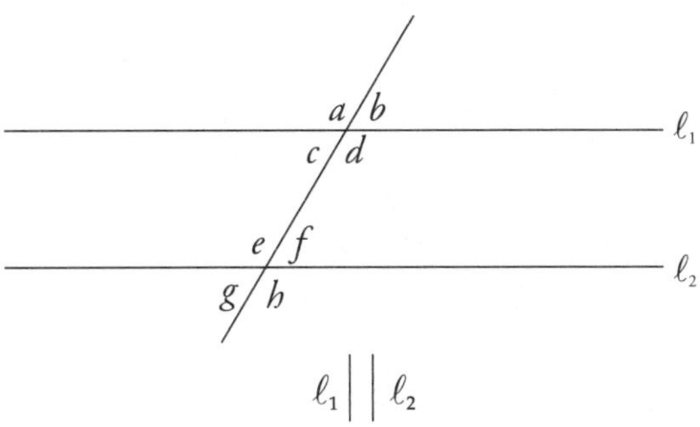

Four-Sided Figures

Thinking Inside the Box

Here's a progression of quadrilaterals from least specific to most specific:

quadrilateral = 4-sided figure

↓

parallelogram = a quadrilateral in which opposite sides are parallel

↓

rectangle = a parallelogram in which all angles equal 90°

↓

square = a rectangle in which all angles and all sides are equal

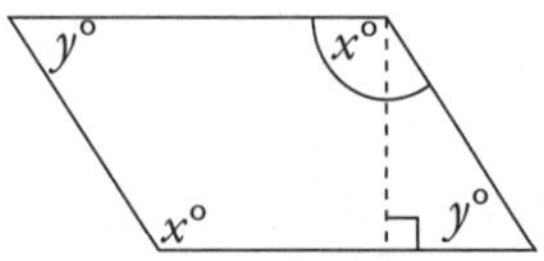

Parallelogram

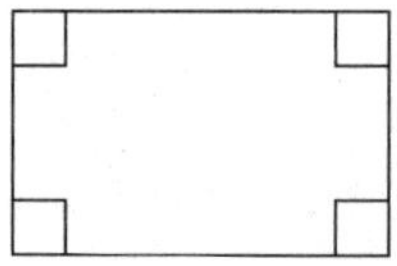
Rectangle

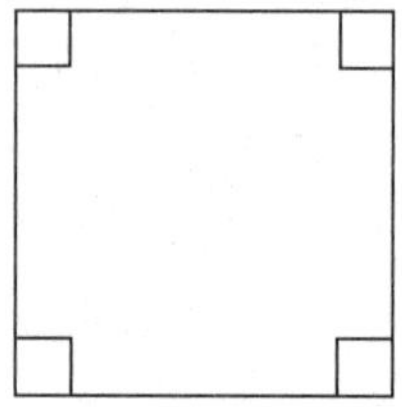
Square

A figure with two sets of parallel sides is a **parallelogram**. In a parallelogram, the opposite angles are equal, and any adjacent angles add up to 180 degrees. (In the left-hand figure above, $x + y = 180$ degrees.) Opposite sides are also equal. The sum of all angles of a parallelogram is 360 degrees.

If all of the angles are also right angles, then the figure is a **rectangle**. And if all of the sides are the same length, then the figure is a **square**.

The *area* of a square, rectangle, or parallelogram is *length* × *width*. (In the parallelogram above, the length is shown by the dotted line.)

The *perimeter* of any figure is the sum of the lengths of its sides. A quadrilateral with sides of 6, 8, 10, and 8 has a perimeter of 32.

Drill 1

Suggested Time Limit for Questions 1 through 4: 6 minutes. Answers can be found in Part IV.

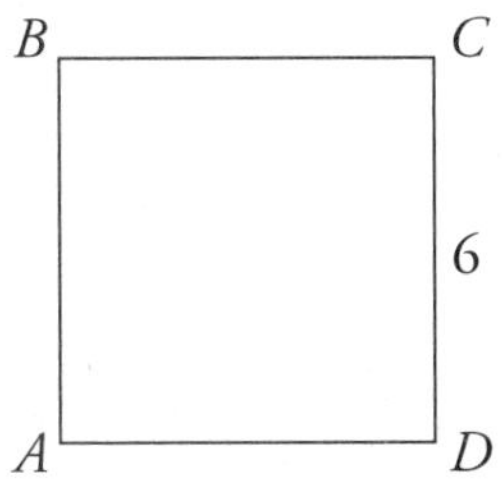

a. What is the area of square *ABCD* above? __________

b. What is the perimeter of square *ABCD* above? __________

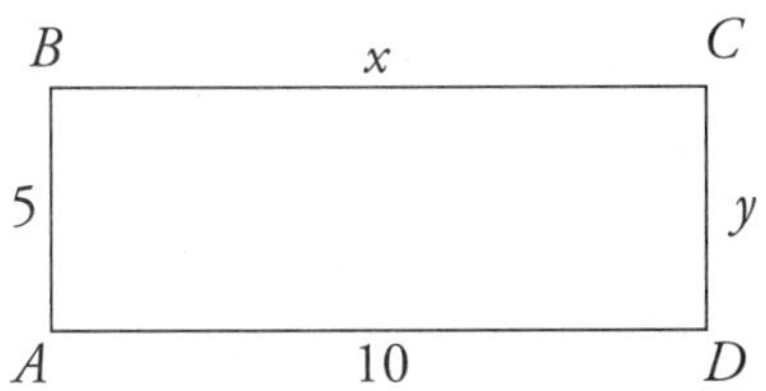

c. If *ABCD* is a rectangle, x = __________
y = __________

d. What is the perimeter of rectangle *ABCD* above? __________

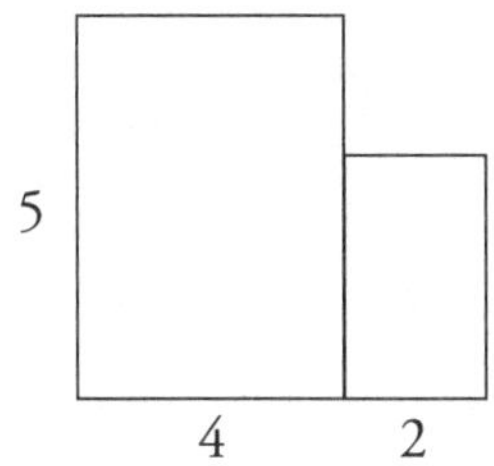

e. If the above figure is composed of two rectangles, what is the perimeter of the figure? __________

1 Mark for Review

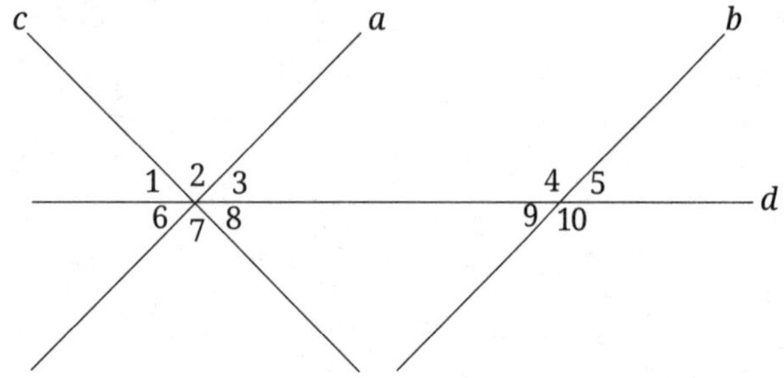

In the figure, lines a and b are parallel. Which of the following pairs of angles must have equal degree measures?

I. 1 and 5
II. 2 and 7
III. 3 and 9

Ⓐ I only

Ⓑ II only

Ⓒ III only

Ⓓ II and III only

2 Mark for Review

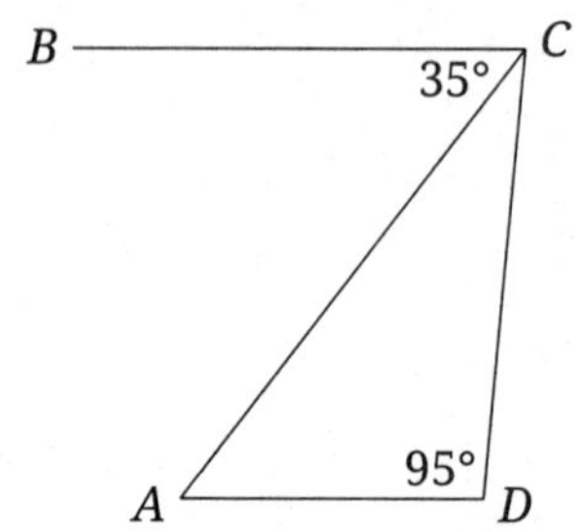

In the figure, $\overline{BC}$ is parallel to $\overline{AD}$. What is the measure of angle ACD?

Ⓐ 35°

Ⓑ 40°

Ⓒ 50°

Ⓓ 55°

3 Mark for Review

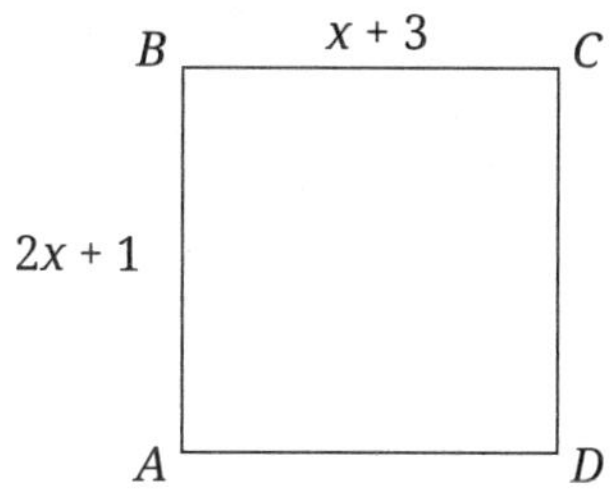

If $ABCD$ is a square, what is the area of the square?

Ⓐ 2

Ⓑ 4

Ⓒ 20

Ⓓ 25

4 Mark for Review

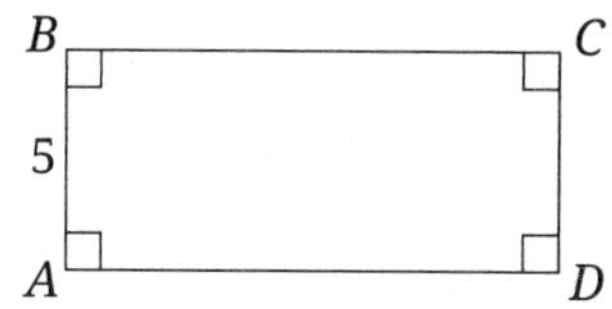

The diagonal of rectangle $ABCD$ is 13 inches long. What is the area of rectangle $ABCD$?

TRIANGLES

The sum of the angles inside a triangle must be equal to 180 degrees. This means that if you know two of the angles in a triangle, you can always solve for the third. Since you know that two of the angles in the following figure are 90 and 60 degrees, you can solve for the third angle, which must be 30 degrees. (Note: The little square in the bottom corner of the triangle indicates a right angle, which is 90°.)

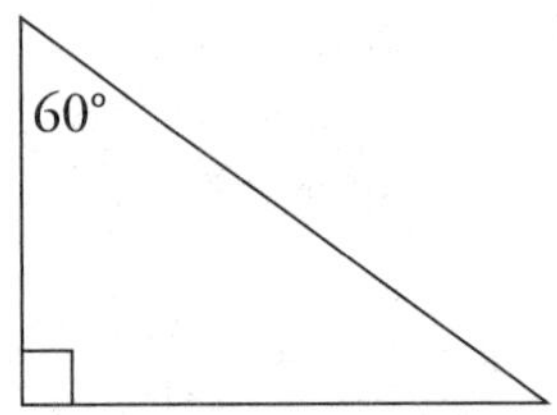

An **isosceles triangle** has two sides that are equal. Angles that are opposite equal sides must be equal. The figure below is an isosceles triangle. Since $AB = BC$, you know that angles x and y are equal. You also know that the sum of angles x and y is 150 degrees (180 degrees in the triangle minus the 30-degree angle = 150). Therefore, angles x and y must be 75 each (150 ÷ 2).

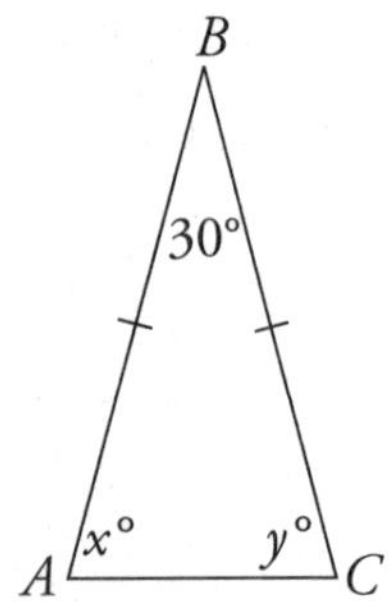

The **area** of a triangle is $\frac{1}{2}$ × *base* × *height*. Note that the height is always perpendicular to the base.

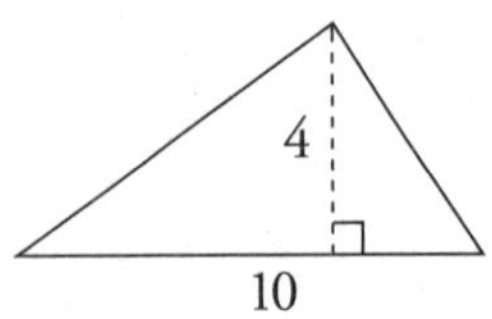

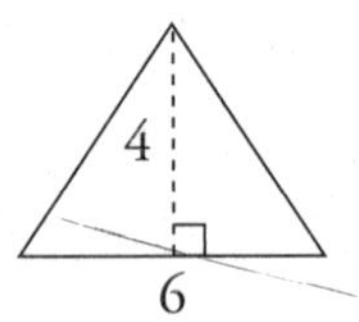

Area = $\frac{1}{2} \times 10 \times 4 = 20$ Area = $\frac{1}{2} \times 6 \times 4 = 12$

An **equilateral triangle** has all three sides equal and all of its angles equal to 60 degrees.

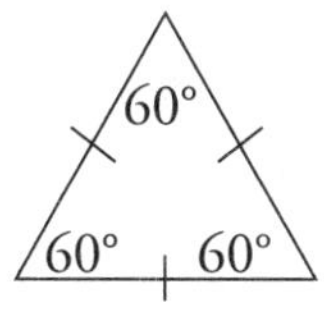

Here's an example of a PSAT question on triangles.

---

1 Mark for Review

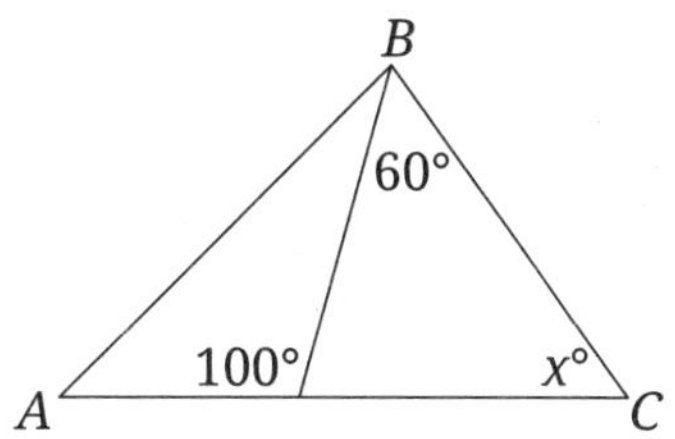

In triangle ABC, what is the value of x?

Ⓐ 30

Ⓑ 40

Ⓒ 50

Ⓓ 60

Here's How to Crack It

The question asks for the value of x, which is an angle measure in a triangle. Redraw the figure on your scratch paper. We know that the angle adjacent to the 100° angle must equal 80° since we know that a straight line is 180°. Fill it in on your diagram. Now, since we know that the sum of the angles contained in a triangle must equal 180°, we know that $80 + 60 + x = 180$, so $x = 40$. That's (B).

Being Aggressive on Geometry Questions

The most important problem-solving technique for tackling PSAT geometry is to learn to be aggressive. This means, whenever you have a figure, ask yourself, *What else do I know?* Write everything you can think of on your scratch paper. You may not see right away why it's important, but write it down anyway. Chances are good that you will be making progress toward the answer, without even knowing it.

The PSAT is also fond of disguising familiar figures within more complex shapes by extending lines, overlapping figures, or combining several basic shapes. So be on the lookout for the basic figures hidden in complicated shapes.

The Pythagorean Theorem

Whenever you have a right triangle, you can use the Pythagorean Theorem. The theorem says that the sum of the squares of the legs of the triangle (the sides that form the right angle) will equal the square of the hypotenuse (the side opposite the right angle).

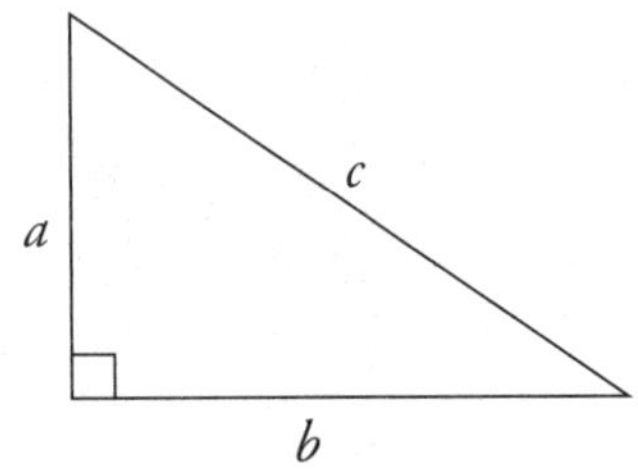

$$a^2 + b^2 = c^2$$

Two of the most common ratios of sides that fit the Pythagorean Theorem are 3-4-5 and 5-12-13. Since these are ratios, any multiples of these numbers will also work, such as 6-8-10 and 10-24-26.

Try the following example.

2 Mark for Review

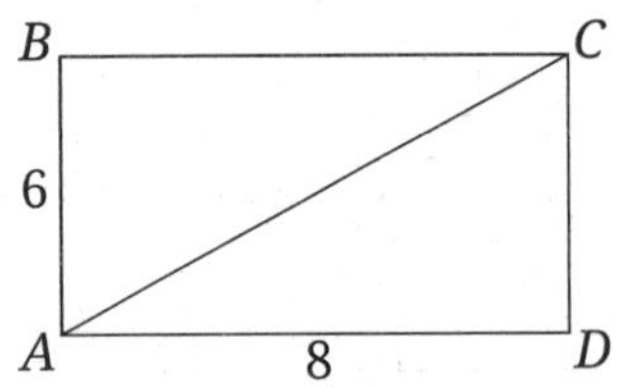

If *ABCD* is a rectangle, what is the perimeter of triangle *ABC*?

Here's How to Crack It

The question asks for the perimeter of triangle *ABC* based on the figure. Redraw the figure on your scratch paper. We can use the Pythagorean Theorem to figure out the length of the diagonal of the rectangle—since it has sides 6 and 8, its diagonal must be 10. (If you remembered that this is one of those well-known Pythagorean triples, you didn't actually have to do the calculations.) Therefore, the perimeter of the triangle is 6 + 8 + 10, or 24.

Special Right Triangles

There are two specific right triangles, the properties of which may play a role in some harder PSAT math questions. They are the right triangles with angles 45°-45°-90° and 30°-60°-90°. These triangles are on the reference sheet that you can click open at any time, so you don't have to memorize them.

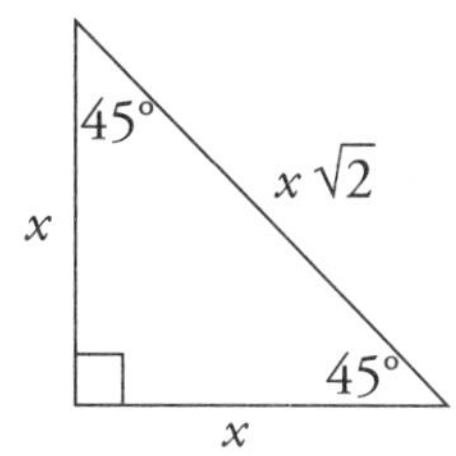

An isosceles right triangle has angles that measure 45, 45, and 90 degrees. Whenever you have a 45°-45°-90° triangle with sides of x, the hypotenuse will always be $x\sqrt{2}$. This means that if one of the legs of the triangle measures 3, then the hypotenuse will be $3\sqrt{2}$.

This right triangle is important because it is half of a square. Understanding the 45°-45°-90° triangle will allow you to easily find the diagonal of a square from its side or find the side of a square from its diagonal.

Here's an example.

3 Mark for Review

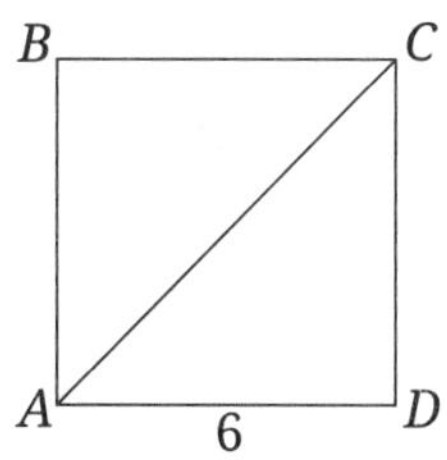

In square $ABCD$, what is the perimeter of triangle ABC?

Ⓐ $6\sqrt{2}$

Ⓑ 8

Ⓒ $12 + \sqrt{2}$

Ⓓ $12 + 6\sqrt{2}$

Here's How to Crack It

The question asks for the perimeter of triangle *ABC* based on the figure. This question looks like a question about a square, and it certainly is in part, but it's really more about the two triangles formed by the diagonal. Redraw the figure on your scratch paper to get started.

In this square, we know that each of the triangles formed by the diagonal $\overline{AC}$ is a 45°-45°-90° right triangle. Since the square has a side of 6, you can use the 45°-45°-90° right triangle rule to determine that each of the sides is 6 and the diagonal is $6\sqrt{2}$. Therefore, the perimeter of the triangle is $6 + 6 + 6\sqrt{2}$, or $12 + 6\sqrt{2}$, and the answer is (D).

The other important right triangle to understand is the 30°-60°-90° right triangle.

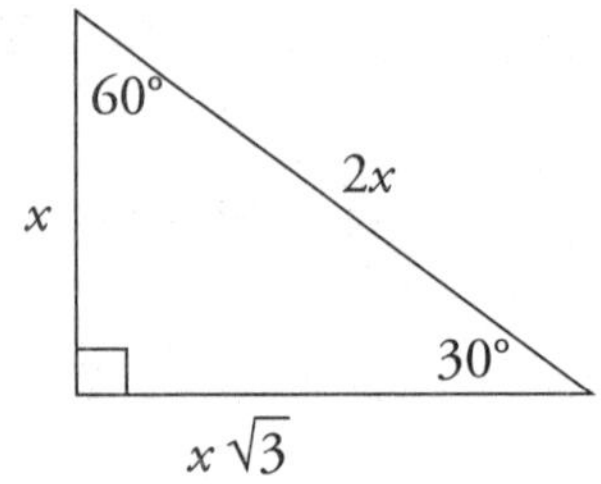

A 30°-60°-90° triangle with a short side of x will have a hypotenuse of $2x$ and a middle side of $x\sqrt{3}$. If the smallest side (the x side) of the triangle is 5, then the sides measure 5, $5\sqrt{3}$, and 10. This triangle is important because it is half of an equilateral triangle, and it allows us to find the height of an equilateral triangle, which is what we'll need in order to find the area of an equilateral triangle.

Try the following.

4 Mark for Review

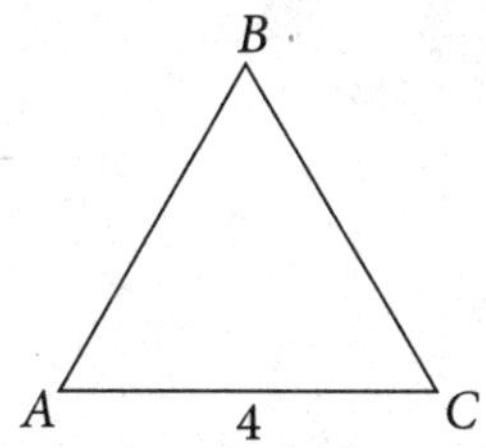

Triangle ABC is equilateral, with sides of length 4. What is its area?

Ⓐ 3

Ⓑ $4\sqrt{2}$

Ⓒ $4\sqrt{3}$

Ⓓ 8

Triangle Tip
An easy way to figure out the height of an equilateral triangle is to take half of its side and multiply it by the square root of 3.

Here's How to Crack It

The question asks for the area of an equilateral triangle with a given side length. First, redraw the figure on your scratch paper. To find the area of the triangle, you need to know the base and the height. The question tells you that the base $\overline{AC}$ is 4; now you need to find the height, which is *perpendicular* to the base. You can create the height by drawing a line from angle B straight down to the base. Now you have two 30°-60°-90° triangles, and you can use the rules of 30°-60°-90° triangles to figure out the height. Half of the base would be 2, and that's the side across from the 30° angle, so you would multiply it by $\sqrt{3}$ to get the height.

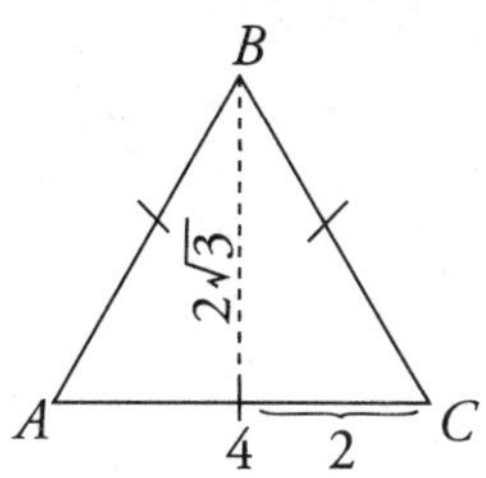

Now we know that the base is 4 and the height is $2\sqrt{3}$, so when we plug those numbers into the formula for area of a triangle, we get $A = \frac{1}{2} \times 4 \times 2\sqrt{3}$, which equals $4\sqrt{3}$. Thus, (C) is the correct answer.

SOHCAHTOA

Trigonometry will likely appear on your PSAT. But fear not! Many trigonometry questions you will see mostly require you to know the basic definitions of the three main trigonometric functions. SOHCAHTOA is a way to remember the three functions:

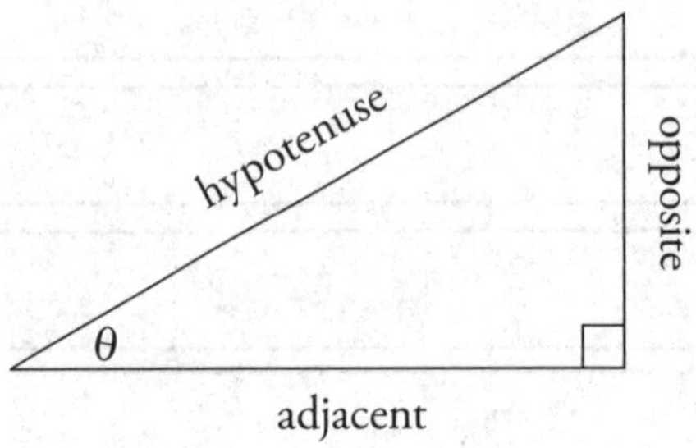

$$\text{sine } \theta = \frac{\text{opposite}}{\text{hypotenuse}} \qquad \text{cosine } \theta = \frac{\text{adjacent}}{\text{hypotenuse}} \qquad \text{tangent } \theta = \frac{\text{opposite}}{\text{adjacent}}$$

Let's see an example.

5 Mark for Review

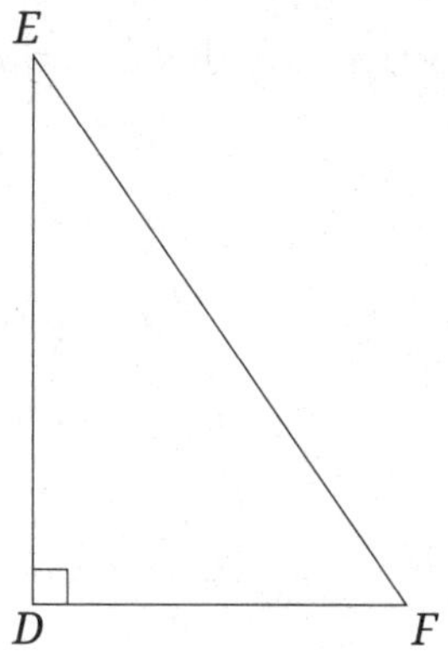

In triangle *DEF* shown, $\cos(E) = \frac{\sqrt{33}}{7}$. What is the value of $\tan(F)$?

Ⓐ $\frac{4}{7}$

Ⓑ $\frac{\sqrt{33}}{7}$

Ⓒ $\frac{7\sqrt{33}}{33}$

Ⓓ $\frac{\sqrt{33}}{4}$

Here's How to Crack It

The question asks for the value of the tangent in a right triangle. Start by redrawing the triangle on your scratch paper so you can mark it up. Next, write out SOHCAHTOA since the question is all about the trig functions. The CAH part of SOHCAHTOA defines the cosine as $\frac{\text{adjacent}}{\text{hypotenuse}}$, and the question states that the cosine of angle E is $\frac{\sqrt{33}}{7}$. Label the side adjacent to angle E as $\sqrt{33}$ and the hypotenuse as 7.

The TOA part of SOHCAHTOA defines the tangent as $\frac{\text{opposite}}{\text{adjacent}}$. The side opposite angle F is already labeled as $\sqrt{33}$. Use the Pythagorean Theorem to solve for the third side: $a^2 + \left(\sqrt{33}\right)^2 = 7^2$. This becomes $a^2 + 33 = 49$. Subtract 33 from both sides of the equation to get $a^2 = 16$. Take the positive square root of both sides of the equation to get $a = 4$. Label the side adjacent to angle F as 4.

Now that all three sides are labeled, plug in the correct sides to find the tangent of angle F, which is $\frac{\sqrt{33}}{4}$. The correct answer is (D).

Use Your Tools!

The online tools won't be very useful on this question because you can't mark the figure. But your scratch paper is enormously helpful on geometry and trig questions. Use it to redraw figures, label figures, write out formulas, and perform calculations. Your scratch paper should look something like this after finishing the previous question.

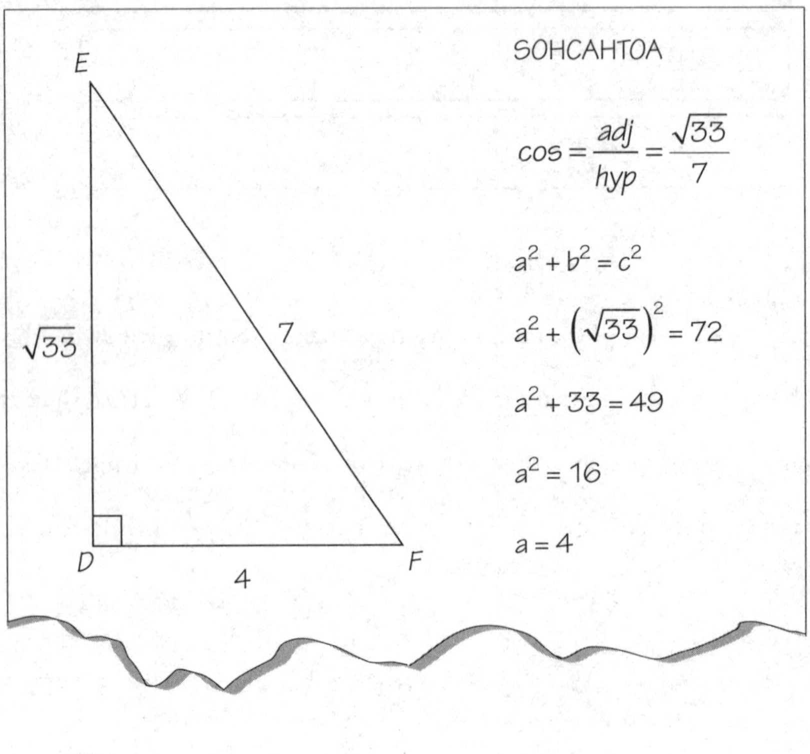

Similar Triangles

Similar triangles have the same shape, but they are not necessarily the same size. Having the same shape means that the angles of the triangles are identical and that the corresponding sides have the same ratio—that is, they are proportional to each other. Look at the following two similar triangles:

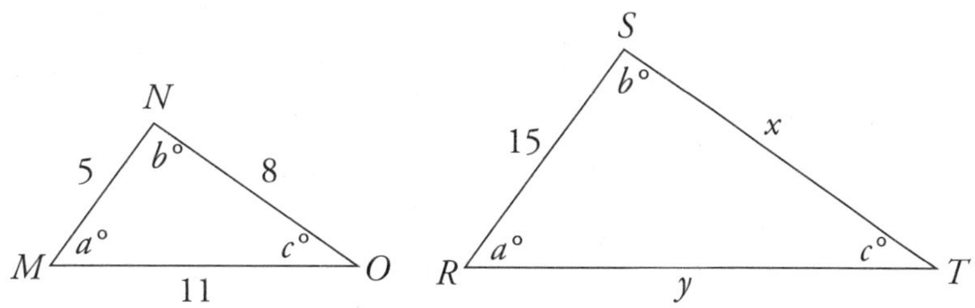

Both of the triangles above have the same set of angles, but they aren't the same size. Whenever this is true, the sides of one triangle are proportional to those of the other. Notice that sides $\overline{NO}$ and $\overline{ST}$ are both opposite the angle that is $a°$. These are called corresponding sides, because they correspond to the same angle. So, the lengths of $\overline{NO}$ and $\overline{ST}$ are proportional to each other. In order to figure out the lengths of the other sides, set up a proportion: $\frac{MN}{RS} = \frac{NO}{ST}$. Now fill in the information that you know: $\frac{5}{15} = \frac{8}{x}$. Cross-multiply and you find that $x = 24$. You could also figure out the length of y: $\frac{MN}{RS} = \frac{MO}{RT}$. So, $\frac{5}{15} = \frac{11}{y}$, and $y = 33$. Whenever you have to deal with sides of similar triangles, just set up a proportion.

Give it a try.

6 Mark for Review

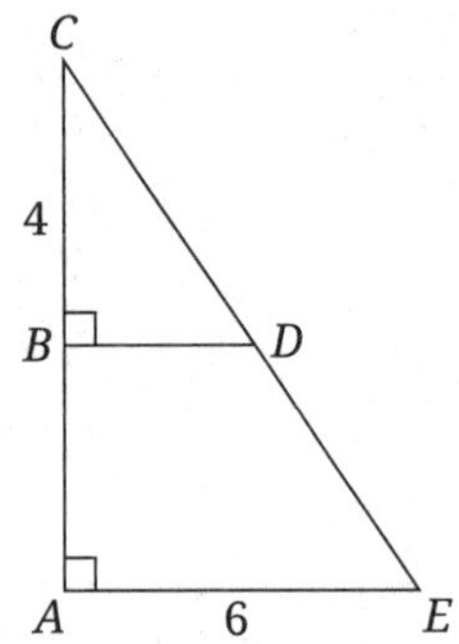

Note: Figure not drawn to scale.

If the area of triangle ACE is 18, what is the area of triangle BCD?

Here's How to Crack It

The question asks for the area of triangle BCD. Start by redrawing the figure on your scratch paper. It might help to draw the two triangles separately. The formula to find the area of a triangle is $A = \frac{1}{2}bh$. Plugging in the area and base of triangle ACE as given in the question and the figure gives you the equation $18 = \frac{1}{2}(6)h$. Simplify the fraction and you will get $18 = 3h$. Divide both sides by 3 and you can see that the height of triangle ACE is 6. Label this on your scratch paper. Because triangle ACE and triangle BCD have the same angle measures, they are similar. Therefore, create a proportion to find the length of $\overline{BD}$. The proportion should look like this: $\frac{\text{height of small triangle}}{\text{base of small triangle}} = \frac{\text{height of large triangle}}{\text{base of large triangle}}$ or $\frac{4}{x} = \frac{6}{6}$, if x represents the length of $\overline{BD}$. Simplify your fractions and cross-multiply to see that $x = 4$. Plug the base and height of triangle BCD into the area formula: $A = \frac{1}{2}(4)(4)$. Simplify the equation and you will see that the area of triangle BCD is 8.

Drill 2

Suggested Time Limit for Questions 1 through 6: 10 minutes. Answers can be found in Part IV.

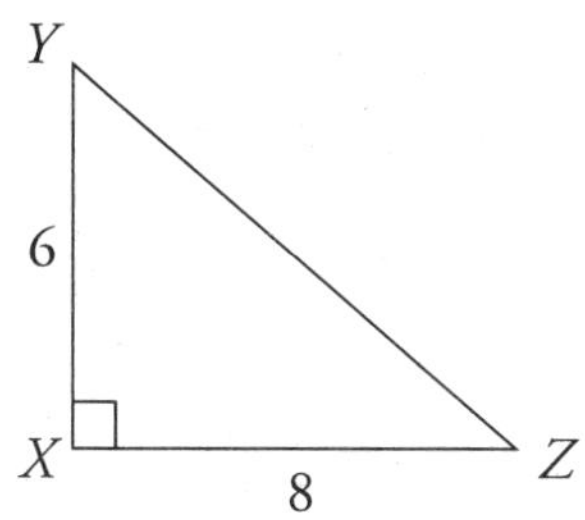

a. What is the area of triangle XYZ above? ________

b. What is the length of YZ? ________

c. What is the sine of $\angle Z$? ________

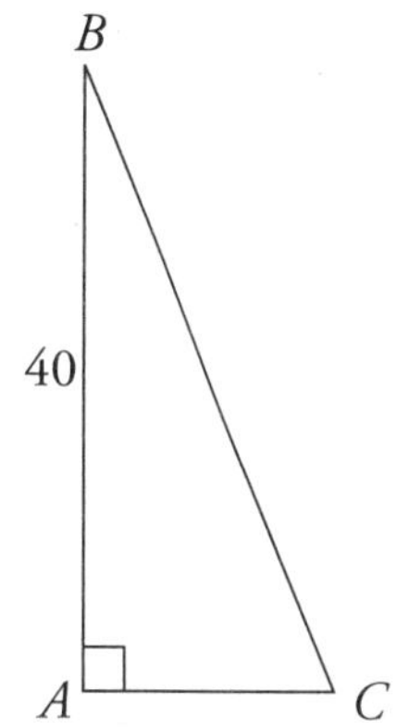

d. If the area of the triangle above is 400, what is the length of AC? ________

e. What is the length of BC? ________

f. What is the cosine of $\angle C$? ________

1 Mark for Review

In similar triangles LMN and PQR, angles L and P are both 90°, and angles N and R have the same measure. If $\cos(Q) = \frac{24}{145}$, which of the following is the value of $\sin(N)$?

Ⓐ $\frac{24}{145}$

Ⓑ $\frac{143}{145}$

Ⓒ $\frac{143}{24}$

Ⓓ $\frac{145}{24}$

2 Mark for Review

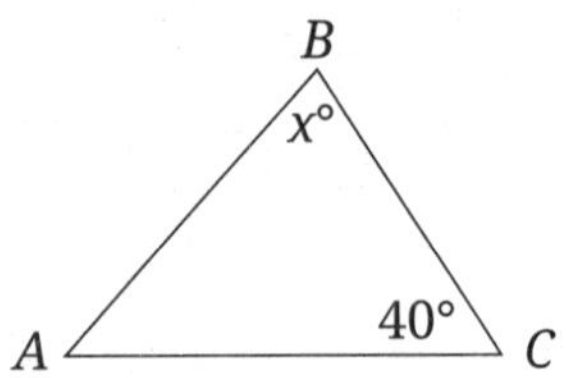

Note: Figure not drawn to scale.

In triangle ABC, if $AB = BC$, what is the value of x?

3 Mark for Review

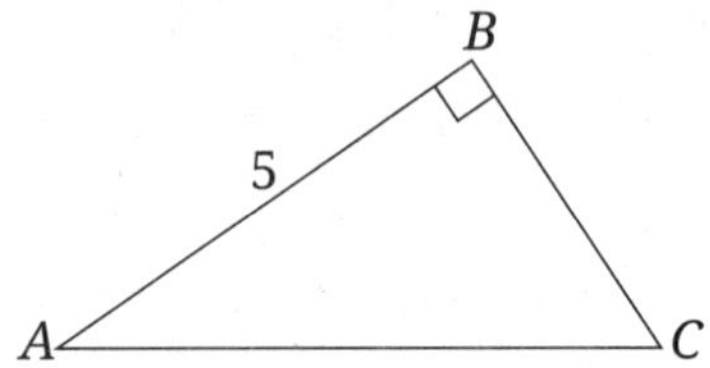

Note: Figure not drawn to scale.

In the figure, if triangle ABC is isosceles, what is the perimeter of the triangle?

Ⓐ 12.5

Ⓑ $10\sqrt{2}$

Ⓒ $10 + 5\sqrt{2}$

Ⓓ $15\sqrt{2}$

4 Mark for Review

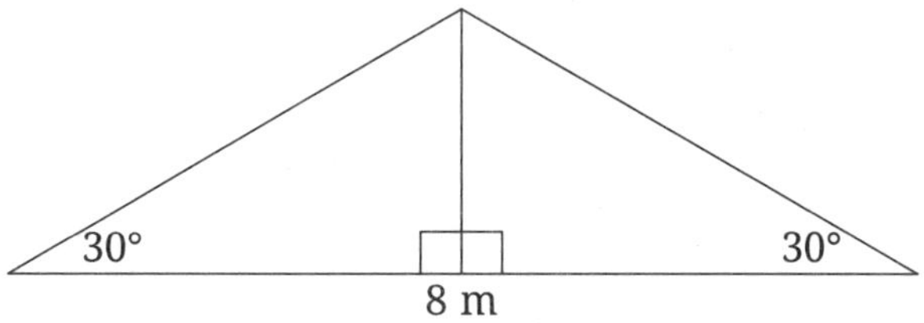

The owner of a barn needs to paint the front of the barn's roof. As shown in the figure, the roof measures 8 m along the bottom, and the sides of the roof meet the bottom at a $30°$ angle. If one bucket of paint can cover 5 m^2, what is the minimum number of buckets the owner needs to purchase?

Ⓐ 1

Ⓑ 2

Ⓒ 3

Ⓓ 4

5 Mark for Review

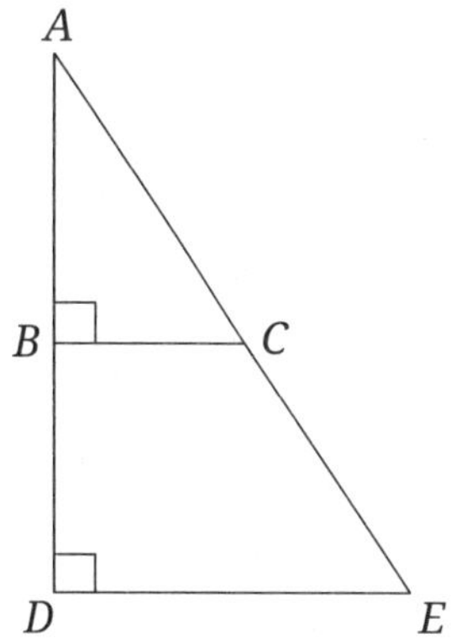

Note: Figure not drawn to scale.

In the figure, if $AB = 5, AC = 13$, and $DE = 24$, what is the value of BD?

Ⓐ 5

Ⓑ 8

Ⓒ 10

Ⓓ 12

6 Mark for Review

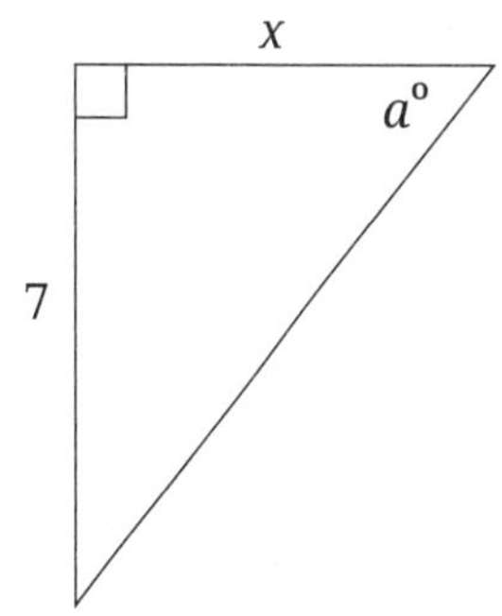

In the triangle, $\tan a° = \frac{14}{15}$. What is the value of x?

CIRCLES

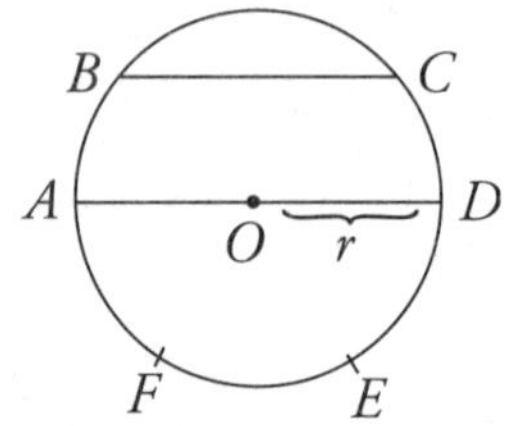

The **radius** of a circle is the distance from the center to the edge of the circle. In the figure above, $\overline{OD}$ is a radius, and so is $\overline{OA}$.

The **diameter** is the distance from one edge, through the center, to the other edge of the circle. The diameter will always be twice the measure of the radius and will always be the longest line you can draw through a circle. In the figure above, $\overline{AD}$ is a diameter.

A **chord** is any line drawn from one point on the edge of the circle to the other. In the figure above, $\overline{BC}$ is a chord. The diameter is the longest chord in a circle.

An **arc** is any section of the circumference (the edge) of the circle. $\overset{\frown}{EF}$ is an arc in the figure above.

The **circumference** is the distance around the outside edge of the circle. The circumference of a circle with radius r is $2\pi r$. A circle with radius of 5 has a circumference of 10π.

The **area** of a circle with radius r is πr^2. A circle with a radius of 5 has an area of 25π.

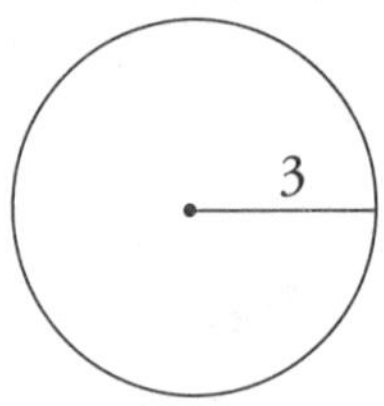

Area = 9π

Circumference = 6π

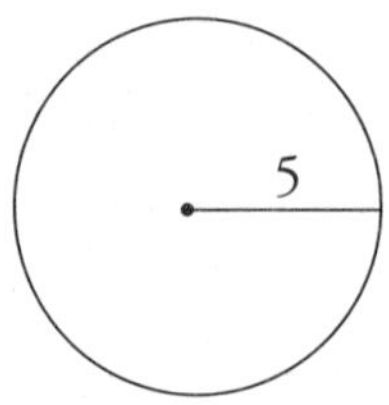

Area = 25π

Circumference = 10π

Quick Review
- An interior angle is an angle formed by two radii.
- A sector is the portion of the circle between the two radii.

Proportionality in a Circle

Here's another rule that plays a role in more advanced circle questions.

> Arc measure is proportional to interior angle measure, which is proportional to sector area.

This means that whatever fraction of the total degree measure is made up by the interior angle, the arc described by that angle is the same fraction of the circumference, and the pie piece created has the same fraction of the area.

Take a look at the figure below.

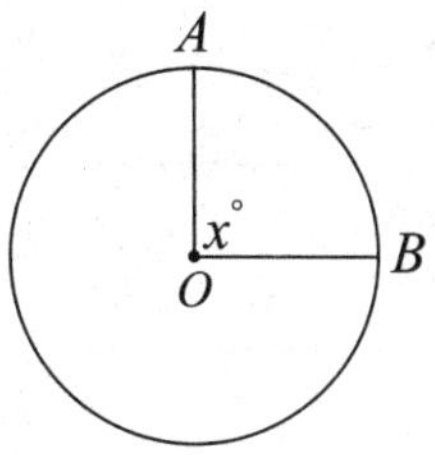

If angle x is equal to 90 degrees, which is one-quarter of 360 degrees, then arc $\overset{\frown}{AB}$ is equal to one-quarter of the circumference of the circle and the area of the sector of the circle enclosed by radii $\overline{OA}$ and $\overline{OB}$ is equal to one-quarter of the area of the circle.

To see how this works, try the following question.

7 Mark for Review

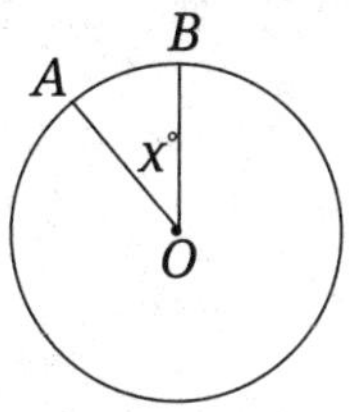

The circle with center O has a radius of 4. If $x = 30$, what is the length of minor arc AB?

(A) $\frac{\pi}{6}$

(B) $\frac{2\pi}{3}$

(C) 3

(D) $\frac{3\pi}{2}$

Here's How to Crack It

The question asks for the length of minor arc *AB*. Since the interior angle *x* is equal to 30°, which is $\frac{1}{12}$ of 360°, we know that minor arc *AB* will be equal to $\frac{1}{12}$ of the circumference of the circle. Since the circle has radius 4, its circumference will be 8π. Therefore, arc *AB* will measure $\frac{1}{12} \times 8\pi$, or $\frac{2\pi}{3}$, (B).

8 Mark for Review

Points *A* and *B* lie on a circle with center *O* such that the measure of angle *OAB* is 45°. If the area of the circle is 64π, what is the perimeter of triangle *AOB*?

Ⓐ $8 + 8\sqrt{2}$

Ⓑ $16 + 8\sqrt{2}$

Ⓒ $16 + 16\sqrt{2}$

Ⓓ $32 + 16\sqrt{2}$

Here's How to Crack It

The question asks for the perimeter of triangle *AOB*. This time a diagram isn't given, so drawing the circle on your scratch paper should be your first step. Since points *A* and *B* lie on the circle, $\overline{OA}$ and $\overline{OB}$ are both radii and equal in length, making ΔAOB isosceles. The question indicates that $\angle OAB$ is 45°, which means that $\angle OBA$ is also 45°, which makes ΔAOB a 45°-45°-90° triangle (remember those special right triangles?).

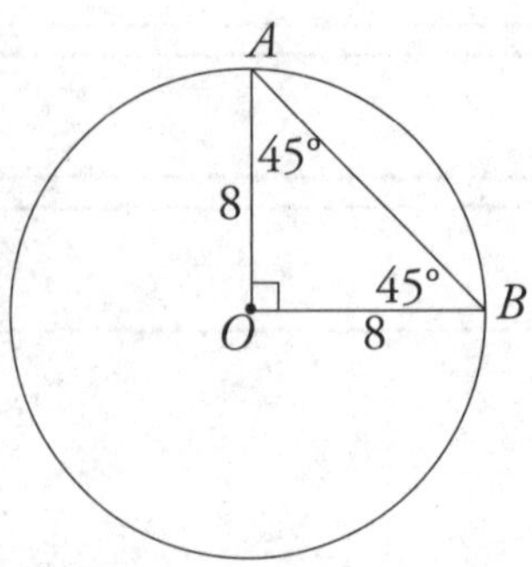

Given the circle's area of 64π, the radii of the circle (which are the legs of the isosceles right triangle) are 8 and the hypotenuse is $8\sqrt{2}$, making the perimeter $8 + 8 + 8\sqrt{2}$, or $16 + 8\sqrt{2}$, which is (B).

Tangents to a Circle

A tangent is a line that touches the edge of a circle at exactly one point. A radius drawn to the point of tangency forms a 90-degree angle with the tangent line. This comes up occasionally on hard questions, so take a look at the example below. As you work through this question, if you're thinking that you'd never know how to do it yourself, there's still a valuable lesson here, and it's that this question is not in your POOD, so you should look instead for a plug-in or something you're more familiar with.

9 Mark for Review

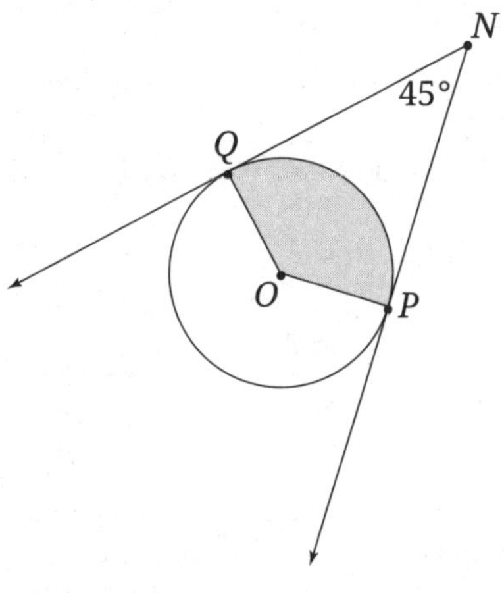

In the figure, $\overline{NP}$ and $\overline{NQ}$ are tangent to the circle with center O at points P and Q, respectively. If the area of the shaded region is 24π, what is the circumference of the circle?

Ⓐ 8π

Ⓑ 12π

Ⓒ 16π

Ⓓ 40π

Here's How to Crack It

The question asks for the circumference of the circle. The key is remembering that any line or line segment drawn tangent to a circle is perpendicular to a radius drawn from the center of the circle to that tangent point; this means both $\angle OQN$ and $\angle OPN$ equal 90°. With $\angle QNP$ given as 45°, that leaves the central $\angle QOP$ of quadrilateral *QNPO.* Since all quadrilaterals contain 360° and the three angles mentioned so far account for 90 + 90 + 45 = 225°, that remaining angle must be 360 – 225 = 135°. As all circles contain 360° of arc, this means the shaded area represents $\frac{135}{360}$, or $\frac{3}{8}$, of the area of the entire circle.

Remember, we want to write down the formulas for quantities the question talks about, so that's $A = \pi r^2$ and $C = 2\pi r$. So far, we don't have anything we can put directly into a formula, so what do we know? We're told that the area of the shaded sector is 24π, so we can use that to figure out the area of the whole circle, because we know it's proportional to the central angle. In fact, we've figured out that this part of the circle is $\frac{3}{8}$ of the whole, so the proportion looks like this: $\frac{3}{8} = \frac{24\pi}{x}$. Cross-multiply to get $3x = 192\pi$, and then divide both sides by 3 to get $x = 64\pi$. Now we can use the first formula and solve for $r = 8$. We can put this right into the second formula and get $C = 16\pi$, so the answer is (C).

The Equation of a Circle

One last thing you may need to know about a circle is what the equation of a circle in the *xy*-plane looks like.

The equation of a circle is as follows:

$$(x - h)^2 + (y - k)^2 = r^2$$

In the circle equation, the center of the circle is the point (h, k), and the radius of the circle is r.

Let's look at one.

10 Mark for Review

What is the equation of a circle with center (2, 4) that passes through the point (–6, –2)?

Ⓐ $(x + 2)^2 + (y + 4)^2 = 100$

Ⓑ $(x + 2)^2 + (y + 4)^2 = \sqrt{20}$

Ⓒ $(x - 2)^2 + (y - 4)^2 = 100$

Ⓓ $(x - 2)^2 + (y - 4)^2 = \sqrt{20}$

Here's How to Crack It

The question asks for the equation of a circle with a given center and containing a certain point. Take the given center and put it into the circle equation above. Plugging in $h = 2$ and $k = 4$, you get $(x - 2)^2 + (y - 4)^2 = r^2$. Eliminate (A) and (B) because they show the left side of the equation with incorrect signs. In the circle equation, x and y are the coordinates of a point on the circle. Plugging in the point (–6, –2), you get $(-6 - 2)^2 + (-2 - 4)^2 = r^2$, which simplifies to $(-8)^2 + (-6)^2 = r^2$, or $64 + 36 = r^2$. This means $r^2 = 100$, so the equation is $(x - 2)^2 + (y - 4)^2 = 100$, and (C) is correct.

Another method is to use the built-in calculator. Enter the equation for each answer choice, and then scroll and zoom as needed to see which graphed circle has a center at (2, 4) and passes through the point (–6, –2). Only (C) does, so it is correct.

Using either of these methods, the correct answer is (C).

There is a chance that you might see a circle equation that is not in the form shown above. If this happens, do not complete the square. Instead, use the built-in calculator. It will graph the circle no matter what form the equation is in. If the question asks for the radius or diameter, click on the gray dots on the top and bottom, and subtract the y-values to find the length of the diameter.

Drill 3

Suggested Time Limit: 6 minutes. Answers can be found in Part IV.

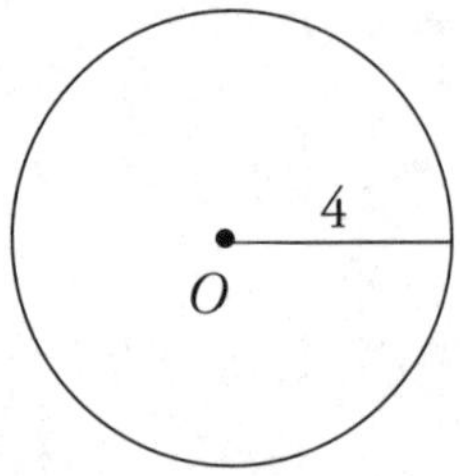

a. What is the area of the circle above with center O? ___________

b. What is its circumference? ___________

1 Mark for Review

What is the center of a circle with equation $x^2 + y^2 - 2x + 8y + 8 = 0$?

Ⓐ (–1, 4)

Ⓑ (1, –4)

Ⓒ (–2, 8)

Ⓓ (2, –8)

2 Mark for Review

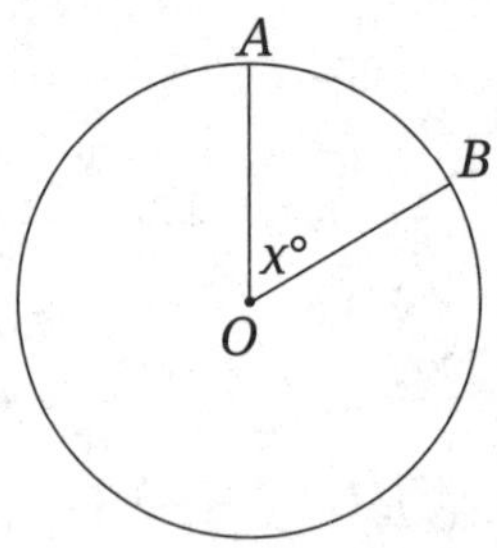

The circle shown has its center at O. If $x = 60$ and the length of minor arc AB is 2π, what is the area of circle O?

Ⓐ 6

Ⓑ 6π

Ⓒ 12π

Ⓓ 36π

3 Mark for Review

A circle with center O has diameter $\overline{AB}$. Segment $\overline{AC}$ is tangent to the circle at point A and has a length of 5. If the area of the circle is 36π, what is the perimeter of triangle ABC?

Ⓐ 15

Ⓑ 25

Ⓒ 30

Ⓓ 60

4 Mark for Review

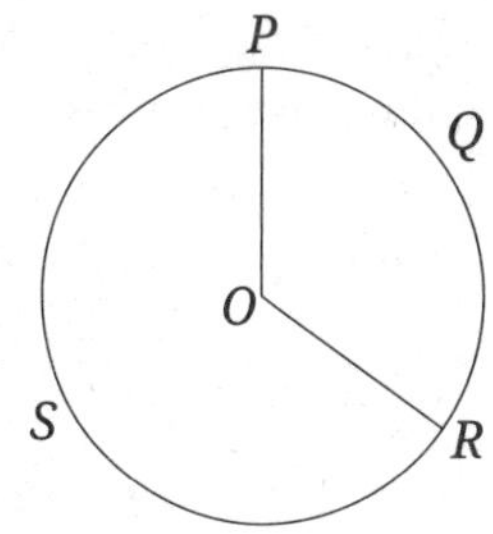

Note: Figure not drawn to scale.

Arc PSR is $\frac{4}{3}$ the length of arc PQR. The length of major arc PSR is 6π units. What is the radius of the circle?

VOLUME

Volume questions on the PSAT can seem intimidating at times. The PSAT sometimes gives you questions featuring unusual shapes such as pyramids and spheres. Luckily, the reference sheet contains all the formulas you will ever need for volume questions on the PSAT. Remember to click it open whenever you need a geometry formula that you don't have memorized.

Let's look at an example.

11 Mark for Review

The volume of cylinder A is twice that of cylinder B. If the combined volume of the two cylinders is 114π, what is the volume of cylinder A?

(A) 38π

(B) 76π

(C) 114π

(D) 228π

Here's How to Crack It

The question asks for a specific value, and there are numbers in the answer choices. Rather than writing and solving equations, recognize that one of the four answers has to be the volume of cylinder A, and try them until one of them fits the information in the question. Eliminate (C) and (D) because they don't make sense: the volume of one cylinder cannot be equal to or greater than the combined volume of both cylinders. Try (B), 76π. The question states that *the volume of cylinder A is twice that of cylinder B*, which also means that the volume of cylinder B is half the volume of cylinder A. If the volume of cylinder A is 76π, the volume of cylinder B is 38π. The question also states that the combined volume is 114π. It is true that $76\pi + 38\pi = 114\pi$, so all of the math checks out. It's impossible for a second volume to also work, so stop here. The correct answer is (B).

PLUGGING IN ON GEOMETRY

Did you recognize the technique you used on the previous question? That's right, it was PITA! You can also plug in your own numbers on geometry questions, just as you can for algebra. Anytime that you have variables in the answer choices or hidden variables, use Plugging In! As long as you follow all the rules of geometry while you solve, you'll get the answer.

Take a look at this question.

12 Mark for Review

A triangle has a base of x units and a height that is 4 times the base. In terms of x, what is the area of the triangle?

Ⓐ $2x$

Ⓑ $5x$

Ⓒ $2x^2$

Ⓓ $4x^2$

Here's How to Crack It

The question asks for the area of a geometric figure. The other dimensions are given in terms of a variable, so pick a number and plug it in. Make $x = 2$. The triangle now has a base of 2 and a height of $4(2) = 8$. The equation for the area of a triangle is $\frac{1}{2}\ base \times height$. Plug the values for the base and the height into the equation to get $Area = \frac{1}{2}(2)(8)$, or $Area = 8$. This is the target value; circle it.

Now plug $x = 2$ into each answer choice and eliminate any answer that does not equal your target value of 8.

A)	$2(2) = 4$	Not 8; eliminate!
B)	$5(2) = 10$	Not 8; eliminate!
C)	$2(2)^2 = 2(4) = 8$	Is 8; keep!
D)	$4(2)^2 = 4(4) = 16$	Not 8; eliminate!

Notice that the wrong answers are all the result of simple mistakes, like forgetting to take one-half or adding the base and height instead of multiplying them. When you use real numbers instead of variables, you're much less likely to make that kind of mistake. Here, you did some basic arithmetic and got (C) as the right answer.

Drill 4

Suggested Time Limit: 10 minutes. Try to use Plugging In on the following questions. Answers can be found in Part IV.

1 Mark for Review

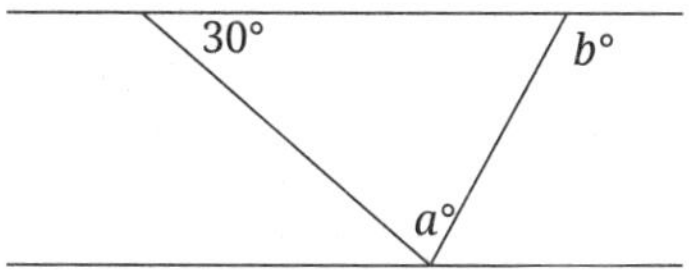

In the figure, what is the value of b, in terms of a?

Ⓐ $30 - a$

Ⓑ $30 + a$

Ⓒ $60 + a$

Ⓓ $80 - a$

2 Mark for Review

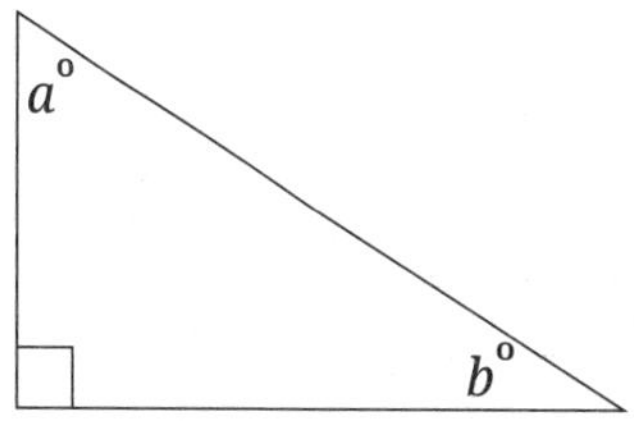

In the figure, if $\sin a° = x$, which of the following represents $\cos b° =$

Ⓐ x

Ⓑ $1 - x$

Ⓒ $\frac{1}{x}$

Ⓓ $x - 1$

3 Mark for Review

Cone A and Cone B are both right circular cones of the same height. If the radius of Cone A is $\frac{3}{4}$ of the radius of Cone B, which of the following is the ratio of the volume of Cone A to the volume of Cone B?

Ⓐ 27:64

Ⓑ 9:16

Ⓒ 3:4

Ⓓ 4:3

4 Mark for Review

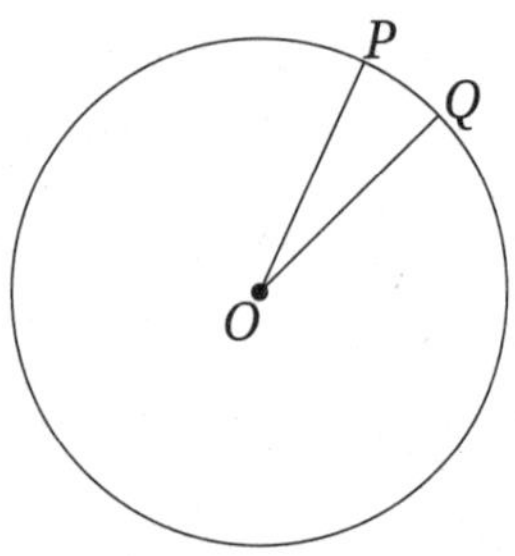

In the figure, O is the center of the circle, the radius of the circle is x, and the length of minor arc PQ is $\frac{\pi x}{18}$. What is the area of sector POQ?

Ⓐ $\frac{\pi x^2}{36}$

Ⓑ $\frac{\pi x^2}{18}$

Ⓒ $\frac{\pi x^2}{9}$

Ⓓ $\frac{\pi x^2}{3}$

5 Mark for Review

Three spherical balls with radius r are contained in a rectangular box. Two of the balls are each touching 5 sides of the rectangular box and the middle ball. The middle ball also touches four sides of the rectangular box. What is the volume of the space between the balls and the rectangular box, in terms of r?

Ⓐ $r^3(3 - 4\pi)$

Ⓑ $4r^2(14 - \pi)$

Ⓒ $4r^3(6 - \pi)$

Ⓓ $12r^2(r - \pi)$

6 Mark for Review

A rectangular box is half as long as it is wide and one-third as wide as it is tall. If the volume of the box is 96, then what is its surface area?

Summary

- Be sure to review your basic geometry rules before the test; often, questions hinge on knowing that vertical angles are equal or that the sum of the angles in a quadrilateral is 360°.
- On all geometry questions, draw figures on your scratch paper and aggressively fill in everything you know.
- When two parallel lines are cut by a third line, the small angles are equal, the big angles are equal, and the sum of a big angle and a small angle is 180°.
- The perimeter of a rectangle is the sum of the lengths of its sides. The area of a rectangle is *length* × *width*.
- The perimeter of a triangle is the sum of the lengths of its sides. The area of a triangle is $\frac{1}{2}$ *base* × *height*.
- Knowing the Pythagorean Theorem, common Pythagorean triples (such as 3-4-5 and 5-12-13), and special right triangles (45°-45°-90° and 30°-60°-90°) will help you figure out angles and lengths in a right triangle.
- For trigonometry questions, remember SOHCAHTOA:
    - sine = $\frac{opposite}{hypotenuse}$
    - cosine = $\frac{adjacent}{hypotenuse}$
    - tangent = $\frac{opposite}{adjacent}$

- Similar triangles have the same angles, and their side lengths are proportional.
- The circumference of a circle is $2\pi r$. The area of a circle is πr^2.
- Circles that show an interior angle (an angle that extends from the center of the circle) have proportionality. The interior angle over the whole degree measure (360°) equals the same fraction as the arc enclosed by that angle over the circumference. Likewise, both of these fractions are equal to the area of the segment over the entire area of the circle.
- When you see a line that is "tangent to" a circle, remember two things:
    - The line touches the circle at exactly one point.
    - The radius of the circle that intersects the tangent line is perpendicular (90°) to that tangent line.
- The formulas to compute the volumes of many three-dimensional figures are supplied in the reference sheet that can be clicked open at any time during the Math section.
- When plugging in on geometry questions, remember to use your knowledge of basic geometry rules; e.g., there are still 180° in a triangle when you're using Plugging In.

Part IV
Drill Answers and Explanations

CHAPTER 7

Reading Comprehension Drill (page 162)

1. **A** This is a Vocabulary question, as it asks for a *most logical and precise word or phrase.* Read the passage and highlight what can help you fill in the blank. The blank describes what chemicals in pool water may do to local habitats, so look for and highlight clues about that relationship. The passage states that the chemicals from pool water *can cause immense environmental damage and even kill plant and animal life* and *will continue to cause great harm.* Therefore, write "destroy" or "wipe out" in the Annotation box.

    - (A) is correct because *decimate* (to remove a large percentage of) matches "destroy."
    - (B) is wrong because *buttress* (support) is the **Opposite** of the annotation.
    - (C) is wrong because *overlook* goes **Beyond the Text**—it's logical to assume some pool and spa owners could overlook the damage caused by their systems, but *overlook* doesn't match "destroy."
    - (D) is wrong because although *refute* is a negative word, it doesn't match "destroy. "

2. **B** This is a Purpose question, as it asks for the *main purpose of the text.* Read the passage and identify who or what the passage focuses on: the eco-friendly parking structure that the city of Palo Alto wants to erect. Then, highlight any sentences that use structural language when discussing this focus and any attitudes expressed toward this focus. The inclusion of the word *thereby* in the last sentence indicates it may be a main idea, so highlight that *Palo Alto city planners hope that the presence of these charging stations will encourage more residents to switch to electric vehicles, thereby reducing the city's carbon footprint from gas emissions.* This is one of several benefits that the city hopes will come about due to its new eco-friendly parking structure. Write down in your annotation box that a good main purpose of the passage would be to "explain potential benefits of parking structure."

    - (A) is wrong because it's **Half-Right**—the passage does describe an initiative *designed to improve environmental conditions*, but it's never compared to *planned initiatives in other municipalities.*
    - (B) is correct because it's consistent with the highlighting and annotation.
    - (C) is wrong because it goes **Beyond the Text**—there is a planned *increase in the number of electric vehicle charging stations*, but there is no mention in the passage of the residents of Palo Alto demanding this increase.
    - (D) is wrong because, if anything, it's the **Opposite** of the passage—no other ways to *improve environmental conditions* are described in the passage besides the parking structure, but regardless, the structure is described as positive rather than as something inefficient.

3. **C** This is a Dual Texts question, as it asks what *the author of Text 2* would *most likely say about the scientists' belief regarding soil microbiota from Text 1.* Follow the Dual Texts Basic Approach. Text 1 states that the *scientists know of soil microbiota* but *believe some other organism must be responsible for the plants' invasiveness and hardiness.* Now, read Text 2 and see what its author says regarding the same idea. Text 2 states that *the crop of garden lupines in the soil containing soil microbiota not only grew much larger* but also *secreted a much stronger scent* than the crop without. So, note in the annotation box that Text 2 would "disagree—microbiota are the ones responsible for hardiness."

   - (A) is wrong because it's **Half-Right**—Ramula and her team have indeed found evidence contrary to the scientists' belief, but there's no *celebratory* tone in Text 1.
   - (B) is wrong because it's the **Opposite** of the annotation—Ramula and her team have indeed demonstrated that soil microbiota is linked to plant growth, and the author of Text 2 would not find the scientists' belief *understandable.*
   - (C) is correct because it's consistent with the annotation by showing a disagreement.
   - (D) is wrong because it's **Recycled Language.** It misuses *control, plant,* and *spread* from Text 1—Text 2 never states that Ramula and her team were able to control plant spread with the research they conducted.

4. **C** This is a Retrieval question, as it asks for a detail *according to the text.* Look for information in the text that indicates why *the Cornish language* was *declared extinct.* The passage states directly that *the language experienced a sharp decline in users from 1300 to 1800, after which no record of any living user could be found for decades.* The correct answer should be as consistent as possible with this detail.

   - (A) is wrong because it claims that Cornish had *complex syntax,* but the passage doesn't mention any actual features of the language's construction.
   - (B) is wrong because it's **Recycled Language**—the *linguists* in the passage aren't said to have any *expectation* regarding Cornish's rate of growth. They are merely working on *reviving* the Cornish language.
   - (C) is correct because it's consistent with the highlighted detail.
   - (D) is wrong because it claims that Cornish *stopped spreading into new regions because it was surpassed by other languages,* but no other languages are mentioned in the passage.

5. **B** This is a Main Idea question, as it asks for the *main idea of the text.* Look for and highlight a sentence that the other sentences build toward or give examples of. The author first states *A little while, a year agone, I knew her for a romping child* but then later states *And turning with a quick surprise, I wondered at her stateliness, I wondered at her altered eyes.* The lines indicate that the speaker is registering his surprise at how different the woman looks from before. The correct answer should be as consistent as possible with this main idea.

- (A) is wrong because it goes **Beyond the Text**—we don't know from the passage whether the speaker and the woman ever had a romantic relationship.
- (B) is correct because it's consistent with what was highlighted.
- (C) is wrong because it states that *the speaker is an expert in observing subtle changes in others,* but the fact that he only notices big changes in one person in the text.
- (D) is wrong because it states that *the speaker uses intricate and complex thought processes to impress those around him*, but while the passage gives the speaker's thoughts, it would be **Extreme Language** to say his thoughts are intricate and complex or that anyone is impressed by them.

6. **B** This is a Claims question, as it asks which quotation *most effectively illustrates the claim.* Look for and highlight the claim in the text, which is that the *poem demonstrates a character's ignorance of a deception created by his enemy.* The correct answer should reference and be consistent with each aspect of this claim.

- (A) and (D) are wrong because each fails to reference both the Earl's ignorance of the deception and the deception itself.
- (B) is correct because it's consistent with the claim—the earl believes his son has returned because he sees his son's flag, but another of his sons warns him that it is an impostor who carries the son's banner, meaning that the Earl did not know about the deception.
- (C) is wrong because it's **Half-Right**—it references the deception and the circumstances that led to the capture of the son's banner, but there is no evidence in this answer that the Earl is ignorant of this fact.

7. **D** This is a Charts question, as it asks for *data from the graph* that will *complete the example.* Follow the Charts Basic Approach. Read the title, variables, and key from the graph. Then, read the passage and highlight the claim connected to the incomplete statement, which is that a *notable aspect* of the study *is that consumer satisfaction with general performance does not always correlate with satisfaction with specific performance areas,* so the correct answer should offer data from the graph that is as consistent as possible with this claim.

- (A) and (C) are wrong because they are each the **Opposite** of the claim—stating that general performance was *equivalent to* or *only slightly below* video performance across several years or both general performance and audio performance hit their lowest totals in the same year would possibly be evidence of a correlation, but the correct evidence should indicate a lack of a correlation.
- (B) is wrong because it's also the **Opposite** of the claim for showing a clear trend—that general performance satisfaction *was consistently higher than video performance satisfaction* for all five years of the survey. Not only does this go against the claim, but it also goes against the graph for the years 2019–2021.

- (D) is correct because it's consistent with the claim, as it shows that general performance satisfaction does not show any type of set relationship with video performance.

8. **A** This is a Conclusions question, as it asks what *most logically completes the text.* Look for the main focus of the passage, which is barefoot running. Then, use structural language to find and highlight the main points made regarding this focus. The passage states that barefoot running *has increased in popularity since the year 2000* among exercise enthusiasts as a way to prevent injury, but *the practice dates back thousands of years.* Also, *Latin American and African groups* have apparently used barefoot running for a long time and continue to use it *despite the availability of modern footwear in those regions.* Write "practice has been around a long time, groups have kept using it over modern footwear" into the annotation box as a good conclusion.

    - (A) is correct because it's consistent with the main points of the highlighted sentences and the annotation.
    - (B) is wrong because it's **Extreme Language**—there is no support given to conclude that people in Latin America and Africa cannot *afford* the footwear. It is implied that they choose not to wear it.
    - (C) is wrong because it goes **Beyond the Text**—while it's likely at least some exercise enthusiasts correctly predicted the trend, no support for this is given in the passage.
    - (D) is wrong because it also goes **Beyond the Text**—region-specific footwear sounds like a logical way to boost sales to regions that may have passed on modern footwear, but nothing about footwear manufacturers or their practices is mentioned in the passage.

CHAPTER 8

More Question Formats Drill (page 181)

1. **B** This is a Vocabulary question, as it asks what "settled" *most nearly means.* Treat "settled" as if it were a blank—the blank describes the snow on the cathedral towers, so look for clues regarding the snow. The passage states that *many a statue wore a long white bonnet on its grotesque or sainted head.* This imagery is describing how the snow coated the various features of the cathedral towers. Therefore, write "covered" or "coated" in your annotation box.

    - (A) is wrong because *Resolved* goes **Beyond the Text**—it's an alternate definition of *settled* that does not match "covered."
    - (B) is correct because *Accumulated* could match "covered" in this context, as both would mean the snow is building up on the roof of the cathedral.

- (C) is wrong because *Disappeared* is the **Opposite** of the snow covering much of the cathedral's roof.
- (D) is wrong because *Survived* doesn't match "covered."

2. **B** This is a Purpose question, as it asks for the *function of the underlined portion in the text as a whole.* Read the passage and focus on structural language that can help explain the function of the underlined portion. The underlined sentence describes the Code Girls' efforts, so look before the underlined sentence to determine why the Code Girls' efforts were referenced. The first sentence states that *The Code Girls... may finally be receiving their due recognition from World War II historians.* Therefore, the underlined sentence is giving an example of how historians are finally recognizing the Code Girls. Write down in your annotation box that a good function of the underlined portion would be to "explain further how historians are finally recognizing the Code Girls."

   - (A) is wrong because it's **Right Answer, Wrong Question**—the first sentence explains that the US Navy hired the Code Girls, but the first sentence is not the underlined sentence.
   - (B) is correct because it's consistent with the highlighting and annotation.
   - (C) is wrong because, if anything, it's the **Opposite** of the passage—there is no evidence in the passage that being a Code Girl was a *typical* role for women, and the role is actually described as *secretive* and therefore not something most people would even know about.
   - (D) is wrong because no *other heroic women* are discussed in the passage besides the Code Girls.

3. **C** This is a Purpose question, as it asks for the *overall structure of the text.* Read the passage and look for a shift in the passage that will indicate where the passage switches from one focus to the next. The passage states that *Until this discovery, it was believed that individual hair cells reacted independently to set frequencies.* Before this shift, a discovery is made that *microscopic hair cells...react to low-frequency sound.* After the shift, the passage discusses *A significant outcome of this breakthrough.* Write down in your annotation box that the structure of the passage is to "mention a discovery and then discuss its impact."

   - (A) is wrong because it's **Half-Right**—there's no mention in the passage of any scientists being *skeptical of the results.*
   - (B) is wrong because it's also **Half-Right**—it does sound like the Swedish team may be doing something new or *innovative,* but the methods used by previous researchers are not described as *superior.* In fact, the previous researchers were not able to discover what the Swedish team discovered.
   - (C) is correct because it's consistent with the highlighting and annotation.
   - (D) is wrong because no *hypothesis* is given, and any *steps taken* by the Swedish team occur before, not after, the shift in the passage.

4. **C** This is a Dual Texts question, as it asks *which statement* the two authors would *agree* on. Follow the Dual Texts Basic Approach. Text 1 states that *Robinson's versatility made him both adaptable enough to work with others and talented enough to work on his own.* Now, read Text 2 and see what its author says regarding the same details, understanding that the two authors won't agree on their main conclusions. Text 2 states that *Robinson was considered so charismatic and skilled a dancer that he was eventually allowed to perform solo and as part of a mixed-race collaboration with white actress Shirley Temple.* So, note in the annotation box that the authors would agree that "Robinson's success came due to his charisma and talent."

    - (A) is wrong because it goes **Beyond the Text**—Robinson worked with several different artists, but it's not known from the passage that he *drew inspiration* from them.
    - (B) is wrong because it also goes **Beyond the Text**—it's logical that other entertainers *deeply admired* Robinson, but no such claim is made in the passage.
    - (C) is correct because it's consistent with the highlighting and annotation.
    - (D) is wrong because the *restrictions faced by Robinson* are described only in Text 2, and even there, it's not stated that the public was *largely unaware* of those restrictions.

5. **D** This is a Claims question, as it asks which finding *would most directly undermine the team's hypothesis.* Read the passage and highlight the claim, which is that *the team theorized that the zebra stripes must confuse the biting flies' landing and biting patterns* which *reduces the number of bites each cow receives.* Because the question task is to undermine, or weaken, a claim, the correct answer should be as inconsistent as possible with this hypothesis.

    - (A) is wrong because it mentions *the number of bites caused by insects other than biting flies,* which are not referenced by the claim.
    - (B) is wrong because it's the **Opposite** of what the question asked for; it would strengthen, not weaken, the claim if *biting flies were more prevalent near cows that did not have the zebra stripes.*
    - (C) is wrong because it's an **Opposite** trap for the same reason—it strengthens the link between zebra stripes and reducing bites from biting flies.
    - (D) is correct because it directly contradicts the team's hypothesis that zebra stripes lower the number of bites caused by biting flies, stating that the presence of zebra stripes instead *increased* the number of bites.

6. **A** This is a Charts question, as it asks for *data from the table to support the underlined claim.* Follow the Charts Basic Approach. Read the title and headings in the table. Read the passage and highlight the underlined claim, which is that *even in countries with the largest communities of Esperanto speakers, Esperantujo represent only a tiny fraction of each nation's total population.* The correct answer should offer data from the table that is as consistent as possible with this claim.

- (A) is correct because it's consistent with the claim and the table—it shows that Brazil has the largest *Esperantujo* population of all three countries given, and yet, they represent only a *tiny fraction* of Brazil's population.

- (B) is wrong because it's **Half-Right**—it's consistent with the table but irrelevant to the claim, which focuses on *countries with the largest communities of Esperanto speakers.*

- (C) is wrong because it's the **Opposite** of the table—Brazil's population does not encompass 0.003% of the global population, but rather, Brazil's *Esperantujo* account for 0.003% of Brazil's population. Additionally, Brazil has 7,000 *Esperantujo,* not 63,000, which is taken from the passage.

- (D) is wrong because it's also the **Opposite** of the table—it is not that *0.001% of all Esperantujo live in Japan*, but rather, *Esperantujo* make up 0.001% of Japan's population.

CHAPTER 9

Mastering the POE Drill (page 197)

1. **C** This is a Vocabulary question, as it asks for a *most logical and precise word or phrase.* Read the passage and highlight what can help you fill in the blank. The blank describes the dog and human relationship, so look for and highlight clues about that relationship. In the dog and human relationship, the dog *grants the* elderly *person a true companion,* and the human is described as *providing the dog with shelter, food, medical care, and affection.* The human here is responding to the dog's positive contributions with some of their own, so write "gives back" or "returns the favor" in your annotation box.

    - (A) is wrong because *diverges* (separates from) is the **Opposite** of "gives back."

    - (B) is wrong because *exaggerates* is **Extreme Language**—the passage doesn't support that the human is going too far; rather, the human gives the appropriate positive reply to the dog.

    - (C) is correct because *reciprocates* matches "gives back."

    - (D) is wrong because *counters* suggests a negative interaction between dog and human, which is the **Opposite** of what is stated in the passage.

2. **C** This is a Purpose question, as it asks for the *main purpose of the text.* Read the passage and identify who or what the passage focuses on: a discussion of the aftermath of World War I. The inclusion of *Some could, some could not* in the third line indicates a comparison, so highlight that *Some could, some could not, shake off misery.* This contrast due to how different groups felt about the war is repeated in the fourth and fifth lines, in which one spirit claims the war was necessary and the other asks why that

would be true. Write down in your annotation box that a good main purpose of the passage would be to "show different feelings regarding the war."

- (A) is wrong because it goes **Beyond the Text**—two spirits are mentioned, but it's not stated that the speaker had *a conversation* with them.
- (B) is wrong because it's the **Opposite** of the passage—the war had definitely ended according to the introductory text.
- (C) is correct because it's consistent with the highlighting and annotation.
- (D) is wrong because it also goes **Beyond the Text**—as logical as it is to *lament the passing of those lost in battle* during war, the speaker does not do this in the passage, and the emotions of *misery* and *Pity* aren't said to be felt directly in connection to the deaths of anyone.

3. **A** This is a Dual Texts question, as it asks how *the author of Text 2* would *most likely respond to the underlined claim in Text 1.* Follow the Dual Texts Basic Approach. The underlined claim in Text 1 states that *domesticated felines…did not respond when called by their owners.* Highlight this claim and see what should be highlighted in Text 2 regarding the same idea. Text 2 states that *cats increased their behavior intensity when directly addressed by the voice on their owners' audio* but did not show the same increase when listening to the audio from strangers. So, note in the annotation box that "Text 2 would disagree—cats do respond to owner's voice."

- (A) is correct because it's consistent with the author of Text 2 showing disagreement with Text 1's claim.
- (B) is wrong because it's the **Opposite** of the annotation—Text 2 would not *strongly concur* with the claim from Text 1.
- (C) is wrong because it goes **Beyond the Text**—as likely as it is that domesticated cats inherited their instincts from feral, or wild, ancestors, that doesn't mean the author of Text 2 would praise the claim. In fact, the annotation states that the author disagrees with the claim.
- (D) is wrong because it's **Half-Right**—the author of Text 2 probably would criticize the claim, but the author of Text 1 never assumes that cats responded to the human voice before being domesticated.

4. **A** This is a Retrieval question, as it asks for a detail *according to the text.* Look for information in the text that indicates what made *Alexei become a monk.* Read the passage and highlight the reason given for Alexei's career choice. The passage states that *This particular way had caught his attention only because he had happened to meet a man who made an overwhelming impression on him—the famous Zosima, the elder of our monastery.* The correct answer should be as consistent as possible with this detail.

- (A) is correct because it's consistent with the highlighted sentence.

- (B) is wrong because it's **Extreme Language**—Alexei is said to have *love* for his fellow men, but not that this love is *overwhelming.*
- (C) is wrong because it's the **Opposite** of the passage—Alexei would not want to *isolate himself from others*, as he loves his fellow men.
- (D) is wrong because it's both **Extreme Language** and **Recycled Language**—it's not claimed that becoming a monk is the *only* way to do anything, nor are *darkness* and *wickedness* in the passage described as things Alexei will *battle*.

5. **D** This is a Main Idea question, as it asks for the *main idea of the text.* Look for and highlight a sentence that the other sentences build toward or give examples of. The passage first introduces a claim but then states that *paleontologists disagree with this claim, arguing that the plates on the animal's back are more akin to ridges similar to those present on the backs of modern chameleons than they are to the features of any dinosaur.* This sentence captures the main idea—there is debate about what "dinosaur of Ta Prohm" is meant to depict. The correct answer should be as consistent as possible with this main idea.

    - (A) is wrong because it's **Extreme Language**—it's not stated that analyzing ancient sculptures is the *best* way to determine anything.
    - (B) is wrong because it's also **Extreme Language**—the sculpture does not *prove* anything according to the passage.
    - (C) is wrong because it goes **Beyond the Text**—just because the paleontologists believe *the plates on the animal's back are more akin to ridges similar to those present on modern chameleons* does not mean they are *certain that the sculpture is depicting a modern organism.*
    - (D) is correct because it's consistent with the highlighted sentences and the various viewpoints offered during the passage.

6. **D** This is a Claims question, as it asks which finding *would most directly support the skeptic's claim.* Read the passage and highlight the claim, which is that *the length and rigor of training are more likely to have attracted those in lower classes, as they would be more willing to devote such time to improve their situation.* The correct answer should be as consistent as possible with this claim.

    - (A) is wrong because it's the **Opposite** of the question task—it would weaken the claim if *bunraku* plays contained similar elements *regardless of the social status of the author.*
    - (B) is wrong because it's irrelevant to the claim, which is about which classes would have been drawn to *bunraku* initially rather than anything regarding modern times.
    - (C) is wrong because it's also the **Opposite** of the question task—if it were true that the *shamisen* was an *expensive* instrument, this would support the idea that upper classes, who could afford more expensive items, might have been the ones involved in *bunraku* at first.

- (D) is correct because it is consistent with the highlighted claim—since the *kugutsu-mawashi* often lived in poverty, they'd be an example of folks from *lower classes* being drawn to *bunraku* at first.

7. **A** This is a Charts question, as it asks for *data from the graph to complete the assertion.* Follow the Charts Basic Approach. Read the title, variables, units, and key from the graph. Read the passage and highlight the assertion, which is that *The most dramatic growth occurred in states like Alaska,* so the correct answer should be related to the data for Alaska and show some type of dramatic growth.

    - (A) is correct because it's consistent with the assertion and the graph.
    - (B) is wrong because it's the **Opposite** of what's presented for Alaska in the graph—Alaska's average home price is not *around $30,000* in 1950; it's much closer to $20,000.
    - (C) is wrong because it's **Half-Right**—it presents the correct value for Alaska in 1950, but by 1990, Alaska's average home price was $120,000, not $140,000.
    - (D) is wrong because it's **Right Answer, Wrong Question**—these values accurately describe Ohio's growth, not Alaska's.

8. **C** This is a Conclusions question, as it asks what *most logically completes the text.* Look for the main focus of the passage, which is hobby tunneling. The passage states that tunnel hobbyists *simply continued digging once the initial job was completed* and that many of them *stated that the effort required to make their tunnels seemed disproportionate to the stated purpose.* Write "hobby tunneling must be about more than just completing a goal" into the annotation box as a good conclusion.

    - (A) is wrong because it is the **Opposite** of the examples given in the passage, where the reasons are clearly stated.
    - (B) is wrong because it's **Extreme Language**; the text doesn't support the idea that tunnel hobbyists should *only* build tunnels on their own properties.
    - (C) is correct because it is consistent with the highlighting and annotation.
    - (D) is wrong because it states that *hobby tunneling can improve mental condition more than physical condition,* but this is **Recycled Language** as the passage never states which is bolstered more by hobby tunneling.

CHAPTER 11

Punctuation Drill (page 233)

1. **B** In this Rules question, periods and question marks are changing in the answer choices, so it's testing questions versus statements. The sentence after the blank says that *Solar and his* team *designed a study to find out*, so they must be finding out the answer to a question. Thus, the sentence with the blank must be a question. Eliminate answers that aren't correctly written as questions.

   - (A) is wrong because it has a question mark but is written as a statement.
   - (B) is correct because it's correctly written as a question.
   - (C) and (D) are wrong because they are statements.

2. **C** In this Rules question, verb forms are changing in the answer choices, so it's testing sentence structure. The phrase after the word *computer* describes how and why the *mussels* are used. Eliminate any answer that does not make the phrase clear and correct.

   - (A), (B), and (D) are wrong because they are in main verb form but a second main verb isn't appropriate at this point in the sentence.
   - (C) is correct because it states that the mussels are being used *to monitor the water quality*, which provides a clear and correct meaning.

3. **D** In this Rules question, punctuation including a period is changing in the answer choices, so it's testing how to connect clauses. Look for independent clauses. The first part of the sentence says *Cristina Ibarra's documentary…follows two girls…*, which is an independent clause. The second part says *for over 100 years the ball…has been part of the celebration…*, which is also an independent clause. Eliminate any answer that can't correctly connect two independent clauses.

   - (A) is wrong because some type of punctuation is needed in order to connect two independent clauses.
   - (B) is wrong because a coordinating conjunction (*and*) without a comma can't connect two independent clauses.
   - (C) is wrong because a comma without a coordinating conjunction (FANBOYS) can't connect two independent clauses.
   - (D) is correct because the period makes each independent clause its own sentence, which is fine.

4. **A** In this Rules question, punctuation including a period is changing in the answer choices, so it's testing how to connect clauses. Look for independent clauses. The first part of the sentence says *These winners share an average age (64) and geographical diversity with those in other categories*, which is an independent clause. The second part of the sentence says *though they have not attended the same schools...*, which is a dependent clause. Eliminate any option that doesn't correctly connect an independent + a dependent clause.

   - (A) is correct because independent + dependent can be connected with a comma. Although the dependent clause comes second, there is a contrast in meaning, which requires a comma.
   - (B) and (D) are wrong because independent + dependent cannot be connected with punctuation other than a comma.
   - (C) is wrong because there is no reason to use a comma after *though*.

5. **D** In this Rules question, punctuation with a transition is changing in the answer choices. A semicolon appears in the answers, so look for independent clauses and ignore the transition word for now. The first part of the sentence says *For example, diapers were originally made of cloth*, which is an independent clause. The second part of the sentence says *diapers are mainly disposable now, so the phrase "cloth diaper" is used to describe diapers in their original form*, which is also an independent clause. Next, consider which clause the transition belongs in. The second part of the sentence contrasts with the first part of the sentence, which states that diapers were *originally made of cloth*, so *however* belongs in the second part of the sentence. Eliminate options that incorrectly link the independent clauses or place *however* in the first part of the sentence.

   - (A) is wrong because it puts *however* with the first independent clause.
   - (B) and (C) are wrong because two independent clauses cannot be connected with commas alone.
   - (D) is correct because it puts *however* with the second independent clause and puts a semicolon between the two independent clauses.

6. **B** In this Rules question, punctuation including a period is changing in the answer choices, so it's testing how to connect clauses. Look for independent clauses. The first part of the sentence says *Nearly every player...reads music using the treble clef or the bass clef, except for one*, which is an independent clause. The second part of the sentence says *the violist, who typically reads music using the alto clef*, which is the one exception and is not an independent clause. Eliminate any option that doesn't correctly connect the independent clause to the exception.

   - (A) is wrong because a semicolon is used when the second part is an independent clause, which is not the case here.
   - (B) is correct because a colon is used when the second part of the sentence elaborates on the first.
   - (C) is wrong because some type of punctuation is needed to separate the independent clause from the exception.

- (D) is wrong because the period makes the second part its own sentence, which doesn't work because it's not an independent clause.

7. **C** In this Rules question, punctuation between a title (*animal behaviorist*) and a name is changing in the answer choices, so it's testing describing phrases. The words *animal behaviorist* are a title for Slobodchikoff, so no punctuation should be used. Eliminate answers that use punctuation.

    - (A) and (B) are wrong because they use punctuation between the title and the person's name.
    - (C) is correct because titles before names have no punctuation.
    - (D) is wrong because it puts a single punctuation mark between the subject (*research*) and its verb (*has revealed*).

8. **A** In this Rules question, punctuation is changing in the answer choices. Look for independent clauses. The sentence includes a noun phrase that says *a high-strength material used in personal armor, sports equipment, and musical instruments,* which is a describing phrase and not an independent clause. Noun phrases beginning with "a" or "an" are always Extra Information and should be set off with matching commas, parentheses, or dashes. Eliminate answers that do not have one of these options.

    - (A) is correct because it uses dashes before and after the Extra Information.
    - (B) is wrong because a colon can only follow an independent clause but the part before the colon isn't an independent clause.
    - (C) is wrong because the dashes do not include the entire noun phrase.
    - (D) is wrong because it has a comma before the noun phrase but doesn't have a matching comma after it.

9. **B** In this Rules question, commas are changing in the answer choices. The answers contain commas in several places, so use Process of Elimination to eliminate any answers that don't use commas correctly.

    - (A) is wrong because the phrase *among World War I veterans* is Specifying Information and shouldn't be separated from the rest of the sentence with commas.
    - (B) is correct because no punctuation is needed here.
    - (C) is wrong because there is no reason to put a comma between *tremendous* and *unemployment.*
    - (D) is wrong because it puts a single comma between a subject (*unemployment*) and its verb (*was seen*).

10. **B** In this Rules question, commas and semicolons are changing in the answer choices. The sentence already contains a semicolon near the end, and the part after it is not an independent clause, which suggests that the sentence contains a list separated by semicolons. Use the second and third examples to determine the structure of each item: Type of Publication, Comma, Title of Publication, Comma, Year. Make an annotation of this pattern and eliminate any answer that doesn't follow it.

- (A) is wrong because the first item ends after the year, so there should be a semicolon between the year and the type of publication for the second item.
- (B) is correct because it follows the pattern of the third item.
- (C) and (D) are wrong because they don't have a comma after the title of the publication.

CHAPTER 12

Grammar Drill (page 250)

1. **D** In this Rules question, verbs are changing in the answer choices, so it's testing consistency with verbs. Find and highlight the subject, *co-writers*, which is plural, so a plural verb is needed. Write an annotation saying "plural." Eliminate any answer that is not plural.
    - (A), (B), and (C) are wrong because they are singular.
    - (D) is correct because it's plural.
2. **A** In this Rules question, verbs are changing in the answer choices, so it's testing consistency with verbs. In this case, the verb is part of a list of two things that Baingana did, the first of which is *studied.* Highlight the word *studied*, which the verb in the answer should be consistent with. Eliminate any answer that isn't consistent with *studied.*
    - (A) is correct because *obtained* is in the same tense and form as *studied.*
    - (B), (C), and (D) are wrong because *obtaining, to obtain*, and *having obtained* aren't consistent with *studied.*
3. **B** In this Rules question, pronouns are changing in the answer choices, so it's testing consistency with pronouns. Find and highlight the word the pronoun refers back to, *A hikaye*, which is singular, so a singular pronoun is needed. Write an annotation saying "singular." Eliminate any answer that isn't singular or doesn't clearly refer back to a *hikaye.*
    - (A) is wrong because it is plural.
    - (B) is correct because *it* is singular and is consistent with *A hikaye.*
    - (C) and (D) are wrong because *one* and *you* would both refer to people, which isn't consistent with *A hikaye.*
4. **D** In this Rules question, pronouns and apostrophes are changing in the answer choices, so it's testing consistency with pronouns. The underlined portion does not refer back to a specific noun, so it is not a pronoun. Eliminate any answer that is a pronoun.

- (A), (B), and (C) are wrong because they're all pronouns.
- (D) is correct because it is not a pronoun.

5. **A** In this Rules question, verbs are changing in the answer choices, so it's testing consistency with verbs. Find and highlight the subject, *He*, which is singular, so a singular verb is needed. All of the answers work with a singular subject, so look for a clue regarding tense. The other verbs in the passage are *has focused* and *is*, which are both in present tense, so highlight those verbs and write an annotation saying "present." Eliminate any answer not in present tense.

    - (A) is correct because it's in present tense and correctly refers to something that has happened *since 1976*.
    - (B) and (C) are wrong because they're in past tense.
    - (D) is wrong because although it is in present tense, it's not consistent with the idea that he has done something *since 1976*.

6. **B** In this Rules question, verbs are changing in the answer choices, so it's testing consistency with verbs. In this case, the verb is part of a list of two things that the alfalfa could do, the first of which is *grow*. Highlight the word *grow*, which the verb in the answer should be consistent with. Eliminate any answer that isn't consistent with *grow*.

    - (A), (C), and (D) are wrong because *fertilizing*, *fertilized*, and *fertilizes* aren't consistent with *grow*.
    - (B) is correct because *fertilize* is in the same tense and form as *grow*.

7. **C** In this Rules question, apostrophes with nouns are changing in the answer choices. Determine whether each word possesses anything. The *company* possesses the *posts*, but the *posts* don't possess anything. Eliminate any answer that doesn't match this.

    - (A) and (B) are wrong because *companies* is plural, and the text says *a* before the underlined portion, so the noun should be singular.
    - (C) is correct because *company's* is possessive and *posts* is not.
    - (D) is wrong because *posts* shouldn't be possessive.

8. **C** In this Rules question, verbs are changing in the answer choices, so it's testing consistency with verbs. Find and highlight the subject, *interest*, which is singular, so a singular verb is needed. All of the answers work with a singular subject, so look for a clue regarding tense. The previous two sentences use past tense verbs: *became*, *vowed*, and *worked*. Highlight those verbs and write an annotation that says "past." Eliminate any answer not in past tense.

    - (A) is wrong because it's in present tense.
    - (B) is wrong because it's in future tense.

- (C) is correct because it's in past tense.
- (D) is wrong because it's in present perfect tense and incorrectly refers to something that started in the past and continues to the present, but the passage's use of past tense and reference to Wauneka's experience in *1918* suggest that she's not currently living.

9. **D** In this Rules question, pronouns are changing in the answer choices, so it's testing consistency with pronouns. Find and highlight the word the pronoun refers back to, *birds*, which is plural, so a plural pronoun is needed. Write an annotation saying "plural." Eliminate any answer that isn't plural or doesn't clearly refer back to *birds*.

    - (A) is wrong because although *them* is plural and can refer back to the birds, it doesn't provide a clear meaning in this context, since the sentence doesn't clearly indicate who or what would be presented *as part of a courtship ritual*.
    - (B) and (C) are wrong because they are singular.
    - (D) is correct because *themselves* is plural and makes clear the meaning that the birds are presenting themselves *as potential mates*.

10. **A** In this Rules question, pronouns are changing in the answer choices, so it's testing consistency with pronouns. Find and highlight the word the pronoun refers back to, *the beaver*, which is singular, so a singular pronoun is needed. Write an annotation saying "singular." Eliminate any answer that isn't singular or doesn't clearly refer back to *the beaver*.

    - (A) is correct because *it* is singular and is consistent with *the beaver*.
    - (B) and (D) are wrong because *this* and *one* don't refer back to a specific thing.
    - (C) is wrong because it is plural.

11. **A** In this Rules question, verbs are changing in the answer choices, so it's testing consistency with verbs. Find and highlight the subject, *Work*, which is singular, so a singular verb is needed. Write an annotation saying "singular." Eliminate any answer that is not singular.

    - (A) is correct because it's singular.
    - (B), (C), and (D) are wrong because they are plural.

12. **C** In this Rules question, the subjects of the answers are changing, which suggests it may be testing modifiers. Look for and highlight a modifying phrase: *Analyzing the genomes of existing populations and fossil DNA*. Whoever is *Analyzing the genomes* needs to come immediately after the comma. Eliminate any answer that doesn't start with someone who can analyze genomes.

    - (A), (B), and (D) are wrong because *donkeys*, *research*, and *genetic information* can't analyze genomes.
    - (C) is correct because *scientists* can analyze genomes.

CHAPTER 13

Rhetoric Questions Drill (page 264)

1. **C** This is a Transitions question, so follow the basic approach. Highlight ideas that relate to each other. The preceding sentence describes what type of actions *Monopoly rewards*, and this sentence says *the original version...had a much different objective.* These ideas disagree, so an opposite-direction transition is needed. Make an annotation that says "disagree." Eliminate any answer that doesn't match.

    - (A) and (D) are wrong because *Likewise* and *In effect* are same-direction transitions.
    - (B) is wrong because *Regardless* is used when something will occur despite something else, which is not the case here.
    - (C) is correct because *By contrast* is an opposite-direction transition used when two ideas are opposites of each other.

2. **A** This is a Transitions question, so follow the basic approach. Highlight ideas that relate to each other. The preceding sentence states that *the play...has been updated with each production*, and this sentence describes one way it was updated. These ideas agree, so a same-direction transition is needed. Make an annotation that says "agree." Eliminate any answer that doesn't match.

    - (A) is correct because *For instance* is used when the sentence is an example of the preceding sentence.
    - (B) is wrong because *Moreover* is used when the idea is an additional point to the previous sentence, which isn't the case here.
    - (C) is wrong because *Similarly* is used to compare two separate things, which isn't the case here.
    - (D) is wrong because *Subsequently* is used when the next idea occurs as a result of the first idea, which isn't the case here.

3. **C** This is a Transitions question, so follow the basic approach. Highlight ideas that relate to each other. The preceding sentence states that *they found nanoplastics in the mouths and guts of the larvae*, and this sentence states that *they also found nanoplastics in different parts of the fish.* These ideas agree, so a same-direction transition is needed. Make an annotation that says "agree." Eliminate any answer that doesn't match.

    - (A) is wrong because *To that end* is used when the preceding idea is used to state a specific goal that the following sentence shows what was done to achieve it, which isn't the case here.
    - (B) is wrong because this sentence isn't a more specific version of the preceding sentence.

- (C) is correct because *Similarly* is used to compare two ideas, in this case what was found in *the larvae* and what was found in *the fish*.
- (D) is wrong because *Nevertheless* is an opposite-direction transition.

4. **B** This is a Transitions question, so follow the basic approach. Highlight ideas that relate to each other. The preceding sentence states that *Although conservation efforts have been enacted, it may be too late*, and this sentence says *hope is not lost*. These ideas disagree, so an opposite-direction transition is needed. Make an annotation that says "disagree." Eliminate any answer that doesn't match.
    - (A) and (D) are wrong because *Therefore* and *For example* are same-direction transitions.
    - (B) is correct because *Still* is used when the second idea happens despite the first idea.
    - (C) is wrong because *Instead* is used when the second idea is an alternative to the first idea.

5. **B** This is a Transitions question, so follow the basic approach. Highlight ideas that relate to each other. The preceding sentence states that *The sculpture* looks like *a large, silver bean* and this sentence says the *sculpture has been nicknamed "The Bean."* These ideas agree, so a same-direction transition is needed. Make an annotation that says "agree." Eliminate any answer that doesn't match.
    - (A) and (D) are wrong because *Though* and *Nonetheless* are opposite-direction transitions.
    - (B) is correct because *Indeed* supports and reinforces the preceding idea.
    - (C) is wrong because the second idea is not a conclusion based on the preceding idea.

6. **B** This is a Rhetorical Synthesis question, so follow the basic approach. Highlight the goal(s) stated in the question: *present a possible explanation for chimpanzees not "saying goodbye."* Eliminate any answer that doesn't fulfill this purpose.
    - (A) and (C) are wrong because they say chimpanzees don't *"say goodbye"* but don't offer a reason why.
    - (B) is correct because it gives an *explanation* for why *chimpanzees may not "say goodbye"*: they are able to *communicate...over long distances* by drumming.
    - (D) is wrong because it doesn't mention saying *goodbye*.

7. **C** This is a Rhetorical Synthesis question, so follow the basic approach. Highlight the goal(s) stated in the question: *highlight the various literary accolades that Erdrich has received*. Eliminate any answer that doesn't fulfill this purpose.
    - (A) and (D) are wrong because each mentions only one *literary accolade*.
    - (B) is wrong because it doesn't mention any *literary accolades*.
    - (C) is correct because it cites two *literary accolades* Erdrich won.

8. **B** This is a Rhetorical Synthesis question, so follow the basic approach. Highlight the goal(s) stated in the question: *introduce crème brûlée to an audience familiar with caramelization.* Eliminate any answer that doesn't *introduce crème brûlée* in a way that assumes the audience is *familiar with caramelization.*

- (A) and (D) are wrong because they describe *caramelization* even though the audience is already familiar with it.
- (B) is correct because it introduces *crème brûlée* and doesn't explain *caramelization* since the audience is familiar with it.
- (C) is wrong because it doesn't give a general introduction stating what *crème brûlée* is.

9. **B** This is a Rhetorical Synthesis question, so follow the basic approach. Highlight the goal(s) stated in the question: *introduce the main point to an audience unfamiliar with US city and state names.* Read the bullet points to identify the *main point* (that many city and state names have *French origins*) and eliminate any answer that doesn't *introduce the main point* in a way that assumes the audience is *unfamiliar with US city and state names.*

- (A) is wrong because the audience is *unfamiliar with US city and state names,* so the answer needs to clarify whether the names are cities or states.
- (B) is correct because it introduces *the main point* and does provide examples of both *US city and state names* since the audience is *unfamiliar with* them.
- (C) is wrong because it refers only to city names, not *state names.*
- (D) is wrong because it refers only to state names, not *city names.*

10. **D** This is a Rhetorical Synthesis question, so follow the basic approach. Highlight the goal(s) stated in the question: *emphasize the two results of the study.* Read the bullet points to identify what the *two results* are: *reduced mowing was connected to an increase in the abundance of arthropods* and *an increase in the taxa richness (or biodiversity) of arthropods.* Eliminate any answer that doesn't accurately identify these two results.

- (A) and (B) are wrong because each addresses only one of *the two results of the study.*
- (C) is wrong because it doesn't identify either result.
- (D) is correct because it describes *the two results of the study.*

CHAPTER 14

Drill 1 (page 275)

1. **c** Examples: –7, 0, 1, 8

2. **d** Examples: 0.5, 2, 118

3. **g** Examples: –0.5, –2, –118

4. **f** Examples: –4, 0, 10

5. **b** Examples: –5, 1, 17

6. **a** Examples: *Factors* of 12 are 1, 2, 3, 4, 6, and 12. Factors of 10 are 1, 2, 5, and 10.

7. **i** Examples: *Multiples* of 12 include –24, –12, 0, 12, 24, and so on. Multiples of 10 include –20, –10, 0, 10, 20, 30, and so on.

8. **h** Examples: 2, 3, 5, 7, 11, and so on. There are no negative *prime numbers*, and 1 is not prime.

9. **e** Examples: 3 and 4 are *distinct* numbers. –2 and 2 are also distinct.

10. **j** Examples: In the number 274, 2 is the *digit* in the hundreds place, 7 is the digit in the tens place, and 4 is the digit in the ones place.

Drill 2 (page 276)

11. **p** Examples: –1, 0, 1, and 2 are *consecutive* numbers. Be careful—sometimes you will be asked for *consecutive even* or *consecutive odd* numbers, in which case you would use just the odds or evens in a consecutive list of numbers.

12. **n** Examples: 6 is *divisible* by 2 and 3, but not by 4 or 5.

13. **l** Examples: When you divide 26 by 8, you get 3 with a *remainder* of 2 (2 is left over). When you divide 14 by 5, you get 2 with a remainder of 4 (4 is left over).

14. **k** Examples: When you add 2 and 3, you get a *sum* of 5. When you add –4 and 1, you get a sum of –3.

15. **r** Examples: When you multiply 2 and 3, you get a *product* of 6. When you multiply –4 and 1, you get a product of –4.

16. **m** Examples: When you subtract 2 from 3, you get a *difference* of 1. When you subtract –4 from 1, you get a difference of 5.

17. **q** Examples: When you divide 2 by 3, you get a quotient of $\frac{2}{3}$. When you divide –4 by 1, you get a quotient of –4.

18. **o** Examples: The absolute value of –3 is 3. The absolute value of 41 is 41.

Drill 3 (page 287)

1. **B** The question asks for the relationship between two variables. Translate one piece of information at a time in order to build the equation. Translate *is* as equals, translate *2 more than* as + 2, and translate *one-fourth of the number b* as $\frac{1}{4}b$. The translated equation is $a = 2 + \frac{1}{4}b$. Rearrange the terms on the right side of the equation to get $a = \frac{1}{4}b + 2$. The correct answer is (B).

2. **B** The question asks for an equivalent inequality. One method is to enter the inequality in the question into an entry field in the built-in calculator, then enter each answer choice inequality one at a time in another entry field, and eliminate ones that do not show the same graph. Only the inequality in (B) results in the same graph, so (B) is correct.

   To solve algebraically, subtract 3 from both sides of the inequality to get $-15 \leq 3x$. Divide both sides of the inequality by 3 to get $-5 \leq x$, which matches (B).

   Using either of these methods, the correct answer is (B).

3. **C** The question asks for a system of equations that can be solved to find the number of skis and the number of snowboards rented over the three-day weekend. Translate the given information into equations one piece at a time, and eliminate after each piece. One piece of information states that *180 total skis and snowboards were rented.* Since s represents the number of skis and b represents the number of snowboards, translate this as $s + b = 180$. Eliminate (A) and (D) because they do not include this equation. Another piece of information states that *the resort collected $4,600 in total rental fees.* Thus, the second equation must equal 4,600. Eliminate (B) because the second equation equals 460, not 4,600. The correct answer is (C).

4. **–19** The question asks for the negative solution to an equation with absolute values. The most efficient method is to enter the equation as written into the built-in calculator. Scroll and zoom to see the solutions represented by vertical lines at $x = -19$ and $x = 9$. The question asks for the negative solution, which is –19.

   To solve algebraically, recall that, with an absolute value, the value inside the absolute value bars can be either positive or negative, so this equation has two possible solutions. To start solving for x, treat the absolute value symbols the same as you would parentheses. Add $4|x + 5|$ to both sides of the equation to get $|x + 5| = 14$. The value in the absolute value bars could equal 14 or –14, so set $x + 5$ equal to each. When $x + 5 = 14$, subtract 5 from both sides of the equation to get $x = 9$. When $x + 5 = -14$, subtract 5 from both sides of the equation to get $x = -19$. The question asks for the negative solution, which is –19.

   Using either of these methods, the correct answer is –19.

5. **B** The question asks for the value of a constant given an equation. A linear equation has infinitely many solutions when the x-terms are the same and the constants are the same. Distribute on both sides of the equation to get $30x + 40 = 30x + 8k$. The x-terms are the same, so set the constants equal to each other to get $40 = 8k$. Divide both sides of the equation by 8 to get $5 = k$. The correct answer is (B).

6. **C** The question asks for a certain number that works for the given information. Translate the English into math in order to write an equation. In math terms, "is" means equals, "more" is addition, and "times" is multiplication. The equation becomes $x = 7x + 3$. Solve the equation for x. Subtract $7x$ from both sides to get $-6x = 3$. Divide both sides of the equation by -6 to get $x = \frac{3}{-6}$. Reduce to get $-\frac{1}{2}$. The correct answer is (C).

7. **D** The question asks for an inequality that represents all values of r. Translate the question one piece at a time, and eliminate after each piece. The total number of recipes Ann will include in her book is the sum of 32 main dish recipes, 18 dessert recipes, and r additional recipes. The book will include up to 98 recipes, meaning the greatest possible number of recipes in the book is 98. This information can be written as the inequality $32 + 18 + r \leq 98$. Subtract 32 and 18 from both sides of the equation to get $r \leq 48$. Isolate r in the answer choices to find the one that matches $r \leq 48$. For (A), add 50 to both sides of the equation to get $r \geq 148$. Eliminate (A). For (B), add 50 to both sides of the equation to get $r \leq 148$. Eliminate (B). For (C), subtract 48 from both sides of the equation to get $r \leq -48$. Eliminate (C). For (D), add r to both sides of the equation to get $48 \geq r$. The correct answer is (D).

8. **C** The question asks for the equation that represents a situation. Translate the information in bite-sized pieces and eliminate after each piece. One piece of information says *the carpenter uses 2.1 planks of wood to create one set of blocks*. Since b represents the number of sets of blocks, multiplying 2.1 by b, or $2.1b$, represents the total number of planks of wood used to make sets of blocks. Eliminate (A), (B), and (D) because they do not include the term $2.1b$. Choice (C) also correctly translates the number of planks of wood used to make t sets of tops as $0.7t$ and the total number of planks of wood as $= 28$. The correct answer is (C).

9. **A** The question asks for the value of an expression given a system of equations. The most efficient method is to enter both equations into the built-in calculator, and then scroll and zoom as needed to find the point of intersection. The lines intersect at $(3.5, -7)$, so $y = -7$. The question asks for the value of $3y$, which is $3(-7) = -21$, so (A) is correct.

To solve algebraically, recognize that, when a PSAT question asks for the value of an expression, there is usually a straightforward way to solve for the expression without needing to completely isolate either variable. To solve for $3y$, find a way to make the x-terms disappear. First, multiply the entire second equation by -1 to get $-2x - 15 = 2y - 8$. Now the two equations have the same x-term with opposite signs, so stack and add the two equations:

$$\begin{array}{r} 2x - 6 = y + 8 \\ \underline{+\ -2x - 15 = 2y - 8} \\ -21 = 3y \end{array}$$

The question asks for the value of $3y$, so stop here and pick (A).

Using either of these methods, the correct answer is (A).

10. **A** The question asks for the cost of ten eggs. Translate the English into math to create a system of equations and then solve the equations to find the price of eggs. The first purchase can be written as $5e + 4f = 5.50$. The second purchase can be written as $9e + 8f = 10.50$. At this point, one option is to solve algebraically. Multiply the first equation by –2 to get $-10e - 8f = -11.00$, stack the equations, and add.

$$\begin{array}{r} -10e - 8f = -11.00 \\ \underline{9e + 8f = 10.50} \\ -e = -0.50 \end{array}$$

Therefore, $e = 0.50$. Multiply 0.50 by 10 to find the price of 10 eggs, which is \$5.00, making (A) correct.

After translating the two equations, another option is to use the built-in calculator. Replace e with x and f with y so the calculator will show a graph. The lines intersect at (0.5, 0.75). Since x represents eggs, 1 egg costs \$0.50. Multiply this by 10 to get \$5.00 as the price of 10 eggs, making (A) correct.

Using either of these methods, the correct answer is (A).

Drill 4 (page 293)

a. 3^5

b. 3^1

c. 3^6

d. x^8

e. x^4

f. x^{12}

g. $2\sqrt{2}$

h. –4

Drill 5 (page 301)

a. –6

b. 6

c. –1

d. –1

e. 1

1. **B** The question asks for the value of a constant in one of the two given equations. The slope-intercept form of the equation of a line is $y = mx + b$, where m is the slope and b is the y-intercept. So, the slope of the line given by the first equation is 6. The question states that the two equations represent perpendicular lines. The slopes of perpendicular lines are negative reciprocals, so the slope of the second line is $-\frac{1}{6}$. The second equation is also in slope-intercept form with a slope of c, so $c = -\frac{1}{6}$. The correct answer is (B).

2. **D** The question asks for the y-intercept of a line with a given equation. One method is to use the built-in calculator. Enter the equation as written in an entry field, and then scroll and zoom as needed to find the y-intercept. It is at (0, 4), so (D) is correct.

To solve algebraically, put the equation into slope-intercept form, $y = mx + b$, in which b is the y-intercept. Manipulate this equation to solve for y. Subtract $2x$ from both sides of the equation to get $3y = -2x + 12$, and then divide both sides of the equation by 3 to get $y = -\frac{2}{3}x + 4$. Therefore, the y-intercept is 4, and (D) is correct.

Using either of these methods, the correct answer is (D).

3. **D** The question asks for an equation that represents a graph. One method is to enter each answer choice equation into the built-in calculator to see which one graphs the line in the question. Only the graph of the equation in (D) looks the same, so (D) is correct.

Another method is to compare features of the graph to the answer choices. In the line shown, the point at which the line crosses the y-axis is 1, so the y-intercept is 1. Use the two points on the line, (0, 1) and (8, 0), to calculate the slope: $\frac{y_2 - y_1}{x_2 - x_1} = \frac{(0 - 1)}{(8 - 0)} = -\frac{1}{8}$. The correct answer must be the equation of a line with a slope of $-\frac{1}{8}$ and a y-intercept of 1. Rewrite the answers in the slope-intercept form of the equation, $y = mx + b$, where m is the slope of the line and b is the y-intercept. In (A), the equation becomes $2y = x - 8$, or $y = \frac{1}{2}x - 4$. The slope of this line is $\frac{1}{2}$, and the y-intercept is –4, so eliminate (A). In (B), the equation becomes $4y = -x - 8$, or $y = -\frac{1}{4}x - 2$. The slope of this line is $-\frac{1}{4}$, and the y-intercept is –2, so eliminate (B). In (C), the equation becomes $8y = 3x + 8$, or $y = \frac{3}{8}x + 1$. The slope of this line is $\frac{3}{8}$, and the y-intercept is 1, so eliminate (C). In (D), the equation becomes $8y = -x + 8$, or $y = -\frac{1}{8}x + 1$. The slope of this line is $-\frac{1}{8}$, and the y-intercept is 1, which is the same as the slope and y-intercept of the line shown in the graph.

Using either of these methods, the correct answer is (D).

4. **2** The question asks for the sum of the x-coordinates of the two points of intersection of a system of equations. One method is to enter each equation into its own entry field in the built-in calculator, and then scroll and zoom as needed to find the two points of intersection. They are at (0, 4) and (2, 8), so the x-coordinates are 0 and 2. Add these two values of x to find the sum: $0 + 2 = 2$, making 2 correct.

Another method is to solve algebraically. Since both equations are set equal to the same value, set the right sides of the two equations equal to each other and solve for x. The equation becomes $4x^2 - 6x + 4 = 2x + 4$. Subtract $2x$ and 4 from both sides to set the equation equal to 0, so the equation becomes $4x^2 - 8x = 0$. Divide both sides of the equation by 4 to get $x^2 - 2x = 0$. Factor x out of the equation to get $x(x - 2) = 0$. Therefore, the two possible values for x are $x = 0$ and $x = 2$. Add these two values of x to find the sum: $0 + 2 = 2$.

Using either of these methods, the correct answer is 2.

5. **B** The question asks for the equation of a line that is parallel to a line shown in a graph. Parallel lines have equal slopes. Therefore, because the line in the graph has a negative slope, the correct answer will also have a negative slope. Eliminate (C) and (D) because they have positive slopes. Now find the exact slope of the line shown and compare it with the remaining answers to see which line equation has the same slope. The slope of a line is determined by the equation $\frac{y_2 - y_1}{x_2 - x_1}$. Use the points (0, –1) and (–3, 0), and calculate the slope of the line: $\frac{-1 - 0}{0 - (-3)} = -\frac{1}{3}$. The answers are all in the slope-intercept form of an equation, $y = mx + b$, where m = slope. Only (B) has a slope of $-\frac{1}{3}$. The correct answer is (B).

6. **A** The question asks for the slope of a line graphed in the *xy*-plane. The line is descending from left to right, so it has a negative slope. Eliminate (C) and (D) because they have positive slopes. Use two points on the line to calculate the slope using the formula $slope = \frac{y_2 - y_1}{x_2 - x_1}$. The line passes through points at (0, 2) and (1, –2). Plug those values into the slope formula to get $slope = \frac{2-(-2)}{0-1}$, which becomes $slope = \frac{4}{-1}$, or $slope = -4$. The correct answer is (A).

7. **B** The question asks for the slope of a line shown in a graph. Use the two points on the line, $\left(-\frac{7}{2}, \frac{16}{3}\right)$ and $\left(\frac{11}{2}, -\frac{17}{3}\right)$, to calculate the slope: $\frac{y_2 - y_1}{x_2 - x_1} = \frac{-\frac{17}{3} - \frac{16}{3}}{\frac{11}{2} - \left(-\frac{7}{2}\right)} = \frac{-\frac{33}{3}}{\frac{18}{2}}$. Continue simplifying to get $-\frac{33}{3} \times \frac{2}{18} = -\frac{66}{54} = -\frac{11}{9}$. The correct answer is (B).

8. **C** The question asks for an inequality that represents a graph. One method is to enter the inequality from each answer choice into the built-in calculator to see which graph looks most like the graph in the question. The graph of the inequality in (C) looks the same as the graph in the question, so (C) is correct.

Since there are variables in the answer choices, another approach is to test points from the graph in the answer choices. Pick a point in the shaded area of the graph, plug it into the inequalities in the answer choices, and eliminate any answers that don't work. Try the point (–2, 0). Plug $x = -2$ and $y = 0$ into (A) to get $0 \geq -3(-2) + 2$, which becomes $0 \geq 6 + 2$, and then $0 \geq 8$. This is not true, so eliminate (A). Next, plug $x = -2$ and $y = 0$ into (B) to get $0 \leq -3(-2) + 2$, which becomes $0 \leq 6 + 2$, and then $0 \leq 8$. This is true, so keep (B), but try the same point in the remaining answer choices. Choice (C) becomes $0 \geq 3(-2) + 2$, then $0 \geq -6 + 2$, and finally $0 \geq -4$; keep (C). Choice (D) becomes $0 \leq 3(-2) + 2$, then $0 \leq -6 + 2$, and finally $0 \leq -4$; eliminate (D).

Two answers worked with the first point, so try a second point from the shaded area of the graph, such as (0, 4). Choice (B) becomes $4 \leq -3(0) + 2$, then $4 \leq 0 + 2$, and finally $4 \leq 2$; eliminate (B). Choice (C) becomes $4 \geq 3(0) + 2$, then $4 \geq 0 + 2$, and finally $4 \geq 2$; keep (C). Only (C) worked both times, so it is correct.

Using either of these methods, the correct answer is (C).

Drill 6 (page 311)

1. **–625** The question asks for the value of an expression. Use the given equation $5x^2 = 125$ to find the value of x. Divide both sides of the equation by 5 to get $x^2 = 25$. Squaring a negative number makes the result positive, so x could be 5 or –5. The question states that $x < 0$, so in this case $x = -5$. Plug $x = -5$ into $5x^3$ to get $5(-5)^3$. This equals $5(-125)$, or –625. The correct answer is –625.

2. **C** The question asks for a value on a graph. First, check the units on each axis of the bar graph. The number of types of flowers is on the x-axis, so find 4 on the x-axis. Look at the top of the bar for 4, and then look left to the y-axis, using the mouse pointer or the edge of the scratch paper as a ruler. The y-axis shows the number of floral arrangements, and the top of the bar for 4 types of flowers is slightly above 60. Thus, the number of floral arrangements that contained 4 types of flowers must be a little more than 60. Eliminate (A) and (B) because 30 and 44 are less than 60. Eliminate (D) because 70 is too far from 60. The correct answer is (C).

3. **2** The question asks for a value in a system of equations. The correct value of y is the y-coordinate of the solution to the system, so the most efficient method is to enter both equations into the built-in calculator. Scroll and zoom as needed to find the point of intersection at (11, 2). The question asks for the value of y, which is 2. The correct answer is 2.

4. **A** The question asks for a value based on a graph. First, check the units on each axis of the line graph. Dogs are on the x-axis and cats are on the y-axis. The question asks how many dogs were vaccinated if 6 cats were vaccinated, so find 6 on the y-axis. Move right from there to where the line crosses the horizontal line for 6, using the mouse pointer or edge of the scratch paper if needed, and then move down from there to the x-axis. The x-value of the point on the line when the number of cats is 6 is 2. Thus, 2 dogs were vaccinated if 6 cats were vaccinated. The correct answer is (A).

5. **9** The question asks for the value of x. One method is to use the built-in calculator. Enter the equation as written; for the square root symbol, either open the keypad using the icon in the lower left or type "sqrt" and the calculator will insert the symbol. Scroll and zoom as needed to see that the only solution is represented by a vertical line at $x = 9$, making 9 correct.

   To solve algebraically, isolate x on one side of the equation. Start by squaring both sides of the equation to get $(5 - \sqrt{x})(5 - \sqrt{x}) = x - 5$. Use FOIL on the left side of the equation to get $25 - 5\sqrt{x} - 5\sqrt{x} + x = x - 5$. Combine like terms to get $25 - 10\sqrt{x} + x = x - 5$. Subtract x and 25 from both sides of the equation to get $-10\sqrt{x} = -30$. Divide both sides of the equation by –10 to get $\sqrt{x} = 3$. Square both sides of the equation to get $x = 9$. The correct answer is 9.

   Using either of these methods, the correct answer is 9.

6. **–3** The question asks for one of the x-coordinates of the solution to a system of equations. The most efficient method is to enter both equations into the built-in calculator and then scroll and zoom as needed to find the points of intersection. The graphs intersect at (–3, –18) and (9, 54). The question states that $x < 0$, so the correct x-value is –3.

To solve algebraically, substitute $6x$ for y in the first equation to get $6x = x^2 - 27$. Put the quadratic into standard form by setting one side equal to 0. Subtract $6x$ from both sides of the equation to get $0 = x^2 - 6x - 27$. Next, factor this equation. Find two numbers that multiply to –27 and add to –6. These are 3 and –9. Thus, the quadratic factors into $(x + 3)(x - 9) = 0$. Now set each factor equal to 0 to get two equations: $x + 3 = 0$ and $x - 9 = 0$. Subtract 3 from both sides of the first equation to get $x = -3$. Add 9 to both sides of the second equation to get $x = 9$. The negative value of x is –3, making it correct.

Using either of these methods, the correct answer is –3.

CHAPTER 15

Drill 1 (page 321)

1. **C** The question asks for an equivalent expression. There are variables in the answers, so plug in. Make $x = 2$ and plug it into the expression. The expression becomes $-2(2) - [3(2) - 8(2)]$. Simplify the expression to get $-4 - (6 - 16)$, which becomes $-4 - (-10)$. Subtracting a negative is the same thing as adding, so the result is $-4 + 10 = 6$. This is the target value; circle it. Now plug $x = 2$ into the answer choices and eliminate any that do not match the target value of 6. Choice (A) becomes $-13(2) = -26$. This does not match the target, so eliminate (A). Choice (B) becomes $-7(2) = -14$; eliminate (B). Choice (C) becomes $3(2) = 6$. This matches the target, so keep (C), but check (D) just in case. Choice (D) becomes $9(2) = 18$; eliminate (D). The correct answer is (C).

2. **D** The question asks for the equation that represents values given in a table. The table includes four pairs of x and y values, and the correct equation must work for every pair of values. Plug in values from the table and eliminate equations that don't work. Because $x = 0$ and $x = 1$ are likely to make more than one answer work, try the third row of the table and plug $x = 2$ and $y = -9$ into the answer choices. Choice (A) becomes $-9 = 8 - 9(2)$, then $-9 = 8 - 18$, and finally $-9 = -10$. This is not true, so eliminate (A). Choice (B) becomes $-9 = 8 - 2$, and then $-9 = 6$; eliminate (B). Choice (C) becomes $-9 = 7 - 2$, and then $-9 = 5$; eliminate (C). Choice (D) becomes $-9 = 7 - 8(2)$, then $-9 = 7 - 16$, and finally $-9 = -9$. Only (D) works with this pair of values, so stop here. The correct answer is (D).

3. **C** The question asks for an equation that models a specific situation. There are variables in the answer choices, so plug in. The variable c appears on the more complicated side of the equations in the answers, so plug in a value for c, which is the number of correct answers. The total number of questions is 50, so c must be less than 50. Make $c = 46$. Now work the question in bite-sized pieces. The student got 46 questions correct and 4 questions wrong. The student earned 1 point for each of the 46 correct answers and lost $\frac{1}{4}$ point for each of the 4 incorrect answers. The student's score would be $(1)(46) - \frac{1}{4}(4) = 46 - 1$. Subtract $46 - 1 = 45$. This is the target answer; circle it. Now plug $c = 46$ into the answer choices to see which one matches the target value. Choice (A) becomes $S = 50 - 0.25(46) = 50 - 11.5$. This becomes 38.5,

which does not match the target, so eliminate (A). Choice (B) becomes $S = 50 - 0.75(46) = 50 - 34.5$. This becomes 15.5, so eliminate (B). Choice (C) becomes $S = 46 - 0.25(50 - 46) = 46 - 0.25(4)$. Continue simplifying to get $46 - 1 = 45$. This matches the target. Keep (C), but check (D) just in case. Choice (D) becomes $S = 46 - 0.75(50 - 46) = 46 - 0.75(4)$. Continue simplifying to get $46 - 3 = 43$. Eliminate (D). The correct answer is (C).

4. **B** The question asks for an expression that models a specific situation. There are variables in the answer choices, so plug in. Make $m = 10$. If David goes over his limit by 10 megabytes, then David pays \$25 + \$0.05(10) = \$25.50. This is the target value; circle it. Now plug $m = 10$ into the answer choices to see which one matches the target value. Choice (A) becomes 25 + 1.05(10) = \$35.50. This does not match the target, so eliminate (A). Choice (B) becomes 25 + 0.05(10) = \$25.50. Keep (B), but check the remaining answers just in case. Choice (C) becomes 0.05(25 + 10) = \$1.75. Eliminate (C). Choice (D) becomes 1.05(25 + 10) = \$36.75. Eliminate (D). The correct answer is (B).

5. **D** The question asks for the value of a constant in the equivalent form of an expression. Although there are numbers in the answer choices, a question with a variable that asks for an equivalent expression is still a good chance to plug in. Make $x = 2$ and plug it into the expression. The expression becomes $2^2 + 4(2) - 4$, which becomes $4 + 8 - 4$, or 8. Plug $x = 2$ into the equivalent form of the expression to get $(2 + 2)^2 - a$, which becomes $(4)^2 - a$ and then $16 - a$. Since the two expressions are equivalent, set them equal to each other to get $8 = 16 - a$. Add a to both sides of the equation to get $a + 8 = 16$, and then subtract 8 from both sides of the equation to get $a = 8$. The correct answer is (D).

6. **B** The question asks for a net percentage increase. No information is given about the initial value, so plug in. Make the initial value 100 because 100 works well with percentages. Next, translate the information one piece at a time. One piece of information says that the value *decreased by 37% from the end of August to the end of November. Percent* means out of 100, so translate 37% as $\frac{37}{100}$. Take 37% of 100 to get $\frac{37}{100}(100) = 37$. Translate *decreased by* as subtraction to get $100 - 37 = 63$ as the population at the end of November. Another piece of information says that the population *increased by 112% from the end of November to the end of February.* Take 112% of 63 and add it to 63 to get $63 + \frac{112}{100}(63) = 63 + 70.56 = 133.56$. This is the population at the end of February. A resort population should be a whole number, but the decimal result from plugging in 100 will still lead to the correct answer.

   The question asks for the net percentage increase from the end of August, when the population was 100, to the end of February, when the population was 133.56. This is an increase of $133.56 - 100 = 33.56$, which is 33.56% of 100. The correct answer is (B).

Drill 2 (page 327)

1. **D** The question asks for the value of the variable n in the given equation. Since the question asks for a specific value and the answers contain numbers in increasing order, plug in the answers. Begin by labeling the answers as n and starting with (B), 3. Plug $n = 3$ into the equation and work the steps of the question. The equation becomes $2(3 + 5) = 3(3 - 2) + 8$, or $2(8) = 3(1) + 8$. This simplifies to $16 = 11$, which is false. Eliminate (B). Next, try (C). Plug $n = 4$ into the equation to get $2(4 + 5) = 3(4 - 2) + 8$, or $2(9) = 3(2) + 8$. This simplifies to $18 = 14$, which is false. Eliminate (C). Next, try (D). Plug $n = 8$ into the equation to get $2(8 + 5) = 3(8 - 2) + 8$, or $2(13) = 3(6) + 8$. This simplifies to $26 = 26$, which is true. Since (D) works, stop here. The correct answer is (D).

2. **C** The question asks for the point that satisfies a system of inequalities. There are specific points in the answers, so plug in the answers. Test the ordered pairs in each inequality from the question and look for a pair that makes both inequalities true. Start by plugging (A) into the first inequality to get $2(-4) - (-1) > -3$. This becomes $-8 - (-1) > -3$, or $-7 > -3$. Since this is not true, eliminate (A). Now plug the point in (B) into the first inequality to get $2(-3) - (-2) > -3$. This becomes $-6 - (-2) > -3$, or $-4 > -3$. Since this is not true, eliminate (B). Now plug the point in (C) into the first inequality to get $2(-1) - (-1) > -3$. This becomes $-2 - (-1) > -3$, or $-1 > -3$. This is true, but the point must work in both inequalities. Plugging the point in (C) into the second inequality gives $4(-1) + (-1) < 5$. This becomes $-4 + (-1) < 5$, or $-5 < 5$. This is also true. The point in (C) satisfies both inequalities in the system.

   Another method is to use the built-in calculator. Enter each inequality in an entry field to see a graph of the solutions to the system of inequalities. Next, enter each (x, y) point from the answer choices in its own entry field, and the calculator will plot the points. It's even possible to give the points labels to see which one matches which answer choice.

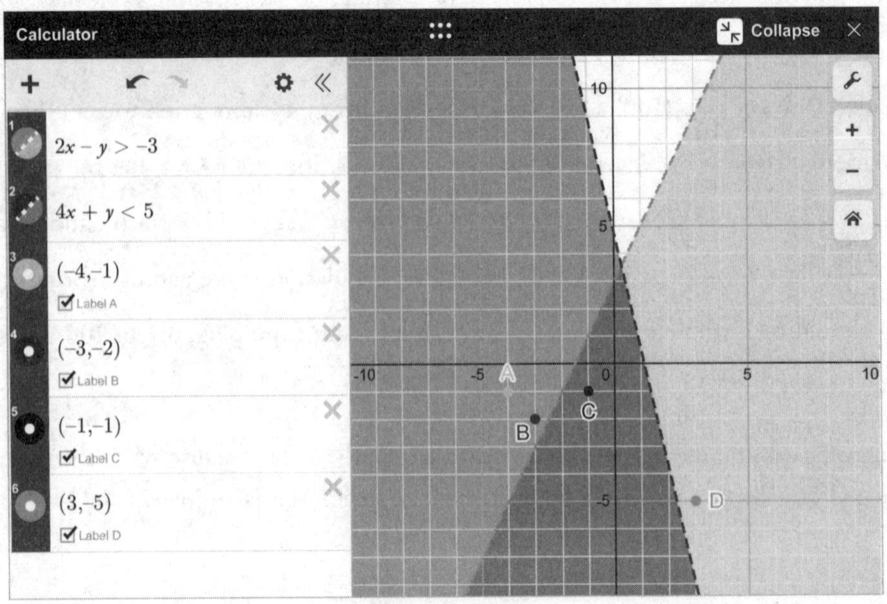

Only (C) is in the darker shaded region where the two inequalities overlap, so it is correct.

Using either of these methods, the correct answer is (C).

3. **C** The question asks for the table that contains values that are solutions to an equation. When given an equation and asked for a table of values, plug values from the table into the equation to see which ones work. All of the tables include an x-value of 0 with different corresponding y-values, so start there. Plug $x = 0$ into the equation to get $y = -0 + 9$, or $y = 9$. Eliminate (A), (B), and (D) because they have different y-values when $x = 0$. The correct answer is (C).

4. **C** The question asks for a value based on two means. The question asks for a specific value and there are numbers in the answer choices, so plug in the answers. Start with one of the middle numbers and try (B), 2. Use the $T = AN$ equation to find the two means. When $x = 2$, the Total for the first mean is $8 + 2 = 10$, and the Number of things is 2, so the equation becomes $10 = (A)(2)$. Divide both sides of the equation by 2 to get $5 = A$. When $x = 2$, the Total for the second mean is $5 + 9 + 2 = 16$, and the Number of things is 3, so the equation becomes $16 = (A)(3)$. Divide both sides of this equation by 3 to get $\frac{16}{3} = A$. The two means are not equal, so eliminate (B).

It might be difficult to determine whether a bigger or small number is needed, so pick a direction and try (C), 4. When $x = 4$, the Total for the first mean is $8 + 4 = 12$, and the Number of things is 2, so the equation becomes $12 = (A)(2)$. Divide both sides of the equation by 2 to get $6 = A$. When $x = 4$, the Total for the second mean is $5 + 9 + 4 = 18$, and the Number of things is 3, so the equation becomes $18 = (A)(3)$. Divide both sides of this equation by 3 to get $6 = A$. The two means are equal, so (C) is correct.

Another method is to enter the two means with x into the built-in calculator and set them equal to each other.

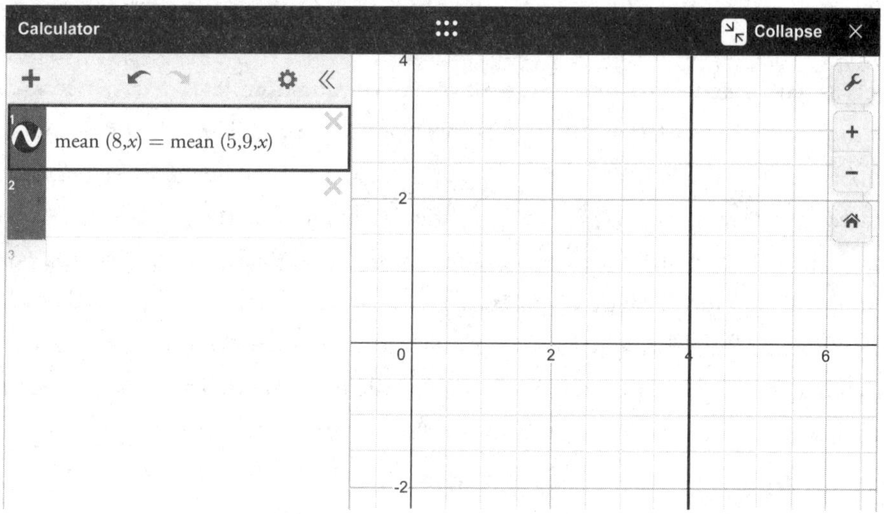

The graphing area shows a vertical line at $x = 4$, so (C) is correct.

Using either of these methods, the correct answer is (C).

5. **C** The question asks for a value given a specific situation. Since the question asks for a specific value and the answers contain numbers in increasing order, plug in the answers. Rewrite the answer choices on the scratch paper and label them "number of dinner plates." Next, pick one of the middle numbers and try (B), 450. The question states that *the company has 450 more dinner plates than coffee mugs.* This would mean that the company has 450 – 450 = 0 coffee mugs. Eliminate (B) because the company must have some coffee mugs given that the other employee counted some. Also eliminate (A) because then the company would have a negative number of coffee mugs. Next, try (C), 600. If the company has 600 dinner plates, it has 600 – 450 = 150 coffee mugs. The question also states that *the company has 4 times as many dinner plates as coffee mugs.* If the company has 150 coffee mugs, it has (4)(150) = 600 dinner plates. In both cases, the number of dinner plates is 600 and the number of coffee mugs is 150, so stop here. The correct answer is (C).

6. **A** The question asks for a possible value of a variable in a system of inequalities. Since the question asks for a specific value and the answers contain numbers in increasing order, plug in the answers. Begin by labeling the answers as y and start with (B), 5. The point that is in the graph of the system becomes (8, 5). Plug both values into the second inequality to get $8 - 7(5) \geq -12$. Multiply on the left side of the inequality to get $8 - 35 \geq -12$, and then $-27 \geq -12$. This is not true, so eliminate (B). It may be difficult to tell whether a larger or smaller number is needed, so pick a direction and try (C), 12. Plug the point (8, 12) into the second inequality to get $8 - 7(12) \geq -12$. Multiply on the left side of the inequality to get $8 - 84 \geq -12$, and then $-76 \geq -12$. This is also not true, so eliminate (C). That was the wrong direction, so the answer must be (A). To check, plug the point (8, 2) into the second inequality to get $8 - 7(2) \geq -12$. Multiply on the left side of the inequality to get $8 - 14 \geq -12$, and then $-6 \geq -12$. This is true, so stop here. The correct answer is (A).

7. **D** The question asks for the number of a certain type of item. Since the question asks for a specific value and the answers contain numbers in increasing order, plug in the answers. Begin by labeling the answers as "enchanted items" and start with (B), 4. The question states that *enchanted items are worth 15 points each,* so the player has 4 × 15 = 60 points from enchanted items. The question also states that the player *has 9 items,* which means the player has 9 – 4 = 5 normal items. Since *normal items are worth 4 points each,* the player has 5 × 4 = 20 points from normal items. The player thus has 60 + 20 = 80 total points. This does not match the information in the question that the player has 102 points, so eliminate (B). The result was too small by 22 points, so try a larger number and plug in (D), 6. The player has 6 × 15 = 90 points from enchanted items. The player has 9 – 6 = 3 normal items and 3 × 4 = 12 points from normal items. The player thus has 90 + 12 = 102 total points. This matches the information in the question, so stop here. The correct answer is (D).

Drill 3 (page 342)

a. 90
b. 320
c. 6
d. $x = 8$
e. 5
f. 10
g. 120%
h. 108
i. $1,000
j. 1%
k. 40
l. 1.5

1. **D** The question asks for an unknown value in relation to three known values. This relationship is a proportion, so set up two equal fractions, being sure to match the units. $\frac{10 \text{ pecks}}{2.5 \text{ bushels}} = \frac{x \text{ pecks}}{4 \text{ bushels}}$. Solve for x by cross-multiplying: $(4)(10) = (2.5)(x)$. Divide both sides of the equation by 2.5 to get $x = 16$. The correct answer is (D).

2. **D** The question asks for an expression that represents a specific situation. Eliminate answer choices that translate parts of the question incorrectly. The air squad is decreasing the size of the fire by a certain percent over time, so this question is about exponential decay. When the decay rate is a percent of the total, the formula is *final amount* = (*original amount*)(1 – *rate*)$^{\textit{number of changes}}$. In this case, $F(t)$ is the *final amount*, and the *number of changes* is t hours. The *original amount* is 10, so it should be outside the parentheses on the right side of the equation. Eliminate (A) and (B) because they have 10 inside the parentheses. The *rate* is 7%, or 0.07, so the number inside the parentheses should be 1 – 0.07, or 0.93. Eliminate (C) because it has the wrong value inside the parentheses. The correct answer is (D).

3. **84** The question asks for a mean based on two other means. For means, or averages, use the formula $T = AN$, in which T is the total, A is the average, and N is the number of things. For the first three tests, 80 is the average and 3 is the number of things. The formula becomes $T = (3)(80) = 240$. Use the formula again for the last two tests, with 90 as the average and 2 as the number of things to get $T = (2)(90) = 180$. Now, use the formula one more time to find the average for all five tests. The total for all 5 tests is $240 + 180 = 420$, so the formula becomes $420 = A(5)$. Divide both sides by 5 to get $84 = A$. The correct answer is 84.

4. **C** The question asks for an amount after a period of time. The amount remaining to pay on the student loans is decreasing by one-half every 5 years, so use the formula for growth or decay by a multiplier. That formula is *final amount* = (*original amount*)(*multiplier*)$^{\textit{number of changes}}$. In this case, $20,000 is the *original amount*. If the amount decreases by $\frac{1}{2}$, there is $1 - \frac{1}{2} = \frac{1}{2}$ left after every decrease, so $\frac{1}{2}$ is the *multiplier*. Read carefully to find the *number of changes*. The question states that the amount is reduced *every 5 years* and asks about *after 20 years*. The number of changes is thus $\frac{20}{5} = 4$. The formula becomes $\text{final amount} = (20{,}000)\left(\frac{1}{2}\right)^4$. Use a calculator or solve by hand to get $\text{final amount} = (20{,}000)\left(\frac{1}{16}\right)$, and then *final amount* = $1,250. The correct answer is (C).

5. **A** The question asks for a value given a proportional relationship. Begin by reading the question to find information about the proportional relationship. The question states that the *solution has a concentration of 125 milligrams of solute per cubic centimeter.* Set up a proportion, being sure to match up the units. The proportion is $\frac{125 \text{ milligrams}}{1 \text{ cubic centimeter}} = \frac{1{,}000 \text{ milligrams}}{x \text{ cubic centimeters}}$. Cross-multiply to get $(125)(x) = (1)(1{,}000)$, which becomes $125x = 1{,}000$. Divide both sides of the equation by 125 to get $x = 8$. The correct answer is (A).

6. **A** The question asks for the difference between two times. The question gives information about averages, so use the formula $T = AN$, in which T is the total, A is the average, and N is the number of things. For Everett's drive, the total is 594 miles, and the average is 66 miles per hour. The formula becomes $594 = (66)(N)$. Divide both sides of the equation by 66 to get $N = 9$ hours. For the parents' drive, the total is 594 miles, and the average is 54 miles per hour. The equation becomes $594 = (54)(N)$. Divide both sides of the equation by 54 to get $N = 11$ hours. To find the difference between the two travel times, subtract them: $11 - 9 = 2$. The correct answer is (A).

7. $\frac{5}{6}$ The question asks for a probability, which is defined as $\textit{probability} = \frac{\textit{number of outcomes you want}}{\textit{number of possible outcomes}}$. Read the table carefully to find the right numbers. The question asks for the probability that a cell phone user in 2022 is a contracted user, so look at the row labeled 2022. In 2022, there were 225 contracted users, so that is the *number of outcomes you want.* There were 270 total cell phone users in 2022, so that is the *number of possible outcomes.* Therefore, the probability is $\frac{225}{270}$. Reduce the fraction to get $\frac{5}{6}$, or express it as a decimal, which is $0.8\overline{33}$. Fill in either the fraction or the decimal. To fill in a repeating decimal, include as many places as will fit or round at the end. In this case, both result in .8333. The correct answer is $\frac{5}{6}$, .8333, or an equivalent form.

8. **6** The question asks for a measurement and gives conflicting units. The question provides the conversions that 1 gallon = 8 pints and 1 pint = 16 fluid ounces. Set up proportions one at a time, being sure to match up units. First, convert fluid ounces to pints with the proportion $\frac{1 \text{ pint}}{16 \text{ fluid ounces}} = \frac{x \text{ pints}}{768 \text{ fluid ounces}}$. Cross-multiply to get $(16)(x) = (1)(768)$, which becomes $16x = 768$. Divide both sides of the equation by 16 to get $x = 48$ pints. Next, convert pints to gallons with the proportion $\frac{1 \text{ gallon}}{8 \text{ pints}} = \frac{x \text{ gallons}}{48 \text{ pints}}$. Cross-multiply to get $(8)(x) = (1)(48)$, which becomes $8x = 48$. Divide both sides of the equation by 8 to get $x = 6$ gallons. The correct answer is 6.

CHAPTER 16

Drill 1 (page 353)

1. **B** The question asks for a value given a function. Since the answers are numbers that could represent the a-value, or the input, one option is to plug in the answers. Start with the easy number in (B), and plug 3 into the function for a to get $h(3) = 5(3)^4$, which becomes $h(3) = 5(81)$, and then $h(3) = 405$. This matches the output value given in the question, so (B) is correct.

   The other option is to solve algebraically. In function notation, the number inside the parentheses is the x-value that goes into the function, or the input, and the value that comes out of the function is the y-value, or the output. The question provides an output value of 405, so set $h(a)$ equal to 405 and solve for a. The equation becomes $405 = 5a^4$. Divide both sides of the equation by 5 to get $81 = a^4$, and then take the fourth root of both sides of the equation to get $\pm3 = a$, making (B) correct.

   Using either method, the correct answer is (B).

2. **C** The question asks for the equation of a function. Notice that there are variables in the question and in the answer choices, so try to plug in. Since m represents months, plug in a number that works easily with the question. The number must be within the range $0 \leq m \leq 36$, so choose $m = 10$. After 10 months, the total amount paid will be \$3,200 (the down payment) + \$380 × 10 months, or 3,200 + (380)(10) = \$7,000. This is the target value; circle it. Now plug $m = 10$ into each answer choice to see which one matches the target value. Choice (A) becomes $f(10) = 380 + 3{,}200(10)$, which is much larger than the target value, so eliminate (A). Choice (B) becomes $f(10) = 3{,}200 + 36(10)$, or 3,560. This does not match the target value, so eliminate (B). Choice (C) becomes $f(10) = 3{,}200 + 380(10)$, or 7,000. This matches the target value, so keep (C), but check (D) just in case. Choice (D) becomes $f(10) = 10{,}480 - 380(10)$, or 6,680. This does not match the target value, so eliminate (D). The correct answer is (C).

3. **C** The question asks for the value of the constant a. The question states that the number of bonus points increases by 25 when the number of purchases (p) increases by 4. To avoid working with multiple variables, pick a starting number for p. If $p = 0$, then the number of bonus points is $B(p) = a(0) + 7$, or 7. When the number of purchases is increased by 4, the number of bonus points increases by 25. So, if $p = 0 + 4 = 4$, then $B(p) = 7 + 25 = 32$. To find the value of a, plug $B(p) = 32$ and $p = 4$ into the equation and solve for a. The equation becomes $32 = a(4) + 7$, or $32 = 4a + 7$. This simplifies to $25 = 4a$, or $a = 6.25$. The correct answer is (C).

4. **B** The question asks for the value of a constant in the (x, y) coordinates of a point on a line. One option is to use the formula $slope = \frac{rise}{run}$ twice using the three points on the line given in the table. Another option is to use the built-in calculator. Open a table in an entry field using the plus button, then enter the points (–1, –2) and (3, 4) into the table, then click and hold the icon of a circle with points, and

then switch on the Lines toggle. Since the third point is (c, c), scroll and zoom to find a point on the line where the x- and y-coordinates are the same. Another option is to enter (c, c) in a second entry field and use the slider to find a point on the line.

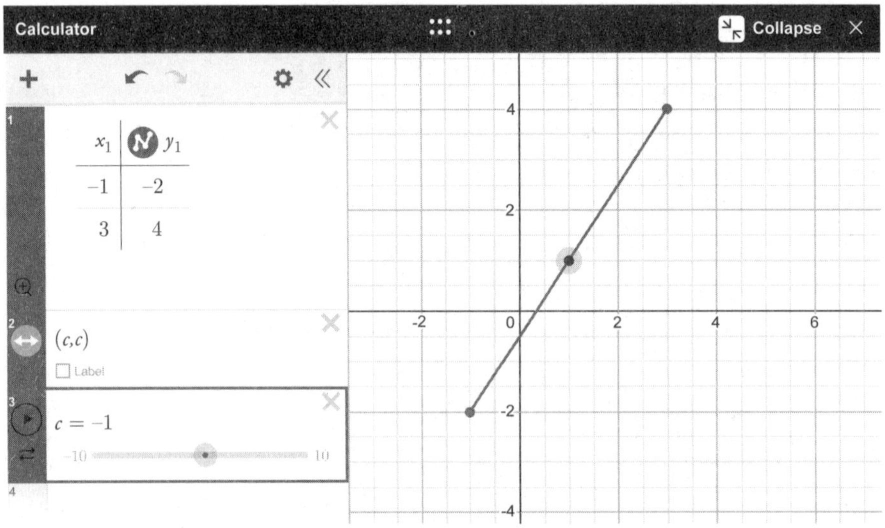

Either way, there is a point on the line at (1, 1), so $c = 1$. The correct answer is (B).

5. **C** The question asks for a description of a function that models a specific situation. Compare the answer choices. Two choices say the function is increasing, and two say it is decreasing. Since the sandwich shop sells more sandwiches each day compared to the day before, this is an increasing function. Eliminate (A) and (B) because they describe a decreasing function. The difference between (C) and (D) is whether the function is linear or exponential. Since the number of sandwiches sold each day is twice the number sold the previous day, the relationship between the number of sandwiches sold and the day is exponential. Eliminate (D) because it describes a linear function. To check, plug in a number. Make 10 the number of sandwiches sold on Monday. The number of sandwiches sold on Tuesday is (2)(10) = 20, the number of sandwiches sold on Wednesday is (2)(20) = 40, and so on. The number of sandwiches sold increased by 20 – 10 = 10, and then by 40 – 20 = 20. These are different numbers, so the increase is exponential, not linear. The correct answer is (C).

6. **B** The question asks for the equation of a function. In function notation, the number inside the parentheses is the x-value that goes into the function, and the value that comes out of the function is the y-value. The question gives two pairs of values, and the correct function must work for both. Start by plugging $x = 2$ and $f(x) = -5$ into each answer choice and eliminate any that don't work. Choice (A) becomes $-5 = 5(2) - 25$, then $-5 = 10 - 25$, and finally $-5 = -15$. This is not true, so eliminate (A). Choice (B) becomes $-5 = 10(2) - 25$, then $-5 = 20 - 25$, and finally $-5 = -5$. This is true, so keep (B), but check the remaining answers. Choice (C) becomes $-5 = 10(2) - 5$, then $-5 = 20 - 5$, and finally $-5 = 15$. This is not true; eliminate (C). Choice (D) becomes $-5 = 10(2)$, then $-5 = 20$. This is not true; eliminate (D). Choice (B) also works when $x = 4$ and $f(x) = 15$ since $15 = 10(4) - 25$. The correct answer is (B).

Drill 2 (page 366)

1. **B** The question asks for the value of x in an equation. One method is to use the built-in calculator. Enter the equation as written into an entry field, and then scroll and zoom as needed to see the solutions represented by vertical lines at (–5, 0) and (1, 0). Only –5 is in the answer choices, so (B) is correct.

   Since the question asks for a specific value and the answers contain numbers in order, another method is to plug in the answers. Begin by rewriting the answer choices on the scratch paper and labeling them "x." Start with the easier of the answers in the middle, and try (C), 5. Plug $x = 5$ into the equation to get $12 - (5 + 2)^2 = 3$, which becomes $12 - (7)^2 = 3$, then $12 - 49 = 3$, and finally $-37 = 3$. This is not true, so eliminate (C). A larger x-value will lead to a smaller result on the left side of the equation, so also eliminate (D). Try (B) next, and plug $x = -5$ into the equation to get $12 - (-5 + 2)^2 = 3$, which becomes $12 - (3)^2 = 3$, then $12 - 9 = 3$, and finally $3 = 3$. This is true, so stop here and pick (B).

   Using either of these methods, the correct answer is (B).

2. **14** The question asks for the value of x when the graph of a function reaches its minimum. A parabola reaches its minimum or maximum value at its vertex, so find the x-coordinate of the vertex. One method is to enter the equation into the built-in calculator, and then scroll and zoom as needed to find the vertex. The vertex is at (14, –6), so the x-coordinate is 14.

   Another approach is to know the vertex form of a parabola. That form is $y = a(x - h)^2 + k$, where (h, k) is the vertex. In this quadratic, $(x - h) = (x - 14)$, so $-h = -14$. Divide both sides of this equation by –1 to get $h = 14$.

   Using either of these methods, the correct answer is 14.

3. **D** The question asks for the equation of a parabola with a vertex of (–5, –2). One method is to enter the equation from each answer choice one at a time and eliminate any that do not have a vertex of (–5, –2). Eliminate (A), (B), and (C) because each has a different vertex, leaving (D) as correct.

   Since there are variables in the answer choices, another method is to plug in. Plug $x = -5$ and $y = -2$ into each answer choice equation, and eliminate ones that don't work. Choice (A) becomes $-2 = (-5)^2 - (10)(-5) - 23$. Simplify the right side of the equation to get $-2 = 25 + 50 - 23$, which becomes $-2 = 52$. This is not true, so eliminate (A). Choice (B) becomes $-2 = (-5)^2 - (10)(-5) + 23$. Simplify the right side of the equation to get $-2 = 25 + 50 + 23$, which becomes $-2 = 98$; eliminate (B). Choice (C) becomes $-2 = (-5)^2 + (10)(-5) - 23$. Simplify the right side of the equation to get $-2 = 25 - 50 - 23$, which becomes $-2 = -48$; eliminate (C). Choice (D) becomes $-2 = (-5)^2 + (10)(-5) + 23$. Simplify the right side of the equation to get $-2 = 25 - 50 + 23$, which becomes $-2 = -2$; keep (D). Only (D) works, so it is correct.

   Using either of these methods, the correct answer is (D).

4. **D** The question asks for the interpretation of a statement in context. In function notation, the number inside the parentheses is the x-value that goes into the function, or the input, and the value that comes out of the function is the y-value, or the output. The number inside the parentheses, 7, is the x-value,

and x represents the number of years. Eliminate (A) and (B) because they state that 7 is a multiplier or a percentage, not the number of years. The question states that the output, $f(x)$, is equal to the car's value, in dollars. Plug 7 into the function to get $f(7) = 35{,}000(0.82)^7$, which becomes $f(7) \approx 8{,}725$. Thus, the number 8,725 represents the car's value after 7 years. Eliminate (C) because 8,725 is the car's value after 7 years, not a decrease in value. The correct answer is (D).

5. **C** The question asks for the number that represents the initial height of the projectile. One method is to enter the equation into the built-in calculator. The initial height is the height, on the y-axis, when the time, on the x-axis, is 0. Find the y-intercept, which is (0, 45). Thus, the height when the projectile was launched was 45 feet, and (C) is correct.

   Another method is to plug in. Since t represents the time since the projectile was launched, t was 0 when the projectile was launched. Plug $t = 0$ into the equation to get $h(0) = -5(0)^2 + 20(0) + 45$, which becomes $h(0) = 0 + 0 + 45$, and then $h(0) = 45$. Thus, the height when the projectile was launched was 45 feet, and (C) is correct.

   Using either of these methods, the correct answer is (C).

6. **B** The question asks for an equation that matches the graph. The answer choices are quadratic equations that have already been factored, so use the roots from the graph to eliminate wrong answers. The roots, or solutions, of a graph are where it crosses the x-axis: look at the graph to see that the correct solutions will be −3 and 1. Eliminate (C) and (D), which have a 4 in one of the factors instead of 1 and 3. To decide between (A) and (B), plug in a point from the graph. The vertex appears to be at (−1, 4). Plug $x = -1$ and $y = 4$ into (A) to get $4 = -(-1 - 3)(-1 + 1)$. This becomes $4 = -(-4)(0)$ or $4 = 0$. This is not true, so eliminate (A), but check (B) just in case. Choice (B) becomes $4 = -(-1 + 3)(-1 - 1)$ or $4 = -(2)(-2)$. This simplifies to $4 = 4$. The correct answer is (B).

7. **3** The question asks for the value of a function. In function notation, the number inside the parentheses is the x-value that goes into the function, and the value that comes out of the function is the y-value. Therefore, $x = a$ and $f(x) = f(a) = 10$. Plug $x = a$ into the function to get $f(a) = a^2 - a + 4$. Since $f(a) = 10$, replace $f(a)$ with 10 to get $10 = a^2 - a + 4$. To solve for a, subtract 10 from both sides of the equation and factor. The equation becomes $0 = a^2 - a - 6$, which can be factored into $0 = (a - 3)(a + 2)$. Set both factors equal to 0 to get $a = 3$ or $a = -2$. There are two possible solutions to this equation, but the question states that a is *non-negative*, so −2 cannot be a solution. The correct answer is 3.

8. **B** The question asks for a value of the constant c in the given quadratic equation. Since the question asks for a specific value and the answers contain numbers in increasing order, plug in the answers. Begin by labeling the answers as c and starting with (B), 135. The equation becomes $x^2 + 24x + 135 = (x + 9)(x + p)$. The left side of the equation is a quadratic in standard form, and the right side is a factored quadratic; this means that 135 from the left side of the equation should equal $9p$ once the right side is expanded to standard form. Divide 135 by 9 to get $x^2 + 24x + 135 = (x + 9)(x + 15)$. Test whether this is the right answer by using FOIL to expand $(x + 9)(x + 15)$ into $x^2 + 15x + 9x + 135 = x^2 + 24x + 135$. The middle term is $24x$, which matches the value given on the left side, so stop here. The correct answer is (B).

9. **B** The question asks for an equation that models a specific situation. Translate the question in bite-sized pieces and eliminate after each piece. One piece of information says that the correct equation should be a parabola. The standard form of a parabola equation is $y = ax^2 + bx + c$. The equation should include an x^2 term, so eliminate (D), which is a linear equation. The value of a tells whether a parabola opens upward (positive a) or downward (negative a). Since the water from the fountain shoots up and down, the parabola should open downward and have a negative value for a. Eliminate (C), which has a positive value for a. Compare the remaining answers. The important difference between (A) and (B) is the c term. The question states that the fountain's spout is 8 feet above the ground. Since y is the height of the water and x is the time from the spout, $y = 8$ when $x = 0$. Plug $x = 0$ into (A) to see whether it becomes $y = 8$. Choice (A) becomes $y = -0^2 + 15 = 15$. This means $y = 8$ does not appear in (A), so eliminate (A). The correct answer is (B).

10. **D** The question asks for the equation of a function that is a translation of another function. One method is to plug in and use the built-in calculator. Make $c = 2$, and plug 2 into the g function for c to get $g(x) = -\frac{2+7}{x} - 2$. Enter this into an entry field in the calculator to see the graph. In a second entry field, enter the equation in (A) with 2 in place of c, which is $h(x) = -\frac{2+12}{x-2} - 2$. The resulting graph is to the right of the original graph, not the left, so eliminate (A). To save time, keep the equation in the second entry field and change it as needed to look like the equation in (B). This graph is left but not up; eliminate (B). Do the same for (C), and the graph is up but not left; eliminate (C). Do the same for (D), and the graph is both left and up, so (D) is correct.

To solve by hand, translate the graph one direction at a time. When a function is translated up or down, the y-value changes. Add 5 to both sides of the equation to translate the graph up 5 units. The equation becomes $g(x) + 5 = -\frac{c+7}{x} - 2 + 5$, or $g(x) + 5 = -\frac{c+7}{x} + 3$. Eliminate (A) and (B) because they have $-\ 2$ instead of $+\ 3$. To translate the graph 2 units to the left, add 2 to the x-value in the function to get $g(x + 2) + 5 = -\frac{c+7}{x+2} + 3$. Now both translations have been applied, and the equation for function h is $h(x) = -\frac{c+7}{x+2} + 3$, making (D) correct.

Using either of these methods, the correct answer is (D).

CHAPTER 17

Drill 1 (page 375)

a. 36

b. 24

c. $x = 10, y = 5$

d. 30

e. 22

1. **D** The question asks for the pairs of angles that must have equal degree measures on a figure. Start by redrawing the figure on the scratch paper. Then label the figure with the given information. Mark lines *a* and *b* as parallel. In Statement (I), angles 1 and 5 do not have to be equal because a side of angle 1 is line *c*, which intersects only one parallel line in the figure; there is not enough information to determine whether any angle formed by line *c* is equal to one formed by line *b*. Thus, the angles in Statement (I) do not have to be equal; eliminate (A). Angles 2 and 7 are vertical angles (angles opposite each other when two lines intersect), and vertical angles must be equal. Therefore, the angles in Statement (II) have to be equal, so eliminate (C). Any time a line crosses two parallel lines, all of the small angles have the same measure, and all of the big angles have the same measure. Both angle 3 and angle 9 are small angles formed where the same line (line *d*) crosses one of the parallel lines. Since the angles in Statement (III) must be equal, eliminate (B). Only Statements (II) and (III) are true. The correct answer is (D).

2. **C** The question asks for the value of an angle on a figure. Start by redrawing the figure on the scratch paper. Then label the figure with the given information. Mark $\overline{BC}$ and $\overline{AD}$ as parallel. It may not be immediately obvious how to get the value of angle *ACD*, so see what else can be determined. Anytime a line crosses two parallel lines, all of the small angles have the same measure, and all of the big angles have the same measure. The big and small angles are *supplementary angles*: the sum of the measure of any big angle plus any small angle equals 180°. In this figure, angle *BCD* and angle *ADC* are supplementary big and small angles. Because angle *ADC* has a measure given of 95°, subtract 95 from 180 to see that angle *BCD* must have a measure of 85°. Subtract 35 from 85 to see that angle *ACD* must have a measure of 50°. The correct answer is (C).

3. **D** The question asks for the area of square *ABCD*. The lengths of the sides are given as variable expressions instead of numbers, so solve for *x* first. In a square, all sides are equal, so $2x + 1 = x + 3$. First, subtract 1 from each side so that $2x = x + 2$. Then subtract *x* from each side so that $x = 2$. Plug that value of *x* into the expression $x + 3$ to get $2 + 3 = 5$, which is the length of each side. The formula for the area of a square is $A = (length)(width)$, so the area is $(5)(5) = 25$. The correct answer is (D).

4. **60** The question asks for the area of rectangle *ABCD*. Start by redrawing the figure on the scratch paper. Then label the figure with the given information. The length of one side is 5, and the question states that the length of the diagonal, *BD* (or *AC*), is 13. The formula for the area of a rectangle is $A = (length)(width)$, so find the width first. Since the corner of the rectangle is a right angle, either recognize that this is a 5:12:13 Pythagorean triple or use the Pythagorean Theorem:

$a^2 + b^2 = c^2$. Plug in *AB* for *a* and *BD* for *c* so that $5^2 + b^2 = 13^2$. Then solve for *b*, which will be *AD*, the length of the other side of the right triangle, and thus the width of the rectangle. First, simplify: $25 + b^2 = 169$. Then subtract 25 from both sides and take the square root: $\sqrt{b^2} = \sqrt{144}$. Then, $b = 12$. Since $AD = 12$, plug the length and width into the formula for the area of a rectangle to get $A = (5)(12) = 60$. The correct answer is 60.

Drill 2 (page 389)

a. 24

b. 10

c. $\frac{6}{10}$, $\frac{3}{5}$, or 0.6

d. 20

e. $20\sqrt{5}$

f. $\frac{20}{20\sqrt{5}}$, $\frac{1}{\sqrt{5}}$, or $\frac{\sqrt{5}}{5}$

1. **A** The question asks for the value of a trigonometric function given similar triangles. Start by drawing two triangles on the scratch paper, being careful to match up the vertices. Since the triangles are similar, and two pairs of angles have already been identified as having the same measure, the third pair of angles also has the same measure. Next, write down SOHCAHTOA. The CAH part of the acronym defines the cosine as $\frac{\text{adjacent}}{\text{hypotenuse}}$, and the question states that the cosine of angle *Q* is $\frac{24}{145}$. Label the side adjacent to *Q* as 24, and label the hypotenuse as 145. Label the equivalent sides in the second triangle, keeping in mind that these are proportions, not the actual side lengths. The scratch paper should look something like this.

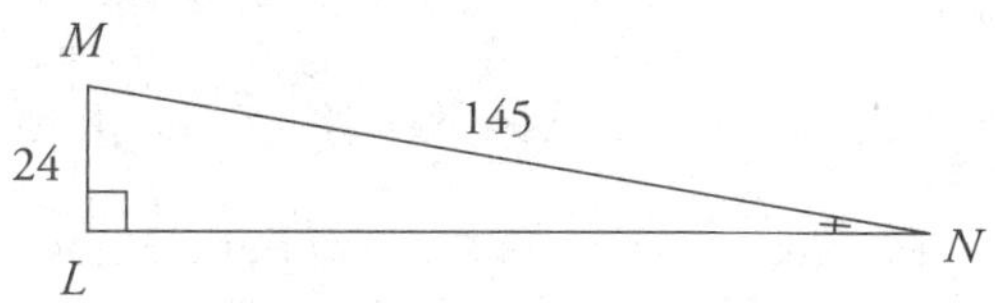

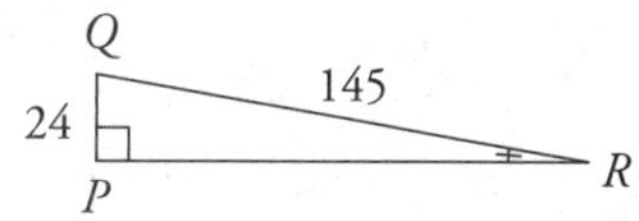

Next, find the value of sin(*N*). The SOH part of the acronym defines the sine as $\frac{\textit{opposite}}{\textit{hypotenuse}}$. The side opposite angle *N* is 24, and the hypotenuse is 145, so the sine of angle *N* is $\frac{24}{145}$. It will always be the case that the two angles in a right triangle that are not the right angle add up to 90°, and that the sine of one equals the cosine of the other. The correct answer is (A).

2. **100** The question asks for the value of an angle on a figure. Start by redrawing the figure on the scratch paper. Then label the figure with the given information. Because $AB = BC$, ABC is an *isosceles triangle,* which has two sides that are equal. In an isosceles triangle, angles that are opposite equal sides must be equal. Therefore, angle A and angle C have the same measure, so angle A is also 40°. Angle A and angle C have a combined measure of 80°. The sum of the angles inside a triangle must equal 180°. Subtract 80 from 180, and x must measure 100°. The correct answer is 100.

3. **C** The question asks for the perimeter of an isosceles triangle. Start by redrawing the figure on the scratch paper. Then label the figure with the given information. The question says that the triangle is isosceles, and there is a right angle present in the figure. An isosceles right triangle has angles that measure 45°, 45°, and 90°. Since $AB = 5$, that means $BC = 5$ as well. Using the 45°-45°-90° right triangle rule, $AC = 5\sqrt{2}$. Therefore, the perimeter of the triangle is $5 + 5 + 5\sqrt{2}$ or $10 + 5\sqrt{2}$. The correct answer is (C).

4. **B** The question asks for the minimum number of buckets of paint needed to cover the front of a barn's roof. Start by redrawing the figure on the scratch paper. To find the answer, solve for the total area. The formula for the area of a triangle is $A = \frac{bh}{2}$. The figure provides that the base, b, is 8 m. The two smaller right triangles both have angles of 30° and 90°, so the other angle must be 60° in both. Since they share a side (the height), the two triangles are the same size, and the 8 m base is equally split to be 4 m for each right triangle. To find the height, use the 30°-60°-90° right triangle rule: if the short side (opposite 30°) is h, the middle side (opposite 60°) is $h\sqrt{3}$. Make $4 = h\sqrt{3}$ and divide both sides by $\sqrt{3}$ to get $h \approx 2.4$. Then set $A = \frac{(8)(2.4)}{2} = (4)(2.4) = 9.6$. To cover 9.6 m^2, the owner will need $\frac{9.6}{5}$ buckets, which is 1.92. Since 1 bucket is not enough, round up to 2. The correct answer is (B).

5. **A** The question asks for the length of a line segment in a figure containing triangles. Start by redrawing the figure on the scratch paper. Then label the figure with the given information. When given two or more triangles and information about the lengths of the sides, look for similar triangles. Both triangles share angle DAE, and each has a right angle. Since all triangles have 180°, the third angles in each triangle must also be equal. The two triangles must have the same set of angles, but they aren't the same size; they are *similar triangles,* so the sides of one triangle are proportional to those of the other. $BD = AD - AB$, and AB is given; find AD to get the answer. In the small right triangle, two sides are given, so use the Pythagorean Theorem to find the third: $a^2 + b^2 = c^2$. Plug in AB for a and AC for c so that $5^2 + b^2 = 13^2$. Then solve for b, which will be BC, the length of the other side of the right triangle. First, simplify: $25 + b^2 = 169$. Then subtract 25 from both sides and take the square root: $\sqrt{b^2} = \sqrt{144}$.

Therefore, $b = 12$. Another way to solve for b would be to recognize the Pythagorean triple: 5-12-13. Since $BC = 12$, set up a proportion with corresponding sides: $\frac{AB}{AD} = \frac{BC}{DE}$ or $\frac{5}{AD} = \frac{12}{24}$. Cross-multiply: $(AD)(12) = 120$. Divide both sides by 12 to get $AD = 10$. Now solve: $BD = AD - AB = 10 - 5 = 5$. The correct answer is (A).

6. **7.5** The question asks for the value of x, the length of a side of a right triangle. The value of tan $a°$ is given, and the length of the side opposite that angle is 7. SOHCAHTOA says that tangent $\theta = \frac{opposite}{adjacent}$. The needed side is adjacent to that angle, so set up a proportion: $\frac{14}{15} = \frac{7}{x}$. Cross-multiply to get $14x = 105$. Divide both sides by 14, so $x = 7.5$. The correct answer is 7.5.

Drill 3 (page 398)

a. 16π

b. 8π

1. **B** The question asks for the coordinates of the center of a circle. Enter the equation of the circle into the built-in calculator. The center is not marked, but scroll and zoom as needed to see that it is at (1, –4). The correct answer is (B).

2. **D** The question asks for the area of the circle. The parts of a circle are directly proportional to one another. In this circle, the fraction of the central angle of 360° is the same as the fraction of the arc length of the total circumference. Set up the proportion $\frac{central\ angle}{360°} = \frac{arc\ length}{circumference}$, and then plug in the given information to get $\frac{60°}{360°} = \frac{2\pi}{circumference}$. Cross-multiply to get $60(circumference) = 360(2\pi)$. Divide both sides by 60 to get $circumference = 12\pi$. Since the formula for circumference is $2\pi r$, the radius of the circle is 6. Then, find the area using the formula πr^2. If $r = 6$, then the circle has an area of $\pi(6)^2 = 36\pi$. The correct answer is (D).

3. **C** The question asks for the perimeter of triangle ABC. Start by drawing the figure according to the description in the question. The figure should look like the following:

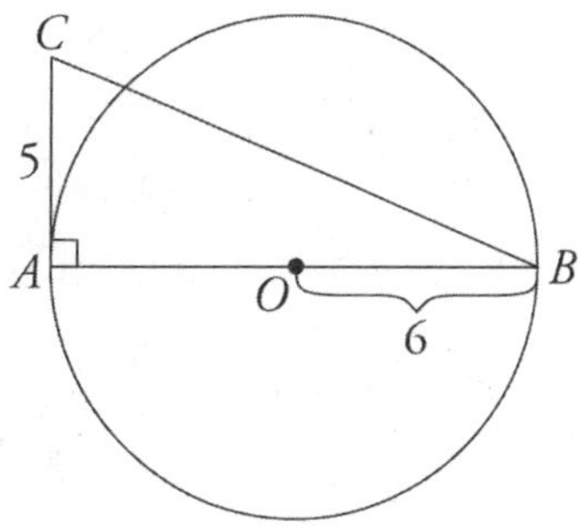

Next, write down the equations needed to answer the question. Since the area of the circle is 36π, and the formula is $A = \pi r^2$, the radius of the circle is 6. Therefore, the diameter of the circle is 12. Since a line that is tangent to a circle forms a 90° angle with the radius at the point of tangency, the side lengths of this right triangle are a 5-12-13 Pythagorean triple. To find the perimeter of the triangle, add the side lengths to get $5 + 12 + 13 = 30$. The correct answer is (C).

4. **5.25** The question asks for the radius of the circle. Start by translating English to math. *Arc PSR is* $\frac{4}{3}$ *the length of arc PQR* means $\overparen{PSR} = \frac{4}{3}\overparen{PQR}$. Since $\overparen{PSR}$ is 6π, substitute for $\overparen{PSR}$ to get $6\pi = \frac{4}{3}\overparen{PQR}$. Multiply both sides by 3 to cancel out the fraction to get $18\pi = 4\overparen{PQR}$. Divide both sides by 4 to get $\frac{18\pi}{4} = \overparen{PQR}$, or $\overparen{PQR} = 4.5\pi$. The two arcs, $\overparen{PSR}$ and $\overparen{PQR}$, add up to the circumference of the circle, so $C = 6\pi + 4.5\pi = 10.5\pi$. Since $C = 2\pi r$, the radius of the circle is 5.25. The correct answer is 5.25.

Drill 4 (page 403)

1. **B** The question asks for the value of an angle in the figure. There are variables in the answer choices, so plug in. Make $a = 90$. The third angle will be 60°. Since the 60° angle and b° are supplementary angles, $60 + b = 180$. Subtract 60 from both sides to get $b = 180 - 60 = 120$. This is the target value; circle it. Now plug $a = 90$ into the answer choices to see which one matches the target value. Choice (A) becomes $30 - 90 = -60$. This does not match the target, so eliminate (A). Choice (B) becomes $30 + 90 = 120$. Keep (B), but check (C) and (D) just in case. Choice (C) becomes $60 + 90 = 150$. Eliminate (C). Choice (D) becomes $80 - 90 = -10$. Eliminate (D). The correct answer is (B).

2. **A** The question asks for the value of a trigonometric function. There are variables in the answer choices, so plug in. You are given a right triangle, so plug in for the sides of the triangle. Use the Pythagorean triple 3-4-5 to make the math easy. Add these side lengths to the figure as follows:

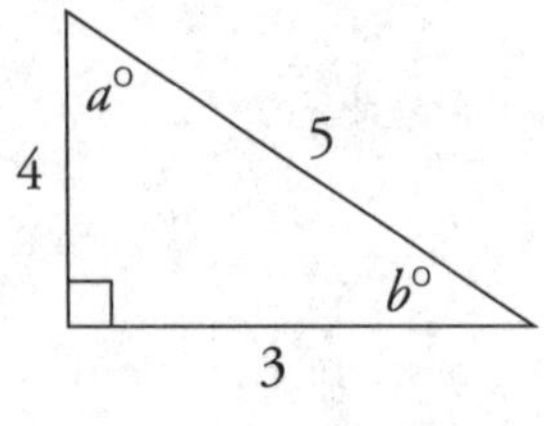

$\sin\theta = \frac{opposite}{hypotenuse}$, so calculate $\sin a° = \frac{3}{5}$. Let $x = \frac{3}{5}$. Since $\cos\theta = \frac{adjacent}{hypotenuse}$, then calculate $\cos b° = \frac{3}{5}$. This is the target value; circle it. Now plug $x = \frac{3}{5}$ into the answer choices to see which one matches the target value. Choice (A) becomes $\frac{3}{5}$. Keep (A), but check (B), (C), and (D) just in case. Choice

(B) becomes $1 - \frac{3}{5} = \frac{2}{5}$. This does not match the target, so eliminate (B). Choice (C) becomes $\frac{1}{\frac{3}{5}} = \frac{5}{3}$. Eliminate (C). Choice (D) becomes $\frac{3}{5} - 1 = -\frac{2}{5}$. Eliminate (D). The correct answer is (A).

3. **B** The question asks about the ratio of the volumes of two cones with the same height but different radii. The question also describes a relationship between unknown numbers, so plug in. The relationship between the radii of the cones is provided, so plug in numbers that fit this relationship. Plug in $r = 6$ for Cone A and $r = 8$ for Cone B. Let $h = 3$. The formula for the volume of a cone is $V = \frac{1}{3}\pi r^2 h$, so plug in the values for r and h to determine the volume of each cone. The volume of Cone A is $\frac{1}{3}\pi(6)^2(3) = 36\pi$, and the volume of Cone B is $\frac{1}{3}\pi(8)^2(3) = 64\pi$. Therefore, the ratio of volume A to volume B is $36\pi{:}64\pi$, which reduces to 9:16. The correct answer is (B).

4. **A** The question asks for the area of a sector of the circle. There are variables in the answer choices, so plug in. Plug in $x = 3$. Write down the equations needed to answer the question. The equation for area of a circle is $A = \pi r^2$, so the area of the circle is $\pi(3)^2 = 9\pi$. The equation for circumference is $C = 2\pi r$, so the circumference of the circle is $2\pi(3) = 6\pi$. The length of arc PQ is $\frac{\pi(3)}{18} = \frac{\pi}{6}$. The parts of a circle have a proportional relationship. In this circle, the fraction of the arc length out of the total circumference is the same as the fraction of the sector area out of the total area. Set up the proportion $\frac{\textit{arc length}}{\textit{circumference}} = \frac{\textit{sector area}}{\textit{total area}}$, and then plug in the given information to get $\frac{\frac{\pi}{6}}{6\pi} = \frac{\textit{sector POQ}}{9\pi}$. Divide the fraction on the left side of the equation to get $\frac{1}{36} = \frac{\textit{sector POQ}}{9\pi}$. Cross-multiply to get $9\pi = 36(\textit{sector POQ})$, and then divide both sides by 36 to get $\textit{sector POQ} = \frac{\pi}{4}$. This is the target value; circle it. Now plug $x = 3$ into the answer choices to see which one matches the target value. Choice (A) becomes $\frac{\pi(3)^2}{36} = \frac{\pi}{4}$. Keep (A), but check (B), (C), and (D) just in case. Choice (B) becomes $\frac{\pi(3)^2}{18} = \frac{\pi}{2}$. This does not match the target, so eliminate (B). Choice (C) becomes $\frac{\pi(3)^2}{9} = \pi$. Eliminate (C). Choice (D) becomes $\frac{\pi(3)^2}{3} = 3\pi$. Eliminate (D). The correct answer is (A).

5. **C** The question asks for the volume of the space between the spheres and the rectangular box. Since no figure is provided, start by drawing the figure according to the description in the question. The figure should look like the following:

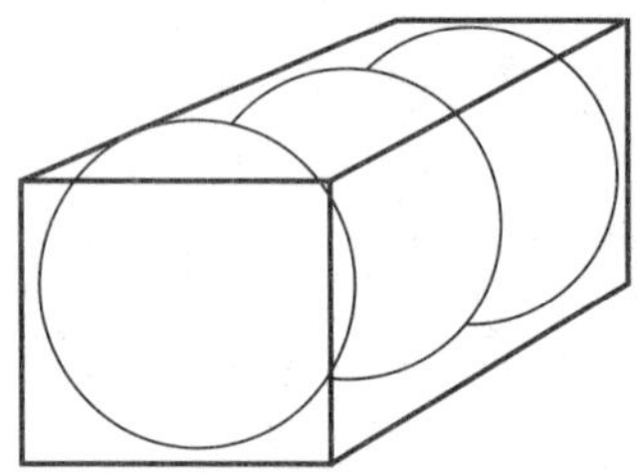

There are variables in the answer choices, so plug in. Make $r = 2$. Therefore, the diameter of the sphere is 4, which is also the width and height of the box. There are 3 spheres in a row, so the length of the box is $3(4) = 12$. The formula for volume of a rectangular solid is $V = lwh$, so plug in the values for the length, width, and height to get $(12)(4)(4) = 192$. The formula for volume of a sphere is $V = \frac{4}{3}\pi r^3$. So, the volume of each sphere is $\frac{4}{3}\pi(2)^3 = \frac{32\pi}{3}$. There are 3 spheres, so multiply this result by 3 to get a total volume of 32π. Therefore, the volume of the spaces between the balls and the box is $192 - 32\pi$. This is the target value; circle it. Now plug $r = 2$ into the answer choices to see which one matches the target value. Choice (A) becomes $(2)^3(3 - 4\pi) = 8(3 - 4\pi)$. Distribute the 8 to get $24 - 32\pi$. This does not match the target, so eliminate (A). Choice (B) becomes $4(2)^2(14 - \pi) = 16(14 - \pi)$. Distribute the 16 to get $224 - 16\pi$. Eliminate (B). Choice (C) becomes $4(2)^3(6 - \pi) = 32(6 - \pi)$. Distribute the 32 to get $192 - 32\pi$. Keep (C), but check (D) just in case. Choice (D) becomes $12(2)^2(2 - \pi) = 48(2 - \pi)$. Distribute the 48 to get $96 - 48\pi$. Eliminate (D). The correct answer is (C).

6. **160** The question asks for the surface area of a rectangular solid. The values of the side lengths are relative to each other, so write the side lengths using a single variable. Translate English to math to find that $l = \frac{1}{2}w$ and $w = \frac{1}{3}h$, or $h = 3w$. Since $V = lwh$, substitute the values for l, w, and h into the equation to get $96 = \left(\frac{1}{2}w\right)(w)(3w)$. Simplify the right side to get $96 = \frac{3}{2}w^3$. Multiply both sides by $\frac{2}{3}$ to get $w^3 = 64$, then take the cube root of both sides to get $w = 4$. Use this value for w to find the values of l and h. The length becomes $\frac{1}{2}(4) = 2$ and the height becomes $3(4) = 12$. The surface area is the sum of the areas of all the faces of the rectangular box, or $2lw + 2lh + 2wh$. Substitute the values for l, w, and h to get $2(2)(4) + 2(2)(12) + 2(4)(12) = 16 + 48 + 96$. Add these values to find that the surface area is 160. The correct answer is 160.

Notes

Notes